D0215099

62734

CP cloth lst 15⁰⁰

GOVERNMENT AND LOCAL POWER IN JAPAN

500 to 1700

GOVERNMENT AND LOCAL POWER IN JAPAN

500 to 1700

A Study Based on Bizen Province

BY

JOHN WHITNEY HALL

PRINCETON, NEW JERSEY
PRINCETON UNIVERSITY PRESS
1966

Copyright © 1966 by Princeton University Press
ALL RIGHTS RESERVED
L. C. Card: 65-14307

Publication of this book has been aided
by the Whitney Darrow Publication Reserve Fund of Princeton University Press.

Printed in the United States of America
by Princeton University Press, Princeton, New Jersey

To Miki Yukiharu

PREFACE

THIS BOOK received its inspiration between 1951 and 1952 when I spent my first extended period of residence in Okayama Prefecture and succumbed to the area's lure as a subject for historical study. Okayama offers its history freely as an exciting and moving panorama. It begins with the visible signs that in human memory most of the land of the Okayama plain had been sea and that the hills which rise above its broad stretches of rice fields were once islands. It comes alive in the present as one watches the reclaiming of still new land for modern industry and the scooping of new channels for ocean-going vessels. Man has lived long and industriously in the area of ancient Kibi, as the region used to be called, and the evidence of this long history, given unity by its geography of rivers and hills, provides a microcosmic record of the evolution of human society in Japan.

Readers of the previously published results of this first period of field research in Okayama, in the volume entitled *Village Japan*, will discover there the beginnings of a method and of a plan. The method is simply the technique of concentrating field observation and documentary analysis upon a single geographical region and thus to define a historical case study which, though limited in scope, nonetheless contains all the institutional ingredients of the larger national community. The plan is the hope to persevere in the investigation of Okayama so as to complete a series of studies which will trace its history from ancient times to the point at the end of the nineteenth century when Japan stood on the threshold of becoming a modern state. This volume, then, is the first of several projected works and serves as an introduction to a considerably more detailed analysis of the political institutions of Okayama during the Tokugawa period, which in due time should follow.

Being an introductory work it must partake more of a survey than of a narrowly confined regional analysis. I have departed somewhat from the standard style of local study by attempting from time to time in the course of local events to draw connections to the wider flow of national history or to read into observations made at the local level implications for a broader understanding of Japanese history. By doing so I no doubt reveal that my interests are ultimately more national than local. Though Okayama has become a second home in Japan, it is nonetheless as the region reveals the secrets of national history that it delights me most. And Okayama is full of such delights.

That this plan to study a local region over a span of sixteen centuries is even remotely possible is itself a historical fact of some significance. Japan has preserved the story of its past not only in the remarkably rich deposits of historical artifacts and institutional continuities but also through the work of generations of diligent historians. In this volume I must count myself the beneficiary of the works of three generations at least. First there are those often anonymous scholars of the Tokugawa period who in Chinese style compiled local histories or gazetteers which they filled with extracts from old documents or with commentaries on the legends which had grown up around historical persons or locations of the region. Following them, the twentieth century produced first a generation of local antiquarians who refurbished these older works, who vigorously pursued the fields of historical geography and antiquarian archaeology, and who carefully combed the standard historical texts for local references. The greatest of this generation in Okayama is Nagayama Usaburō, whose several massive volumes have served as basic references for my study. He himself proved a rare and enthusiastic guide to the many historic monuments of old Kibi, which he vividly brought to life for me with stories of ancient heroes or climactic battles.

But a third generation is now in the field. Historians attached to Okayama University, bibliographers in the university and prefectural libraries, archaeologists with professional training who have come into Okayama from central university posts or who are attached to such institutions as the Kurashiki Archaeological Museum—these are the men who today are reworking the history of Okayama by the application of new methodology and the uncovering of new sources of documentation from out of the ground or from hitherto undiscovered archives.

In the face of such richness of historical study it would be presumptuous for one from afar to suggest that he might prepare a study notably different from what these Japanese precursors have already done in greater depth and detail. My debt to my Japanese guides and mentors is great, and, as the following pages will show, I have freely relied upon their labors for tasks which I myself could hardly have duplicated. My object, in this first volume especially, has been to synthesize and to interpret. And if to them I have contributed anything of value, it must simply be the occasional nuance with which an outsider to Japanese culture will express a well-known fact from a slightly different point of view. It in no sense belittles my debt to these scholars to say, however, that my greatest dependence has been upon the region of Okayama itself, its hills, fields, coastline, and villages. For above all it has been the region which has excited my interest and which has given me what sense I may have acquired of the flow of history and of the boundaries of the historically possible and plausible in Japan. Okayama has taught a brand of history which is not contained in books.

But Okayama is also its people, and among them I must count many who have been of very special help to me in the preparation of this book. I start with the late Governor Miki whose gracious hospitality and interest in my work has made my visits to Okayama both pleasant and rewarding. At Okayama University Professor Fujii Shun, whose family lineage traces back to the earliest rulers of Kibi, first acquainted me with the contents of the ancient documents of the area. Professor Mizuno Kyōichirō has diligently filled out the Ashikaga chapter of Okayama history which had hitherto remained almost unknown. Professor Taniguchi Sumio uncovered the vast riches of the Ikeda House archives as well as conducting basic research in Tokugawa institutions. My debt to him will increase as I take up the second of my contemplated volumes on Okayama. Finally I must recognize a very special indebtedness toward Mr. Kanai Madoka of the Historiographical Institute of Tokyo University who singlehandedly performed the difficult task of reconstructing the land map of the Kamakura period, who drew a number of base maps upon which I have relied heavily, and who deciphered the complex figures of the 1203 wheat tax. Both Professor Taniguchi and Mr. Kanai have offered me valuable suggestions in the editing of my manuscript, and Professor Taniguchi also helped in securing illustrations. I am especially indebted to the Okayama Prefecture Government, which graciously granted permission to use certain of the photographs.

A book of this kind which has been in preparation for many years and under various circumstances is indebted in the final analysis to a large number of persons who have aided directly in its preparation and to institutions which supported its author's research and writing. Among the latter, at various periods and under various circumstances, I have received the support of the Carnegie Corporation, the Guggenheim Foundation, the University of Michigan's Horace H. Rackham School of Graduate Studies, Princeton University's Council of the Humanities, and Yale University's Concilium on International Studies. Individuals who have helped in the preparation of the manuscript include Miss Adrienne V. Suddard, who offered editorial advice and helped prepare the index, and Mr. Robert Williams, who drew the maps.

JOHN WHITNEY HALL

Bethany, Connecticut
September 1964

CONTENTS

LIST OF ILLUSTRATIONS

following page

LIST OF MAPS

GOVERNMENT AND LOCAL POWER IN JAPAN

500 to 1700

INTRODUCTION

JAPAN's growing role in world affairs has directed increasing attention to its historical past. The first Oriental nation to project itself upon the world stage, a country which in the last century has undergone the most startling of cultural changes, Japan appears as something of a modern prodigy whose history is probed for answers to the riddle of its restless emergence as a modern power. Histories of Japan there are in abundance, and among these many have described with imagination and skill the fascinating pageant of the past in Japan. Yet too often this history has appeared to Western eyes more exotic than real, more contradictory than plausible. Too often our writers have unrolled a brocade of oddly composed figures: of warlike tribal chieftains, elegant aristocrats emulating the arts of China, Buddhist monks engrossed in meditation, fanatical samurai fighting and dying for their lords, dedicated Christians and equally dedicated enemies of the Cross, docile subjects, and cold-blooded assassins.

The exotic quality of Western writing on Japanese history derives in part from the remoteness of Japanese culture from so much that is familiar to the Western observer. The Japanese have literally lived on the farthest fringe of the civilized world. And for the European, the Japanese have been the farthest in that romantic easterly direction of any people of the Orient. Only as steam and air travel have bridged the Pacific have Americans come to speak of Japan as a "New Far West" which yet seems strangely Eastern in its paradoxes.[1]

In the nineteenth century, when Westerners rediscovered Japan, the clothing, food, and domestic architecture which they found seemed incredibly quaint and impractical. And yet this same "land of birds and butterflies" as it was once called, was the first of the countries of Asia to master the ways of Western life and thought.[2] This modern paradox has seemed to be only the last of many which confront the Western reader of Japanese history. How is one to account for the contrasting images of a quiet people in love

[1] *Show* devoted its May 1963 issue (vol. 3, no. 5) to Japan under the title "Japan: The New Far West." The reference was intended to be humorous, to be sure, and played on the concept of "Westernization" in Japan as much as on the fact that travel to Japan has become so easy.

[2] The quotation is from Sir Edwin Arnold who headed a long line of romantic Western commentators on Japan.

with nature and shadows yet periodically roused to violent warfare or fanatical assassination, worshippers at the feet of Chinese
civilization yet aggressively proud of their own heritage, artists
of uncanny delicacy and sensitivity among warriors and officials
capable of utmost arrogance and brutality, a people so seemingly
Oriental yet so energetically modern?

The Western historian has not found it easy to discover unity
and meaning in the seeming contradictions of Japanese history
or the unfamiliar behavior of its main actors. And this is particularly true the farther back he goes in Japanese history. The very
names with which the story is studded seem to deny the possibility of coherence. What is the thread linking the separate beads of
Yamato, Nara, Heian, Kamakura, Muromachi, Azuchi, Momo-
yama, Edo, and Tokyo? How can one explain except by reference
to inscrutable behavior, for instance, the political condition of the
thirteenth century when the real rulers of Japan were usurpers
of the power of the shogun, who presumably ruled in the name of
the emperor, who himself was a puppet of the court regent, who
in turn had no influence because he was overshadowed by the
office of ex-emperors?

Such are the seeming conundrums with which Japanese history
confronts the Western writer, causing him to resort to concepts
of "uniqueness" in Japanese behavior or of an "imitativeness"
which responds to every passing influence from abroad. One explanation is as common as another among historians groping for
the elusive Japanese "essence." The strong currents of Buddhist
influence, of Chinese political philosophy, of Sung and Ming
aesthetics have been used to explain a variety of turning points
in Japan's premodern history. And against these there have been
counterposed the periodic outcroppings of native practices and social values which seem to articulate an almost mechanical dialectic
from the interplay of the foreign and the native in Japanese culture. But more often the Western historian, despairing of explanation, has sheepishly made a virtue of telling his story as a "bewildering history."[3]

Most of this difficulty in arriving at an understanding of Japanese history stems from the propensity to look at Japan through
alien eyes, to seek explanations in terms of Western preconcep-

[3] For an extreme example see Vincent McHugh, "Japan: Their Bewildering History," *Holiday*, 30.4 (October 1961), 76-111.

tions about the nature of society, the political process, or religious consciousness. If the Western observer could but shift his viewpoint and accept Japanese history on its own terms, taking explanations from the content of Japanese culture and from the value system of the Japanese people themselves, the results would be quite different, and certainly more comprehensible. Behind the colorful pageant of Japan's cultural history, behind the seeming erratic shifts in political or social behavior, the outlines of continuity are inescapably visible. In the basic relationships within Japanese society, such as those between government and social classes, between power and wealth, between individual and society, Japanese institutions have shown a remarkable constancy. The brocade of Japanese history has been woven on a warp of enduring material. This is not to say that we should think to find some single controlling factor or some single thread which will unravel all the mysteries of Japanese history. The patterns of cultural behavior in Japan have been quite varied. But this variety has been contained within well-defined limits, and the predominant motifs have frequently repeated.

The following study of Japan in premodern times, embracing a span of nearly thirteen centuries, is directed toward the illumination of some important elements of continuity in Japanese history. It is an effort to explain through the detailed analysis of a microcosm—the small province of Bizen—the fundamental institutions of political organization and social and economic structure upon which Japanese government has rested. It seeks historical depth both by limiting the study in terms of its geographical scope and by restricting the number of variables to which it gives attention. The geographic base is the province of Bizen, one of sixty-six divisions of old Japan. In area it covered perhaps five hundred square miles, and by the eighteenth century it had acquired a population of something over 400,000 people. Within the confines of Bizen our attention is concentrated upon the unfolding of two sets of relationships: first, the combination of traditions and techniques by which the Japanese organized power and exercised authority and, second, the connections between the holders of power and the sources of wealth, mainly the land. Our study, therefore, deals chiefly with such subjects as theories of legitimacy and practices of administration, concepts of social stratification and social rights, and practices of land tenure and taxation. Within the limited world of Bizen it seeks to gain a sufficient intimacy with Japanese life to find meaning in the historic continuities and changes in the way premodern Japanese governed themselves.

For the historian one of the most fascinating aspects of the study of Japanese political institutions is the fact that isolation has placed limitations on the number and duration of contacts which Japan has had with outsiders and has protected Japan from the possibility of foreign invasion and cultural engulfment. The drama of political change in Japan was, until recent times at least, almost completely an indigenous affair, and the roles and the motivations of its main actors were created and sustained by the conditions of the Japanese environment. To this extent Japan offers the ingredients of a closed system in which the norms of political life have been relatively fixed and in which influences intruding from outside have been few and easily identified. Within this system have evolved certain clearly established patterns, each originally a response to a particular set of conditions at a particular period of Japan's past, which provided the boundaries and moving forces of political behavior in later eras. To look at Japanese political history through Japanese eyes is to see these recurring, interacting, subtly changing, indigenous patterns in the perspective of their centuries-long continuity.

The oldest and in many ways the most deeply rooted of these historically ingrained systems of political organization grew out of the earliest period of Japanese history for which we can reconstruct the political community. We have called this the "familial" system, rather than use the more common term "clan" which gives rise to too many ambiguous connotations. (The Japanese elite family organization, the *uji*, was by no means a clan in either the Germanic or Chinese sense.)[4] During the Yamato period, that is, from roughly the middle of the third century to the middle of the seventh, government in Japan was exercised by a hierarchy of ruling families whose authority, though secured originally by military force, was ultimately rationalized on the basis of lineage and exerted along the lines of kin relationship. The prime sanctions for authority were prestige of family status and the supposed religious power possessed by family chiefs according to their position within the social hierarchy. At the apex of the familial system stood the imperial family around which there developed the be-

---

[4] I have also thought it best to avoid the term "familistic" used by Max Weber.

liefs and practices of political Shinto. The "familial state," in which sovereignty was held by the head of the house claiming lineal descent from the Sun Goddess and in which all subjects were conceived of as being members of a great extended family, became the form of national organization which Japanese periodically looked back to as most ideally theirs. Once it had become established and institutionalized during the fourth or fifth centuries it was to have tremendous staying power throughout the remainder of Japanese history, as indicated by the continuous respect paid the imperial house, the almost religious veneration given to political and social eminence, and the continuing propensity to channel authority along family lines. The familial ingredient in Japan's political heritage, while being transformed under changing conditions of culture and political ideology, nonetheless formed a constant and important element linking the social hierarchy to the power structure at all levels. The tendency of the Japanese to fictionalize superior-inferior relations by conceiving of them in familial terms is the best example of this.

Contrasted with this deeply indigenous style of exercising authority was another which we have called imperial-bureaucratic. In origin this tradition was considerably affected by Chinese influence, although it would be wrong to see it as wholly alien to the Japanese way of government. The tendency of familially based power groupings to become "rationalized" and to develop what Max Weber would call a patrimonial officialdom for purposes of administration was a recurring feature of Japanese political history. The Chinese model of bureaucratic organization thus fitted into the urge toward centralization and rationalization of government which frequently manifested itself in Japan. The bureaucratic concept of government and administration received the greatest commitment from the Japanese during the Nara and early Heian periods, that is, during the eighth through tenth centuries. To this concept belongs the principle of imperial rule under heavenly mandate, the ordered hierarchy of court ranks, the centralized national bureaucracy, and the exercise of authority through a systematically codified legal and administrative apparatus. Since it was first put into effect in Japan when society in China, but even more in Japan, was strictly divided between aristocracy and commoners, the bureaucratic tradition came to rest upon an assumption that authority was an inherent quality of aristocracy. The aristocracy, as partners in the exercise of sovereignty with the emperor, were by definition imbued with the right to govern. Beyond this, the idea that bureaucracy and law could exist in the abstract above and independent of the hierarchy of aristocratic families was adopted less whole-heartedly in Japan than in China. The familial structure of government which had characterized the earlier period was never entirely discarded but remained as the skeleton upon which bureaucratic procedures were overlaid. Japan never abandoned the essentially patrimonial style of authority. And the government of the Heian period provides a particularly clear example of fusion between a highly aristocratic conception of society and certain bureaucratic techniques imported from China.

The deterioration of civil aristocratic power during the Heian period gave rise to a third distinctive tradition of political organization which was in large measure the creation of the lower aristocracy. This group, increasingly preoccupied with military functions, had by the eleventh century become identified as a distinct class, the *bushi* or samurai. The *bushi* style of government has customarily been called feudal, a characterization which should not offend us if we are careful to limit the sense in which the term is used. What particularly distinguished the *bushi* manner of exercising authority was its reliance on the lord-vassal relationships resulting from agreements in arms between members of the fighting aristocracy. The military bond added a dimension of compulsion to a system of authority in a world which had become dangerously disorganized.

The *bushi* gained their first major power breakthrough with the establishment of the office of shogun in 1192, but it was not until the fifteenth and sixteenth centuries that feudal practices became the norm in Japan. For many centuries the practices of feudal organization applied to only certain clear-cut areas within Japanese government, primarily to the areas of shogunal jurisdiction and to certain features of local administration exercised by military governors and land stewards. Throughout much of the early centuries during which the *bushi* were gaining power, the Japanese polity was held together by the remnants of the imperial bureaucracy or at least the idea of an imperial state to which both the court aristocracy and the warrior aristocracy subscribed. Feudal authority from the beginning justified itself as a delegation from the imperial system. Furthermore, the feudal system in Japan commonly retained many features of the earlier familial organization. Vassals in Japan for instance were generally called "children of the house" or "housemen," and the feudal power structure was typically buttressed by real or fictional family ties. The feudal tradition added a number of ingredients to the political culture of Japan. In particular it brought into being a definite warrior aristocracy, the members of which conceived of their national role as protectors of the state uniquely competent to exercise political leadership. It added the power of the sword to the authoritarianism inherent in the other traditions.

The high point of feudalism in Japan occurred during the sixteenth century; thereafter the feudal elements of Japanese society were gradually diluted. The revival of Confucianism as the prime social philosophy was indicative of a renewed reliance on bureaucratic techniques in government. If during the early phase of feudal development in Japan the imperial system had maintained the framework of national organization within which feudalism spread, then during the Tokugawa period it was the feudal system which maintained the structure within which the bureaucratic and legal principles reminiscent of the imperial system began to infuse the political life of Japan.

Not that the Tokugawa period should be thought of as a throwback to the somewhat primitive procedures of state organization which characterized the Nara period. Clearly in the course of Japanese history there had been a constant growth in cultural richness and in technological complexity. By the Tokugawa period Japanese culture was fundamentally different from that of the eighth century. Greater and more varied economic production, a dramatic growth in urbanization, the spread of literacy, and an overall rise in standard of living, all made for a much more complex and sophisticated way of life. Whereas government in the eighth century relied on the thinnest crust of an educated aristocracy, Japan by the eighteenth century was a society of large mass groups and classes in which the samurai made up a sizable five percent or more. Moreover, the samurai class of the Tokugawa period constituted a body of educated officials vastly superior in quality of education and administrative experience to the Nara aristocracy. While the eighth century officials had tried to enforce uniform codes of administrative procedure, their effort had been largely premature. Their codes having been imported from China

contained provisions too far out of touch with Japanese conditions. In the seventeenth century, despite the strong influence of
Confucian theory upon Japanese law, the basic elements of the
new procedural codes were of strictly indigenous origin and had
grown out of more than a century of experimentation by the great
territorial houses. The greatest legal innovation of this period, the
practice of legislation by class, or social group, was clearly an out-
growth of the functional differentiations which were becoming apparent in Japanese society.

The three systems of authority which we have described served
principally as methods of supralocal or elite organization within
Japanese society. Underlying all of these systems were the practices which linked power in the hands of the elite to wealth and
the ability to enforce authority, namely land and labor. The key
to the organization of land and man in Japan was the agrarian
community. Village Japan itself gave rise to an important pattern
of political organization which formed a continuing though quali-
tatively changing foundation beneath the elite structure. Village
life in turn was strongly affected by prevailing conditions of agriculture, namely the intensive wet rice system of cultivation and
the concomitant need for a dense population organized for communal cooperation. The rural community in Japan since earliest
times tended to manage its local affairs within a system of corporate existence under the leadership of community headmen.
These headmen played a dual role. They were first of all representatives of the locality and of the village, but they were also in
touch with higher authority and hence performed a key function
in the delivery of tax grain and labor service. Village communities
consisting of cultivators and headmen traditionally handled their
own affairs with a minimum of interference from above, but always as units of the superior system of local administration. Thus,
depending upon which of the dominant traditions prevailed within
the elite level of government, the ties between supralocal and
local government were based on familial concepts, bureaucratic
procedures, or feudal controls.

Rural life has had little direct effect upon the shaping of Japan's
political history, and to this extent the villages may seem to form
an inert mass upon which the play of elite politics took place. Yet
the problem of village control has always been a prominent concern of Japanese rulers, and the interaction between the large and

the small communities in Japan has not been without its influence upon the lives of the elite. In particular the conditions of village organization have strongly affected the pattern of land use and management and in this way have touched the roots of elite society and its sources of power.

Perhaps the reason that village organization has played such an important role in the affairs of the elite is that the level of control over land production exercised by the Japanese elite has been relatively removed from the land itself. In other words, their main concern has been man and his labors rather than the land as such. In the Yamato period emphasis was frankly on manpower, that is, on the communities of workers known as *be*. Under the imperial-bureaucratic system, taxes were assessed on the head and labor was more important than the grain tax. Under the feudal system, military and labor service were important elements of the superior rights of profit from the land. Throughout premodern Japanese history control of the rights over profit from the land—in other words, control over the workers of the land—has served as the basis of political power. Even in the Tokugawa period the territorial aristocracy was enfeoffed in terms of villages and units of production (rice) rather than in terms of specific parcels of land. It was not until Japan's modern revolution that land in economic terms, or wealth secured from other sources than the villages, or the ability to control men's minds became alternative bases of political power.

Thus up through the middle of the nineteenth century the evolution of Japan's political institutions has had a remarkably stable quality. This is not merely because the elements of power and the sources of wealth were limited and homogeneous, but also because of the isolation of the Japanese islands and the fact that the political struggle was confined within such a narrow sphere. We have already noted that the interplay of political traditions was slow and that one system of authority never suddenly displaced another. In surveying the history of Japanese political institutions it would be hard to say that anything like a real revolution ever took place. There were, of course, many periods of violent warfare and bloodshed among the ruling families. And yet these did not result in the overthrow of an entire political system or of an entire ruling group. The elite of one age were generally only pushed aside by those of the next. And so the familial chiefs of the seventh century remained as the local elite of the eighth; the court aristocracy of the eleventh century retained an identity even into the twentieth century, and even the members of the feudal aristocracy received patents in a modern nobility after 1885.

If the Japanese political establishment was not subject to violent division leading to dynastic overthrow, neither was it greatly troubled by revolutionary outbursts which might have posed a threat to the social order from below. The first Westerners who visited Japan in the sixteenth century commented on the remarkably secure hold of the territorial rulers over their officials and subjects. Undoubtedly the Japanese political community has been characterized by a strong tendency to accept authority among individuals in all stations of life and by a prevalence of authority situations within the sub-units of the political system such as family, fief, or village. This condition had another manifestation which helps to explain the frequency of group tenure of authority or of group responsibility and the relative ease with which individuals have subordinated themselves to family, group, or authoritarian interests. In common with most political cultures of the Orient, the Japanese have accepted the existence of social stratification as ordained by nature and have recognized without reluctance the prerogatives which have attended such stratification. The stress upon group rather than individual has been an outcome of the importance of the group as the recipient of status. And status itself has served as its own prime rationale for the exercise of political authority.

In its most generalized form, perhaps, the sense of group served to heighten the Japanese consciousness of the political community as a whole, reinforcing that particular pattern of unity around the imperial family which the Japanese have labeled "the polity" (*kokutai*). From the time of the early Yamato hegemony, the structure of political power in Japan had consisted of a coalition of families around the emperor, and the Japanese political community was sufficiently small that there were no powers to contend with outside the imperial sway. The significance of this fact cannot be understated. For since there was never but one power hierarchy, struggles for national hegemony took place within a limited group and consisted of conflicts or intrigues among a closed elite. Thus war in Japan was always civil war, and intrigue was always carried out from within the group. This made for strong pressures toward compromise and coalition at every step. From the time of the original rise of the imperial family, political ascendancy tended to be the result of incomplete civil war. The resulting power structure generally consisted of a coalition of closely allied and recently defeated families held together in a delicate balance.

Historically the imperial family was once a party to the violent struggle for power in Japan. But once the initial hegemony was established, and although the imperial family gradually lost real military and political power, its symbolic position as mediator between the members of the oligarchy and as the prime source of legitimacy remained of such importance that the emperor could never be assailed. A few attempts were made to overthrow the imperial family by intrigue from within the oligarchy, notably by the Soga chiefs during the seventh century and again by the priest Dōkyō during the eighth. Each time these attempts were frustrated by a closing of the ranks among the remaining aristocratic families who felt threatened by the "usurper." Five times powerful military families arose to political hegemony in Japan: the Taira, Minamoto, Ashikaga, Toyotomi, and Tokugawa. Yet in each instance these families achieved their victory as the result of a military conquest which carried through from within the oligarchic structure rather than attacking it from without. The resulting hegemonies therefore included former enemies who had given up the struggle as the balance of power turned against them. Even during the age of great feudal wars no group was able to obtain a base of power outside of the polity from which it might have attacked and destroyed the system of legitimacy over which the emperor presided. In the fifteenth and sixteenth centuries the emperor was reduced to a condition of near oblivion and outright economic distress, yet the idea of the national hierarchy remained. As new military leaders fought to the top they looked to the emperor for the tokens of legitimacy and to the system of court ranks over which he presided for a means of ritualizing the pyramid of power. It is no accident that Japan entered the modern era following a political coup d'état carried out in the name of the emperor.

The slow organic nature of the changes which affected the structure of government in Japan is nowhere better illustrated than in the practices dealing with land tenure and property rights. We have already noted that the particular form of intensive agriculture practiced in Japan had profoundly influenced the tenure system so that superior rights over land were generally limited to the rights of profit and management and not that of outright ownership. Inferior rights of cultivation were equally persistently retained in the hands of the workers of the soil. The evolution in practices of tenure and taxation have thus revolved around two distinct poles: possession as practiced by the elite has taken the form of proprietorship and has consisted of rights of management and taxation; the rights of cultivation have remained separable from proprietorship.

We know too little about the pre-seventh century land system to be able to say much more about it than that it was tied in with the system of familial organization and with the groups of hereditary workers attached to the elite families. There was no clear-cut theory of proprietorship. This was first clarified legally during the seventh century when the government codified its claim not only to the rights of governance but also of proprietorship over the rice lands of the country. The breakdown of this system of public domain came about as rights of proprietorship were gradually acquired away from the government by the aristocracy and the religious institutions along with certain immunities and exemptions from taxation and governmental inspection. The *shōen*, or private proprietorship, which resulted from this process put into the hands of court families and religious orders most of the powers over the workers of the land which had formerly been exercised by the state. For this reason the proprietary rights were themselves divisible into several functional levels with respect to the land and its management. As the military aristocracy gained possession of various proprietorships they divided them among themselves, linking their possession to conditions of military service. In other words, they became the basis of the feudal fief. But it was not until the sixteenth century that the military families secured proprietary control over all lands in Japan, at which time they automatically had secured possession of the territorial rights of governance as well.

Characteristic of the history of land tenure in Japan was its very slow evolution and the persistent overlap of one system of tenure as another began to develop. Despite the fact, for instance, that the Chinese-inspired system of public proprietorship began to be circumvented as early as the middle of the eighth century, public domain was still to be found (in a greatly modified form, to be sure) as late as the fifteenth century. While the practice of linking *shōen* proprietorships to the system of feudal authority began as early as the eleventh century, the *shōen* system itself persisted into the sixteenth century. It was in fact not until after 1585, when Hideyoshi imposed a nationwide cadastral survey upon Japan, that a new legal basis was laid for the distribution of superior and inferior rights to the land. To the military aristocracy went the rights (and responsibilities) of territorial proprietorship and governance under the authority of the military hegemon. To the cultivators went the rights of copyhold as established in the village cadastral registers. This was the system which provided the foundation for daimyo rule in the provinces during the Tokugawa period. Not until the Meiji Restoration did the central government finally regain the rights of governance and of eminent domain, giving to the people only the rights of ownership in its modern sense.

These are the main themes of institutional continuity and change which we shall hope to illuminate through our study of the history of Bizen province. The study need not be isolated from the narrative of political events in Bizen and cannot be cut away from the course of national history as it flowed through the province. But it will naturally play down the record of personal or idiosyncratic events in its search for pattern and commonality. Bizen is of interest to us as a case study through which we can observe at close range the functioning of political institutions common to most of the rest of Japan. There is no attempt to claim for Bizen, however, a place among Japanese provinces which makes its study typical or particularly significant, and the meticulous student may well question whether generalizations from the case of Bizen are at all representative. But the local historian is fortunate in having at his command a wide variety of monographic studies with which he can correct his provincialism. And Bizen need not be excused as being too far from the main stream of Japanese political development. Located midway between the capital and the frontier provinces, it has had a history which has avoided the extremes of both center and periphery. The one qualification which might be made is that Bizen by being located to the west of the capital has had a longer and richer cultural history under more propitious economic conditions than if it had been located in the mountainous region a similar distance to the east.

The contemporary traveler to Okayama, the heart of old Bizen, will find himself struck by two extremes of the historical process almost simultaneously. For the soil of Bizen today shows its age in the intensity with which it has been worked by its human inhabitants. Even the casual eye quickly picks up the contours of ancient burial mounds, of dyked rivers long channeled to flow between the fields of rice, of stretches of paddy land reclaimed in past ages from the waters of the sea. Yet on top of the ancient base the present citizens of the area engaged in almost frenzied efforts to build their cities and improve their lives. The ocean dredge is ever active in reclaiming still new strips of land for industrial use, and new lines of concrete laid with intricate bridgework over ancient waterways are linking Okayama to Tokyo by truck and bus. The record of Bizen's development from the days of the early tumuli is indeed impressive, and though we in this study look at Bizen impersonally and analytically, the story of human achievement and cultural growth cannot altogether be lost upon us.

GOVERNMENT AND LOCAL POWER IN JAPAN

500 to 1700

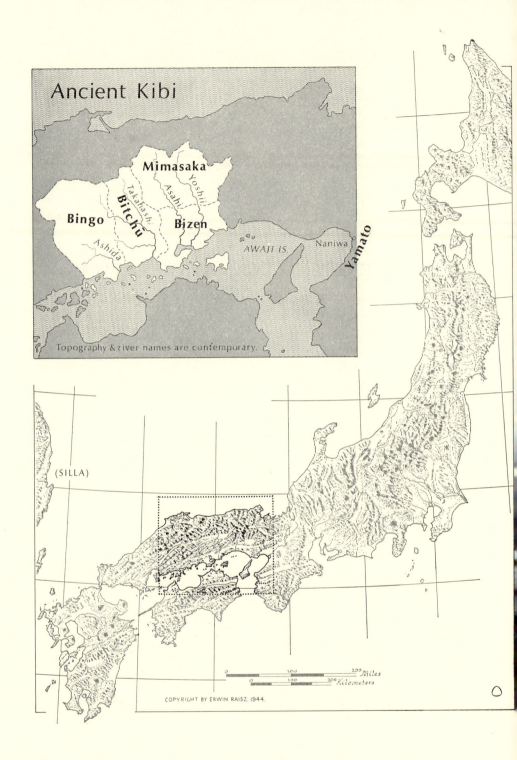

Ancient Kibi

Mimasaka

Bingo

Bitchū

Bizen

Takahashi

Asahi

Yoshii

Ashida

AWAJI IS.

Naniwa

Yamato

Topography & river names are contemporary.

(SILLA)

```
0        100        200 Miles
0      100      200  300 Kilometers
```

COPYRIGHT BY ERWIN RAISZ. 1944.

I. THE FAMILIAL SYSTEM IN EARLY KIBI

Bizen was one of four provinces created in the seventh century by subdividing the ancient region of Kibi. The name Bizen, which signifies "the fore-part of Kibi," indicates that it lay closest to the capital among the Kibi provinces. What the original significance of the name Kibi was we do not know, but by early historic times it had come to refer to a locale possessing strong political and cultural cohesion and extending over all of present Okayama Prefecture and a portion of Hiroshima Prefecture to the west. Topographically this area was based upon the drainage systems of four large rivers which in east-west order bear the modern names of Yoshii, Asahi, Takahashi, and Ashida. Bizen, the easternmost of the subdivisions of Kibi, consisted in the main of the river-mouth plains of the Yoshii and Asahi rivers.

As in a number of other similar parts of western Honshu bordering on the Inland Sea, the physical features of the Kibi region have undergone considerable change in the last two millennia owing to the erosion of hills and the silting-in of bays and river mouths along the coast. At the time when our story begins, some sixteen centuries ago, the topography of Bizen was visibly different from what it is today. At that time three rivers, the Yoshii, Asahi, and Takahashi, all flowed into the Inland Sea within twenty miles of each other at a point considerably above what was then the large island of Kojima. The name Kojima means "child island," and presumably derives from the early geographical relationship of the island to the "parental" mainland.[1] Today Kojima is no longer an island, but is joined to the mainland by a rich stretch of alluvial soil. The mouths of the three main rivers are widely separated from each other. The steady silting-in of the shallow waters which once lay between the mainland and off-shore islands like Kojima has given a constant dimension of growth to the agricultural base of the region. The fertile plain formed by the expanding deltas of the rivers of this region became the heart of historic Bizen and provided the soil on which the modern city of Okayama was to emerge.

A mild climate, broad river valleys, and easy access to the sea account for the early settlement of Kibi in prehistoric times. Here

[1] Nagayama Usaburō, *Okayama-ken tsūshi* (2 vols., Okayama, 1930), 1.55. Hereafter cited as *Tsūshi*.

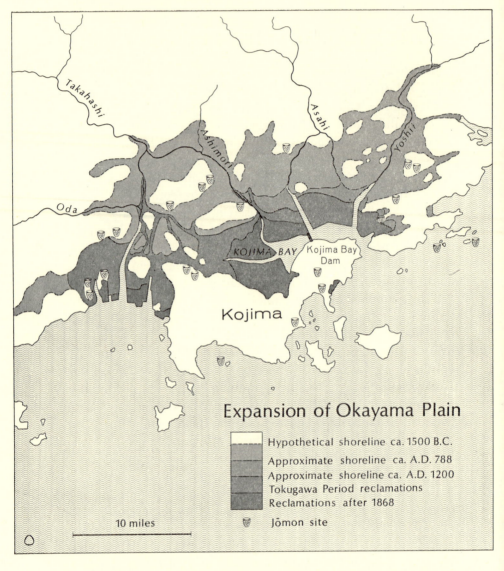

Expansion of Okayama Plain

Hypothetical shoreline ca. 1500 B.C.
Approximate shoreline ca. A.D. 788
Approximate shoreline ca. A.D. 1200
Tokugawa Period reclamations
Reclamations after 1868
Jōmon site

10 miles

was one of the cradles of Japanese civilization, its history closely paralleling that of Yamato to the east, where the political center of Japanese culture established itself. Today the region abounds in archaeological remains which attest to the continuity of human life from remote prehistoric times. Hardly a town is without its amateur archaeological association, each with its collection of Stone or Iron Age artifacts uncovered in the surrounding fields and hills. The Kurashiki Museum of Archaeology is one of several modern organizations active in the scientific study of the prehistory of Kibi.

Archaeological evidence of human life in Bizen begins with scattered finds of paleolithic flake and core stone implements dating back some eight or more millennia. But our concern is with the beginning of the political community in Bizen, and for this our story begins quite late, perhaps in the third or fourth century of our era. It begins essentially with the appearance of large burial mounds erected by the first regional chieftains of the area. These mounds, called *"kofun"* by the Japanese, are often referred to as "dolmens" by Western writers, though the simple term tumuli is probably more appropriate. The earliest in Kibi date from about the beginning of the fourth century; the latest were built in the seventh century. These dates roughly define what has been called the *"kofun* age" in Japan, a time during which recorded and archaeological evidence begin to fuse for us and when our conceptions of the earliest social and political institutions of Japan can take on substance.

It is during the age of tumuli that Kibi first acquired political identity. Chinese records, which provide the earliest authentic descriptions of Japan, relate that Japan of the third century consisted of some 50 districts (or *kuni*), and we may presume that Kibi-no-kuni was one of these. The Kibi region probably acquired its identity somewhat later than similar districts of northern Kyushu, and it is perhaps only with the rise of Yamato that Kibi came into prominence. Although the provinces into which Kibi was later divided ultimately merged without great distinction into the ranks of "the 66 provinces," from the fourth to seventh centuries this region was one of the most culturally advanced and politically important outside of Yamato. Today Okayama Prefecture boasts a density of tumulus remains greater than that of any locale outside of central Japan. A count in 1918 revealed over 4000 large and small *kofun*.[2] Among these are some of the most spectacular in terms of size and richness of content to be found anywhere in Japan. Within the present boundaries of what was once Kibi, archaeologists have identified over 140 gigantic "keyhole" (*zempō-kōen*) tumuli of the type reserved for chieftains of great influence. Twenty of them are readily visible in the environs of Okayama City. The largest of these tombs, that of Kamo-Tsukuriyama in Takamatsu township just west of Okayama, is a massive man-made mound measuring nearly 90 feet high and over 1100 feet long.

[2] *Tsūshi*, 1.309-317.

Such mounds were heaped over spacious stone burial crypts which have yielded pottery, bronze, and iron artifacts of advanced manufacture.

Tsukuriyama appears long ago to have been plundered of its most significant contents, but other dolmens excavated either by amateur antiquarians or more recently by professional archaeological teams have gathered from the ancient tombs of Kibi a rich accumulation of artifacts from which we can gain considerable insight into the early life of this region.[3] Kibi's rulers, as revealed by the articles buried with them, bore the conspicuous marks of higher civilization and political and social distinction. Earthenware figurines placed both within and outside the tombs reveal house types ancestral to the present thatched-roofed farmhouses of western Honshu. They also depict men and women dressed in continental-style garments, the men in riding outfits which were the fashion in Northeast Asia. Iron and bronze horse equipment, iron breastplates and helmets, iron swords and arrow points tell us much about the style of warfare in which the Kibi chieftains engaged. Iron agricultural implements reveal the secret of agrarian improvements which expanded the economic base upon which the tumulus builders depended. Ornaments of semi-precious stones and particularly bronze mirrors of both foreign and domestic manufacture tell us of some of the embellishments which distinguished the elite life of this period.

Comparison of the artifacts found in Kibi with those in other regions of Japan reveals that Kibi was in close contact with Yamato, the center of Japanese culture, and also with the continent. To date, for instance, the region has yielded 94 bronze mirrors. Many of these were most certainly imported directly from China, and among these some look intriguingly like articles received from the Chinese court in return for tribute. Others were

[3] A thorough and well-illustrated report on the excavation of Kanakura-yama tumulus is characteristic of the newest professional archaeological studies. See Nishitani Shinji and Kamaki Yoshimasa, *Kanakura-yama kofun* (Kurashiki, 1959). For a general illustrated survey see Iwatsu Seiuemon and Kamaki Yoshimasa, eds., *Okayama-ken jūyō bunkazai zuroku, Kōko shiryō hen* (Tokyo, 1957). The *Okayama-ken tsūshi* and more recent surveys of Okayama history all contain useful chapters on the tumulus period. Occasional articles in more general historical series help to put the Kibi area in perspective. See Nishikawa Hiroshi, "Kofun bunka ni arawareta chiiki shakai" (*Nihon kōkogaku kōza*, 5, 1955) Kondō Yoshirō, "Nihon kofun bunka" (*Nihon rekishi kōza*, 1, *Genshi-kodai*, 1958), and Inoue Tatsuo, "Iwai no hanran to Nansen" in the same volume.

clearly of domestic manufacture, and of these several share the same mold as mirrors found in Yamato tombs.[4] It is not so much the individual finds of the dolmen period but rather the total assemblage that is most characteristic and impressive. When we consider the total number of the burial mounds, the gigantic size and weight of the boulders fashioned into the inner crypts, the many styles and origins of articles both of religious and secular significance found in the tombs, we are able to visualize not only a society of some material sophistication but also one whose leaders were men of considerable power and political influence. Here clearly was the origin of the political community in Kibi.

Unfortunately for Japan as a whole and for individual regions such as Kibi in particular, the documentary evidence which might fill out the details of the social and political institutions of Japan prior to the seventh century do not compare in richness and reliability with the archaeological record. Because of the belated spread in Japan of the knowledge of writing and the practice of keeping records, there are almost no written records which might accompany the findings from the tumuli, particularly for regions outside of Yamato. The national histories set down in the eighth century are concerned primarily with events at the political center of Japan. Although it is presumed that house histories from Kibi may have gone into the writing of the *Nihon shoki*, it is not at all possible to gain from the fragmentary references to local events contained in this work any clear conception of the internal events of Kibi or of the region's political institutions. It seems incredible, for instance, that no written record or inscription links any of the great graves of Kibi with the men for whom they were built. Nonetheless we must proceed with what little evidence we have to add political and social substance to the archaeological evidence.

By the age of the tumulus builders, it is clear, Kibi was by no means politically isolated; the region was, in fact, part of a growing national order. At a time not yet agreed upon with any certainty, but judged by Japanese historians to have occurred in the late third or early fourth century, the basis of a primitive political hegemony was laid in the Yamato region to the east of Kibi. Here a group of families (*uji*) drawn together under the leadership of the powerful chieftain claiming descent from the Sun Goddess

[4] Kobayashi Yukio, *Kofun jidai no kenkyū* (Tokyo, 1961), 97-159.

(Amaterasu-Ōmikami) had succeeded in pacifying the Yamato plain and had begun to push out from Yamato into adjoining regions. The first incident which appears to fuse legend, archaeology, and written history around the area of Kibi is the story of what was unquestionably the conquest of Kibi by this emergent Yamato power.

Local legend associated with shrines and place names of Kibi and the earliest national historical records, the *Kojiki* and *Nihon shoki*, relate that the Yamato ruler Sujin, probably of the early fourth century, sent out military chiefs along four routes from central Japan. According to the *Kojiki*, one of these, said to be the son of the Yamato ruler Kōrei, named Ō-Kibitsu-hiko-no-mikoto, was dispatched westward along the Inland Sea.[5] Ō-Kibitsu-hiko met and conquered formidable opposition just west of present Okayama City. Having pacified the area, he and his brother, Waka-hiko-take-no-kibitsu-hiko-no-mikoto, are said to have settled in the region, giving it the name Kibi-no-kuni. Ō-Kibitsu-hiko himself is commemorated in the main shrine of the locale, Kibitsu Jinja.[6] A great keyhole mound near the shrine is still revered as his burial place. According to the *Nihon shoki*, it was the younger brother, however, whose offspring peopled the area with members of the Kibi family, and continued to represent the Yamato interest within the region.

While the narrative of Ō-Kibitsu-hiko's exploits is probably embellished by legend and may, in fact, be a composite of several individual stories, later references in the chronicles to members of the Kibi family are unquestionably factual. There is sufficient reason to accept, therefore, the existence of a powerful tomb-age family surnamed Kibi in the Okayama region. Its branches, spreading east and west, extended the area of the family's dominance in subsequent generations. The current, though perhaps fictional, genealogy of the Kibi lineage states that Kibitsu-hiko had three offspring, two of whom were daughters and were taken as wives or concubines into the household of the Yamato chieftain. The third child, a son named Misuki-tomomimi-takehiko-no-mikoto, had seven children. Each of these attained prominence

---

[5] Pertinent passages are quoted and annotated by Nagayama in *Tsūshi*, 1. 157-159.

[6] Nagayama Usaburō, *Kibi-gun shi* (3 vols., Okayama, 1937-38), 1. 92-100. Hereafter cited as *Kibi-gun shi*.

in one way or another. One son is said to have become a local chieftain in the region of Suruga, another in Echizen. One daughter became the wife of the fabled Yamato-takeru-no-mikoto, another the consort of the Yamato ruler Ōjin. Of the three remaining sons, Mitomo-no-wake-no-mikoto continued the succession of the main Kibi lineage. His brothers and his three sons established branch lineages with hegemonies over separate districts within Kibi.[7]

While the Kibi family carried out the conquest of Kibi and remained dominant in most of the area for several centuries, it was not the only ruling group to enter the region from Yamato. During the slightly later reign of Ōjin, it is recorded that the third generation offspring of Nuteshi-wake, son of the Yamato ruler Suinin, was set over the region of Fujino as a reward for his military services. Fujino at that time referred to the area embracing the upper valley of the Yoshii River and included the districts of Iwanashi and Wake of later years. The family which took root from this migration used the name Iwanashi-no-wake, and eventually simply "Wake." The origin of this name was obviously derived from the fact that the family began as a branch (*wake*) of the Yamato line.[8]

These stories of the Kibi and Wake families, taken in conjunction with what we know about the events in Yamato at the time, reveal a picture, necessarily dim and uncertain, of an emerging military hegemony centered on the Yamato plain. The late third and early fourth centuries were a period of extensive warfare, as the Yamato rulers consolidated their position in central Japan and then embarked upon further conquests. Legends clustered around the names Sujin and Yamato-takeru tell of the conquests by which the central core of the Japanese islands was securely tied to the Yamato hegemony and the remoter areas, containing different ethnic groups such as the Kumaso and Hayato, were pacified. The conquest of Kibi came relatively early in this process. Once it was pacified, its conquerors stayed on as local rulers, continuing to serve in the fighting forces of the Yamato chieftain. Eventually we find members of the Kibi family group fighting

[7] *Tsūshi*, 1. 191-194. Nagayama relies on the "Kibitsu Jinja ki" which contains the tradition perpetuated by the shrine of Kibitsu.

[8] Miyoshi Iheiji, ed., *Okayama-ken, Wake-gun, Fujino-son shi* (Okayama, 1953), 3-5; *Tsūshi*, 1.379-385.

even in Korea. The cultural identity of Kibi with Yamato is clearly borne out by the style of tumuli and the objects they have been found to contain, particularly the many mirrors of identical manufacture held in common between the Kibi and Yamato graves.[9]

The evolving Yamato polity was based first of all on conquest, but it was held together and given institutional stability by a number of other techniques which provided for a routinization of authority in a manner common to early familial societies. Efforts to elevate the position of the Yamato chieftain to a position of sovereignty was accomplished rather early. A vocabulary of political and social titles distinguished the Yamato chieftain as sovereign (*sumera-mikoto*) and endowed with the prerogative to govern (*shiroshimesu*).[10] The establishment for public worship of a shrine to the ancestral deity of the sovereign family and ritual identification of the family with the protective deity of Yamato, Ōmono-nushi-no-kami, provided the elements of religious sanction. But it was chiefly through the spread of an extended kinship system and the tightening of marriage or fictive kinship bonds with an increasingly large body of subservient family lines that the authority of the Yamato chieftain was extended, first throughout Yamato and then to more distant regions. This particular pattern of interrelationship between lines of political authority and kinship ties was one to which the Japanese elite was to return time and time again throughout premodern history.

Between the sovereign family, its outlying branches, and its direct subordinates the earliest channels of authority, those created during the third and fourth centuries, consisted of real or artificial kinship ties. Groups like the Kibi and Wake, presumably branches of the sovereign lineage, were "kept in the family" by regular intermarriage and by the granting of intimate titles. Subjugated groups such as the Izumo were also interconnected through marriage and required to pay homage. In both instances one of the strongest continuing methods of cementing close but subservient ties was the taking of wives and "tribute" men and women from the families of the subordinate chiefs. Tribute females (*uneme*) frequently found their way into the group of recognized wives of the Yamato chieftains. Tribute males (*toneri*)

---

[9] Kobayashi, *op.cit.*
[10] Ishii Ryōsuke, *Nihon hōsei shiyō* (Tokyo, 1949), 12. Hereafter cited as Ishii, *Hōsei shiyō.*

served as guards and servants of the sovereign. While in the service of the sovereign, such individuals must also have remained as hostages on behalf of their own family. Passages relating to Toneri-kibi-no-yugibe-no-ōsora and Kibi-no-Kamutsumichi-no-uneme-ōamachi in the record of the ruler Yūryaku contained in the *Nihon shoki* are two of many references which indicate that Kibi men and women were sent to Yamato for tribute purposes.[11]

Kinship relations were constantly expanded and generalized to cover wider and more inclusive conditions of political organization. The Yamato rulers devised rather early a system of social classification and ranks which gave justification to their claim of sovereignty. A division of lineages into direct branches (*kōbetsu*), those of local but unrelated origin (*shimbetsu*), and those of foreign origin (*bambetsu*) provided a gross indication of the relationship of all elite lines to the Yamato chieftain. Gradually also the diverse vocabulary of social distinction was brought under control and fashioned into a uniform hierarchy of titles (*kabane*) descending from the sovereign. Since the Kibi and Wake families traced their descent from the sovereign line, they were included among the *kōbetsu*. Kibi chiefs appear in the earliest records with such titles as *mikoto, wake, hiko,* or *mimi*. Several generations later as the system of titles became standardized, the heads of the chief families of the Kibi lineage were designated *omi*, a title given almost exclusively to branch members of the sovereign line originating with or before the ruler Kōgen.[12]

But there was constantly in evidence a tendency to push beyond this sort of rough federation of local chiefs to something more clearly resembling a government of officials serving a supreme authority. Gradually the Yamato chiefs began to claim over local chiefs an administrative authority based on the concept that they were officials (*tsukasa*) of the sovereign accountable to his pleasure (*yosashi*).[13] This effort is best illustrated in the use of titles of local authority such as *kuni-no-miyatsuko* and *agata-nushi,* and those of service to the sovereign, chiefly *tomo-no-miya-tsuko.*

Terms for geographical units of local rule such as *kuni* or *agata*

---

[11] Wakamori Tarō and Nagano Masashi "Reimeiki Nihon no shakai to seikatsu," (*Shin Nihon shi taikei, 1, Kokka no seisei* (1952), 179-180.

[12] Ōta Akira, *Zentei Nihon jōdai shakai soshiki no kenkyū* (rev. ed., Tokyo, 1955), 89; 404-405.

[13] Ishii, *Hōsei shiyō,* 13.

appear to go back a considerable time in Japanese practice. In the legend of the original pacification of Yamato it is related that several of the local chiefs who had come over to the cause of the new sovereign were set up as *agata-nushi* or *kuni-no-miyatsuko* in the Yamato region. The records of succeeding Yamato rulers tell the story of the extension of their authority through the acquisition of control over an increasing number of *kuni* from which they could derive tribute. The relationship between *kuni* and *agata* is not altogether clear. In certain instances the terms appear to be used interchangeably; in others the term *agata* seems to stand for a smaller subdivision of the *kuni*.[14]

In Kibi the earliest appearance of these territorial titles is found in the record of the ruler Ōjin in the third and fourth generations after Ō-kibitsu-hiko's conquest. The time was perhaps at the very end of the fourth century. As the story in the *Nihon shoki* goes, Ōjin, whose wife was a Kibi woman, had been on a hunt on Awaji Island in the Inland Sea. On his return he visited Kibi and in the course of his stay confirmed the titles of the members of the Kibi *uji* over Kibi and its parts. To the chief of the Kibi lineage, Mitono-wake, went the superior title of Kibi-no-kuni-no-miya-tsuko. The others were assigned as follows:

> At that time Mitomo-wake went to greet him accompanied by his brothers, children, and grandchildren, and prepared a banquet. The sovereign, seeing the reverence with which Mitomo-wake served him, was pleased. He therefore divided the country (*kuni*) of Kibi and allotted [Chinese character for enfeoffed] its parts to his children. To the *agata* of Kawa-shima he assigned his eldest son Inahaya-wake. He originated the line of Shimo-tsu-michi-no-omi. Next he assigned the second son Nakatsu-hiko to the *agata* of Kamu-tsu-michi. He originated the lines of Kamu-tsu-michi-no-omi and Kaya-no-omi. Next he granted to Otohiko the *agata* of Mino. He orig-inated the line of Kasa-no-omi. Next he assigned the *agata* of Sono to his elder brother Urakori-wake. He originated the line of Sono-no-omi. Finally he granted to [his consort] Ehime the *agata* of Hatori.[15]

[14] Ōta, *op.cit.*, 698-699; Inoue Mitsusada, "Kokuzō-sei no seiritsu," in *Shigaku zasshi*, 60.11 (November 1951), 964-1005. Henceforth cited as Inoue, "Kokuzō."
[15] *Nihon shoki*, Kokushi Taikei edition, 1.187.

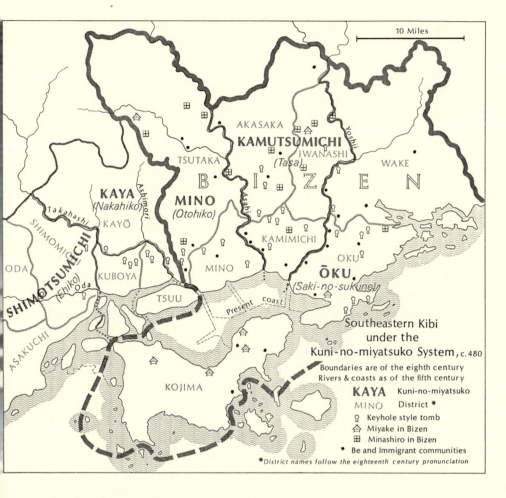

The significance of this passage is heightened when we learn that the *agata* designated by Ōjin are equivalent, or nearly so, to many of the administrative divisions, later called districts (*kōri* or *gun*), which remained in use, either formally or informally, from the seventh century to the present day. In particular the districts of Kaya, Mino, and Kamutsumichi retained the same names and roughly the same boundaries from this time for over 1500 years. There is strong evidence that throughout much of central Japan the basic territorial divisions upon which later government was to rest had already begun to take shape.

The practice of adding to the number of *kuni-no-miyatsuko* proved the most effective method by which the Yamato sovereign could spread his authority once the initial process of conquest was complete. By the time of the ruler Ōjin the process appears to have gone a considerable distance, and the "King of Wa" boasted in A.D. 478, "From of old our forebearers have clad themselves in armor and helmet and gone across the hills and waters, sparing no time for rest. In the east, they conquered fifty-five countries of hairy men; and in the west, they brought to their knees sixty-six countries of various barbarians."[16] *Kuni-no-miyatsuko* or *agata-nushi* were, of course, not all uniformly related to the Yamato chieftain. Some were heads of local groups whose subjugation was uncertain. Others were strongly attached to Yamato by blood ties. But the Yamato rulers were constantly at work to convert local chiefs to the more subservient type of *kuni-no-miyatsuko*, and this required frequent interference in local affairs.

Some such underlying political motive no doubt was at the bottom of Ōjin's further modification of the regional organization of Kibi. Toward the end of his reign, during the early decades of the fifth century, it is recorded that he revised the system he had established on his previous visit to Kibi, renaming existing *agata* into *kuni*, and assigning new titles. The area of central and eastern Kibi, with which we are chiefly concerned, was divided at this time into the *kuni* (rather than *agata*) of Ōku, Kamutsumichi, Mino, Kaya, Hatori, and Shimotsumichi (an amalgamation of Sono and Kawashima). Except for Ōku, which was assigned to Saki-no-sukune, the other *kuni* were given under the title of *kuni-no-miyatsuko* to the same members of the Kibi family who had formerly served as *agata-nushi*.[17] It is possible that behind this action may have been an effort to break up the strong regional influence of the Kibi chiefs and that the occasion which permitted this was Mitomo-no-wake's death. At any rate, from this time the Kibi family was apparently divided into two competing factions, one based geographically on the Takahashi River and headed by the Shimotsumichi line, the other centered on the Asahi River and headed by the Kamutsumichi line. Thereafter the regional title *Kibi-no-kuni-no-miyatsuko*, previously held by Mitomo-no-wake, was passed back and forth between the heads of these two lines.[18]

As was to prove the case so often in Japanese history, a power

16 Tsunoda Ryūsaku, tr. *Japan in the Chinese dynastic histories: Later Han through Ming dynasties* (So. Pasadena, Calif., 1951), 23. The quotation is from the *Sung shu*, c. A.D. 513.

17 *Tsūshi*, 1.168-169; Ōta, *op.cit.*, 83.

18 Inoue, "Kokuzō," 976.

structure that placed its prime reliance on kinship or marriage bonds, while able to maintain the hierarchy of authority effectively during the early stages of political consolidation, tended to lose its cohesion as time wore on, succumbing to the fractional pull of intrafamily rivalries and feuds. From all indications the relationship of Kibi to Yamato was both intimate and precarious during the fifth and sixth centuries. Heads of the Kibi branch lines, such as Mino or Shimotsumichi, though considered chiefs of *kuni* for administrative purposes, held the status of *omi* which placed them high in the hierarchy of social ranks around the sovereign. Despite their distance from Yamato, Kibi chiefs were often directly involved in Yamato affairs. It may well be that the Kibi chiefs were in the habit of providing loyal support to the Yamato rulers. Yet understandably the written record dwells on the less happy side of Kibi-Yamato relations, citing examples of friction and even of open rebellion.

Perhaps the most dramatic incident in the history of Kibi-Yamato relations took place during the rule of the notorious sovereign Yūryaku, who lived during the last half of the fifth century. Yūryaku appointed Tasa, chief of the Kamutsumichi branch of the Kibi family, to the governorship of Mimana, Japan's distant Korean colony. His motives may well have been, as some historians suspect, to move Tasa out of the way so as to weaken Kibi influence. Or his motives may have been purely personal; for with Tasa gone to Korea, Yūryaku is said to have abducted the beautiful wife he left behind. And Tasa, on hearing the news, turned rebel in Korea. Yūryaku, true to his character, devised the scheme of ordering Tasa's son, Otogimi, to lead a Yamato force against his father. Otogimi complied and moved toward Korea; but he intended eventually to join his father in rebellion. Before this could happen, however, Otogimi's wife discovered his intention and killed her own husband to prevent him from turning against his sovereign.[19] Too much of this story sounds romanticized, but there is every evidence that a clash of power was building up between Kibi and Yamato. Previous to the Tasa episode, Yūryaku had become incensed over what he took to be the disrespectful behavior of the head of the Shimotsumichi branch of the Kibi line and had sent a force of Mononobe warriors who reportedly wiped out all seventy members of this branch of the family. Yet the

---

[19] *Tsūshi*, 1.204.

Shimotsumichi line carried on to produce eminent leaders in the eighth century, so that it would be wrong to take the chroniclers too literally. Several other incidents involving intrigues or uprisings of members of the Kibi family are contained in the chronicles. Each one of these failed, and each failure must have served to weaken, but not destroy, one or another branch of the Kibi line. By the beginning of the sixth century evidence from yet another source indicates that the Kibi family was losing its ability to dominate quite so dramatically the region with which its name was identified. Archaeologists tell us that there was a perceptible decrease in size and grandeur of local tombs built after the middle of the sixth century.[20]

Much of the same uncertainty that has affected our attempt to describe the position of Kibi in the Yamato political hegemony must attend any effort to picture the conditions of life within the Kibi region itself. Evidence derived from early historical writings, the archaeological record, the connotations surrounding certain place names, and the legends clustering around the most ancient shrines in the area offers at best tangential information about the society, life, and religious practices of the tomb age inhabitants of Kibi. There is no certain evidence, for instance, either written or legendary, which identifies the builders of the tumuli in Kibi, so that we can only infer that they were the work of the several chieftains of the Kibi and Wake families. Yet the tombs are stark evidence of the existence of local chieftains of great power. Today we can only marvel at the size of the largest of these huge mounds, at the tremendous expenditure of manpower it must have taken to float and drag the great boulders which comprised the burial crypts, and the labor taken to heap the earthen mounds above the stones. A recent estimate of the earth-moving task required for a burial mound of the type exemplified by Kibi-Tsukuriyama puts the volume of earth at over 1,400,000 cubic meters. Assuming that one man could move one cubic meter a day, it would have taken a thousand laborers four years to complete the mound alone. In addition, there was the added labor of digging a broad moat about the mound and various other lesser requirements such as making clay figures (*haniwa*) and distributing them about the tomb. It is recorded that the tomb of the Yamato ruler Nintoku took twenty years to complete. All of this required effective po-

[20] Inoue Tatsuo, *op.cit.*, 111.

litical control over a large populace and periodically the ability to draw huge quantities of manpower away from the primary function of food production.[21]

What sort of authority did the Kibi or Wake chiefs exercise over the mass of the inhabitants within their spheres of influence? Undoubtedly they relied upon the same combination of military power, the claim to social superiority backed by religious sanctions, and the loose network of kinship connections of the type which served the Yamato family in its assertion of overall supremacy. They could, of course, invoke the backing of the Yamato sovereign as well.

The stories of the Kibi and Wake families illustrate how closely they were identified with certain areas as "natural" indigenous rulers. Kibi and Wake chiefs went by names that coincided with entire districts. This in turn gives us some idea of the extent over which the separate chiefs exercised authority. The continued prestige of the shrine of Ō-kibitsu-hiko at Magane, as well as the fact that the chief provincial shrines of Bizen and Mimasaka are dedicated to Ō-kibitsu-hiko and that at least five other extant shrines bear his name or those of his relatives, points to the close relationship between ruling authority and religious practice at this time.[22] The same condition held for the Wake family, whose influence eventually penetrated the inner province of Mimasaka and left as its mark eight shrines dedicated to Wake ancestors.[23] Although few of these shrines are actually associated with extant burial mounds, there is no question but that tumuli did serve as centers of religious worship and that, as in the case of Kibitsu shrine of Bitchū, the efficacy of such worship was thought to extend beyond family membership to an entire region.

Chinese records containing the observations of continental travelers to Japan in the third century report the marked differentiation between the common people and those of rank. They note the almost religious reverence that the ordinary people showed their rulers. Early Japanese myths and legends and the later historically documented activities of the Yamato sovereign confirm this picture of local chieftains who combined acts of

[21] Furushima Toshio, *Nihon nōgyō shi* (Tokyo, 1956), 33.
[22] *Tsūshi*, 1. 534-547.
[23] Nagayama Usaburō, *Okayama-ken nōchi shi* (Okayama, 1952), 181. Hereafter cited as *Nōchi shi*.

governance with leadership in religious observance. As religious leaders, they performed rites at local shrines, thereby assuring the welfare of the area over which the powers of the shrine were thought to extend. In the process a great deal of the charisma of the local deities rubbed off upon the officiating leaders. As George Sansom has observed, European sovereigns "might call themselves sovereign 'by the grace of God,' but the emperors of Japan described themselves as 'manifest gods. . . .' "[24] This strong tradition of identity between secular and sacerdotal authority which typified the historic status of the Japanese sovereign applied equally to other *uji* chieftains during this period. In Kibi the most significant local religious observances were those performed by the head of the Kibi family at Kibitsu shrine. Conversely, the privilege of performing such rites provided the Kibi chief with a potent source of prestige.

But how was this strong social and religious charisma translated into political authority? Of the precise form of local government we know almost nothing. Yet, on the other hand, we have enough general knowledge about the organization of Japanese society as a whole to be able to describe the institutional channels through which authority was exercised. From the structural and functional point of view three types of social groups, *uji*, *be*, and *yatsuko*, made up the local community. The first we have translated "family" or "lineage group"; the second has no easy English equivalent and so will remain untranslated; the third may be rendered "slave."

Much remains to be revealed about the exact nature of the first two of these social categories. Some scholars have in fact denied any fundamental difference between them, at least in their earliest manifestation.[25] Recently scholars have put the formation of *be* at a considerably later date than heretofore supposed. By the tomb age, however, we are not troubled by problems of origin. By then it was apparent that elite families were organized as *uji*, while subordinate bodies of workers were by and large grouped into *be*. *Uji* were organized in principle on the basis of consanguinity, while *be* were held together more by shared locale or occupation. Yet it was characteristic of both types of organization that, as a means of assuring cohesion, kinship bonds were frequently as-

[24] George Sansom, *A History of Japan to 1334* (Stanford, 1958), 45.
[25] Nakamura Kichiji, *Nihon shakai shi* (Tokyo, 1952), 62-63.

1. The city of Okayama lies on both sides of the Asahi River which cuts through the center of the Bizen Plain. Okayama castle once occupied the point of the bend just below the island which was turned into a recreation park by the Ikeda daimyo.

2A-B. Below Okayama the plain stretches out in a wide belt between the Inland Sea and the hill lands of the interior.

3. Reclamation projects have filled in the sea between Okayama and what were once the hills of Kojima Island.

4. Drying racks laden with the fall rice harvest reveal the region's productiveness.

5. Rice seedlings are transplanted by hand into paddy fields in the spring.

6. A farm lies between growing rice and upland fields and woodlots.

7. Entrance to the village shrine, where farmers worship their protective *kami*.

8. At the fall festival, villagers offer thanks for a successful harvest.

9. These newly reclaimed fields will soon be cultivated by the farmers who recently occupied the government-built houses in the distance.

10. Powerful suction pumps dredge the bottom of the Inland Sea to create industrial land and port facilities for Okayama Prefecture.

11. The great keyhole style tomb of Kamo Tsukuriyama lies across the Bizen border in Bitchū. Its base is now occupied by a village, and the small clearing on its crest contains the protective shrine of the locality.

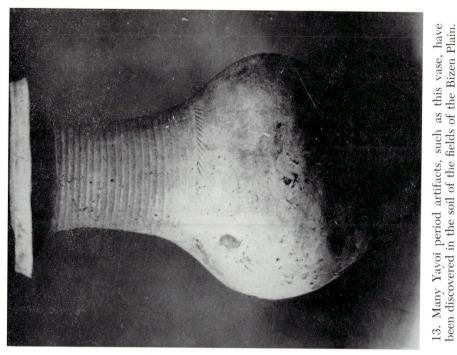

13. Many Yayoi period artifacts, such as this vase, have been discovered in the soil of the fields of the Bizen Plain.

12. This 9-inch bronze mirror was found in a tomb now located in the city limits of Okayama.

sumed where none in fact existed. An *uji* frequently included households which had only a "guest" relationship to the main lineage; *be*, though consisting of households of heterogeneous lineage, frequently behaved as if blood-linked.[26] For both groups authority tended to be exercised along the lines of real or fictional kinship channels. The result was the formation of familial groupings of characteristic Japanese style to which modern sociologists have attached the term *dōzoku*.[27]

Slaves, though never of great number, formed an important adjunct to the economy, supplementing the manpower available to the elite. Though they may never have existed in any greater proportion than five percent of the entire populace, they nonetheless gave evidence that the culture condoned slavery, and they helped to accentuate the economic differentiation between the elite and the inferior levels of society. Japanese slaves also appear to be closely bound up in the household organization of their masters, being used more as domestic servants than in large groups for the working of agricultural lands.[28]

In the lower levels of the society of the *uji* period, then, many conditions and gradations of unfree and bound status were prevalent. The relationship between *be* and *uji* was basically unfree. But *be* were not slave communities. They are probably most properly conceived of as village units tied to the superior *uji* under some sort of fictive kinship concept and required to yield up fixed amounts of produce and labor and, most likely, individuals for household service. In other words, they were managed under the patriarchal authority of the *uji* heads, though the idea is often set forth that they were "owned."[29] It was this combination of superior *uji* and subordinate *be* that formed the minimal units of the political community in Kibi. The great majority of the inhabitants of the region, of course, resided in *be* communities. Most

[26] Nakamura Kichiji, "Kodai," in Sonraku Shakai Kenkyūkai, *Sonraku kenkyū no seika to kadai* (Tokyo, 1954), 156-157; Inoue Mitsusada, "Bemin shiron," in *Shin Nihonshi kōza*, case 4 (Tokyo, 1948).

[27] Ariga Kizaemon, "Nihon jōdai no ie to sonraku," in *Tōa shakai kenkyū*, 1 (1943).

[28] Shimizu Mitsuō, *Jōdai no tochi-kankei* (Tokyo, 1943), 38. To be sure a number of Japanese scholars maintain that Japan had an ancient "slave state" and that slavery was the basis of *shōen* economy until the sixteenth century. But the main line of interpretation from the time of Takikawa Masajirō's *Nihon dorei keizai shi* (Tokyo, 1930) has been to play down the role of slavery in the Japanese land system.

[29] Nakamura Kichiji, "Kodai," 146-158.

were engaged in tilling the soil, others in fishing or the performance of special craft or service functions. Controlling the *be* and
subsisting above them were the *uji*, to whose members belonged
the affairs of government, religion, and warfare.

The local power structure of Kibi took the shape of regional
hierarchies of *uji-be* units held together in loose equilibrium under
the influence of the Yamato hegemony. Dominating eastern Kibi
were the great *uji* of Kibi, Wake, and Saiki. Each one of these
lineages formed the center of a regional authority based first on
the extension of its own kinship organization and secondly upon
conquest or other forms of coercion. At the heart of each of these
regional hegemonies was an extended or great *uji*. From the *Nihon
shoki* passage relating Ōjin's visit to Kibi we can learn a good deal
about the structure of the great *uji* of Kibi. By the end of the fifth
century, the Kibi *uji* had become a complex familial organization
consisting of a loose cluster of families which acknowledged a real
or imagined common ancestry and submitted to the authority of
a central family, whose head served as the lineage chief, or *uji-no-
kami*.

Within such an extended *uji*, the chief maintained a position
of leadership as the supposed lineal descendant of the progenitor
of the *uji*. It was the prerogative of the *uji* chief to lead *uji* members in political and military affairs and in ceremonies of veneration toward the line's progenitor as a means of expressing family
solidarity. Frequently the protective deity of a powerful lineage
became identified with the locality over which the *uji* exercised
its political influence. This came about either by projecting the
uji-gami as a local guardian deity, or by the process of absorbing
previously venerated territorial *kami* into the *uji*'s ancestral cult.
At any rate, it became common for at least the most powerful local
uji chiefs to combine in their persons priestly as well as secular
power extending beyond the immediate membership of the *uji*
to include a geographical region. In Kibi most of these connections between family and shrine lost their meaning as the lineages
passed out of existence. Occasionally, as in the case of the Kaya
(later pronounced "Kayō") branch of the Kibi *uji*, this relationship
has continued. Today the shrine of Kibitsu is still tended by a
family which traces its lineage back directly to the Kaya family.
What saved this family was undoubtedly the fact that it attached
itself as hereditary wardens to the shrine and hence weathered

the political and military struggles which eliminated the other Kibi lines.

The extended *uji* were not permanently stable organisms. For they were constantly expanding or breaking up. The Kibi *uji* segmented almost immediately upon its arrival in Kibi into a number of branches, and the process of fragmentation continued generation after generation. The manner by which branch families were held within the extended *uji* structure is revealed in the practice of maintaining two sets of surnames, that of parent *uji* and that of branch. Most often, as in the case of the Kibi *uji*, branches adopted the names of the localities to which they moved. Thus within two generations after Mitomo-wake a member of the Kibi *uji* was identified as Kibi-no-shimotsumichi-no-omi-sakitsuya, a composite name made up of lineage name + branch name + title + given name. The fractional pull between *uji* ties and locality is illustrated in the tendency for each branch family to establish its own ancestral shrine within its area of residence. How many generations passed before branch lines began to drop the superior *uji* name is difficult to determine, but there is strong evidence that the fourth degree of relationship to the main line served as a first break point in *uji* connections.[30]

The composition of the great *uji*, especially the regional hegemons, was filled out by numerous subordinate families brought into subservience either by conquest or on a voluntary basis. Unfortunately we are given almost no information about the lesser ranks of *uji* society and of the manner by which the lesser *uji* related to the Kibi or Wake chiefs. We can surmise, on the basis of the example of the Yamato hegemony, that such *uji*, once brought into the range of control by superior local families were treated under various fictive kinship categories as remote branches, subjected families, voluntary allies, or "servant" families. We know very little also about the elements of authority which local chiefs could wield over the heads of lesser *uji*. The rendering of submission and veneration by virtue of superior charisma must have been more or less routine. Military service may also have been expected. Beyond this it is doubtful that any regular remission of tribute, other than gift tokens, could have been demanded. Each branch family or subject *uji* was expected to hold down its par-

[30] Abe Takehiko, "Jōdai keishisei no han-i ni tsuite," *Shigaku zasshi*, 55.2 (February 1944), 138-154.

ticular locale with its own resources. Yet in the face of the evidence of the great effort required to build the tumuli, we must imagine that at times the supreme chief could recruit the labors of the entire locale. If the Kibi-no-kuni-no-miyatsuko derived no regular tribute from all the many *uji* under his authority, he must at least have been able to require service contributions for "public" and "military" purposes. For its own private needs each *uji* unit of a regional hegemony was dependent upon its own workers and followers.

The relationship between *uji* and *be* was probably fairly uniform throughout Japan. It may well be that most *be* were originally *uji* which became subordinated to other more powerful *uji*.[31] Lesser branches of *uji* after several generations are known to have "fallen" into *be* status. War captives and a constant flow of immigrants from the continent also filled the lower social orders. By the late tomb period, the special condition of *be* members as a partially unfree, subordinate class had become the norm. Also it would seem that powerful *uji* such as those of the Yamato group or regional hegemons such as Kibi or Wake were constantly at work increasing the number of *be* which supported them. Many *be* were created by such *uji* for the purpose of tilling newly reclaimed land or to engage in some special craft. These were called *kakibe*. *Be* attached to the sovereign family were generically referred to as *tomobe* or as *nashiro*. The Yamato rulers also relied upon a variety of service *uji* (known as *tomo-no-miyatsuko*) to oversee the many *be* serving them. Thus for each major service or commodity the Yamato chief could draw upon the resources of his *be* through the agency of a service *uji*. Whether the Kibi *uji* had the use of service groups of the *tomo-no-miyatsuko* type is difficult to determine, yet it would seem unusual that the practice was limited to the ruling family alone. We do know, at least, that agricultural *be* communities served the Kibi *uji* and that some of these bore the name of Kibi-*be*. The appearance of the surname Wakebe in eighth century records shows also that the Wake must have controlled *be* bearing the name of their lineage.[32]

If at any time a locale such as Kibi could have existed as an independent political entity, completely free from outside inter-

[31] Nakamura Kichiji, *Nihon shakai shi*, 76-77.

[32] Ōta, *op.cit.*, 172; Hirano Kunio, "Taika zendai no shakai kōzō," in *Iwanami kōza, Nihon rekishi, 2, Kodai, 2* (Tokyo, 1962), 98.

ference, it could only have been before what we have called the
Yamato conquest of the area. The Kibi family from the first acknowledged the supremacy of Yamato, and this brought with it
certain tangible signs of subservience. But it may well be that
for a few generations after the entrance of the Kibi into this
region, the influence of Yamato rulers was obliged to pass entirely
through the hands of Kibi chiefs before it touched the lesser *uji*
and the *be* communities of Kibi. This condition was short-lived,
however, so that the picture we have of Kibi in the fifth century
shows a considerable influx of direct Yamato interference.

The intrusion of Yamato authority in Kibi is revealed not only
in the ability of Yamato rulers to control titles and make appointments among *uji* chiefs of the area, but also by their acquisition of
various lands, granaries, and productive *be*. Agricultural communities held in direct tribute relationship by the ruling family
were generally given names to commemorate some deceased sovereign or his consort. These formed a special type of *be* called
nashiro or *koshiro*. Many such communities have left their names
upon the present-day map of Kibi. Thus lands commended to the
memory of the famous Yamato general Yamato-takeru-no-mikoto
were worked by groups known as Takebe; for the consort of the
ruler Nintoku, Yatabe; for yet another consort of Nintoku, Kat-
suragibe; for a child of the same ruler, Kusakabe; for the consort
of the ruler Ingyō, Osakabe; for a child of Ingyō, Karube.[33] Scattered throughout the Kibi area, also, were numerous craft and
service communities which provided tribute for the Yamato court.
Such were the Kumebe and Mononobe, providers of military
service; the Yugebe and Yahagibe, makers of bows and arrows;
the Suebe, Hajibe and Imbe, makers of pottery; the Shitoribe,
Ayabe, Hatabe, Hatoribe communities of weavers; the Ukaibe,
Totoribe, Yamoribe, groups of hunters and fishers.[34]

The fact that the names of such *be* are liberally found among
the place names of present day Okayama leads us to suppose that
the Yamato rulers acquired a large number of direct connections
in Kibi during the fifth and sixth centuries. How the tribute from
such communities was assimilated into the Yamato system we
cannot determine precisely. It may well be that the several *kuni-
no-miyatsuko* (in other words Kibi and Wake chiefs) were re-

[33] *Tsūshi*, 1. 216-225; Ōta, *op.cit.*, 162-165.
[34] Tsūshi, 1. 244-252.

quired to supervise these special *be* and deliver quotas of tribute
to Yamato. On the other hand, there is evidence that the Yamato
rulers were constantly dispatching men of a more subordinate
status into the Kibi area for such supervisory purposes. The heavy
influx of continental immigrants appears to have had strategic
significance, for such groups tended to be more dependent upon
the Yamato authority. At a slightly later date, when special
granaries were attached to Yamato land or *be* holdings in Kibi,
there is evidence that the Yamato rulers sent out a supervisory
staff selected from among their lower officialdom.

This evidence of Yamato intrusion into Kibi in such a way as
to compete with local control of manpower and land raises a number of questions regarding the economic structure of the Kibi
regional hegemony, particularly with regard to the relationship
between political authority, economic production, and the concepts of land ownership. We are obviously dealing with a period
of social development in which modern concepts of private ownership are inappropriate. It is probably correct to assume that prior
to the emergence of the great *uji*, land was largely a communal
property and that frequent relocation or redistribution of cultivated plots mitigated against the sense of particular attachment
of individual to land. Moreover, the earliest evidence relating to
the *uji* shows that the great families were concerned not so much
with land as with manpower in the form of *be*. It was the human
rather than the material linkages to the sources of production that
were emphasized; hence, during the fifth and sixth centuries when
the Yamato rulers acquired what was essentially their own lands
in Kibi, their acquisition was accompanied by the creation of new
be to provide a means of working the lands and a mechanism for
the production of tribute.

The slow development of clearly defined concepts of land
tenure in Japan is not surprising, for it is obviously a product of
the particular conditions of agricultural technology that reached
an early stage of maturity during the Yamato period. The fact
that the most important economic activity in Japan at this time
was the production of rice by irrigated cultivation had important
implications for many aspects of Kibi life. There is every evidence
that the Kibi region was particularly well suited to agriculture.
The size and prevalence of tombs in Kibi lead us to conclude that
by the fifth century the area maintained a relatively dense popu-

lation with ample resources. Technologically the people seem to have been highly advanced by the standards of the time. Archaeological finds confirm the use of iron in agricultural implements. In fact, Bitchū has given its name to a particular type of four-pronged hoe-fork.[35] Despite the implications of the fact that the name Kibi may originally have meant "millet," we can be sure that rice was already widely cultivated throughout central Japan at this time. The combination of wet rice culture and the use of iron implements gave Kibi a rich productive base. But not only did rice cultivation provide the means of supporting a dense population and an influential ruling class, the requirements of wet rice cultivation were already having a profound effect upon the patterns of life and society and upon concepts of political authority and land tenure. Rice in fact proved to be a potent conditioning factor in that important zone of contact between human society and the land and its resources.

Even at the most primitive level of technology, irrigated rice cultivation carried with it certain advantages that made for high yield per unit of cultivation. The technique of flooding constantly replenishes the soil and makes possible its repeated use. Water can serve as a deterrent to weeds and insects; it also minimizes the need for fertilization and crop rotation. In this sense it provided an extremely secure and uniform base for an agricultural population like Kibi's.[36] On the other hand, wet rice cultivation tended to encourage a type of intensive farming in which attention was focused on the maximum production per unit of cultivation through the use of complex irrigation systems and the maximum expenditure of human labor. Both the necessities of irrigation and the heavy emphasis on manpower thus characterize the wet style of rice cultivation.[37]

It was characteristic of Japanese agriculture that it was almost exclusively dominated by wet rice cultivation. Why, for instance, was so little attention given to animal husbandry? Was it that the early and successful development of the paddy field system left no margin for other types of economy, was it because of religious or customary inhibitions against eating animal products, an idea

[35] Furushima Toshio, *Nihon nōgyō shi*, 34-35.
[36] Sakamoto Keiichi, "Suiden shakai no seikaku," *Jimbun gakuhō*, 3 (March 1953), 143-149.
[37] *Ibid.*, 149-152.

later reinforced by Buddhism, or was it because of the prevalence of the bamboo grass (*sasa*) that was unsuited to grazing?[38] The now successful introduction of dairying into Okayama Prefecture would tend to direct the answer toward the first two suggestions. The paddy field system was firmly established in Japan—in fact, in most of East Asia—by the Yamato period.

A system of intensive agriculture requiring heavy application of manpower both stimulated and depended upon a dense sedentary population concentrated upon alluvial plains and river valleys. Rice cultivation under irrigation could provide extremely high yields. But paddy field technology is complex and laborious. The preparing of dyked fields and the planting and transplanting of rice are labor-consuming operations that permit relatively little use of draught animal power. Thus agricultural Japan from this remote past clearly required an unusual concentration of population on the land. In turn, the pressure of this population must have served to intensify the method of cultivation so that it could produce sufficient food for all mouths, requiring elaborate parceling of land into small, intensively worked plots.

Irrigated rice cultivation could affect its users in yet another way, for it imparted a stabilizing, even self-perpetuating, inertia to the technology while emphasizing the social factors of organizing manpower among the cultivators. One is struck by the almost exact identity between the hoe, both forked and bladed, the ploughs, and other cultivating equipment identified by archaeologists as belonging to this period and the equipment used until the end of the nineteenth century in this area. Such simple tools remained sufficient for the kind of "hand cultivation" required by the paddy field system. On the other hand, the "land-and-water technology" of this form of agriculture became increasingly complex and refined. The construction of irrigated plots themselves was never a simple matter. Paddy fields had to be constructed to hold water at an even level. In preparing them the cultivator often had to start several feet below the surface of the land and build up with carefully graded soils. Each plot had to be dyked and linked to an irrigation source. The same irrigation system had to provide for proper drainage as well during the times when the fields are dried. This complicated network of terraced fields and interlacing irrigation and drainage ditches was neither easily

---

[38] F. Joüon des Longrais, *L'est et l'ouest* (Tokyo, Paris, 1958), 92.

assembled nor easily modified. It inevitably became the cherished heritage of an entire community, generation after generation.

The irrigation technology of tomb age Kibi was, to be sure, still in its rudimentary stages, but there is evidence of the existence of artificial ponds and dyked fields, a sign that intensive technology was already established.[39] Even in protohistoric times, and with increasing intensity thereafter, we can imagine that wet rice farming placed an imprint upon the communities of Kibi. Upon the smallest social units, the household and *be*, it placed the maximum need for internal cohesion and cooperation. We can imagine also that communal organization for cultivation and work on irrigation systems tended to favor the continuance of concepts of communal ownership (or use) of land and water rights, particularly with regard to the rice lands. Somewhat later in the sixth century when evidence of tenure concepts permits a more adequate view of the land system of Japan, it appears that while *uji* or household ownership of dry land, forest, and house plots existed, paddy land still retained its communal character.[40]

Wet rice cultivation thus had manifold social implications that could put their stamp upon Kibi even in these remote times. Lack of crop diversity and the heavy labor needs of paddy field cultivation served to limit individual initiative and deemphasize factors of economic independence within the communal group. Reclamation of land, the opening up of new paddies, the control and use of water were operations requiring the joint efforts of extended communities or the economic resources of the politically powerful.[41] The tendency then was toward settled communities closely locked in cooperative organizations such as the *uji* and *be*. The interrelation between the economic system of primitive Japan and the general pattern of family organization in which authority followed along the lines of social hierarchy, in which emphasis on manpower and family ties predominated over land and abstract concepts of authority, was not accidental. It may well be that the entire culture of a region such as Kibi was more "inner-directed," its leaders more intent upon the exploitation of available manpower than the acquisition of new territory, and the agrarian population more absorbed in the intensification of production from existing fields rather than the expansion of cultivation.

[39] *Nōchi shi*, 186.
[40] Torao Toshiya, *Handen shūju-hō no kenkyū* (Tokyo, 1961), 415.
[41] Sakamoto Keiichi, *op.cit.*, 157-162.

Despite our limited knowledge of the social and economic institutions of Kibi as a unit of local political life prior to the seventh century, enough is known to have revealed to us a pattern of life of great significance to the later history of the area. The units in this pattern were the ruling *uji*, hierarchically arranged along familial lines, an agrarian base stressing irrigation and intensive application of manpower, and between these a form of political and social control centered in the communal village and legitimized by pseudo-kinship concepts and locally rooted religious beliefs. As we shall see, these fundamental institutions of the tomb period and the manner of integration between them were to prove ancestral to some of the most basic and long-enduring practices of government and social and economic organization in Japan. And while the cultural style and technology of life in Kibi was to change many times before the advent of modern times, there was in fact only one major near break with the concepts which underlay the "familial state" system of these early years. This near break came in the seventh century in the reform program based on Chinese models, to which we must now turn.

II. THE CREATION
OF THE IMPERIAL STATE SYSTEM

THE court revolution of 645, with the accompanying Taika Reform, is commonly assumed to be the great turning point in early Japanese history, the dividing line between the familially organized Yamato hegemony and a new centralized order built in the image of the great empires of the continent. But as so often happens in historical interpretation, the reputation of a "great event" has been used in this instance to catch up a cluster of changes that occurred much more haphazardly and less dramatically over a period of several centuries. While the coup d'état of 645 brought about a crucial shift in the balance of political power at the Yamato court and, as a consequence, assured a decisive commitment to certain reform policies, it by no means signaled the beginning of radical social and political innovation under continental inspiration. It neither marked the origin of such reforms, nor witnessed their fulfillment.[1] This is especially true for a local area such as Kibi where the impetus for cultural and institutional change was not automatically responsive to factional shifts within the Yamato court.

While there is a deceptive flatness to the narrative record of Japanese history from the fourth to the seventh century, historians and archaeologists have been able to identify below the surface a number of important structural movements in Japanese culture between the time of the fashioning of the Yamato hegemony and the time of the Taika Reform. They see, in fact, the gradual shift from a society organized primarily along familial lines toward one in which the various aspects of society were becoming increasingly differentiated on functional grounds and in which secular operations of government tended to separate out from the traditional *uji* and *be* communal practices. The stimulus for such changes was both internal and external.

Most apparent of the internally motivated changes was the steady increase in the effective power exercised by the Yamato rulers. Up through the period of early conquest and the ultimate

---

[1] Of the abundant literature on the Taika Reform I have relied mainly on the recent works of Inoue Mitsusada. A convenient summary of his views is contained in his "Ritsuryō taisei no seiritsu," in *Iwanami kōza, Nihon rekishi, 3, Kodai 3* (Tokyo, 1962), 1-31. Henceforth cited as "Ritsuryō taisei."

consolidation of Japan's scattered and independent chieftains under a single hegemon, the basic structure of the Yamato polity had been that of a federation of *uji.* By the fifth century, however, the Yamato rulers were engaged in an effort to override the extreme aspects of decentralization within this system and to assert a more direct voice in local affairs. The attempt to rationalize the exercise of authority by local chieftains as a delegation under the title *kuni-no-miyatsuko* was a clear example of this. The increase in number of *be* directly controlled by the Yamato family also represented a direct intrusion of Yamato influence into peripheral areas. In addition, the new communities of Chinese and Korean immigrants who took up residence in outlying areas were often attached to Yamato as special service groups. In some parts of the country, notably the northeast, the Yamato rulers even developed the practice of recruiting private military garrisons from among the *kuni-no-miyatsuko* families.

A significant breakthrough in the direction of increased central power came with the creation in Yamato, and in numerous outlying districts, of properties held under the direct ownership of the Yamato rulers. These were the sovereign estates, or *miyake,* which began to expand with great vitality after the middle of the sixth century. We know too little about the actual operation of the *miyake* to describe them with any great certainty, yet it is probably safe to conceive of them as a form of property holding in which the emphasis was placed upon land rather than upon family or upon *be* organizations. By dedicating *miyake* each to some deceased member of the Yamato family, these lands were held as heritable possessions by the various branches of the Yamato family. In their locales, *miyake* were worked either by labor drawn from adjoining lands or by artificially created agrarian communities known as *tomobe. Miyake* were superintended either by delegation through the *kuni-no-miyatsuko* or through special agents sent out from Yamato. In either case they intruded upon the territorial autonomy of outlying *uji.*

In Kibi the spread of *miyake* quite clearly followed the gradual decline of the Kibi family. There is, in fact, a hint that the growth of *miyake* was pushed at the expense of local autonomy, perhaps as a means of bringing the Kibi region more directly under Yamato control. Leaving their names on the map of Okayama today are the sites of numerous *miyake.* Under the year 555, the *Nihon shoki* records: "Iname-no-Sukune, Soga-no-Ōomi and Hozumi-no-Iwa-yumi-no-Omi were dispatched to the five *agata* of Kibi to establish the *miyake* of Shirai."[2] And in the next year the following passage was recorded: "Soga-no-Ōomi, Iname-no-Sukune and others were dispatched to the district of Kojima in Kibi to establish a *miyake*. Mizuko, Katsuragi-no-Atae was made steward."[3] This mention of the island of Kojima, which is conspicuously absent from the early historical records of Kibi, suggests that the island may not have been included in the Kibi family's sphere of influence. It is quite probable that it had developed instead into an important outpost of Yamato strength, for it is frequently mentioned in the annals of the ruling house.[4] A reason for this may have been that Kojima provided a convenient way-stop in the communication route between Yamato and Dazaifu, the administrative center of Japan's overseas contacts located in northern Kyushu at the end of the Inland Sea.[5] At any rate, four *miyake* sites can be identified in Kojima today, and one of these may well have been the administrative center to which Soga-no-Iname traveled.

The spread of *miyake* is bound up with yet another fundamental change which affected even more deeply the nature of Japanese society in the sixth century. The *miyake* represented a new conception of property and of the relationship between political power and land. *Uji* society had put its emphasis not upon land, but upon manpower and the social requisites necessary to secure it. Wealth was assessed in terms of the size of the *uji*, the extent of its branches and service groups. The hierarchies of power and wealth were in fact one. Perpetuation of power came through the inheritance of family status and the secular and religious authority accompanying such status. Wealth accrued to social position and flowed through lines of kin-based hierarchal relationships. Land appears to have been controlled under a vague conception of communal ownership vested in the chieftain; hence, there was no free acquisition or free disposal.

Such a conception of landed property is obviously fundamen-

[2] *Nihon shoki*, Chap. 19, Section 48.

[3] *Ibid.*, 19.48.

[4] Fujii, Taniguchi, and Mizuno, eds., *Okayama-ken no rekishi* (Okayama, 1962), 61-64. Hereafter cited by title only. Also Fujii Shun, "Kodai-shi jō no Kibi no Kojima," in Kodaigaku Kyōkai, *Nihon kodai shi ronsō* (Tokyo, 1960), 588-604.

[5] Hiroshima Shiyakusho, *Shinshū Hiroshima-shi shi* (6 vols., Hiroshima, 1961), 1 (*Sōsetsu*), 238.

tally different from one in which property becomes identified on what we would call economic terms. And basic to this difference were the practices of considering land private and heritable on the one hand, and subject to public or state control on the other. In other words, they followed the tendency of the ruling families to differentiate their social and political roles and develop a more overtly defined attitude toward the ingredients of wealth and political power.

The shift toward differentiated rather than communal owner-ship is most evident in the activities of the Yamato rulers, but it did not stop there. Although we lack in Kibi the documentary evidence to show that local *uji* pursued an aggressive policy of land acquisition, it is possible to trace the growth of the Kibi and Wake families and follow their spread into the upper valleys of the coastal plain and beyond into Mimasaka. This spread at first resulted from a natural proliferation and branching of the two *uji*. But as land naturally suited to rice cultivation was used up, we may suppose that the families engaged in "land improvement" which brought with it the concept of intimate ownership. *Uji* rice lands, known as *tadokoro* and worked by newly created *be*, known as *kakibe*, were making their appearance.

Evidence that the *uji* and their several branches were increas-ingly engaged in private aggrandizement is revealed both in the archaeological record and in the chronicles. By the early sixth century there began to appear in Kibi the first of the small graves of rather humble construction (at least by the standards of the great tumuli) which in a century or so came to cover the entire area in the tens of thousands. Clusters of these tumuli, averaging perhaps 20 feet across, now began to dot the Kibi landscape. And while some may have contained impressive stonework and con-tents, others were clearly of a more modest construction. Japanese archaeologists have been able to show that in terms of local popu-lation the practice of conspicuous burial was extending to a much wider number of the *uji* elite. The breakup of the integral *uji* unit into its branch components seems clearly revealed in this evi-dence.[6] And this conclusion is confirmed by the notices in the chronicles, particularly the government edicts after 645, which

[6] Wajima Seiichi, "Kofun bunka no henshitsu," in *Iwanami kōza, Nihon rekishi*, 2, *Kodai* 2 (Tokyo, 1962), 146-153; Kurashiki Kōkokan, *Kibi no kofun* (Kura-shiki, 1960).

complain of the competition among the *uji* for private wealth and manpower and the exhaustion of the country's resources through the building of ever increasing numbers of graves.

In the chronicles these social and economic developments are linked to the gathering political unrest of the period; and there seems no reason to question this relationship. Kibi was as involved in such unrest as any locale. Frequent participation by Kibi leaders in Yamato intrigues reflect a mounting power struggle between Kibi and Yamato. How much of this conflict was purely political and how much economic, we have no way of deciding conclusively. But we can be sure that both wealth and power were interrelated. Whereas earlier accounts of *uji* feuds and the Yamato conquest of new territories most often concluded with stories of the adjustment of kinship relationships and the degradation of the deities of the defeated *uji*, later accounts tell more frequently of the disposition of property. After the defeat of Kibi-Kamutsumichi-no-omi in an attempted coup d'état after Yūryaku's death, the victorious party confiscated for the Yamato ruler all the *yamabe* (grave keepers) in the family's possession. Confiscation of Mononobe property in 587 provides us with a remarkable inventory of the properties held by that great *uji*: 273 slaves and over 100,000 "paces" of rice land. Land and slaves were clearly commodities of accumulation. As noted with alarm in the Taika Reform edict of 645: "Within the several districts the families divide up the hills, seas, ponds and fields and make of them their own property. They do not cease to struggle among themselves. Some have amassed up to several tens of thousands of paces of riceland. Others have not even enough land into which to stick a needle."[7]

An equally characteristic complaint voiced by the reform edicts of the Taika era, however, was over the breakdown in social order illustrated primarily by the falsification of genealogies and false claims to title and rank. As the chronicles stated: "The minds of the people of the whole country take a strong partisan bias and conceiving a deep sense of me and thee hold firmly each to their names. . . . The names of *kami* and of sovereigns are applied to persons and places in an unauthorized manner. . . . As a consequence the minds of the people have become unsettled and the government of the country cannot be carried on."[8] This disrup-

---

[7] *Nihon shoki*, 25.12.   [8] *Ibid.*, 25.37. (Aston trans.)

tion of the lines of authority which accompanied the economic differentiation of *uji* society was to prove most troublesome to the Yamato rulers. And it was, in fact, largely toward this problem that their efforts to define a more general system of political authority were directed.

These indications of mounting social and economic unrest should not come as a surprise. They were in many ways the predictable outcome of the failure of the *uji* social system to keep pace with changes in the technological and agricultural base. Equally predictable was the direction from which the solution to these problems was to come, namely, the continent of Asia. To the Japanese of the sixth century there could have been no doubt that Chinese political and religious institutions seemed vastly superior to anything they then possessed. There was no disputing, first of all, the great power and influence of imperial China, and this power was based not only on the size of the empire and the great number of its people but also upon the techniques of political organization and the means of channeling human energies. What distinguished the institutions of imperial China from those of the petty states on her periphery was the superior ability to achieve systematic organization of the administrative, economic, military, and religious functions of society. Characteristic of the familial form of organization was its functional dis-separateness. Such a system was sufficient, of course, for a small and relatively undifferentiated community. But the kinship structure became overloaded as society increased in complexity and specialization. It was the advantage of the Chinese system that it provided a more adequate technology of social organization behind new concepts of political and religious authority.

Of course we cannot suppose that the early rulers of Japan or of Korea comprehended the difference between their own society and that of China other than in the overwhelming realization of the superior grandeur of China or except perhaps in small technological details. China as a great power was feared or emulated. Chinese artifacts were desirable and sought after. Chinese immigrants were highly skilled in weaving or metal work and hence were welcomed. And, where possible, Chinese ways of doing things, of writing and recording, of weaving silk or divining the future, were adopted where it seemed practicable. By the middle of the sixth century, however, the peoples of Korea and Japan were absorbing more fundamental aspects of the Chinese institutional complex with certain predictable results. In this the Korean states took the lead over Japan, but in Japan too the obvious realization that there was a conflict between native traditions and new practices learned from China became sufficiently apparent to divide leadership around the Yamato sovereign into two contending camps by the middle of the sixth century.

We can assume that a constant and fairly continuous seepage of material innovations had entered Japan from the continent up to the sixth century. This could have gone on indefinitely with no fundamental disruption of Japan's social fabric. During the sixth century, however, Japan was reacting to two more far-reaching influences: a new technology of state and the new religion of Buddhism. This observation contains nothing new; scholars have long interpreted the significance of the Taika Reform in terms of the impact of Confucian institutions and Buddhist beliefs on Japan. What we must gain sight of, however, is the length of time over which these two influences were at work and how fundamentally they were to meet the basic needs of Yamato society.

The early steps toward increased centralization and functional differentiation in the Yamato government could have taken place without reference to continental models. The extension of the *tomo-no-miyatsuko* and *kuni-no-miyatsuko* systems and later the appointment of great councillors (*ō-omi* and *ōmuraji*) emerged logically out of the Yamato familial system. To move beyond this point to a more bureaucratically organized administration, however, required changes in the theory and execution of government, and it was here that the traditional system was proving most inadequate. As the Yamato rulers pushed the *miyake* system into local territories, for instance, and especially as local chiefs vied with each other for land, certain fundamental questions were raised regarding the concept of state authority, the nature of sovereignty and local power, and the nature of proprietary authority over land. The answers eventually adopted were already in the air, but they came from outside the system in the form of Buddhist ideas of social order and Confucian concepts of the primacy of the state and techniques of administrative and fiscal management. By the sixth century the kingdoms of Korea had all adopted Buddhism as their state religion and most had begun to use the state-controlled system of official ranks, had remodeled their governments according to the Chinese bureaucratic system, and had adopted the land tax procedures devised by the Northern Wei dynasty.

The main channel through which such new concepts and techniques of government entered Japan was apparently the fiscal branch of the Yamato court. This in turn was in large part the doing of the Soga *uji*, which by the mid-sixth century was serving as hereditary great councillors, or *ō-omi*, in Yamato. The Soga family, a comparatively late arrival on the Yamato scene, was a branch of the Yamato line which, about the middle of the fifth century, was placed in charge of the "three treasuries." This meant that the Soga oversaw the collection, storage, and expenditure of various tribute articles produced by service *be* other than those superintended directly by the service *uji* such as the Mononobe, Ōtomo, and Imbe. In practice, the bulk of the service functions managed by the Soga were concerned with the new *be* formed by immigrant Chinese craftsmen and the new Yamato ricelands of the *miyake* type.

Since the sources of income that flowed into the three treasuries were heterogeneous, the Soga relationship to the producers could not rest on usual familial practice. The Soga were not set up, in other words, as *tomo-no-miyatsuko* over *be* which were considered the fictional kin appendages of the Soga chieftain. Rather they served as administrative chiefs over groups of producers (some of which may have been organized as *be*) comprised of immigrants or freshly assembled agricultural workers. Over such groups the Soga exerted not the authority of an *uji* chief backed by the powers of a family deity, but rather the abstract authority of the Yamato sovereign. For control purposes the Soga apparently used officials employed on a bureaucratic basis. A concrete illustration of the Soga method of fiscal administration is revealed in the example of the Shirai *miyake* of Kibi established in 555. A subsequent notice in the chronicles reports that in 569 a superintendent (*tatsukai*) of the *miyake* was selected from among one of the Soga branch families, and a vice-superintendent was appointed from an immigrant family. The latter received the surname Shirai for merit in managing the *miyake*. Cultivators were organized into corps (*tako*) and assigned land on the basis of a cadastral register.[9] Here then was evidence that the Japanese had begun to adopt the continental system of land allocation and taxation. A method of land measurement based upon the *shiro,* a unit prevalent in Korea since the Han dynasty, was apparently also in use. Along with it went a new systematic method of taxation and labor recruitment.[10]

It is no accident that the Soga were instrumental in introducing into Japan not only Chinese practices of administration but also the Buddhist religion. Among the top rank of the various *uji* in Yamato the Soga were unquestionably the most intimately acquainted with conditions in China and Korea. At the same time, the Soga, as a branch of the Yamato *uji,* had a less separate identity than some of the long-established families whose lineages traced back to the age of the native *kami,* or whose territorial bases were firmly fixed in a traditional locality. Just as the Soga had borrowed the prestige of the Yamato sovereign in their fiscal dealings, so also were they open to the possibility of adopting a new religion as a source of political influence.

Buddhism must have been known in Japan several decades before 552, the official date given for its introduction. Surely it was the chosen religion of many of the immigrant families who settled in Japan after the beginning of the sixth century. But its acceptance within the Yamato court was not easily achieved. To the ruling families of Yamato who based their political authority in important part upon their claim of descent from the *kami* native to the Japanese islands, Buddhism presented a real and even frightening threat. The possibility of its contribution to a more stable political hierarchy was not easily seen. For if it was, as it claimed, a religious power superior to all local powers, then what was to become of the religious authority claimed by the various *uji* chiefs or by the *mikoto?* Once the authority of the Shinto *kami* was challenged, then the foundation of *uji* society could be threatened. As it turned out, these fears were only partially justified, even for the lesser *uji.* Buddhism did not displace Shinto, though its spread coincided with the abandonment of Shinto as the sole spiritual support of the social and political order in Japan. Buddhism, in fact, within a short time was to make a vital con-

[9] See the interpretation given the *Nihon shoki* notices by Ueda Masaaki in his "Asuka no kyūtei," in *Nihon rekishi kōza, 1, Genshi-kodai* (Tokyo, 1958), 145-147.

[10] Murao Jirō, *Ritsuryō zaiseishi no kenkyū* (Tokyo, 1961), 35-37.

tribution to the whole apparatus supporting the authority of the Yamato sovereign and the hierarchy of nobles attached to him.

It was in 552 that the issue of Buddhism was squarely put before the great families of Yamato. A predictable clash between the Soga and the traditionally oriented chieftains such as the Mononobe and Nakatomi resulted. There is no record of how the Kibi chiefs stood at this point, but their later behavior as members of a counterreform party in 646 would lead us to believe that they must have opposed the introduction of Buddhism. Yet not for long, or perhaps not by all, for Buddhist relics in Kibi burial mounds reveal an early interest in the new religion.[11] The result of the controversy over Buddhism is well known. The tension between the Soga and the Mononobe, smoldering long before the religious issue had arisen, now broke into open flame. Mutual acts of defiance mounted in intensity until 587 when the Soga annihilated the Mononobe and distributed the major part of the defeated family's property for support of the new religion. From this point for the next thirty years direction of affairs in Yamato passed into the hands of two men openly committed to pressing continental institutions upon Japan. These were Soga-no-Umako, head of the Soga main lineage, who served as *ō-omi*, and the Yamato prince Umayado-no-toyotomimi-no-mikoto, posthumously known as Shō-toku Taishi, who served as regent to the ruler Suiko. Shōtoku Taishi lived until 622, and, although he was never free from the shadow of Soga dominance, he emerged as a vigorous champion of the dignity of the Yamato sovereign.

Whether or not all the acts attributed to Shōtoku Taishi were indeed his own is not of great importance to us at this point. Certainly it was during his lifetime that the Yamato court came to understand the role Buddhism could play as a buttress to the social order, and the dream of rebuilding the political hierarchy in Japan on the Confucian principles of state centralization came into being. During these years the conception that the ruler of Yamato was indeed a sovereign emperor to whom the people of Japan owed allegiance as loyal subjects was first clearly enunciated.

If we may accept the traditional, and undoubtedly idealized, record, much of Shōtoku Taishi's life was dedicated to the increase

[11] See the reproduction of a mirror decorated with four Buddhist figures found in Ōba-yama tumulus, late sixth century, in Kurashiki Kōkokan, *Kibi no kofun*.

of imperial prestige. In his youth he fought for the acceptance of Buddhism as a recognized religion of state, and in his later years he richly endowed Buddhist institutions throughout the Yamato area. For several years he worked to recapture Japan's lost power of interference in Korean affairs, sending expeditions to recapture Mimana between 595 and 602. Then abandoning his military policy, he opened up direct communication with the reunited Chinese empire in 607.

Shōtoku Taishi was less successful in securing the internal political reforms needed to bolster the Yamato hegemony. He attempted, however, to gain for the Yamato sovereign the status of a ruler in the imperial sense, endowed with the moral foundations of sovereignty and surrounded by a regulated court and officialdom. The adoption in 603 of a system of twelve court ranks placed in the hands of the sovereign the power to determine to his interest the order of official precedence. The proclamation in 604 of a code of seventeen articles of government set a new tone of political ethics, borrowing Confucian theories of state in which the relationship between sovereign and subject was proclaimed to be that of Heaven to Earth. At home and abroad Shōtoku Taishi worked for the adoption of a new terminology of sovereignty in Yamato, applying the concepts of imperial China and asserting for the Yamato chief the dignity of "emperor" or "son of heaven."

The death of Shōtoku Taishi in 622 and the passing of Soga-no-Umako from the political scene soon after plunged the Yamato court into a state of political rivalry which far overshadowed any steps toward the continued introduction of continental institutions. In the years following, it became quite clear that the Yamato and Soga families had joined forces only temporarily during the regency of Shōtoku Taishi. Between these two families there existed a basic conflict of interest that made itself increasingly apparent in the next two decades. While both were willing to conceive of a centralized state with authority vested in a sovereign of the Chinese type, it was clear that the Soga and many other powerful *uji* expected that the role of the sovereign would be as nominal as it actually had become by the early years of the seventh century. Whether the Soga actually intended to usurp the throne as has been claimed is immaterial. After 622 they gave every indication of setting themselves up as unrivaled masters of the Yamato court, controlling the Yamato sovereign through the post of great councillor and by intermarriage.

In Yamato after 622, then, the process of political and cultural change under Chinese influence became inextricably interwoven with the domestic competition among the great chiefs. Gradually, in the succeeding years there had begun to emerge a coalition of families, led by Prince Naka-no-Ōe and Nakatomi-no-Kamako, dedicated to seizure of power from the Soga and also to the furtherance of the centralizing political and administrative reforms that Shōtoku Taishi had recommended. Prince Naka had very personal reasons for opposing the Soga, who had pushed him out of succession to the throne. So did his other followers have grievances, frequently of a personal sort. Nonetheless, these men realized that no simple redistribution of the balance of power at the Yamato court, no mere coup d'état that would put them in positions of authority at the expense of the Soga would make any lasting change. The close contact of this group with advisers who had studied at first hand the bureaucratic achievements of T'ang China led them to the conclusion that far-reaching institutional reforms must accompany any direct action on their part. The rest of the story is well known. In 645, at a state ceremonial, Prince Naka himself took the lead in assassinating Soga-no-Iruka. This dramatic and frightening act not only prepared the way for the easy elimination of Soga influence but so stunned the great chiefs that a reform faction led by Prince Naka quite easily gained control of the Yamato court. On New Year's Day of 646 this group, after a thorough political house-cleaning, issued the famous reform edict that established the basis of a new political order. Its provisions are of sufficient interest to be quoted at length:

1. Let the status of imperial serf (*koshiro*) created by former emperors together with the scattered imperial lands (*miyake*) be abolished. Also let the privately held serfs (*kakibe*) and the scattered lands (*tadokoro*) of the *omi, muraji, tomo-no-miyatsuko, kuni-no-miyatsuko,* and *mura-no-obito* be abolished. In their place sustenance households (*hehito*) will be assigned to all of the rank of *mosagimi* and above according to rank. For officials and those with surnames (*hyakushō*) payments of cloth will be made according to rank. . . .
2. From henceforth an imperial city will be established and

provincial and district governors assigned in the home territories (*uchitsukuni*). Barriers, guard and defense forces, post
horses, and transport horses shall be provided. Bells and
tokens shall be made, and the use of mountains and rivers
regulated. . . . Districts of 40 villages (*ri*) will be classed as
large, those of from 30 to 4 villages as medium, and those of
3 villages as small. For the districts let *kuni-no-miyatsuko* of
good character, able to endure the duties of office, be chosen
as governors (*ōmiyatsuko*) and assistant-governors (*suke-
no-miyatsuko*). Let men of skill and intelligence with ability
at writing and arithmetic be selected as administrative chiefs
(*matsurikoto-hito*) and record keepers (*fumi-hito*). . . .

3. Population and tax registers will be drawn up, and laws
   enacted for the taking in and granting out of allotment land.
   Fifty households (*ko*) will comprise a village (*ri*). Each
   village shall have one headman (*chō*) in charge of the supervision of the households and individuals, the planting of
   crops, the cultivation of mulberry trees, the prevention and
   examination of offenses, and the levy of taxes and labor. A
   tan of paddy land shall measure 30 by 12 paces. Ten *tan* shall
   equal a *chō*. For each *tan* the land tax is two sheaves (*tsuka*)
   and two hands (*tawari*) of rice. The tax on a *chō* is 22 sheaves
   of rice. However, in hills or valleys where land is steeply
   graded, or in remote areas of scant population, collection
   should be made according to circumstances.

4. The old labor tax is abolished and in its place a produce tax
   (*mitsugi*) will be collected on rice lands. This will be paid in
   silk, coarse silk, thread, or batting according to the produce
   of each locality. For one *chō* of paddy land the tax rate is one
   jō (10 *shaku*) of fine silk cloth. . . . There shall also be a produce tax levied by household to the amount of 1 *jō* 2 *shaku*
   of coarse cloth each. Subsidiary produce taxes such as salt
   will be collected according to the produce of the locality. One
   hundred households will provide one medium quality horse
   for official use. If a horse is of fine quality, it may suffice for
   200 households. If a horse is purchased, the price shall be
   made up at the rate of 12 feet (*shaku*) of coarse cloth per
   household. For military equipment, each person shall provide
   sword, armor, bow, arrows, banner, and drum. The old practice of requiring one male for assignment to various public

officials from each 30 households is modified to one from each 50 households. Fifty households will make up provision for one servant. The commuted labor tax (*chikarashiro*) is 12 *shaku* of cloth and 5 *shō* of rice per household. Ladies-in-waiting (*uneme*) shall be selected from among the sisters or daughters of district governors. They should be comely and be attended by 1 male and 2 female servants. One hundred families will be responsible for supplying provisions for one lady-in-waiting. The collection of cloth and rice for this purpose shall follow the rule for the provisioning of servants.[12]

There is, of course, some doubt that the Taika edict was issued in the above form, and its inclusion in the *Nihon shoki* may well be a version retouched by later official historians.[13] But whether the document is in its original form or not, it unquestionably contains the essence of the reform policy that culminated in the Taihō administrative and penal code of 702, and reached its clearest manifestation with the completion of the permanent capital of Nara in 710.

It goes without saying that the coup d'état of 645 and the edict of 646 did not change overnight the condition of the entire country. The reform faction was strategically placed in Yamato, but it was never without its opponents even within the Yamato family and particularly among those families long established around the Yamato sovereign or in the outlying regions. For this reason the reform faction moved slowly and pragmatically, making changes where they were most easily brought about and compromising where necessary. The process of bringing rice land under public regulation began at first voluntarily when Prince Naka relinquished his own private lands. Other Yamato lands, the *miyake* and *nashiro*, were also readily brought under central control and management. In 649, eight departments of central administration were created and an officialdom named to staff them. In 652 an imperial headquarters was established at Naniwa and in the next year the first national land distribution and tax census was completed. By the time Prince Naka had ascended the throne in 668 as the emperor Tenchi, he was ready to order the compilation of a comprehensive administrative code, the now lost *Ōmi ryō*.

[12] *Nihon shoki*, Kokushi Taikei edition, 1.431-433.
[13] Torao Toshiya, *op.cit.*, 99-112; Mayuzumi Hiromichi, "Taika-kaishin Shō to Ritsuryō to no kankei," *Rekishi kyōiku*, 9.5 (1961), 12-17.

Upon Tenchi's death a serious succession dispute broke out which engulfed six provinces of central Japan in several months of bloody warfare. Yet it was this war, the so-called Jinshin disturbance, that brought to power an emperor in possession of all the attributes of absolute rule. The emperor Temmu, having built up a strong military force in eastern Japan, swept to power as much on the basis of military might as any Japanese ruler since prehistoric times. A combination of military force, clearcut military victory over his rivals, and the support of the lesser nobility put Temmu in a position of real influence and gave him the ability to act resolutely and decisively. For the first time since the coup d'état of 645 the imperial family itself had sufficient power at hand to exert real leadership.

It was Temmu, therefore, who completed the program begun by Prince Naka and who succeeded in pushing through measures that had long been opposed by vested interests in Yamato. It was Temmu, for instance, who finally succeeded in exchanging lands traditionally held by the upper nobility for new lands under state control. He attempted also to break once and for all ties of personal subservience between the agricultural communities and the nobility. He even had some success in obliging officials to return their sustenance lands to the state after their term of office was terminated.[14]

One measure adopted by Temmu has been misunderstood as a compromise with the desire of the nobility to regain the privileges they enjoyed as *uji* chiefs. His reinstitution of a system of hereditary titles did indeed seem like a return to the old *kabane*. But the fact was that the new titles were so arranged that they concentrated unassailable social prestige within the imperial house and made possible the rewarding of a selected few families who had been most loyal to Temmu. In other words it instituted a new and stable hierarchy of noble families around the throne. Historians have recently come to the conclusion that Temmu's greatest contribution was the drafting of the *Kiyomihara ritsuryō* code of 689, which provided the direct model for the Taihō code of 702.

Before shifting our attention from the center of political activity to the provinces, it is essential for us to try to grasp more fully and completely the meaning of what had transpired in Japan

[14] Inoue Mitsusada, "Ritsuryō taisei," 14.

during the seventh century. Unfortunately, the recorded chronicles of this period tell us little about the motives of the main participants in political reform and almost nothing about the sentiments of the rest of the country, whether they welcomed reform or were the reluctant victims of changes which they basically mistrusted.

It is obviously too facile to assume that the Taika Reform occurred simply as the result of irresistible Chinese influence upon Japan. Nor should we judge the success or failure of the reform movement on the basis of how closely the Japanese copied the institutions of T'ang China. The Chinese model was of course vastly influential and stimulating to the Japanese, and within their capacity to understand the essence of China's greatness, Japan's leaders were certainly tempted to emulate these qualities. On the other hand, throughout the course of the century of reform that we have just traced, those who led the reform were also practical participants in the struggle for political power. Reform was not pushed merely to achieve institutional symmetry. And in the end the Japanese version of the continental model included differences and innovations which were a product of the domestic realities of seventh century Japan. We can assume that behind the policies of the Yamato leaders were specific political objectives and a clear recognition of the limits within which change was possible or desirable.

It is obvious from the reform edict and the subsequent work of the reform leaders that one of their main concerns was the strengthening of the central government and the technological improvement of administration. The creation of an imperial city with a fully developed officialdom, the adoption of systematic codes of law and governmental procedures, the elaborate rationalization of local government, taxation, and military affairs were carried out with zeal and in many ways a remarkable degree of initial success. So long as private interests were not jeopardized this was the sort of achievement about which all the people of Japan could become excited. The real question then is how the reform affected the private interests of the various groups and regions in Japan. Was reform coerced, and if so by whom? Who benefited and who suffered as a result? Were the reformers entirely without personal or group bias, and were those who opposed reform necessarily obstructionists?

In some ways the last half of the seventh century bears resemblance to the last half of the nineteenth century in Japan. At both times Japan was brought face to face with a foreign culture unquestionably superior in terms of political and economic technology. We do not know whether Japan of the seventh century felt a sense of foreign crisis comparable to that which agitated the Japanese of the nineteenth century. Yet it is true that the Yamato court exerted itself strenuously to recapture its Korean base and that Japanese forces met bitter defeat at the hands of the armies and navies of Silla and T'ang China. If the Yamato leaders did not react to a fear of outright invasion from the continent, at least they were motivated by a sense of chagrin over the impotence of their expeditionary forces. There was certainly alive in the Yamato plain a desire to gain strength and to assert the equality of Japan among the states of East Asia.

Was there alive then, especially around the Yamato court, a sense of urgency and indeed a sense of national purpose which would induce the leading *uji* to subordinate their private interests for those of the whole? This of course was the official explanation for what was done. Numerous protestations of loyalty to the emperor smoothed the passage of land from private to public domain or the rearrangement of ranks and posts within the government. But were these not merely rationalizations? The answer is probably both yes and no. There were obviously those who suffered, who lost out, who were victims of the reform movement. But it would be hard to imagine that the reforms could have been carried out to the degree they had been by the beginning of the eighth century had there not been some sort of enthusiasm for them. The question really comes down then to who were the victims and who the gainers from the reforms.

We can leave out of our consideration those powerful families at the center of the Yamato stage who gambled and lost in the power struggle which accompanied the reform movement. They were not victims of the reform policy so much as of their own political ambitions. What of those of wealth and political power in general, however, the *uji* aristocracy whose sources of private wealth and whose territorially entrenched power we have described in the previous chapter? The extension of the ideas of absolute sovereignty, of overriding state authority, of public proprietorship of land, these struck immediately at the roots of an independent hereditary nobility. Why did the great *uji* such as the Kibi not resist the relinquishment of their hereditary rights over their lands and peoples? The answer is undoubtedly that they could not in the face of the overwhelming power held by the emperor in Yamato, but also that such families probably lost much less in terms of personal income and political influence than appears on the surface. In other words, it is most likely that many of their traditional privileges were sufficiently far from real that they saw some advantage in the new dispensation.

We can assume that just as the Yamato rulers at the beginning of the seventh century were concerned over the breakdown of the authority hierarchy and therefore sought new techniques of administration, so also the *uji* chiefs must have felt the need to adopt new ideologies and techniques of local administration and land control. The Taika Reform did not in fact strip the *uji* of all influence or privilege, it merely interposed between the *uji* chiefs and the sources of their wealth and political power the public institutions of the state. The result was a remarkably effective combination of traditional and rational means of exercising authority. Where formerly the prestige and the means of coercion possessed by these families had come from traditional sources inherent in the familial system, they were now backed by the full weight of imperial prestige, the system of law, and the systematically organized machinery of government which centered on the capital at Nara.

The new land policies probably reversed to a degree the trend toward private acquisition of land we noticed earlier. The new codes did not, of course, deny the right to private ownership, but they circumscribed it with respect of the main source of production, namely, the rice lands. Over these the state claimed both sovereignty and ownership, as had the T'ang government at the start of the dynasty. But how much did the former *uji* lose in real terms? While we have no way of judging the discrepancy between the income received by the *uji* prior to the reform and after it, we can be sure that it was not so great as to cause hardship in most cases. The new system made provision for the payment of maintenance and salary in terms of land income, household produce, and labor service on a scale considered commensurate with the social rank and official position of each official. What had once been income from lands and workers held in the name of the *uji* now came from the emperor in the form of a benefice. And it was the state that was responsible for the maintenance of law and order, the collection of dues, and the payment of salaries. The new land tax system thus actually could provide a more stable backing to privileged status. This was particularly true since no attempt was made to make the official system competitive. The result was the assurance of economic support for an aristocratic society whose political preeminence was so secure that it was able to forego any concern with military affairs other than for the purpose of frontier defense for over four centuries.

But while the Taika Reform served to secure the privileges of a new aristocracy, it also brought about a considerable redistribution of power and status within the ruling stratum. It is here primarily that the struggle came, and it is here also that the reformers touched most directly upon the provincial areas such as Kibi. As was to happen twelve hundred years later at the time of the Meiji Restoration, those close to the center of reform tended to win out over those who either objected to reform or who were far from its active center. In the Nara period the establishment of a capital and the creation of a special group of home provinces, the abolition of the *kuni-no-miyatsuko* and their replacement by a system of provincial and district governors inevitably marked the ascendancy of a central aristocracy over the rest of the country. By the beginning of the eighth century, with the completion of the magnificent new capital the new polity had brought about a radical shift in cultural and political balance between the capital and the provinces. While it may well be that scions of the outlying families such as the Kibi found their way into the central aristocracy, in most instances the provincial families were pushed down in the social hierarchy. Reform brought new institutional stability to locales such as Kibi; it also brought to an end for many centuries to come the political and cultural independence of such areas.

Having looked into some of the economic and political consequences of the reform policies adopted in 646, we must return to an assessment of the full range of changes undertaken by Japan in the seventh century. There is no question that Japan had been transformed from a loose federation of *uji* in the fifth century to an empire on the order of imperial China in the eighth. A new theory of state and a new structure of government supported the Japanese sovereign in the style and with the powers of an absolute monarch. The traditional political and economic relationships which had comprised the *uji* system were now channeled through a rationally conceived state apparatus with legally defined official functions and precedents. The landed surface of the Japanese islands had been surveyed, classed according to type, and registered according to use. The various claims upon the land, short of sovereignty, whether of ownership, proprietorship, right of cultivation, or right to income were defined by administrative practice, and any changes made subject to official process. All of this was most advantageous to the official class and was instrumental in creating a new aristocracy which was both synonymous with the state and strategically placed to benefit most from the activities of the state, now systematically supported by tax income from the entire country. The great public works, the palaces, government offices, temples, roads, and irrigation works which marked the heyday of the Nara period were the visible signs of a new concentration of power. Japan had entered upon an age of cultural achievement under the leadership of a new aristocracy, an age which was to last for over four centuries.

But there were problems which the Taika Reforms bequeathed to the new imperial order. Imbedded in the Chinese system of government, and perhaps in the minds of the more idealistic of the reformers, were certain fundamental premises concerning the relationship of private interest to state authority which were never fully accepted in Japan. First of all was the idea of the state itself, which, though embodied in the person of the emperor, was conceived of as independent of and superior to the aristocracy. Critical to this concept was the requirement that the relationship between officialdom and state pass the test of merit, at least to some degree. Such a procedure was indeed far from the comprehension of the Japanese at this time and even down to recent years. As in the familial Yamato system, so in Nara, the official hierarchy tended to remain synonymous with the social hierarchy. The traditional structure of power holding was combined with a more rational system of official functions but, as Max Weber would say, the structure retained its familistic spirit so that the hereditary charismatic rank of each family determined the rank and suitability for office of its members.[15]

[15] Max Weber, *The Theory of Social and Economic Organization* (Henderson and Parsons, translators, Glencoe, Ill., 1947), 368.

This irreducible ingredient of the Japanese social and political order was the quality which in the long run colored the entire operation of the new government from top to bottom. In particular, it was to effect the manner in which the theory of public domain was to be put in practice. For in certain fundamental ways the idea never took in Japan, despite the remarkable way in which the Japanese carried out the technological features of land rationalization. Since the aristocratic hierarchy literally made up the body of the state, it was not long before the aristocracy absorbed into itself the machinery of government. As this happened, the aristocratic rights to income from land, which the state guaranteed as part of the sustenance system, became indistinguishable from the rights of outright ownership. The existence of a ruling emperor and a legally defined state distinct from the body of hereditary aristocracy serving it turned out to be a momentary achievement of the late seventh century. It did not long endure. But the new political powers and sources of wealth accruing to the aristocracy were by no means limited to this moment.

III. BIZEN AND THE INSTITUTIONS OF TAIHŌ

THE administrative reforms which emanated from Yamato after 646 were communicated only slowly to the more distant areas of the Japanese islands. Kibi, despite its intimate connections with the capital, was not immediately affected; nor does it seem that any sudden or violent transformation shook the area. Instead, reforms came gradually and tended to be fitted into or laid over established practices. Much of what we have come to accept as the "reform institutions of Taika" were not in fact put into effect until after 682 when Emperor Temmu placed the weight of his new regime behind the task of provincial administration; in many instances changes awaited the promulgation of the Taihō administrative code in 702. Between 646 and 702, therefore, there stretched a long period of improvization in which the central authorities worked steadily but cautiously toward the reforms they hoped to achieve. Only gradually, as the formal division between the capital (*kyō*) and the provinces (*kuni*) was made explicit, were the areas outside the capital brought under a uniform field administration.

The new provinces, of which there were sixty-six at the end of the ninth century, while taking their names from the older *kuni*, were everywhere considerably larger than the territories over which the *kuni-no-miyatsuko* had been placed. Thus in all areas, including Kibi, the former *kuni* were pushed down in the administrative hierarchy, frequently being perpetuated simply as districts (*kōri*) within the new provinces. This process was symbolic of the entire spirit of the reform as it impinged upon local administration and placed imperially appointed provincial governors over the provinces at a rank markedly above that of the former *kuni-no-miyatsuko*.

While there is a tradition that the old region of Kibi was first divided into new administrative provinces in 670, it was probably not until 703 that the new *kuni* system was actually enforced. Kibi was first divided into three provinces under the names of Kibi-no-michi-no-kuchi (later Bizen), Kibi-no-michi-no-naka (later Bitchū), and Kibi-no-michi-no-shiri (later Bingo). Bizen contained the valleys of the Yoshii and Asahi rivers, Bitchū centered on the Takahashi River, and Bingo on the Ashida. In 713 Bizen was divided into two parts, the northern portion, comprising an

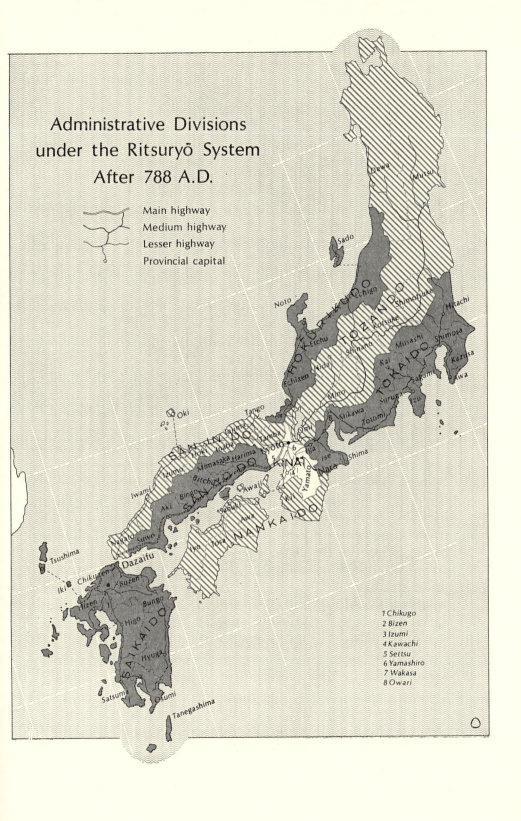

Administrative Divisions under the Ritsuryō System After 788 A.D.

Main highway
Medium highway
Lesser highway
Provincial capital

Dewa
Mutsu
Sado
HOKURIKUDO
TOZANDO
Noto
Etchu
Echigo
Shimotsuke
Hitachi
Hida
Shinano
Kozuke
Musashi
Shimosa
Echizen
Kai
Kazusa
Mino
Sagami
Awa
Oki
Tango
Omi
Suruga
Izu
SAN-IN-DO
Tajima
Hoki
Tamba
Mikawa
Totomi
Izumo
Inaba
Mimasaka
Kyoto
Ise
Shima
Iwami
Harima
KINAI
Nara
Bitchu
SAN-YO-DO
Yamato
Aki
Bingo
Awaji
Sanuki
Kii
Nagato
Suwo
Aua
NANKAIDO
Iyo
Tosa
Tsushima
Dazaifu
Iki
Chikuzen
Buzen
Hizen
Bungo
Higo
SAIKAIDO
Hyuga
Satsuma
Osumi
Tanegashima

1 Chikugo
2 Bizen
3 Izumi
4 Kawachi
5 Settsu
6 Yamashiro
7 Wakasa
8 Owari

inner plateau based on the upper reaches of the Yoshii and Asahi rivers, being cut off to comprise the province of Mimasaka.[1]

We can be reasonably certain that some sort of contest between central and local interests took place in Kibi before the area succumbed to this division and came under central administration. After all, Kibi was the territory of one of the most powerful and influential families outside of Yamato proper. Yet it appears unlikely that the Kibi family had much with which to resist the changes that were destined to deny its members their local independence. Members of the Kibi family had by now divided into several competitive branches. Those with ambition had for many generations involved themselves in the politics of Yamato. Many of them, able to satisfy their political ambitions in the capital, weakened their local ties by long absence. At any rate, no regionally based resistance to the reform of local administration manifested itself in Kibi. The significance of the action of Shitaru, Kibi-no-Kasa-no-omi, who joined the plot led by the imperial prince Furuhito-no-Ōe in 645 against Prince Naka-no-Ōe, is not at all clear.[2] Does the fact that members of the Soga, Mononobe, and Yamato families were fellow conspirators provide evidence that this was a conservative effort to thwart the promulgation of the 646 reform edict? We have no way of knowing.

Whether or not there was open resistance to its reform plans, however, the central government chose to move cautiously in Kibi. Probably the first efforts to influence local administration were based upon the former *miyake*. And it was undoubtedly in such imperial lands that the various fiscal innovations embodied in the reform program were first put into effect.[3] Only after Temmu's rise to power did the central government have the strength to assert visible authority over the Kibi region.[4] In 682 the imperial prince Ishikawa-no-ō was appointed governor-general (*mikoto mochi*) of the entire Kibi region. This was followed in 700 by the appointment of Kamitsukenu-no-Otari to a similar post under the title *sōryō* of Kibi. Regional appointments of this kind were made elsewhere in Japan as well; they were generally confined to those areas in which the remnants of strong local power made it difficult

---

[1] *Okayama-ken no rekishi*, 99.

[2] *Nihon shoki*, 25.12.

[3] Murao Jirō, *Ritsuryō zaiseishi no kenkyū*, 220-239.

[4] Mayuzumi Hiromichi, "Kokushi-sei no seiritsu" in Osaka Rekishigakkai, *Ritsuryō kokka no kiso kōzō* (Tokyo, 1960), 124.

to apply the provincial system immediately.[5] It was these men who probably paved the way for the eventual appointment of imperial governors over the three *kuni* of Bizen, Bitchū, and Bingo. Bizen received the first in its long line of civil governors in 703; Bitchū in 708.[6]

Since the new provincial governors were sent out from among the central aristocratic officialdom, they immediately overshadowed the local families of influence such as the Kibi and the Wake. In the following decades, therefore, the descendants of families who had served as *kuni-no-miyatsuko* gradually lost their prominence in local affairs. Yet in Kibi the process worked slowly as members of the Kibi and Wake families continued to struggle for status both at court and in the areas of their traditional strength. The pages of the official chronicles occasionally reveal their activities. In 757 we hear that Kamutsumichi-no-Hidatsu helped crush the revolt of Fujiwara-no-Nakamaro and consequently received the fourth court rank and the title of *ason*. More outstanding was the story of Kibi-no-Makibi (693-775), head of the Shimotsumichi branch, who distinguished himself in his diplomatic missions to China and by his erudition. In 765 he reached the high post of Minister of the Right and the second court rank. Somewhat later Wake-no-Kiyomaro (733-799) gained recognition for aiding in the downfall of the priest Dōkyō and for his administrative services at the time of the transfer of the capital from Nara to Heian. He achieved the third court rank. All three of these men managed to establish themselves in the central court aristocracy so that their descendants continued for a while as minor officials. Hidatsu's son served in the provincial administration and attained the fourth rank. Makibi's son, Kibi-no-Izumi, in 807 became imperial inspector of the southern circuit and in 810 gained the title of court councillor.[7] His ultimate rank was senior fourth rank upper grade, a large step below that of his father. Kiyomaro's line held on for several generations as scholars at the imperial college. The Kamutsumichi line faded rapidly.

---

[5] See the list of governors of Bizen in Okayama Shiyakusho, ed., *Okayama-shi shi* (6 vols., Okayama, 1938), 1.290-313. Henceforth cited by title only. I follow the interpretation of Mayuzumi, *op.cit.*, 144, and Ōta Akira, *op.cit.*, 760.

[6] *Okayama-shi shi*, 1.290; *Kibi-gun shi*, 1.613.

[7] *Kugyō bunin*, Kokushi Taikei edition, 53.82; Nomura Tadao, "Ritsuryō kanjin no kōsei to shutsuji," in Osaka Rekishigakkai, *Ritsuryō kokka no kiso kōzō* (Tokyo, 1960), 282.

The clearest evidence of the way in which provincial families were eventually cut off from honors and opportunities surrounding the emperor appears in the growing discrepancy between the remnants of the hereditary social honors to which they clung and the new system of titles and ranks defining the official hierarchy from which the servants of the emperor were newly selected. This came about in a typically indirect fashion as the old social elite was bypassed or its remnants allowed to remain after being shorn of real power. By the skillful use of honorary rather than real titles and posts, concessions and compromises were made toward the members of the provincial aristocracy in order to soften the effect of the reform. Thus Temmu's decision to revive a system of honorary titles similar to the old *kabane* cut two ways. It returned to the old *uji* their hereditary titles, but it also re-arranged the hierarchy so that the provincial titles *omi* and *muraji*, which had previously ranked near the top, were now placed near the bottom of a list of eight. The new *kabane*, in order of rank, were: *mahito, ason, sukune, imiki, michi-no-shi, omi, muraji,* and *inagi.* A few of the provincial families such as the Kibi and Wake managed to secure new titles, bettering themselves with the name of *ason.* But they were exceptions. And as we shall see, this title did not serve to assure their possession of high official rank or government posts.

There is one further indication that the central government was sensitive to the problems which might arise from too sudden a destruction of the local familial power groups. There are scattered references in the chronicles to the continued use in certain parts of the country of the title of *kuni-no-miyatsuko.* In 757 Kamu-tsumichi-no-Hidatsu was named *kuni-no-miyatsuko* of Kibi. Later on Wake-no-Kiyomaro was named *kuni-no-miyatsuko* of Mimasaka and Bizen.[8] Obviously these appointments were not administratively significant; the titles were in fact honorary. But they may not have been without a certain local prestige, particularly in the religious sphere. For example, the holders of these titles served as leaders (*haraibashira*) in local Shinto rituals and hence were a symbol of unity around which the inhabitants of these locales could rally.[9] This return to a familiar title of the pre-Taika days

---

[8] *Okayama-shi shi*, 1.431-432; *Okayama-ken no rekishi*, 80-81.

[9] Niino Naoyoshi, "Ritsuryō-sei ka ni okeru 'kuni-no-miyatsuko,'" *Rekishi kyō-iku*, 9.5 (1961), 42-47.

undoubtedly reflected an attempt by the central government to carry over into the new system some stabilizing elements from the past. The critical difference between the old and new *kuni-no-miyatsuko*, therefore, lay in the fact that the latter were placed over the newly created provinces rather than the old geographical units. The final result was the refocusing of local Shinto beliefs toward the new units of local administration, the provinces.[10]

Among the inhabitants of old Kibi who distinguished themselves in the new imperial government, Kibi-no-Makibi and Wake-no-Kiyomaro were both outstanding and unusual. Yet they perhaps exemplify the prevalent pattern of interrelationship between the new capital and the old local hegemonies. Those who made their way to the capital and climbed the ladder of official preferment were few. Those who did so were of the meteoric type—men of outstanding ability in practical affairs (scholarship, administration, or military command) but with little staying power. These momentary successes did not serve to assure security of high office for succeeding generations in the court or in local government.[11] Neither Makibi nor Kiyomaro became governors of their provinces. Though Makibi was named chief of the district of Shimotsumichi at the time of his elevation to Minister of the Right, even this was obviously an honorary appointment.[12] Just as the old *kuni* had been downgraded to the level of district, so also the old *uji* aristocracy was eventually relegated pretty much to the level of district administration.

What assured the deep gap between the provincial and court aristocracy, despite the perpetuation of a more equitable practice of honorific titles, was the system of official ranks which came into use with the Taika Reforms. The rank system finally perfected in 757 and used with almost no change down to 1869 placed unusual emphasis upon proximity to the emperor. Four special ranks (*hon*) were set aside for members of the imperial family. Below these were eight official ranks (*kurai*) which applied to the aristocracy as a whole. These were subdivided into twenty-six separate grades. The first three ranks were each divided into senior and junior grades forming six divisions from senior first rank (*shō ichi-i*) to junior third rank (*ju sammi*). These six grades were limited to a small fraction of the upper aristocracy who

[10] Inoue Mitsusada, "Ritsuryō taisei," 23-26.
[11] Nomura Tadao, *op.cit.*, 267-290. [12] *Kibi-gun shi*, 1.177.

could aspire to the posts of state ministers (*daijin*) and state councillors (*nagon*). The fourth and fifth ranks were each divided into
junior and senior grades with upper and lower levels. They thus
accounted for eight divisions. The highest was senior fourth rank
upper grade (*shō shi-i no jō*), and the lowest junior fifth rank lower
grade (*ju gō-i no ge*). To these ranks belonged the middle class of
court aristocracy. The majority of the aristocracy held ranks within
the twelve grades into which ranks six through eight were
divided.[13] Although the provincial aristocracy could aspire to
court ranks of the above categories, they were, for the most part,
relegated to a system of "outer" ranks quite separate from those
of the central aristocracy. These offered twenty divisions descending from outer senior fifth rank upper grade to lower eighth. The
new rank system effectively divided the aristocracy into four distinct groups between which there could be little mobility: the
high nobility (those above fourth rank), the middle nobility
(those from fourth through fifth rank), the lower aristocracy
(those below the fifth rank), and the local aristocracy (those
outside the capital).[14]

For the Kibi or Wake families, despite the fact that they held
the high honorary title of *ason* (the same as that of the Fujiwara),
their court ranks, except for the rare exception, were low and
were generally classed as "outside." During the middle of the
eighth century members of the Kaya family appear as *ason* ranked
junior sixth lower grade; those of the Shimotsumichi, as *ason*
ranked junior seventh lower grade; and those of the Sono, as
omi outer rank senior sixth upper grade.[15] These men were all district governors and appear to have received "inner" classification
on occasion. Members of the Mino family, also with the title of
ason, nonetheless consistently received "outer" ranks of junior
seventh upper grade.[16] Since the post of governor of a province
the size of Bizen or Bitchū was reserved to the rank of junior fifth
lower grade, we can imagine how the intrusion of the new provincial governors unbalanced the indigenous social and political
hierarchy. The establishment of the new provincial system effectively excluded the old *uji* aristocracy from the most desirable

[13] Joüon des Longrais, *op.cit.*, 185-187, provides the best Western language explanation.
[14] Kodama Kōta, ed., *Zusetsu Nihon bunkashi taikei* (14 vols., Tokyo, 1956),
3.64.
[15] *Kibi-gun shi*, 1.765-766.   [16] *Okayama-shi shi*, 1.491.

positions within the new units of local government. In their place came representatives of the central government backed by all the prestige of the new imperial institutions.

While we can trace the introduction of members of the central officialdom into the new provinces of Bizen, Bitchū, and Mima-saka, we can be less certain of the manner in which they set about organizing provincial government. The first governorships were probably informal affairs involving only periodic tours of official inspection.[17] But eventually, particularly after the promulgation of the Taihō code, the buildings and offices necessary for a full-scale provincial administration were put together. The provinces each built their capital towns, known as *kokufu,* from which the new administrative codes could be applied systematically. These new towns must have been for their locales in every way as impressive to the local population as the imperial city was to the capital area.

The *kokufu* of Bizen was built in the district of Kamutsumichi on what was then the bank of the Asahi River, just north of present Okayama near the village of Kōnoichiba. In those days the Asahi River made a sharp turn to the east after emerging from the foot-hills and entered the sea on the eastern side of the rocky hill of Misao. (It now flows to the west.) Thus the *kokufu* was within reach of the river and its shipping facilities.[18] The *kokufu* of Bitchū was located in the midst of the delta between the Takahashi and Ashimori rivers, in a place now included in the town of Sōja.[19] It too may well have been on the banks of a branch of the Takahashi, which at that time appears to have emptied into the sea to the east of its present mouth. The *kokufu* of Mimasaka was situated near present Tsuyama, and that of Bingo near the present village of Kokufu on the Ashida River above Fukuyama.

Each *kokufu* became the political and cultural center of its province. Public buildings were erected to house administrative offices (*kokuga* or *kokuchō*), storehouses, a school, a military gar-

[17] Inoue Mitsusada, "Ritsuryō taisei," 20.

[18] There is still some debate as to whether the *kokufu* was located in Mino or Kamutsumichi district, but this is largely a problem of how the Asahi River flowed at that time. I have followed Nagayama's conclusions in *Tsūshi,* 1.399-402. Ishida Minoru prefers to place the *kokufu* in Mino district. See his "Okayama-ken jōri no rekishi-chirigaku-teki kenkyū," in *Okayama-ken Chihōshi Kenkyū Renraku Kyōgi-kai kaihō,* 3 (1960), 58.

[19] See Fujii Shun, "Bitchū no kokuga ni tsuite," in *Dokushi Kai Sōritsu Gojūnen Kinen, Kokushi ronshū* (1959), 642; *Kibi-gun shi,* 1.608-609.

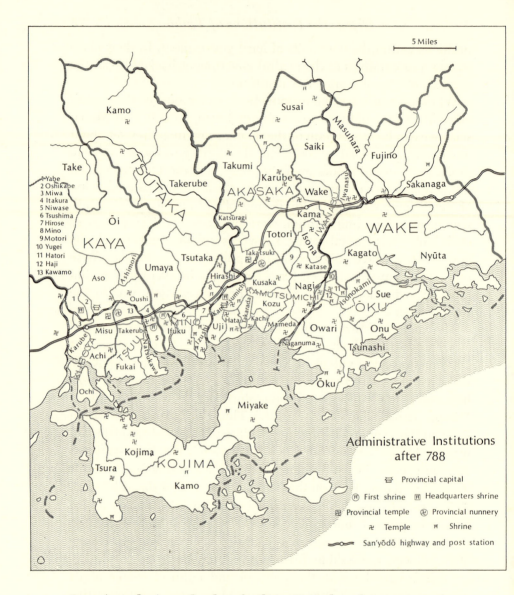

Administrative Institutions after 788

⊟	Provincial capital
冊 First shrine	冊 Headquarters shrine
田 Provincial temple	卍 Provincial nunnery
卍 Temple	冊 Shrine
─○─ San'yōdō highway and post station	

Map labels: Kamo, Susai, Saiki, Fujino, Masuhara, Take, Takumi, Takerube, Karube, AKASAKA, Wake, Sakanaga, 1 Yabe, 2 Oshikabe, 3 Miwa, 4 Itakura, 5 Niwase, 6 Tsushima, 7 Hirose, 8 Mino, 9 Motori, 10 Yugei, 11 Hatori, 12 Haji, 13 Kawamo, Katsuragi, Kama, WAKE, Ōi, KAYA, Totori, Isona, Kagato, Nyūta, TSUTAKA, Umaya, Tsutaka, Takatsuki, Katase, Aso, Ashimori, Hirashi, Kusaka, Nagi, Sue, OKU, Oushi, KAMUTSUMICHI, Kozu, Isonokami, Misu, Takerube, MINO, Hata, Kachi, Mameda, Owari, Onu, Uji, Ifuku, Naganuma, Tsunashi, Achi, Fukai, Ochi, Ōku, Miyake, Kojima, KOJIMA, Tsura, Kamo

rison (*gundan*), and other facilities.[20] Today there exists a rectangular area among the fields near Sōja of about seven and a half acres which bears the name *gosho* (palace). It was here that the central offices of the Bitchū provincial seat were located.[21] Reconstruction of the *kokufu* of nearby Suō has revealed a square area some 2800 feet to a side surrounded by an earthen wall. This was the outer dimension of the town. Within the walls, streets ran

[20] *Kibi-gun shi*, 1.771-773.
[21] Fujii Shun, "Bitchū no kokuga ni tsuite," 643.

north-south and east-west at 350-foot intervals. The governor's offices (*kokuga*) occupied an area 700 feet square.[22]

Near the capital, official temples which served as part of the network of centrally administered provincial guardian temples were also established by government order. Each province was provided with its provincial monastery (*kokubunji*) and its provincial nunnery (*kokubun-niji*). The central government also established a center of shrine administration (*sōja*) and attached this to some existing shrine. The *sōja* of Bizen was attached to the shrine dedicated to Kibitsuhiko on the eastern (or Bizen) side of Kibi Nakayama. It received the first court rank. The Ichi-no-miya of Bitchū was the original shrine of Kibitsu located on the western side of Nakayama.[23] In this matter, as in so many others, we see the effort of the central government to assert its authority over the sources of provincial localism. The new shrine organization incorporated the centers of local worship into a larger system over which the imperial government exercised ultimate authority. The practice of grading local shrines within the imperial hierarchy of ranks was in effect a manner of establishing retroactively the status of the ancestors of the Kibi and Wake families within the new order.

While we have talked up to now about the provincial governor in the singular, it must be explained that the title of governor actually applied to a group of individuals known collectively as *kokushi*. These were the governor (*kami*), vice-governor (*suke*), executive officer (*jō*), and inspector (*sakan*). Together they were called the *shitōkan*, or the four officials of the provincial governor class. Among them, of course, the *kami* ranked highest. As a general rule, officials of the governor class were not selected from among local families but were appointed at the capital and dispatched to the provinces. Their subordinate officials were either brought with them or made up from local personnel. Some of the more important functions of provincial government are revealed in the names of the offices housed within the administrative headquarters. Such were the administrative office (*mandokoro*), militia office (*kondeisho*), police office (*kebiishisho*), land office (*tadokoro*), and finance office (*suitōsho*). As in any bureaucracy, it was

[22] Yamaguchi-ken Bunkashi Hensan Iinkai, ed., *Yamaguchi-ken bunkashi, Tsūshi-hen* (Yamaguchi, 1951), 99-100. Henceforth cited as *Yamaguchi-ken bunkashi*.
[23] *Tsūshi*, 1.546-550.

possible for an official to hold more than one office concurrently. There was obviously a great deal of multiple appointment at the local level.

Lists of appointments to the governorships of Bizen and Bitchū reveal a number of interesting facts.[24] First, it is clear that there was a regular rotation of officials, with few appointments continuing beyond the official limit of six-year terms. Second, the appointments were overwhelmingly from the court aristocracy. While members of local families like the Kamitsumichi, Mino, Kasa, and Kayō occasionally rose to the rank of vice-governor or executive officer, their numbers were extremely few after the middle of the eighth century. Not one held the post of *kami.*

How effective the new provincial government was and how conscientiously the new governors carried out their administrative tasks is difficult to determine. But there is no question that the new system constituted a vast change from the familistic rule of the *kuni-no-miyatsuko* to one based on a systematically organized system of officials with prescribed functions. During the first few centuries the system was in operation, provincial governors faithfully took up residence in the provincial capitals and gave personal attention to local administration. Personal tours to inspect tax collections and religious institutions were frequent.[25] Probably these practices were kept up regularly through the middle of the ninth century. While it rather quickly became common to leave the actual conduct of provincial affairs to subordinates sent out by governors, who themselves stayed in the capital, this was not altogether a way of avoiding responsibility. For provincial affairs bulked large in the routine of central government and it was frequently necessary for the governor to be on hand at the capital. One can imagine that for the Nara and early Heian periods, therefore, direct administrative and fiscal contact was maintained between capital and provinces. The records show a regular remission of grain and local produce taxes to the capital and of labor and military service.

Essential to the maintenance of central control over local administration was the existence of dependable and efficient com-

[24] *Okayama-shi shi,* 1.290-313; *Kibi-gun shi,* 1.613-640.

[25] Takeuchi Rizō, "Zaichō kanjin no bushika," in Takeuchi Rizō, ed., *Nihon hōkensei seiritsu no kenkyū* (Tokyo, 1955), 3. The article was originally published in *Shigaku zasshi,* 48.6 (1937) under a different title.

munications between the capital and the provinces. During the years of effective provincial administration a good deal of attention was given to the development and maintenance of a network of roads and water routes and their incorporation into an official transportation system. The basis for such a system had already been laid. The sea route through the Inland Sea, which connected the Yamato port of Naniwa with the center of overseas affairs at Dazaifu in Kyushu, had been in active use for many centuries. And it is quite possible that Kojima in Kibi served as an important way-station in this water route. The land route probably developed somewhat later. As a general rule the Japanese used land transportation for rapid communications, particularly the transmission of documents, while the sea route was used for bulky commodity shipments.

Each of the *kokufu* was served by its port. These, as we have noted, were generally located inland from the coast on a river which provided easy access to the sea. Thus the port of Bizen was located somewhere in the vicinity of the port village of Kachi and that of Bitchū somewhere near Kamo, which served as its port. Neither of these locations is suitable for shipping today because of shifts in the water courses within the delta plain.

The official highway which served Bizen and Bitchū was, during these days, the single most important of the provincial post roads. Known as the Sanyōdō, its great importance derived from the fact that it was the main route linking Dazaifu with the capital in Yamato. The Sanyōdō of Nara times is another one of those creations of the early Japanese state which was to retain its utility down into modern times. The road was to serve successive generations of Japanese rulers until the twentieth century, when the national motor expressway would use modern engineering techniques to cut across the precarious alluvial soils and the precious rice paddy fields to provide a new kind of rapid communication between Okayama and central Japan. In these earlier days the Sanyōdō was obliged to pick its way carefully along the edges of the hills bordering the river plains and across the upper reaches of the treacherous streams which so often flooded their banks after the monsoon rains.

On official highways, post stations were provided every thirty *ri* (a distance of about ten miles today). Four post stations were therefore established within the boundaries of Bizen. These were at Sakanaga (now Mitsuishi), Kama, Takatsuki, and Tsutaka.[26] Post stations were required by law to provide certain facilities for official travel. On the Sanyōdō they were each obliged to provide maintenance for twenty post horses. This maintenance was drawn from the farming communities of the neighborhood at the rate of one horse for each fifty families. Those families who contributed to the maintenance of the horse were exempted from the corvée and miscellaneous labor taxes. For each post station there were also provided maintenance rice lands to the amount of four *chō* (12 acres). The income from these lands provided upkeep for the station as well as for the procurement and replacement of horses. By the end of the Nara period, however, as the accounting procedures of the central government became more sophisticated, post stations received their support directly from the provincial administration, and the special post station lands were abolished.[27]

Despite the relative ease of reaching Bizen from Nara and despite the official housing provided for the governor and his staff, provincial service was never much relished by court appointees. Life at the capital was preferable. No diaries of Bizen governors tell us of their yearnings for the life of the court or the boorishness they saw in the local inhabitants as do diaries for some of the other provinces. An occasional poem which likens a vista in Bizen to one at the capital is our only hint of the constant tension under which the governors must have lived. Yet provincial administration had its attractions, if mainly in material ways. Provincial officials of the class of governor were entitled to direct demands upon the local tax intake, and their income was provided for in the form of office rice lands. They could draw labor service from the cultivators of this land. Being close to the source of income, provincial officials were able to enrich themselves in ways generally denied those who stayed in the capital. Thus the central aristocracy were induced to accept provincial posts often for highly mercenary reasons, a tendency which put increasing emphasis upon extraction of taxes out of the provinces rather than on good official performance.

While the provincial governors entered Bizen with the full backing of the central government, it was the district chiefs who provided the most consistent and continuous element of government

[26] *Okayama-shi shi,* 1.279-282.   [27] *Hiroshima-shi shi,* 1.240.

at the local level. The districts provided the major element of continuity between the new system of local government and the former familial system. For not only were district chiefs named from among former *kuni-no-miyatsuko*, but the districts themselves tended to correspond to the territories over which the old families had ruled. The new *kuni* were in most instances aggregates of old *uji*-based territories which still had a deep and persistent meaning in terms of geographical boundaries and local mores.

In the new *kuni* of Bizen and Bitchū, the old regions over which the Kibi and Wake chiefs had held sway took their places as *kōri*. There was, of course, a period of adjustment and some giving and taking of boundaries during the eighth century. Bizen in 713 consisted of the five districts of Mino, Tsutaka, Akasaka, Ōku, and Kamutsumichi. Later, in 721, part of Ōku was split off and combined with part of Akasaka to form the independent district of Fujiwara. This area was later divided into the districts of Iwanasu and Wake, probably in honor of the Wake family of that region. By the year 788 the final boundary adjustments had been made, and with the addition of Kojima, Bizen acquired the eight districts it had down to the twentieth century. Mimasaka had seven (later twelve); Bitchū had nine (later eleven); and Bingo had eleven (later fourteen).[28]

The key factor in district administration was its traditional character. District chiefs were by intention appointed from among the descendants of *kuni-no-miyatsuko* families. In the provinces, for instance, the theory of open selection for office did not apply to levels below the governor class. In practice, this meant that the pre-reform distribution of political and social influence remained relatively unchanged, and for many years to come the familiar names of the branches of the Kibi and Wake families were to ap-

[28] *Tsūshi*, 1.7-133. Pronunciations of some of the district names changed in the course of time, thus:

Nara	Heian	Tokugawa	Meiji
Ōku	Ōku	Oku	Oku
Iwanasu	Iwanasu	Iwanashi	Iwanashi
Kamutsumichi	Kamutsumichi	Kamimichi	Jōdō
Tsutaka	Tsutaka	Tsutaka	Tsudaka
Shimotsumichi	Shimotsumichi	Shimomichi	Shimomichi
Kaya	Kaya	Kayō	Kayō

I have attempted to make transliterations match the pronunciations appropriate to the time referred to in each chapter.

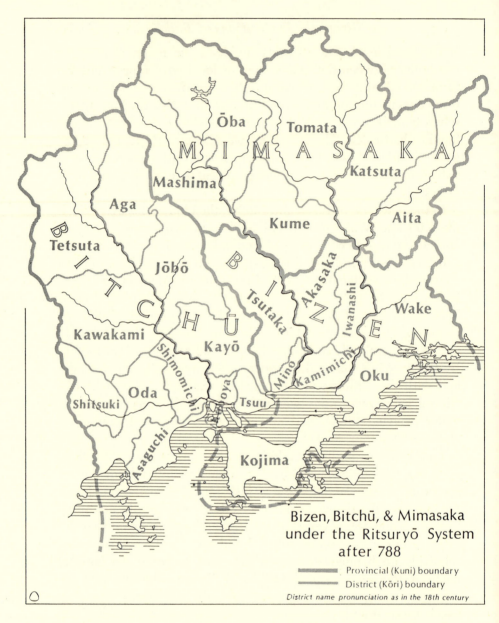

Bizen, Bitchū, & Mimasaka
under the Ritsuryō System
after 788

	Provincial (Kuni) boundary
	District (Kōri) boundary

District name pronunciation as in the 18th century

pear in the rosters of district chiefs. Such men combined in their persons both the prestige attached to them as scions of the great families of the area and the new authority vested in the title of district chief.

Yet it is equally true that the district chiefs under the Taihō regulations were obliged to rationalize their methods of local rule and accommodate themselves to the regulations of the central

government. The generalized local powers they had once held
were now divided among civil, military, and religious officials.
How far the district chiefs moved away from family-based techniques in their administration is not clear, but it is certain that
publicly visible centers of district administration (*gunga*) were
required of them. The new administrative codes prescribed that
the district office should be staffed by four officials referred to as
the chief (*ōmiyatsuko*), vice-chief (*sukenomiyatsuko*), administrative officer (*matsurigotobito*), and a records officer (*fubito*).
The first two of the officers were classed as district chiefs. All four
were known collectively as the "four officials." What records we
have show that the Mino family predominated as chiefs of Mino
and Tsutaka districts, the Wake family generally governed Wake,
Akasaka, and Iwanasu districts in Bizen, while the Shimotsumichi,
Kaya, and Sono families most frequently held appointments over
Shimotsumichi and Kaya districts in Bitchū.[29] In a document of
776 a member of the Sono family signed as district chief of Tsutaka
and a member of the Mino family as vice-chief.[30]

District administration probably never acquired the rationality
that was expected of it. We do not even know whether district
chiefs moved their operations out of their own houses into public
buildings. But we have sufficient evidence of the existence of
official paper work (such as tax receipts and census registers) at
the district level to justify the conclusion that district offices of
some sort were established. The wording of deeds of land sales
made in 774 and 776 indicate that copies were deposited in the
district office (*gūke*).[31] They also indicate that business was conducted according to administrative precedents and that public
appointments were made for such officials as collector of taxes,
chief of taxes, recorder, and the like.

To understand the operation of local administration below the
district chief it is best to start with the administrative households,
or *ko*. These were small divisions of the local population, theoretically based on family organization, but more probably consisting
of small natural communities. They were the prime units of population registration, land allotment, and taxation. In some parts of
the country the *ko* tended to coincide with the extended family,

[29] *Okayama-shi shi*, 1.491; *Kibi-gun shi*, 1.764-765; Taniguchi Sumio, ed.,
Kyōdo no rekishi, Chūgoku-hen (Tokyo, 1959), 11.
[30] *Tsūshi*, 1.407.   [31] *Ibid.*

consisting of a house head and his relatives extending backward and forward for several generations and occasionally horizontally to include several dependent families. But in central Japan the *ko* more often consisted of several families, either of the same or different surnames. From this we can conclude that the *ko* was probably a form of local residential group which was transitional between the earlier *uji* or *be* and the later natural village communities which became the basic units of life in rural Japan. In the tax registers of this period we see that the *ko* varied in size according to locality, and some single surname *ko* are recorded to have consisted of as many as 124 members. The registers include not only house head, children and their families, and attached unmarried members, but also servants and slaves.[32] It is estimated, however, that of all *ko* reported in the remaining cadastral documents of the Nara period, the average size is twenty-five members drawn from two or three conjugal families.[33] For each *ko* the head (*kochō* or *koshu*) bore the responsibility of good conduct and remission of taxes.

A document of the year 739 which remains in the Shōsōin sheds a ray of direct light on conditions in the villages of Kibi during the eighth century. This record, prepared by the provincial headquarters of Bitchū, lists loss of tax revenues due to deaths among the registered tax payers. The deceased, numbering 127 individuals, are listed by name under the heads of the *ko* in which they resided. Several interesting details appear from this document. First, among the *ko* heads (*koshu*) are the familiar names of both the *uji* and *be* prevalent in Bitchū before 645. Titled families such as the Kaya, Kamutsumichi, and Shimotsumichi, appear alongside those of Mononobe, Totoribe, Takebe, and the like. Secondly, while for most *ko* the surname of the dead corresponded to that of the *koshu*, this is not always the case, indicating that quite commonly the *ko* of this area consisted of families bearing a variety of surname lines.[34]

Groups of fifty or fewer *ko* formed the administrative village, called "*ri*." According to the *Wamyō ruiju shō* which records statistics of about the year 930, Bizen contained fifty-one such villages, Mimasaka sixty-five, and Bitchū seventy-two.[35] In Bizen, there-

[32] Kodama Kōta, ed., *Zusetsu Nihon bunkashi taikei*, 3.102-110.

[33] *Ibid.*, 3.68; Takeuchi Rizō, "Manyō-jidai no shomin seikatsu," in his *Ritsuryō-sei to kizoku seiken* (2 vols., Tokyo, 1959), 1.186-188.

[34] *Tsūshi*, 1.404-406.   [35] *Ibid.*, 1.13, 108, 64.

fore, the average district consisted of approximately six villages. Apparently the Nara government had some difficulty in arriving at a stable relationship between the administrative village and the smaller communal elements of rural life. In 715 the name *ri* was abandoned, and the fifty-*ko* units were renamed *gō*. These newly named administrative villages were then divided into two or three smaller units to which the term *ri* was applied. This smaller community may well have been what sociologists call the "natural village." For some reason the *ri* was discontinued as a unit of official organization in 740 and not immediately replaced in the nomenclature of rural administration. Only somewhat later did the term *mura* come to be applied to what was essentially the natural village. In Bizen the word *mura* had made its appearance in land documents by 774.[36]

Despite the fact that the *gō* were clearly arbitrary divisions of the countryside and must have included several natural agricultural communities under a single administrative head, they became one of the most fundamental units of local administration at this time and for many centuries thereafter. The *gō* therefore must have been of an appropriate size for the management of the more intimate aspects of rural life such as census taking, tax collecting, the development of irrigation canals, and the like. The *gō* chief, appointed from among influential *ko* heads, was made accountable for the drawing up of household census registers, allocation of rice land, collection of taxes, and maintenance of law and order within the village. He thus constituted an important mid-stage in the machinery of provincial administration as it descended from the governor to the land cultivator. The administrative village, therefore, although at the outset an arbitrary grouping of rural communities, eventually found a permanent place in the local scene. Large enough not to do violence to the existing settlement pattern, it apparently proved convenient to the administrative technology of the day.

A final unit of local organization which the administrative codes of the Nara period attempted to put into force was the *ho* or "five-family group." The idea of joining five households into mutual responsibility units (*goho* or *ho*) was introduced from China. The *ho*, like the *gō*, was an arbitrary unit, but without administrative functions, though it may have provided a basis for

[36] Takeuchi Rizō, "Manyō-jidai no shomin seikatsu," 190; *Tsūshi*, 1.406.

military defense and police surveillance. We hear little of the *ho*
in Bizen during the Nara period, but in later centuries *ho* names
appeared frequently as territorial subdivisions of *gō*.

From the government's point of view the main purpose of the
new institutions of local administration was to improve the system
of agricultural production and taxation, and it is no accident that
the Taika Reform edicts devoted so much attention to this subject.
The reform measures, as we have seen, sought to establish in Japan
a land tax system based on three new systematic procedures: full
control of manpower, equitable distribution of productive resources (land), and uniform taxation. The task of manpower control was achieved through census registration for which the *ko*
served as the smallest unit and over which the various levels of
administration, the *gō, kōri,* and *kuni* provided the machinery of
supervision.

Technically, the household registers (*koseki*), together with the
rosters of officials and titled aristocracy and the lists of state slaves
or artisans, provided the state with complete data on the numbers
and statuses of the Japanese population. The legal codes began
by making fundamental division between the free and unfree
classes, and then went on to differentiate the numerous gradations of privilege and status among the free subjects of the emperor. Inclusion on population registers or possession of rank
automatically set the status of each individual and specified his
public obligations or privileges. In particular, status defined his
relationship to the sources of wealth, namely, land, manual labor,
and the products of such labor.

Among the so-called free subjects of the state, a fundamental
difference existed between the titled and untitled classes. The
titled, in some manner or other, all shared in the profits for the
land; the untitled were responsible for tax payment in kind and
labor. Yet legally both of these groups bore the same relationship
to the state: both were servants of the emperor and were expected
to repay the beneficence of the sovereign by performance of
services. The titled classes served as officials and were recompensed in terms of land, goods, and labor. The untitled groups
were granted the "use" of elements of production (primarily land)
for which the state expected payment. In terms of the current
theory of state, then, these groups merely represented different

levels in the hierarchy of relationships between sovereign and grateful subjects.

It would be superfluous at this point to describe in detail the many types and gradations of benefice the aristocracy might receive. Those family heads who held titles of the fifth rank or above stood out high above the lower aristocracy, receiving the income from rice lands commensurate to their rank, office, and special merit. They received in addition special payments in commodities, and the services of servants and laborers. Those who held the sixth court rank or lower had distinctly fewer perquisites. But the aristocracy as a whole was permitted to draw income from cultivated land in a variety of amounts and guises.

Though in theory all land was considered the sovereign's property, within any given location, such as Bizen, a wide variety of lands were held or reserved in various degrees of private tenure either on a temporary or permanent basis. For Bizen of the eighth century we do not have sufficient evidence upon which to base a map of land use. We can surmise, however, that hilly or waste land, except perhaps for certain state or imperial forest tracts, would be held communally or under rather loose control of local titled families and religious institutions. Such uncultivated lands probably made up approximately ninety percent of the surface of Bizen and Bitchū. In addition there were the house plots and dry fields, which also were held in perpetuity and so constituted a form of private property. What remained were the rice lands, and it was over these that the state exercised its closest control and asserted the most inclusive claim of ownership.

By the height of the Nara period Bizen had developed as an agricultural region of some consequence with a cultivated area already over a third of what it was to become in the eighteenth century. While the production from this land was as yet relatively limited, the method of exploitation of paddy land was systematic to the extreme. Its chief feature was the practice of land allotment known as the *handen* system. This system, though derived from Chinese models, acquired a number of local features peculiar to Japan. As put into effect in Bizen the new system called for the division of rice land into squares roughly one-half mile to a side. These were divided internally into thirty-six equal and numbered squares (called *tsubo* and equal in area to one *chō*). Each *tsubo* was further divided into ten strips of one *tan* each (at this time approximately .3 acres). These strips were used as the units of distribution to cultivators. Each able-bodied male received two *tan*. (It was assumed that a *tan* produced sufficient rice to support one man for a year.) A woman received two-thirds of the man's share, and a slave one-third. Rice lands allotted in this fashion were called *kubunden*; they became the responsibility of the cultivator who was obligated to keep the land in full cultivation and to pay the required taxes.[37]

While it is generally supposed that the *handen* system did not touch the remoter areas of the Japanese islands until the end of the ninth century, in the Kibi area, the clear remains of systematic field division lines (*jōri*) offer strong evidence that the system was adopted there rather early and completely. Just how the system was put into effect is unknown, since no documents have survived which describe what must have been a gigantic effort at field rationalization. On the other hand, a surprising number of fields in south Kibi retain to this day the dimensions of the *jōri* system and among them many carry the original *tsubo* numbers. It is therefore possible to reconstruct the contours of the *handen* reform as it applied to Bizen and also to account for some of the principles involved in the system.[38]

The experience of the modern Japanese government in effecting a rationalization of paddy land (that is, the straightening of field divisions) in many parts of Japan is enough to indicate that any program of reorganization of the pattern of dykes and water levels within an agricultural region is not lightly carried off. Yet to judge from contemporary evidence, most of the rice land of the Kibi provinces was brought under the *jōri* system of division during the seventh and eighth centuries. How this seemingly superhuman feat was accomplished, and what the attitude of the local inhabitants was to the rationalization program, are still something of a mystery.

It now seems more and more likely that systematic field division for allocation purposes was not a complete innovation with the Taika edict. In the imperially controlled *miyake*, for instance, there is good reason to believe that some sort of allocation system had been put into practice before 646. And if in actuality this did

[37] Iyanaga Teizō in his "Ritsuryō-teki tochi shoyū" in *Iwanami kōza, Nihon rekishi, 3, Kodai, 3* (Tokyo, 1962), 33-78, argues that ownership of *kubunden* lay in between our private and public concepts.

[38] *Nōchi shi*, 242-384, plus 17 supplements; Ishida Minoru, *op.cit.*, 51-62.

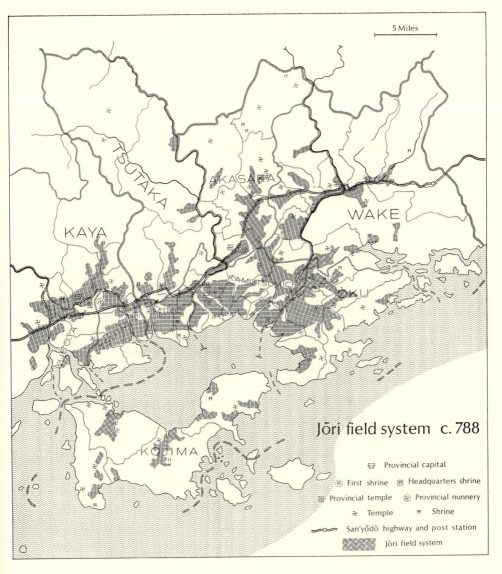

Jōri field system c. 788

⛩	Provincial capital
First shrine	Headquarters shrine
Provincial temple	Provincial nunnery
Temple	Shrine
——○——	San'yōdō highway and post station
▨▨▨	Jōri field system

not extend over much territory, even such a limited application implied a recognition of the effectiveness of regular field division for administrative and tax purposes. The main problem of affecting a carry-over from the pre-Taika system to the *jōri* system of the eighth century was apparently one of measurement. The story of how this was accomplished provides yet another illustration of the ingenuity with which the Japanese took over continental institutions for their own needs.

Prior to 646 the Japanese had adopted a system of area measurement introduced from Korea and known as the Kudara system. The basic unit in this system was a "foot" (*shaku*) of 35.6 centimeters. A unit of six square Kudara *shaku* made up the *bu* and five *bu* comprised the *shiro*. (This was the prime unit of field measurement, since the *shiro* was supposed to produce one *soku* of rice tax.) The Taika Reforms introduced a new system of measure from T'ang China using the T'ang foot of shorter (29.6 centimeters) length. Under the new system, the smallest unit, also called *bu*, consisted of six square T'ang *shaku*. The *tan* was made up of 360 new *bu*, and the *chō* consisted of 10 *tan*.

In the newly adopted allocation system the *tan* was the basic unit of calculation, since one able-bodied mature male received two *tan* as a base allotment. But it was essential that the *tan* be divisible by three, since women received two-thirds of the male allotment and slaves one-third. Thus a *tan* consisting of 360 *bu* was ideal. On the other hand the *tan* was also roughly equivalent to 250 old *bu*. For a while, therefore, a *tan* of 250 old *bu* was apparently carried along with the *tan* of 360 new *bu*. Only after 713 was the attempt made to convert fully to the new system.[39]

If we can surmise then that the *jōri* system had its precedents and hence was not a complete surprise to the Japanese in 646, it is also possible that the system did not have to be extended forcibly by the government, but that in some measure it was able to sell itself. This may seem paradoxical, yet let us remember that we are talking about a time in Japanese history when the principle of private ownership of rice land was still not generally accepted. The paddy system was still very much a community (or even state) resource to which the application of the most efficient technology was considered desirable. Certainly for government at both central and local levels, in an economy without an effective monetary currency, the regular division of fields could provide the most direct method of achieving a systematic and equitable tax yield from the land. Even for the cultivators the system may have had its attraction, for the program of rationalization of field boundaries was undoubtedly linked to other agrarian works, such as the improvement of irrigation facilities. And the systematic method of distribution did eliminate the worst

[39] Murao Jirō, *Ritsuryō zaiseishi no kenkyū*, 22-24; Iyanaga Teizō, *Nara jidai no kizoku to nōmin* (Tokyo, 1956), 23-24, 34.

abuses of the land holding practices which had begun to develop in the seventh century.[40]

It may even be that, as the Taika edicts claimed, the new land tax procedures gave to the cultivators a new security. We have little way of knowing how extensively the *handen* system modified tenure practices which by this time had become customary among the cultivators of Bizen, and there is a good deal of controversy over whether the cultivator was ultimately better or worse off under the new state policies. Yet it is quite evident that the principle of state ownership of rice land was adopted at a time when conditions of land tenure in Japan had not been fully systematized nor the concept of private ownership fully understood. The new codes provided the first uniform public procedures for establishing land rights. The drawing up of census and land registers established for the first time a legal order which clarified not only the status of cultivators but the limits of taxation. For the members of the former *be,* the shift from hereditary producer for an *uji* chief to what was more nearly a condition of state serfdom was probably a desirable one, at least at the outset, for the unfree attachment to land was characteristic of the rice land only.[41] The time was to come, of course, when the holders of *kubunden* felt overburdened by the weight of taxes and the many military and labor services imposed upon them, but in the initial stage the conversion from the status of *be* to free subject (*ryōmin*) must have had its rewards and perhaps even provided a sense of participation in the destinies of the new imperial state.[42]

The tax system brought in by the Taika Reform was complex in its details yet relatively simple in its basic theory. Essentially it put its emphasis upon manpower, seeking to absorb from the cultivators (and craft communities) a maximum of their most useful services. This was collected in the form of agricultural produce (*so*), household craft produce (*chō* or *mitsugi*), corvée labor (*yō*) or its equivalent (*chikarashiro*), and military service (*heishi-yaku*). The unit of taxation was fundamentally the individual.

The grain tax of the Nara period was not heavy by later standards, being about three to five percent of the yield of the field allotments (*kubunden*). Later the practice of forced borrow-

[40] Naoki Kōjirō, *Nihon kodai kokka no kōzō* (Tokyo, 1958), 304.

[41] Torao Toshiya, *Handen shūju-hō no kenkyū*, 416.

[42] Shimizu Mitsuo, *Jōdai no tochi-kankei*, 30.

ing of seed rice at high interest rates increased the government's take of the rice crop and this became a heavy burden on the cultivators. Although the grain tax itself was levied according to the size and quality of cultivated land, it was theoretically collected as a head tax, since all paddy land was supposedly distributed among cultivators on a uniform basis. There is, in fact, some reason to believe that the distribution of *kubunden* was as much for the purpose of providing sustenance for the farming population so that it could carry out other types of labor services as it was to provide a base for the imposition of the grain tax. This emphasis on manpower was the distinguishing feature of taxation throughout the eighth and ninth centuries.[43]

As important as rice to government finances was cloth, which, to a degree served as a medium of exchange and provided the chief means of commuting labor taxes. Both the produce and labor taxes were levied on individual able-bodied males. The former, usually set at a bolt of 26 *shaku* of silk fabric per year, was considered equivalent to 30 days' labor. Corvée was levied by both the central and provincial governments. Service in the capital was set at 10 days per year. This could be commuted to 26 *shaku* of cloth, a practice that became increasingly common. The local corvée was calculated at 60 days and was also commutable. For all of these payments commodities other than silk fabric could be substituted: hemp, cotton, local specialties such as salt, iron products, tiles, and the like.[44]

The Nara experiments with a conscript army were probably the least successful aspect of the Taika reforms. Military service was considered a duty of male subjects and was exacted in lieu of produce and corvée taxes. In theory, one-third of the mature males of a province were placed on the list of conscripts (*heishi*) and were liable to be called up in rotation for service in the provincial military unit. During the years of liability (from age 20 to 59), each conscript was expected to serve one year at the capital and three years on the frontier. While on active service, conscripts were expected to provide their own equipment and provisions, a burden which fell upon the census groups (*ko*) from which the

---

[43] Aoki Kazuo, "Ritsuryō zaisei," in *Iwanami kōza, Nihon rekishi, 3, Kodai, 3* (Tokyo, 1962), 115-146. Note Murao Jirō's stimulating article which discusses the relative burden of taxation on the Nara cultivator: "Ritsuryō seido no hyōka ni kansuru mittsu no mondaiten," *Rekishi kyōiku,* 11.5 (1963), 11-18.

[44] Murao Jirō, *Ritsuryō zaiseishi no kenkyū,* 39.

conscripts were drawn. There were, of course, many adjustments for age and circumstance, and always the possibility of commutation to produce, or payment for a substitute.

The Nara period has not left sufficient documentation for the reconstruction of the overall condition of man and land in Bizen under the Taihō code. Historians have had to rely on the extremely uncertain figures of such later works as the *Kōninshiki*, the *Engishiki*, and the *Wamyō-ruiju-shō* to speculate on the magnitude of the economy of any given province. According to Sawada Goichi, who has extrapolated from the data contained in these sources, the official statistics pertaining to Bizen for the late ninth and early tenth century showed a population of 116,300 persons, rice lands comprising 13,185 *chō* (40,000 acres) and producing a grain tax of 803,300 sheaves (about 16,000 *koku* or 80,000 bushels).[45] The first reasonably accurate statement of this type for Bizen was not available until nearly eight centuries later, by which time the figures for the area under cultivation were double, for population about triple, and for tax rice roughly ten times those given by Sawada. Even by discounting the earlier figures considerably, it would still appear that by the ninth century Bizen had gone far in exploiting its available land for the support of a dense population.

If we take, then, the nearly 40,000 acres of cultivated land reported by Sawada as a very rough base figure, what do we know about the various types of use and tenure to which it was put? First, of course, there were the lands set aside for official purpose such as the endowment of public institutions or support of provincial officials. Of these only a few can be determined with any accuracy. The two official temples (the Kokubunji and Kokubun-niji) were assigned 450 acres during the mid-seventh century. At about the same time other Buddhist establishments acquired land endowments of comparable size. An inventory of properties of Daianji temple of Nara in 747 showed a holding of 450 acres in Bizen.[46] Lands of officials, those assigned to certain of the ministers of state in the central government and to the provincial governors, were not extensive; for each provincial official the legal amount did not exceed seven acres. Lands held by the titled district chiefs and the remnants of old *uji* aristocracy were probably

[45] Sawada Goichi, *Nara-jidai minsei keizai no sūteki kenkyū* (Tokyo, 1927), 188.
[46] *Tsūshi*, 1.411.

of the same order, though a few members of the Kibi and Wake families probably held merit lands of greater size. We must conclude, therefore, that at least through the eighth century, before the eventual extension of vast stretches of privately reclaimed land, the bulk of Bizen's rice lands were held as *kubunden* and subject to the provincial governor's jurisdiction.

One of the best illustrations we have that rice land was fairly evenly distributed and that the provincial tax system was in effective operation during the Nara period is the document of 739 which lists rice payment defaults left by the death of registered taxpayers in Bitchū. In this document 127 individuals are listed as having left at time of death a total of 6479 sheaves (about 650 bushels) in unrepaid seed rice loans. On an average these individuals had borrowed 51 sheaves (5 bushels); the largest loan was 191 sheaves (20 bushels). In repayment both principal and interest were returned to the government, meaning that the government would have received on an average 75 sheaves and as a maximum 286 sheaves. Since, as a rule of thumb, the total harvest of a *tan* (.3 acre) plot of superior paddy land was 50 sheaves, the task of repayment of these loan debts would have been of the order of the total return on 1.5 *tan* for the average and 5 *tan* (1.5 acres) for the maximum. Obviously, then, these individuals must have held lands of considerably greater extent than the amount required to return the seed rice debt. Certainly such fields as were their due under the allotment system had been assigned them, and, moreover, the land tax system was working to the extent that cognizance could be taken of annual variations such as those resulting from the death of cultivators.[47]

What was done with the rice, produce, and labor taxes collected in the provinces differed from province to province and depended on such factors as distance from the capital and the extent of land assigned to the support of aristocratic families or religious institutions. Much of the provincial intake was expended locally; of the remainder, much was eaten up in the process of getting it to the capital. As an example, Tajima, a province comparable in location to Bizen, shipped to Nara in 737, in addition to produce taxes, only about 600 *koku* (about 3,000 bushels) of rice. Yet the

[47] *Tsūshi*, 1.404-406; Sakamoto Tarō, *Nihon zenshi, 2, Kodai, 1* (Tokyo, 1960), 209.

expense of this shipment when added to the amount delivered to Nara absorbed roughly 56 percent of the whole provincial outlay for the year. The same was probably true of Bizen.[48]

In the annual fiscal cycle of Bizen, tax collection procedures began in the sixth month with the submission of census data by the heads of the *ko*. By the end of the month these figures were arranged into a province-wide tax assessment register, a copy of which would be submitted to the central government. Meanwhile, collection of produce taxes would begin in the province. Goods collected in payment of the produce and labor taxes were inspected, tagged, and prepared for storage in provincial storehouses. Bizen produced a wide variety of products. According to the *Engishiki*, payments were made in units of silk fabric, flax, silk thread, earthenware vessels, special forest products, salt, iron, iron implements, vegetables, fish, and many others. Shipment out of the province was generally by water. The governor's office, along with those of several of the district chiefs provided the staff which was assigned to supervise delivery of the tax payments to the appropriate offices in Nara.

The *Engishiki* gives figures for the expense of shipping a unit of rice to the capital. Land freight cost 1.2 *koku* per *koku*; sea freight required one sheaf for each *koku* of cargo, plus one *koku* for the ship captain and .75 *koku* per crew member. Thus a shipment of 50 *koku* of rice from Bizen to the port of Yodo would run to 5.15 *koku*, assuming that a crew of three men was required.[49] Because of the expense of shipping, then, we can understand that bulky taxes such as rice tended to be converted to produce for delivery to the capital. The same was true of labor. In fact, the standard method used for recruiting labor for building projects at the capital was for the government to requisition laborers from nearby provinces, exempt them from the regular corvée duty, and enlist them in paid labor gangs. Cloth and other products shipped in from the more distant provinces in lieu of labor were used to pay for this labor.[50]

In Bizen during the spring and early summer the main task of provincial officials was the collection of produce and the assessment of various labor requisitions. Meanwhile, the rice crop would

[48] Sawada, *op.cit.*, 479-501; Sakamoto Tarō, *ibid.*, 206.
[49] *Tsūshi*, 1.530; *Hiroshima-shi shi*, 1.241.
[50] Iyanaga Teizō, *Nara-jidai no kizoku to nōmin*, 79.

be maturing in the *kubunden*. The grain taxes became due after harvest, between the ninth and twelfth months. Repayment of principal and interest (generally 50 percent, on seed borrowed in the spring) would also come due in the fall. The major portion of the grain collections stayed in the provinces, where it served to support local administrative expenses, public construction, and public works, or where it was stored for seed loans and relief rice. We have no information on how much was sent to the capital. Shipments began at the beginning of the new year and Bizen was required to close its tax books at the capital by the end of the sixth month. From the warehouses in the capital the grain and produce from Bizen would then be used to make up stipends for officials, allowances for laborers, or funds for the procurement of building materials. Some Bizen inhabitants, either in labor groups or conscript units, made their way from the province to the capital each year. Thus, despite the still primitive state of transportation in Japan, Bizen was closely linked to the economic life of the capital.

From the point of view of the common inhabitant of Bizen, the reforms begun in the Taika era eventually had a profound effect upon his way of life. While he still may have lived under the dominance of local families of influence (those who served as district chiefs or household heads), these local magnates no longer had the same autonomous influence they once possessed. For the common cultivator, Bizen had changed from the domain of aristocratic chieftains with nearly unlimited local authority to a provincial division of an imperial state, governed under a systematic code of laws and administered by officials who exercised authority by virtue of their public status and the functions of the specific office to which they received appointment. It cannot be claimed, perhaps, that the villager was freer than before, for he was still tied to certain lands, assigned to him by the state, which he was neither free to dispose of nor free to refuse to cultivate. But to a large extent the personal tie between the cultivator and the recipient of his labors was broken. The nobility, both central and local, were, of course, supported by grants of land from which they received produce and labor services. But the Taihō code specifically prohibited the nobility from interference in these lands. It was expected that the first loyalty of the cultivators would be to the state.[51] In theory the state intervened between all free men and the recipients of their services. But more important still, the nature and the extent of the services required of the cultivator were subject to the official schedules of the central government. The concept of government as an abstract embodiment of law and of authority vested in law, however imperfectly understood, was set against the traditional practices in which authority was expressed in personal, familistic terms. The clearest product of these legal changes were the land tax procedures themselves. The systematic practices of land measurement and classification and the various categories of taxation stipulated in the Taihō code were to remain in use for centuries to come.

By the eighth century, it is obvious, the independent acquisition of conspicuous power was no longer possible in the Bizen countryside. The great fountainhead of wealth and political influence had become the central government, and only those sufficiently close to this source could rise to national prominence or local dominance. In the provinces no longer were great mounds built to the memory of local chieftains, and this was in large measure an indication of the diminishing resources upon which local families could rely. Indeed, from the time of the death of Wake-no-Kiyomaro in 799 to the rise of Ukita Naoie, the first of the great daimyo in the sixteenth century, no nationally prominent figures were to be nurtured in the province of Bizen.

The disappearance of the tumuli after the middle of the seventh century is, of course, not attributable simply to the weakening of the local families. The change of religious beliefs and burial habits brought about by the introduction of Buddhism was a prime contributing cause. In the Nara age the building or endowing of Buddhist centers in large measure took the place of the kind of conspicuous religious display that the *kofun* had exemplified. But while families such as the Kibi and Wake sought to identify with the new religion, seeking to acquire the prestige of association with it, the spread of Buddhism, as unrelentingly as the spread of central authority, served to undermine the local influence of these families.

With Buddhism there came into Bizen an entirely new system

[51] Takeuchi Rizō, "Ritsuryō kan-i sei ni okeru kaikyūsei," in *Ritsuryōsei to kizoku seiken,* 1.160.

of religious beliefs unrelated to local social or political traditions. The old system of Shinto beliefs had provided a religious rationale for the social hierarchy. The new religion came in without reference to the traditional authority structure, and although temples were frequently established as "family temples" by certain noble lineages, the Buddhist establishment as such was less apt to support purely local interests. Buddhism received its primary patronage in Japan from the imperial household and the central nobility, and as such was identified with the entire centralizing process which followed the Taika Reform. The introduction of Buddhism into the Kibi area, therefore, understandably diminished the religious prestige of the old *kuni-no-miyatsuko* families. The local leader was no longer able to monopolize the sources of religious veneration and loyalty within his locale. His only recourse was to join in conspicuous patronage of the new religion.

During the Nara period the provinces of Kibi saw some of the most active building of temples and monasteries of any area outside of the capital region. Today the remains of forty-two temples which originated in the Nara period can be identified in Kibi.[52] While no buildings remain fully intact from this number, broken tiles, occasional monuments, and a large number of foundation stones reveal that the provinces of Kibi were rapidly caught up in the Buddhist craze.

Temples built in Kibi during the Nara period were of two types. Many were branches of the great orders which had their headquarters in the capital and so received imperial or central government support. Others were locally endowed. For some of the latter, support came from a relatively small area, a village, a district, or from one of the families of the local aristocracy. These family or community temples (*ujidera*) were established in a like manner to local shrines, and to some extent they served the same purpose of providing religious focus to family or communal life. But the existence of a professional Buddhist priesthood tended to diminish the political influence which patronage of such temples might provide.

Of the great capital temples, it is believed that Saidaiji, Sairyūji, Genkōji, Kōfukuji, Enkakuji, and Daianji all built branches in Bizen, although there is no certain archaeological evidence that buildings were actually erected during the Nara period. Mention

[52] *Tsūshi*, 1.412-414.

of Daianji lands in Bizen would lead to an assumption that a temple by that name had been built. We know for certain of the existence of the two official branches of Tōdaiji: the Kokubunji and Kokubunniji. Tiles and stone foundation remains permit us a fairly exact reconstruction of what these establishments must have looked like. For example, the nunnery of Bitchū covered an area as large as 450 by 360 feet.[53] The Bizen monastery must have been as large, with a full complement of buildings including main Buddha hall, lecture hall, pagoda, library, and several entrance gates.[54]

For some inexplicable reason many more remains are found today of the temples built under local sponsorship. Tiles and foundation stones dating from the Nara period are evidence of the existence of fifteen or more local temples. Among them the Bizen Ichinomiya Jingūji (the temple of Bizen's first shrine) is one of the most interesting. Although it was later to become quite common for the Buddhist priesthood to encroach upon the centers of Shinto worship, the creation of a temple alongside the first shrine of a province during this time is relatively rare. Of the remaining local temples, Fujino-ji and Wake-ji were patronized by members of the Wake family. Jōdō-ji was probably the family temple of the Kamutsumichi family. Owari-ji in Ōku district was patronized by a family of that name. The Owari had settled in Bizen somewhat later than the Kibi and had become heads of Owari village under the new system of local administration. Two temples, Hatori and Tsu, are of particular interest since their patrons were immigrants. The Hatori-be of weavers apparently flourished in Ōku district and put its name upon a village. The Tsu family, perhaps traders connected with the port which served the provincial capital of Bitchū, flourished in the area of the southern boundary between Bizen and Bitchū. In the 747 document on seed rice default in Bitchū, three members of the Tsu family appear with the honorary title of *omi*. The name Tsuu, given to the district centering on the port of Bitchū, may have come either from this family or from the word for port. A foundation stone of Tsu temple remains today. Measuring five by eight feet and exposed three feet above the ground, it is the largest such stone to be found in the Kibi area.[55]

[53] *Kibi-gun shi*, 1.870.   [54] *Tsūshi*, 1.422-429.
[55] *Ibid.*, 1.445-450.

In the religious life of southern Bizen there are indications of the same two levels of provincial and district activity which characterized the political scene. Coming into the province with the backing of the central government were the branch temples of the central Buddhist orders. They brought with them the superior prestige of the imperial capital and they served to turn the attention of the people of the province toward the capital and the imperial court. The provincial temples served to support the prestige of the local families, particularly those whose surnames still coincided with district or village names. This identity of surname to local temple name was not automatic, and the practice gradually became less common. During the Nara period it illustrated the continued prestige, at a fairly low level of political importance, of families whose roots were in the traditional soil of Bizen.

14. All that is left of the former provincial capital is this lonely marker and a small shrine.

15. The old official highway, the Sanyōdō, retains some of its historic atmosphere, since the modern national highway has taken a new course.

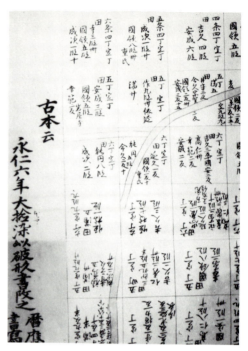

16. An air view of fields in the Bizen Plain reveals remnants of the *jōri* system of land division.

17. A sketch map of fields near the capital of Bitchū Province made in 1298 still records land holdings by *jōri* square numbers.

18. Kibi-no-Makibi (693-775), the last prominent member of the Kibi house, is escorted through the Chinese countryside.°

° From the late 12th century scroll, *Kibi Dainagon Nitto Ekotoba*, in the Bigelow Collection, Museum of Fine Arts, Boston.

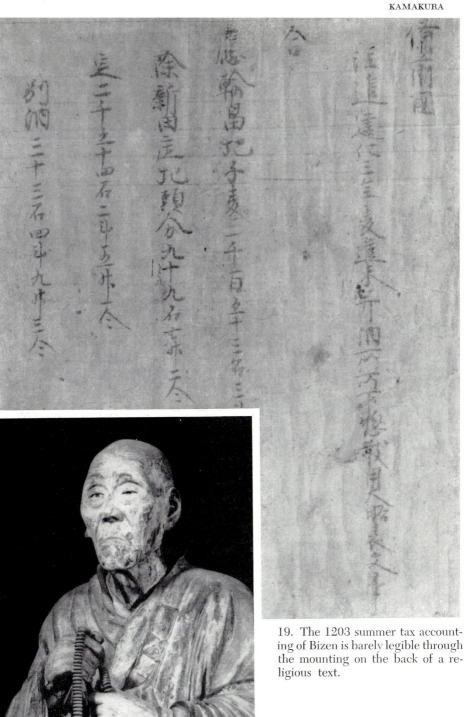

19. The 1203 summer tax accounting of Bizen is barely legible through the mounting on the back of a religious text.

20. The priest Chōgen (1121-1206) devoted considerable energy to extracting taxes from Bizen for the rebuilding of Tōdaiji in Nara.

21. Through this narrow valley beyond the pass of Mitsuishi the Akamatsu ex-tende

22. Akamatsu Norisuke (1314-1371), *Shugo* of Bizen
and Mimasaka, is here depicted as a Zen monk.

ol of Bizen. The River Kinko joins the Yoshi beyond the hill in the distant center.

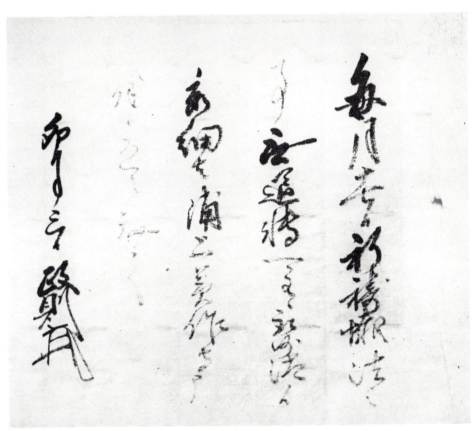

23. Akamatsu Masanori (1455-1496), whose signature is on this document, revived the fortunes of the Akamatsu house after the disastrous Kakitsu affair of 1441.

24. The market at Fukuoka. 25. Saidaiji in its heyday. 26. Saidaiji being burned and sacked.

27. The narrow valley of the Takahashi River permitted only a few major centers of power.

28. Matsuyama, once the stronghold of the Shō and Mimura, is one of the few remaining hilltop castles in Japan today.

29. From Matsuyama castle one looks down steeply to the town of Takahashi below.

IV. THE SHŌEN SYSTEM AND THE RETURN
TO FAMILIAL AUTHORITY

THE system of government which acquired its legal form in the Taihō code continued to function without fundamental modification well into the tenth century. The appearance from time to time of strong emperors, such as Kammu and his immediate successors, kept alive the image of an emperor who could both reign and rule. The transfer of the capital from Nara to Heian between 784 and 794 accentuated the imperial dignity and served for a time to focus attention upon the central government. Bizen was more directly involved in the dramatic transfer of the capital than most of the other provinces. Throughout more than ten years of planning and construction, years which saw the abortive effort to establish the new imperial city of Nagaoka, and then the sudden move to Heian (the present city of Kyoto), one of the most prominent figures at court was Wake-no-Kiyomaro. This son of Bizen brought honor to his province through his service under Emperor Kammu. It was he who in 769 fearlessly brought back the revelation from the shrine of Usa Hachiman that the priest Dōkyō would indeed be a usurper were he to accept imperial dignities. Kiyomaro was banished for this deed, but after Dōkyō's disgrace he returned to the capital with great honor and became a principal adviser to Kammu. He is said to have suggested the site for the new capital of Heian, and as head of the bureau of taxation (Mimbu-no-kami) directed the construction of the palaces and public buildings.[1]

Bizen and the other provinces of Kibi were called upon to take part in the actual building of the new capital as well. Bizen contributed the material and labor for the erection of the Yōmei Gate, one of the largest and most important of the great city entrance ways. It is recorded that this work was carried out under the supervision of the Waka-no-Inukai family of Bizen. How much of an outlay this entailed is unrecorded, but when in 816 palace repairs in Kyoto were imposed upon Bizen and five other provinces a total of 19,800 laborers were called to the capital.[2]

The new capital presided over nearly a century and a half of stable government throughout Japan. In a province such as Bizen

[1] *Tsūshi*, 1.495-497.   [2] *Ibid.*, 1.497.

there was little of moment to disturb a tranquil existence under laws and administrative practices which had by then become quite routine. And yet the very tranquility of provincial affairs portended trouble. After the death of Wake-no-Kiyomaro we hear of no men of Bizen who may have influenced affairs of state at the capital. Capital and provinces were both falling into their own separate routines. Few men of the provinces made their way to the capital except perhaps in minor service capacities or as military officers, and few men of high official rank entered the province. Provincial affairs were left increasingly to the subordinate officials. And while for a time the provinces were able somehow to run themselves, routinization eventually turned to neglect.

That all was not well between the capital and the provinces was apparent in Kammu's time. But the problem was considered chiefly a fiscal one: that of keeping provincial governors honest and the tax collections flowing. Emperor Kammu had attempted to solve these problems by the appointment of special provincial inspectors and audit governors (*kageyushi*). Wake-no-Kiyomaro had served as an inspector in the "Southern Circuit" under Kammu, and in his later years received official commendations for noteworthy administrative services in Bizen. Decline of provincial government was not rapid, and its deepest causes were never fully recognized by the central court, for they were closely linked to the much more fundamental problems of the court's declining interest in the organs of central administration themselves.

Probably the most significant contribution of the Taihō code had been the establishment of the concept of the imperial state as having an existence of its own over and above the body of court nobility which comprised the bureaucracy. The ultimate failure of the Taihō system of government resulted from an abandonment of this concept of the state. The Taihō institutions, complicated in administrative and legal details, were never easy to enforce and were from the start overelaborate for the needs of the Japanese of that time. Modification or simplification was to be expected, and Kammu himself had initiated several simplifying administrative changes in order to draw the reigns of authority more directly under his control. Such changes were not necessarily destined to subvert the power of the emperor. But when, by the reigns of Daigo and Murakami, the emperors gave evidence of relinquishing any claim to real involvement in political affairs, the stage was set for the rapid realignment of the power structure within the court aristocracy in a manner that eventually bypassed the major organs of the central government.

During the ninth century abandonment of such practices as the redistribution of rice land, the minting of currency, and the preparation of official histories gave evidence of a deep-seated change in the relationships between political power, social status, and landed revenue in Japan, a change which in certain superficial respects took the form of a return to pre-Taika conditions of society. Court society had begun to restructure itself in such a way that the social and political hierarchies had very nearly become identical, and as a result the formal apparatus of government as a mechanism for providing competition for power became unnecessary. There had taken place, as Max Weber so appropriately described it, an appropriation of economic advantage and power leading to decentralized patrimonial authority.[3]

Historians have speculated upon a number of causes which help to explain the decline of the central authority particularly over the provinces.[4] Two appear critical. First, the gradual abandonment of provisions for state control of rice lands led ultimately to the growth of vast private proprietorships (*shōen*) through which the aristocratic houses and religious establishments of the capital were able to absorb many of the powers and functions of the central government. Second, abandonment of the principle of public conscription led to the emergence of a provincial military class (*bushi*) which increasingly took over the military and police functions of the state on a hereditary basis and by the thirteenth century began to encroach upon the civil authority of provincial administration as well. Of the two, the spread of the *shōen* system was the first to manifest itself and in the long run was to have the most far-reaching effects upon the political structure of Japan. While it is conceivable that the *bushi* might have attained their political dominance in Japan without the prior existence of the *shōen* system, in actual fact it greatly accelerated the appearance of independent military groups within the provinces.

[3] Max Weber, *op.cit.*, 346-351.
[4] For a general discussion of these problems I have found Naoki Kōjirō's "Ritsuryō-sei no dōyō" particularly useful. See *Nihon rekishi kōza, 2, Kodai-chūsei* (Tokyo, 1959), 35-38.

Among the institutions of Taihō the laws governing land tenure and taxation proved particularly difficult to maintain in the face of strong tendencies toward private ownership and aristocratic and local particularism. The land provisions of the Nara period, of course, had never ruled out the possibility of heritable possession of land. Public ownership had been enforced primarily upon rice lands. The land upon which cultivators' houses were built, dry fields of various sorts, forest land, and wastelands could be, and generally were, privately possessed. Even in the case of paddy field land, temples and shrines were permitted holdings in perpetuity, often free of taxes, for endowment purposes. And court families which had gained special favor from the emperor received merit land (*kōden*) or imperial gift land (*shiden*) that could be held for a specified number of generations or in perpetuity. The imperial family held its own quite extensive private lands (*chokushiden*), while other tracts were set aside as endowments for government offices. In other words, while the principle of state ownership was all inclusive in theory, it was limited in practice to certain specific types of land.

Perhaps it would be more correct to say that the fundamental concern of the state toward land was the authority to tax it and to control its use. In other words it sought to "govern" the land in the full sense of the term. But once the basic reapportionment of political power had been made, and with it the redistribution of the land, there were few interests within the government with any stake in perpetuating the role of the central government as an actual owner. Since the social and bureaucratic hierarchies were never greatly separated even after the Taika Reform, it was merely a matter of time before the aristocracy, and the religious institutions patronized by it, "appropriated to themselves" the rights over land and its fruits which had once been the prerogative of the state. The result of this process was the establishment of large private proprietary domains within which the state relinquished its rights of governance and taxation, retaining only certain residual rights of sovereignty.

The growth of the proprietary domain was the result of no single defect in the Taihō institutions nor any particular form of exploitation by the aristocracy. Rather, the spread of private possession, upon which the proprietorships were based, occurred at many levels and resulted from a number of parallel developments.

How long it took for the sustenance, rank, and office lands assigned to the support of the aristocracy and the religious establishments to slip back into conditions of private holding differed considerably from location to location. In the home provinces the ability of the state to control land assignments persisted well into the ninth century. Yet in the more distant provinces, where we may suppose that the greater portion of lands assigned to the district chiefs was the same as the territories held by these same families before the reform, the sense of continued identity with particular lands was naturally strong. It would have taken constant and strenuous effort on the part of the central government to prevent a return to what amounted to permanent and heritable possession. And this became increasingly true in the capital area as generation after generation certain families held identical ranks and posts.

At the other end of the scale of land rights was the slow but persistent growth of permanent tenures among the cultivators. This resulted both from the gradual abandonment of the practice of land redistribution and from the ability of cultivators to acquire private rice lands outside the public domain. The allotment system was from the first a most complex and cumbersome procedure. The necessity to draw up periodic census records and then to redistribute the holdings of each locale, village by village, proved laborious to the extreme. But basically the problem of the *handen* system was that, whatever its merits at the time of its inception, by the end of the eighth century there were within the government few interests with any strong stake in its continuation. The system could not simply perpetuate itself, for it took constant vigilance to enforce. Moreover, the system was open to abuses which tended to withdraw land from the public domain, despite the fact that a growing population required a constant increase in *kubunden*. There was, of course, a rather significant increase in land under cultivation during the eighth and ninth centuries, but much of this resulted from the extension of private or institutional tenures. Land available for allotment actually tended to diminish in relation to the cultivating population.

For numerous reasons, then, the *handen* system became inoperative, at least as a system of equitable allocation of rice land. Redistribution was gradually abandoned (the last recorded instance in the home provinces occurred in 844), with the result that allotment land lost most of its features of public ownership in the eyes of both the cultivators and the government. For the cultivator, the sense of identity with specific plots of land became increasingly intimate and secure. The government, on the other hand, began to readjust its fiscal policies, gradually shifting the focus of taxation from the individual cultivator to the land itself. Increasingly the land tax became defined according to quotas of grain determined plot by plot according to the productivity of each piece of paddy land. Salaries of officials were no longer calculated in terms of sustenance households but rather in terms of the income from specified amounts of rice land.[5]

Reclamation provided a more direct and less ambiguous means of acquiring private possession of rice lands. The constant demand for more allotment land obliged the government to encourage reclamation and frequently to offer inducements in the form of special land rights over new fields. An ambitious scheme announced in 723 to expand the area of paddy field cultivation in Japan by one million *chō* (about 3 million acres) placed a great deal of reliance on private reclamation. For inducement, land reclaimers were permitted to retain possession of the new rice lands for one, two, or even three generations. A further concession made in 743 when the emperor Shōmu exempted newly reclaimed land from being absorbed into the *kubunden* and permitted its retention in perpetuity by the reclaimer. There is a touch of irony in the fact that this decision, so crucial to the eventual abandonment of the principle of state ownership, should have emanated from the central government itself.

What the government had in mind by its encouragement of land reclamation was obviously the stimulation of many small-scale reclamation works which, when taken together, would help alleviate the pressures on allotment land. While a good deal of this kind of marginal reclamation must have gone on, the new ruling served primarily to encourage the opening up of large tracts of land by those of means: provincial officials, aristocratic families, and religious institutions. Expansion of the rice paddy system was no easy matter, for not only did it require a great expenditure of labor in clearing, filling, flattening, and dyking fields, but also each project faced complex problems of integration into existing

[5] Yasuda Motohisa, *Nihon shōenshi gaisetsu* (Tokyo, 1957), 123. Hereafter cited as Yasuda, *Shōenshi*.

irrigation and drainage systems. The aristocracy and the religious establishments had an obvious advantage when it came to such large-scale operations. These groups had the excess income from land necessary to hire labor gangs and they had the influence necessary to put through new water courses or to acquire favorable water rights.

How successful the reclamation program was in the aggregate we do not know. But before long the government was obliged to set limits to the amount which could be reclaimed by any individual family or institution. These limits themselves are indicative of the amounts being opened up: imperial princes and families of first court rank were limited to 500 *chō*, those of second court rank to 400 *chō*, of fifth court rank to 100 *chō*, of sixth through eighth ranks to 50 *chō*. Among local officials, governors of districts were permitted 30 *chō*, while their subordinates were permitted 10 *chō*. Temples received much more generous limits, beginning with a startling 14,000 *chō* for Tōdaiji.[6] That such limits were reached and even surpassed is indicated by the complaints lodged by the government against the seemingly indiscriminate reclamation by religious institutions and the efforts of court families to circumvent the limits imposed upon them.

A good deal of criticism has been levied at the Nara civil and religious officialdom for their land-hungry efforts to extend their properties. Yet it should be remembered that, failing outright government participation in land development, it required institutions of considerable means to engage in the kind of effort necessary to extend the landed base of Japan's economy by any appreciable amount. To the extent that the aristocracy and the temples expended their wealth in reclamation they were turning back surpluses to the land. Many of the projects carried on in the name of the wealthy were in fact the combined work of entire communities in which the aristocracy or temples provided the margin of additional tools or hired labor necessary to bring the task off. Moreover, no matter how the land was reclaimed, it was not withdrawn from cultivation, but rather was put out to the same extensive cultivation as the *kubunden*. To this extent the great land holders were achieving the desire of the government to provide for a constantly expanding population.

6 *Ibid.*, 20.

The appearance of large private land holdings and the gradual return of rice land to conditions of permanent tenure could go on for some time without greatly disturbing the Taihō administrative and fiscal institutions. Private possession itself was no direct threat to the tax structure of the imperial system. For as long as such land was encumbered by state dues it served the same function as *kubunden*. The real divergence with the Taihō system came as various tax immunities were secured in addition to the rights of private possession. First as tax exemptions were permitted, then as immunities from civil or criminal jurisdiction of local officials were granted, step by step the vital elements of independent state authority over the land were dissipated.

The process of acquiring exemptions from land taxes began slowly and remained fully within the limits of legality for several centuries. The privilege of exemption from the grain tax (*fuyuso*) had been given to many religious establishments from the time of the Taika Reform. Temples and shrines normally carried immunities of some sort for their lands. The court nobility were also permitted exemptions on certain holdings, particularly on merit land. The acquisition of new exemptions by land owners was a matter of some difficulty at first, but there were official procedures which could be followed for the purpose. Newly reclaimed private lands could generally be placed under the category of lands exempted from labor taxes (*zōeki-no-men*). And temples and families of high rank could often claim the extension of immunities from one piece of specially favored holding to others. The process of acquiring exemptions required a specific order (*kanshōfu*) from the central government through the bureau of taxation (*mimbushō*). Gradually, however, exemption became obtainable through the permission of lesser officials and eventually of provincial governors.

Despite the growth of fiscal immunities on private lands, it was always possible that the state should retain its administrative powers over the land, especially with respect to civil and criminal affairs of those who lived upon it. The final immunity, and the one which converted immune lands into true private proprietorships, was protection from official entry and inspection (*funyū*) by the cadastral inspectors and police officers of the provincial government. The right of immunity from entry thus served to withdraw the now extensive private holdings from the purview of the local administration. This was the origin of what the Japanese called the complete *shōen* (or *ichien-chigyō*), territories under private proprietorship in which the proprietor assumed most of the duties of governance as well as all of the fiscal rights which had once belonged to the central government.

Proprietorships of this type appeared sporadically in the eighth century in Japan but grew steadily thereafter. As the privileges and immunities available to *shōen* proprietors were made secure and public, several other related processes combined to add to the size of the *shōen* and also to their territorial homogeneity. The most notable of these was the process of accretion through purchase or commendation whereby immune lands gathered up neighboring holdings into ever larger parcels. Sale of land was permitted for private land, and eventually even *kubunden* could be alienated on something like a permanent lease basis. Commendation (*kishin*) was a favorite means used by owners who wished to place their lands under the protection of larger, and generally more immune, proprietors. Commendation was probably not engaged in primarily for tax evasion, since the rents paid to the proprietor were not so different from the public taxes due to the government. The major attraction of commendation was to gain in some measure greater security of tenure and protection from official interference. Commendation generally involved the transfer of land under conditions less complete than outright sale, since the commender forfeited only a portion of his right of ownership in return for protection. On the other hand, the relationship between commender and proprietor became more personal and probably was considered less capricious than that between the provincial officials and the cultivators of public domain, particularly after the system developed its worst abuses. Thus private agreements between the several levels of persons holding tenure to the land replaced reliance on codified legal practice.

Bizen is not a particularly good province from which to gain insight into the process of *shōen* formation in Japan. The history of the growth of *shōen* in Bizen is poorly documented and what little we know must be pieced together from a rather slender and scattered record culled from a wide variety of sources. No *shōen* in Bizen is sufficiently well documented to show its growth from original grant to full maturity. Of the immune lands held by

Buddhist institutions the earliest record is of Daianji's 150 *chō*
in 747. The temple of Saidaiji, established in Bizen in 780 received a grant of the *shō* of Ōmameda from a member of the
Kamutsumichi family. The important Fujiwara proprietorship of
Shikada-no-shō, first appeared in the records in 813; the temple
Enkakuji is known to have possessed a *shōen* in Bizen in 883 and
Iwashimizu shrine had already acquired Kataoka-no-*shō* by
1024.[7] But this is a meager record, and we must suppose, therefore, that up to the middle of the eleventh century, grants of
immune proprietorships were relatively rare in Bizen.

On the other hand, the ground was being laid for the very rapid
appearance of *shōen* in the twelfth century by the increase of
private holdings, the acquisition of piecemeal immunities, and the
beginnings of commendation. Evidence of reclamation in Bizen
is extensive though not particularly specific. The Daianji land
document of 747 mentions one piece of land reclaimed by a cultivator (*hyakushō*) and another by the Tajihi family, a former
governor of the province. Thereafter the Wake and Kibi families
appear as important landed interests along with the Fujiwara and
Tōdaiji. From archaeological evidence and from the comparison
of areas under cultivation at the beginning and at the end of the
Heian period it is quite clear that large stretches of reclaimed
land were brought under cultivation in Bizen after the eighth
century. Southern Bizen was of course a favorite spot for land
reclamation because of the steady silting-in of the delta region
between the large rivers which converged to flow into the Inland
Sea above Kojima. By at least the tenth century a large area of
new fields had been added below the line of the original *jōri*
squares (see map p. 20), and we may surmise that this was brought
under cultivation as *konden* subsequent to the enforcement of the
original land allotment system. In this area we know that two large
holdings were reclaimed by Daianji and another by Daitokuji.
By 813 we have evidence of the existence of Shikada-no-shō, one
of the most important proprietorships of the Fujiwara house.
Occupying an extensive area on the west bank of the Asahi River,
the Fujiwara must have sponsored its reclamation during the first
years of the ninth century. Further to the north the Wake family
was active in the middle valley of the Yoshii River. In 799 his

[7] *Okayama-ken no rekishi*, 113-119.

son made a grant to the government of 160 *chō* of newly reclaimed land to provide for the erection of a new school at the capital and the establishment of a permanent endowment.[8] In neighboring Bitchū the Kaya family, a branch of the Kibi line now serving as wardens of Kibitsu shrine, appeared as important *shōen* proprietors. The family clearly had been active for several generations as developers of the Ashimori valley (a tributary of the Takahashi River).[9]

The process of accumulation of land through sale in Bizen is revealed in one of the most interesting of all land documents of the eighth century. This is the record of land sale found in the collection of Shōsōin relics and bearing the date 774. The partial translation below provides excellent insight into the complexities of land transfer during the Nara period and especially into the systematic involvement of the government in such matters:

> Deed of sale of dry fields in Bizen, district of Tsutaka, village (*mura*) of Ugaki:
>> Ayabe-no-Akomaro, presenting as his reason that he was unable to pay his taxes proposes to sell the following dry fields: 3 *tan* for the price of 80 sheaves of rice, located as follows. . . . . The above is sold by Ayabe-no-Akomaro, because of tax indebtedness, from out of his dry field holdings to Mino-no-omi Otomasu of the same *gō*.
>
> Two copies of the above deed have been made, one for transmission to the district office (*gūke*), the other for the purchaser. Therefore as proof of this matter this document is prepared and authenticated.

		774, 11, 23
Signed:	Household head (*koshu*)	Ayabe-no-Akomaro
	Chief of taxes (*zeichō*)	Fumi-no-atae-Maro
	Village head (*gōchō*)	Tera-no-Hirotoko
	Witness	Ayabe-no-Kohimaro[10]

Accumulation through commendation, which was so universally practiced throughout Japan, is not revealed in Bizen by any documentary evidence until the twelfth and thirteenth centuries. By that time, however, *shōen* had become quite commonplace, and

[8] *Tsūshi, 1.381; Sekai rekish jiten* (25 vols., Tokyo, 1950-1955) 9.264.
[9] *Okayama-ken no rekishi*, 121.
[10] *Tsūshi*, 1.406.

the types of commendation revealed in Bizen records are those of the outright gift of land to religious institutions in order to secure merit. The following document from the thirteenth century is characteristic of such grants.

Deed of Commendation:
For rice to provide for the reading of the Lotus Sutra every seventeenth day of the month at the Kannon Chapel of Anyōji:
    In total two *tan* taxable at the rate of five *to*. The above is respectfully commended according to precedence by this document. Thus ordered.
1286, 10, 17
Signed: Fujiwara-no-Mitsuhisa[11]

One feature of the *shōen* proprietorships in Bizen was that both *shōen* and public domain tended to retain the boundaries of the subdivisions of local administration (*gō* and *ho*) of the Nara period. This particular feature must have resulted from a conscious policy on the part of the government to avoid fragmentation. In certain instances it must have involved actual exchange between private and public territories. That this was done is revealed in documents of the year 1196 when 260 *chō* of newly reclaimed lands opened by Tōdaiji but scattered widely about Bizen were exchanged for the consolidated *ho* of Noda. The evidence is late, but it is certainly not exceptional, and it is particularly interesting in its revelation of the manner in which the central government was involved in the entire process of authentication of *shōen* rights. In this instance orders were sent by both the left executive officer of the council of state (Sabenkan) and by the office of the cloistered emperor (In-no-chō) to the office of the provincial governor and the provincial office to the following effect:

    In exchange for the return to the state by Tōdaiji of lands for the supply of lamp oil scattered throughout Bizen province amounting to 260 *chō*, the entire *ho* of Noda is created into a single tax free parcel for the supply of oil for the Great Buddha Hall. This land has the following immunities: It is exempt from entry of provincial officials, from dues to the

[11] Fujii Shun and Mizuno Kyōichirō, eds., *Okayama-ken komonjo-shū* (3 vols., Okayama, 1953-56), 1.2. Hereafter cited as *Komonjo-shū*.

central government or to the office of the cloister, and from great and small provincial services.[12]

A document of this sort reveals quite clearly the process whereby consolidated *shōen* came into existence in Bizen. The process was an orderly one involving legal action by the appropriate offices of central and local government. To this extent the *shōen* existed as recognized and legitimate creations within the administrative framework of the Taihō institutions. And as such they came to incorporate into their own internal structures many of the same legal provisions of administration and land law which had existed under imperial public administration. *Shōen* practice, though differing according to location and circumstance and always subject to private idiosyncrasies, nonetheless was fundamentally based upon imperial law and had certain common features.

Shōen law began with the definitions of the rights of proprietorship (*ryōshu-ken*). Commonly it granted to the proprietor the powers of land survey and registration (*kenchū*), of management over land and cultivators (*chigyō*), of land use and alienation (*shitaji-shinchū*), of taxation (*shotō*), and of police and judicial authority (*sata*). In fact, the proprietor could receive nearly all the state's powers of governance except the exercise of sovereignty and the right to determine the legality of proprietary claims.[13]

Proprietorship could be exercised in full or only in part. In fact, as the *shōen* system developed, rights of proprietorship tended to become separated according to the size and rank of the proprietor or according to the history of the original proprietary agreements. The generic term for proprietor was *ryōshu*, to whom belonged the crucial powers of alienation. At various stages in the history of the *shōen*, *ryōshu* predominated at the local level. But at other times they tended to subordinate themselves by commendation to more powerful proprietors connected with the imperial court. *Ryōshu* holding the highest court rank or powerful temple proprietorships were referred to as *ryōke*. Such proprietorships were centered at the capital and were generally sufficiently well protected to provide complete and secure immunity from government interference, but it became common practice for even such high-ranking proprietors to seek the special protection of

[12] *Nōchi shi*, 412.
[13] Nakada Kaoru, *Shōen no kenkyū* (Tokyo, 1948 edition), 63-76; Yasuda, *Shōenshi*, 146-180.

some more exalted court power by commendation to what was called the *honke*. The latter served as the ultimate guarantor of the legality of the *shōen*'s title and immunities. Former *ryōshu* who commended their land to *ryōke* lost their proprietary status but often retained considerable managerial autonomy. Thus in essence it was possible to have a threefold division of the rights and privileges of proprietorship. How these were divided up in actual practice depended, of course, on the internal agreements between *honke, ryōke,* and former *ryōshu.* For the inhabitants of the *shōen* it mattered only to know where the principal managerial powers lay. This function, generally taken over by the *ryōke,* defined the locus of the *shōen*'s headquarters, or *honjo.*

Under the proprietor, the *shōen* came to embrace a regular system of internal customary law deriving in large part from those aspects of imperial local administration which had been displaced by the immunities granted the proprietor.[14] As the various levels of proprietors, managers, cultivators, and tenants worked out their relationships by agreement with each other, and as the increasing acquisition of immunities placed more and more of the responsibility of government into the hands of the proprietor, a virtual system of local administration came into being which looked to the *honjo* as the ultimate authority. In fact, as we shall see when areas as large as the administrative village (*gō*) were brought under a single private proprietorship, the internal organization of such *gō*-converted-to-*shō* remained very nearly what it had been under the imperial system.

A good example of the early but mature *shōen* in Bizen was Shikada-no-shō, the prized possession of the main line of the Fujiwara house.[15] In the case of Shikada-no-shō both the *honke* and *ryōke* were held by the head of the main line of the Fujiwara house. The managerial headquarters (*honjo*) of the *shō* was therefore located in the household organization of the Fujiwara house. Since the *honjo* of Shikada-no-shō was located in the capital, there was a clear separation between the absentee proprietor and the resident administrators and managers. The *shō* itself had been comprised of a variety of local tenures. Some had been land reclaimed directly by the Fujiwara. Some had formerly belonged

---

[14] Ishii Ryōsuke, *Nihon hōseishi gaisetsu* (Tokyo, 1948), 234-237.
[15] Fujii Shun, "Bizen-no-kuni Shikada-no-shō ni tsuite," in Uozumi Sōgorō, ed., *Setonaikai-chiiki no shakaishiteki kenkyū* (Tokyo, 1952), 131-139.

to local landowners, essentially of the *ryōshu* type, who had commended themselves to the Fujiwara under different circumstances.
Over the former the Fujiwara generally placed officers of their
own choosing under a variety of precarious appointments. Over
the latter the commenders generally served as resident subpro-
prietors, retaining various managerial rights as a result of their
act of commendation.

Shōen practice identified several distinct functions within the
category of managership or resident official. Titles such as *jitō,
yoriudo,* or *gesu* each provided for the exercise of supervisory
powers over land and village affairs, tax collection, record keeping, and settlement of *shōen* disputes. The freedom of *shōen* officials differed considerably according to whether the officer was a
delegate of the proprietor or a former local landowner. To take an
example: a document of 1275 reveals that one, Muranushi-no-
Yukishige, commended Kōya, a small local proprietorship, to the
shrine of Kasuga in Nara. He thereby became the resident manager of Kōya-no-shō, over which he retained considerable freedom
of action. At the same time this same individual served as resident
(*gesu*) in Shikada-no-shō. In the latter capacity he was subject to
the direction of several superior officials. Obviously Yukishige was
the head of a Bizen family which had been active in reclamation
and had from time to time commended its lands for protection to
higher authorities.[16] Such an individual frequently held multiple
appointments, accepting whatever status he could acquire in the
process of commendation. On the other hand, resident officers
sent out from the *honjo,* as exemplified by the deputy officer
(*mokudai*) of Shikada-no-shō, were generally residents of the
capital on detached service. Such officers carried considerable administrative authority, by delegation from the proprietor, but had
fewer traditional ties with privately owned land or with subordinate officials.[17]

The bulk of the inhabitants of any *shōen* were families engaged
primarily in cultivation, generally referred to as *shōmin.* Their
condition was extremely varied, and during the ninth and tenth
centuries tended to be in flux, as the shift from allotment land to
hereditary tenures took place. But eventually by the eleventh century the condition of the *shōmin* had settled down to something

---

[16] *Ibid.*, 135.
[17] Yasuda Motohisa, *Nihon zenshi, 4, Chūsei, 1* (Tokyo, 1958), 88-89.

of a uniformity so that it could be described in general terms. By the eleventh century, at least, *shōen* were made up out of an agglomeration of private tenures referred to as *myōden*, the literal meaning of which was "name land." *Myō* were conditions of private rights to cultivation sufficiently secure to be registered under the name of a family head. The holder of these tenures was known as the *myōshu*. As cultivated land within a *shōen* came more and more to be expressed in terms of *myō*, it became customary to levy the land dues upon the *myōshu*.[18] The *myōshu* thus became the responsible units of cultivation and taxation within the *shōen*. As such they served much the same function as the *koshu* under the Taihō system; some, in fact, may have had a pedigree extending back to such a status in Nara times.[19]

Like the *koshu*, the *myōshu* took responsibility for a communal group considerably larger than his immediate conjugal family, though not as large as the older *ko*. The size of the *myō* was probably quite variable. Beginning in the capital region, where the breakdown of the *handen* system had been most advanced, we can trace the gradual formation of consolidated private tenures, in which right of cultivation had been secured in perpetuity under the name of a single individual. Outside of the capital area the size of holdings tended to be large and the origin of the *myō* was more often the result of reclamation. (In Satsuma, *myō* of 150 acres were not uncommon.)[20] But in central Japan the *myō* holdings averaged from about one to three *chō* (three to nine acres) and had frequently originated as *kubunden*. Such units were worked by the *myōshu*'s family operating as a collectivity and drawing on the services of closely related branch families, bondsmen, and tenants. *Myōshu* "families" thus consisted of blood-related and bound houses under the management of a main household head in what had come to be a fairly typical pattern of rural social organization. In terms of land tenure, while the *myōshu* was responsible for the payment of dues from all members of the *myō*, individual members possessed a variety of conditions of occupancy and rights to cultivation. It was these conditions to which *shōen* law gave the status of cultivator (*sakunin*).

[18] Murai Yasuhiko, "Myō seiritsu no rekishiteki zentei," *Rekishigaku kenkyū*, 215 (Jan., 1958), 4-8.
[19] Nakamura Kichiji, *Nihon shakaishi*, 138-145.
[20] Yasuda, *Shōenshi*, 131.

According to *shōen* law, each status in the hierarchy of relationships to the land, whether *ryōke, shōkan, myōshu,* or *sakunin,* was conceived of as possessing certain rights or obligations which in turn permitted certain claims upon the fruits of the land. The nature of these relationships and the extent of these claims was expressed in a concept which became a pivotal part of *shōen* practice, namely, the idea of "function" or *shiki.* Within the *shōen* the idea of *shiki* served to define legally the relationship between land rights and income. For example, the *ryōshu* possessed what was known as the *ryōshu-shiki,* which specified the nature of proprietorship (*ryōchi*) as well as the types and amounts of proprietary dues such as the land rent (*nengu*), the produce payment (*kajishi*), and the service payment (*kuji*).[21] *Shiki* similarly defined the rights and incomes of each lesser "function" within the *shōen.* Each type of *shiki* received the income proper to its designated share. *Shiki* thus became equivalent to landed property itself. They were heritable, divisible, and even alienable within the level of rights and obligations which adhered to them, at each level in the *shōen* hierarchy.

It can be imagined that the legal complexity of the *shiki* system assumed incredible proportions in some instances because of the heterogeneous nature of the land parcels and the multiple types of tenure and divisions of rights to income from the land. Within a *shōen,* for instance, an individual could hold several types of *shiki* or perhaps only a portion of one *shiki,* as he combined many functions in his own person or shared with others the burdens of administration or of cultivation. We must suppose that only under a fairly stable system of law and order could such a practice continue in operation for long. In actuality, the *shōen* must be conceived of as a growth within the imperial law and administration at almost every level. The *shōen* received their immunities by official action. And though they acquired protection from internal interference by provincial officials they continued to depend upon provincial administration for the maintenance of a stable local order. Disputes between *shōen* were settled by reference to the imperial government, and even problems of enforcing *shiki* provisions within *shōen* were brought before the provincial authorities.

[21] Nakada Kaoru, *op.cit.,* 63-76; Yasuda Motohisa, *Nihon zenshi, 4, Chūsei, 1,* 91.

In the final analysis, however, the *shōen* gave rise to a style of land law and local administration which proved quite incompatible with the spirit of the Taihō code. In the first place, the system of authority relationships within the *shōen*, though capable of legal definition under imperial law, were the products of individual contracts. They were both personal and heritable. In the second place, status within the system was recompensed not by office salaries derived from taxation but rather by a form of rent. In the *shōen* the cultivator no longer resided under an impersonal officialdom which imposed a uniform system of taxation, but rather he conceived of himself as owing dues to those above him in return for personal benefices. The *shōen* system thus lay at the bottom of a return to patrimonialism in government and in social relationships in general. It is to this phenomenon that we must now turn.

Not long after the move to the new capital, functional changes in the operations of imperial government began to affect the elaborate bureaucratic machinery set up by the Taihō ordinances. A simplification within the organs of central administration made it possible for a few strategically placed offices to affect a tighter and more direct control of the affairs of state. Chief among the new offices was the post of imperial regent (*sesshō-kampaku*), which, in the hands of the Fujiwara family, robbed the imperial house of its political influence and became the basis of a new centralization of power within the court. Previous to this, the bureau of archivists (*kurōdo-dokoro*) had begun to function as the supreme organ for the conduct of palace affairs and the main channel through which imperial decrees and ordinances were issued. It eventually came to exercise the remnants of legislative and administrative power which still adhered to the civil branch of imperial government, making superfluous the whole apparatus of bureaus and ministries. Likewise another new creation, the office of imperial police (*kebiishichō*), took over powers of arrest, examination, and enforcement from the slow moving guards and provincial levies.

Closely related to these changes in the operation of government was the growing identity between heredity, status, and office-holding within court and provincial officialdom. As we have seen, the Japanese never enforced a system of free selection for office. Official recruitment during the Nara period had its basis in the common practice whereby households inherited status but household heads competed for a variety of offices for which they were eligible by virtue of their inherited status. By the ninth and tenth centuries, however, the element of choice and selectivity in appointment to office had become increasingly narrow, so that many offices were openly tied to one or at most a handful of lineages. Further, as the expectation of holding certain offices generation after generation became more predictable, especially for certain of the great court families, and as these families acquired an increasing number of *shōen* with their attendant managerial problems, we find that they began to build up within their own household establishments much of the apparatus of administration and enforcement which at one time had been the responsibility of the imperial government. For such families the differentiation between public and private rights and responsibilities became increasingly hard to define.

The case of the Fujiwara family is only the most conspicuous example of the way in which court families literally became public institutions with built-in political organs and connective associations with religious centers. Through the example of the Fujiwara house we can see that the aristocracy in Japan continued to organize itself on the *uji* pattern whereby branch families were clustered around a central lineage which served as head of the *uji*. The Fujiwara *uji*, unified during the Heian period under the Northern House (*Hokke*), consisted of a large number of separate families which bore the Fujiwara surname. In this sense, the Heian aristocratic *uji* was probably little different from the *uji* of the pre-Taika period. Yet it would probably be wrong to press the comparison too strongly. The Heian nobility, particularly after the turn into the eleventh century, when the Fujiwara *uji* broke into numerous competing branches, was probably less cohesive than that of the seventh century. Heian court society therefore represented something of a transition between the strongly localized lineage groups of the sixth century and the more easily separated family groups which began to predominate in the thirteenth century.

Within the Fujiwara *uji* of the early Heian period, the chief authority rested with the head of the main line, who held the position of *uji-no-chōja* (family chief). Such an *uji* chief no longer claimed directly the sacerdotal powers of the earlier chieftains.

But it is significant that the Fujiwara house placed great stress upon the support of religious institutions. The family maintained as its ancestral shrine Kasugajinja on the outskirts of the old capital city of Nara and patronized as its family temple Kōfukuji, also of Nara. The head of the *uji* was of course expected to maintain the family rituals and engage in conspicuous patronage of these and many other Buddhist and Shinto establishments.

As head of the Fujiwara, the *uji-no-chōja* also served as the arbiter and administrator (*bettō*) of the family interests. He headed the family council (*hyōjōshū*), which brought together the many Fujiwara branches for discussion of policy problems. He also coordinated the activities of certain functional offices, such as the office of administrative affairs (*mandokoro*), the office of military affairs (*samuraidokoro*), and the court of appeal (*monchūjo*). Together, these offices made up the elements of complete governance over the members of the Fujiwara *uji* and the family's far-flung *shōen* holdings. The *mandokoro* served as a central administrative office, accepting petitions and drafting orders. The *samuraidokoro* asserted the enforcement powers, while the *monchūjo* heard cases of conflicting interest, either within the *uji* membership or within the *shōen*. In effect, the head of the Fujiwara *uji* presided over a subdivision of the imperial government itself.

The pattern of familial organization and house administration exemplified in the Fujiwara *uji* became typical of all of the houses of highest rank and influence within the Heian court aristocracy.[22] And these institutions of house administration were to come into public view from time to time as one after another of these houses gained ascendancy at court and began to exercise control of political affairs through its household offices. What is perhaps less well understood is that the imperial house itself, once the Taihō institutions buttressing it had begun to weaken, also was obliged to look to its own house organization and to assert itself as a separate kinship bloc in the contest for power at court. Behind the gradual abandonment of the Sinified bureaucratic machinery and of the idea of the state as an extension of the imperial person, we find the imperial *uji* working to secure a private hold over the elements of political influence and wealth that had once been

[22] Kuroda Toshio, "Chūsei no kokka to tennō," in *Iwanami kōza, Nihon rekishi, 6, Chūsei, 2* (Tokyo, 1963), 270. Hereafter cited as Kuroda, "Chūsei."

its by definition. Increasingly, the imperial house was obliged to protect its position as a familial power bloc in competition with the Fujiwara, Minamoto, and other court interests. The necessity of gaining a separate existence outside the institutions of the central government was not immediately recognized by the imperial family. It was not until the eleventh century, at a time when the domination of the Fujiwara family over the court was beginning to weaken, that the family was able to proceed with its plans.

The emperor Go-Sanjō, who came to the throne in 1068, happened not to be the product of a Fujiwara marriage. The increased freedom of maneuver this gave him provided the opportunity for a movement to break away from the control which the Fujiwara had exercised over the imperial family for some two centuries. Go-Sanjō's successor, Shirakawa, was able to complete the process. In 1086, he abdicated, but as ex-emperor retained his authority over the imperial family and whatever material and political resources still adhered to the family and its supporters. The result was the establishment in the ex-emperor's detached palace of an office known as the office of the cloister (*in-no-chō*) with a full complement of administrative organs: a manager (*bettō*), administrative officers, an administrative office (*mandoko-ro*), and a contingent of armed guards (*hokumen-no-bushi*). The cloistered ex-emperor (*in*) thus consolidated the familial authority of the imperial family and created a new center of power which could compete with the Fujiwara on their own terms, leaving the enthroned emperor as the symbol of sovereignty.

Perhaps the best illustration of the change in political atmosphere brought on by the spread of the *shōen* and the increasingly patrimonial nature of court power relations is seen in the changing attitude of the imperial house toward the *shōen* problem as a whole. At first the emperors were quite content to see the immune lands grow, since these were frequently assigned as rewards for civil or religious service to the throne. Of all of the court groups, however, the imperial house stood to lose the most from the disappearance of the public domain. The time came, therefore, when the *shōen* so sapped the revenue of the central government that the imperial house could not remain indifferent. Thereafter a succession of emperors made some attempt to arrest the growth of *shōen*.[23] At the beginning of the tenth century, the emperor Daigo undertook the so-called reforms of the Engi era, pushing through the last national census and land survey.[24] As part of this belated effort to reassert the powers of the central government, Daigo sought to "regulate" the *shōen* by investigating titles and screening out unauthorized claims of immunity. The attempt was not overly successful, but it proved to be the first of a series of similar efforts which culminated in the year 1069 when the emperor Go-Sanjō established a records office (*kirokusho*) for the purpose of scrutinizing the titles of all existing *shōen*. As a consequence a number of minor irregularities were discovered and some *shōen* were confiscated. Yet no fundamental attack was made upon the *shōen* system itself.

With the successful establishment of the office of the cloister the imperial family dramatically reversed its policy of *shōen* control and instead began to enter full force into the competition for *shōen*, a competition which was directed primarily against the Fujiwara.[25] In the course of the eleventh and twelfth centuries under the emperors Shirakawa, Toba, and Go-Shirakawa the imperial family converted large pieces of public domain into *shōen* under direct imperial proprietorship.[26] Before long, the imperial house through the office of the cloister had gained title to some 1000 *shōen* in 59 provinces. In Bizen and Bitchū, for instance, it is quite clear that the most dramatic expansion of *shōen* came at this time with the creation of many large imperial holdings. Thus by looking to its own private interests and dropping its reliance on the state as an institutional source of income, the imperial house retrieved for the moment a significant share of the proprietary rights available under the *shōen* system. In fact, by the twelfth century it had become the foremost center of *shōen* holdings, and the most sought after among the court powers by local *shōen* proprietors who wished to commend their holdings for guardianship protection. Except for the fortuitous circumstance that the cloister

[23] Nishioka Toranosuke, "Shōen-sei no hattatsu," in *Shōen-shi no kenkyū* (3 vols., Tokyo, 1956-1957), 1.54. Hereafter cited as Nishioka, *Shōen*.

[24] Hayashiya Tatsusaburō, "Ritsuryō-sei yori shōen-sei e," in *Rekishigaku kenkyū*, 183 (May 1955), 9.

[25] Kodama Kōta *et al.*, eds., *Shiryō ni yoru Nihon no ayumi* (4 vols., Tokyo, 1959), 1 (*Kodai*), 328.

[26] Okuno Takahiro, *Kōshitsu gokeizaishi no kenkyū* (rev. ed., Tokyo, 1942), 35-36. Hereafter cited as Okuno, *Kōshitsu*.

had been an emperor, there was little difference between the cloister and the head of the Fujiwara house as far as its relationship to the emperor was concerned.[27]

Once the imperial house gave up its interest in maintaining the land provisions of the Taihō codes it can be imagined that there remained at court no other group interested in continuing the system of public land ownership. Yet this did not mean that the public domain suddenly ceased to exist and that the lands of a province such as Bizen passed completely under private proprietorship. Even as late as the thirteenth century in Bizen, at least half of the administrative subdivisions of the province were still governed as public domain, and this was not at all uncommon for provinces with a comparable history of close relationship to the central government. We must conclude, therefore, not only that the imperial system of local administration remained operative much longer than is generally supposed, but also that behind this façade of continuity the substance may well have changed beyond recognition. In fact, as we shall see, the methods of provincial administration, particularly with regard to public land, were by the end of the eleventh century becoming practically indistinguishable from the practices of *shōen* management.

The methods of provincial administration laid down in the Taihō code were hardly more easily maintained than those which governed the administration of land holding. In the first place, the provincial system was obviously too ambitious for Japan of the eighth century. Provincial governors were required to travel to their provincial seats, to tour the provinces over which they were appointed, to oversee the shipment of taxes, and to maintain close watch over local affairs at the same time that they kept in touch with the central government. In view of the level of Japan's development in communication, transportation, and bureaucratic training, these requirements were most burdensome and quite difficult in practice. They became especially burdensome for courtiers used to the amenities of life in the capital. Moreover, most of the practical administrative functions in the provinces had been left in the hands of the resident district chiefs. It is understandable, therefore, that there should be a tendency for governors to remain in the capital as much as possible and to leave

27 Kuroda, "Chūsei," 281.

to subordinate officials the liaison functions between capital and province. By the ninth century it was general practice to assign high-ranking courtiers to titular provincial governorships in addition to their other court functions, sometimes merely for stipendiary purposes. Such courtiers handled provincial affairs through their household offices in Kyoto and kept in touch with the provincial capital through deputy officials (*mokudai*) whom they dispatched on their own initiative. That the court's interest in the provinces increasingly turned simply to tax revenues appears in the use of the title *zuryō* (literally, "receiver of land dues") as an alternate designation for officials in the provincial governor class.

Despite the court's lack of concern for the administration of the provinces, and hence the constantly diminishing involvements of the court in provincial affairs, it would be a mistake to believe that there was a cessation of communication between court and provinces. In fact, the diminishing prestige of provincial service and the spread of hereditary holding of office combined to encourage a significant flow of court personnel of middle and low rank into the provinces. Quite frequently, such families settled down to become permanent members of the local aristocracy. By the end of the tenth century the provincial administrative headquarters were being called "the absentee office" (*rusudokoro*) and officials such as the governor's deputy, the deputy governors, and other lesser functionaries were collectively called "resident officials" (*zaichō-kanjin*).[28] At first the deputy was able to represent central authority fairly effectively, borrowing authority as the governor's representative and frequently traveling back and forth from Kyoto to the provincial capital. But while the post of governor's deputy may well have resisted reduction to a hereditary office, the other officials who served in the provincial government held their posts increasingly on a hereditary basis and frequently concurrently with the possession of other hereditary offices such as district chieftainships.[29]

Common among the court families which took up local residence were lesser branches of the Fujiwara and offshoots of the imperial house which bore the surnames Taira and Minamoto.

[28] Takeuchi, "Zaichō," 11-22; also "Bushi hassei-shi jō ni okeru zaichō to rusudokoro no kenkyū," *Shigaku zasshi*, 48.6 (June 1937), 671-694.
[29] Takeuchi, "Zaichō," 22.

These families, reduced to the lower levels of court rank, had little future within the central court circles. In the provinces, however, they ranked high and were able to capitalize upon their superior status and family connections. Provincial posts carried salary lands which could easily be turned into private domains. Reclamation was also a constant possibility. Using their rank and official prerogatives, these courtiers turned local officials were able to carve out positions of influence alongside or above the old local aristocracy. Such families, because of their familiarity with the affairs of the court, also found their way into the management of court-held *shōen*. As they themselves became proprietary *shōen* officials, they helped to accelerate the fusion of the public affairs of the provincial headquarters with the private interests of the *shōen*. By the middle of the Heian period most provincial officials probably served as *shōen* officials as well.[30]

The ultimate revelation of the change in court attitude toward the province as an administrative subdivision of the state occurred when the naming of governorships became the personal prerogative of certain members of the court hierarchy. After the establishment of the office of the cloister particularly, control of a large number of the provincial governorships was taken over by the cloistered emperor as what were called "gift provinces" (*shikoku*) or "salary provinces" (*bunkoku*). The cloistered emperor was able to designate men to fill these posts at will from among his followers. Other influential court families such as the *sesshō-kampaku* house of the Fujiwara and certain great monasteries acquired control over other provinces in this manner. Eventually this practice became standardized into what was called the *chigyō-koku* "proprietary-province" system whereby blocs of provinces were held under the appointment power of one or another influential court figure, who became known as the "provincial proprietor" (*kokushu*). The proprietor not only received a fee for making appointments of governors but received the income from the remaining public land in the province.

The use of the term *chigyō* (proprietorship) in reference to a province is indicative of a fundamental change in the conception of local administration. In the eyes of the court the province had become little more than a domain, the main purpose of which

[30] *Ibid.*, 24-26.

was to supply an income. By the twelfth century a province such as Bizen was divided about half-and-half between public and private sectors. What this meant was that the remaining public lands had become for all practical purposes "public *shōen.*" Local provincial officials served as their managers and the governor functioned as the proprietor's agent. The vestigial public domains, now known as the *kokugaryō* (also *kokuryō* or *kōryō*), were even treated as proprietorships (*ryō*) which could be passed from one family to another. In popular usage the provincial governors were even referred to as *honjo* and the annual tax as rent (*nengu*). By this time, then, if we can say that anything remained of the conception of public interest in provincial administration, it was but weakly implied in the way in which the provincial proprietorship could be shifted about from group to group.[31]

At the lower levels of provincial administration, by this time, there was an almost complete reliance on hereditary practices. The continual conversion of offices into hereditary possessions of powerful families at court or in the countryside meant that the officials with responsibility for administrating public land became attached to the *kokugaryō* in much the same way as *shōen* officials to the *shō.* Such officials were even referred to as possessing *shiki* for their public services. Thus in the *kokugaryō* of Bizen, officials were listed as possessing *gunji-shiki, gōji-shiki,* and *hoji-shiki.* Frequently these were the same men who also held *shōkan-shiki* in adjoining *shōen.*[32] Such multiple and complex holdings of responsibilities and profitable land rights became one of the chief characteristics of the Japanese provincial scene after the middle of the Heian period.

The scanty evidence we have for the condition of land tenure and the internal administration of Bizen province for the eleventh and twelfth centuries would lead to the conclusion that at least until the time of the establishment of the headquarters of the cloistered ex-emperors probably only about a quarter of the territory of Bizen had been taken over by *shōen* proprietorships and that the remaining territory was administered as *kokugaryō.* In Bizen, for reasons not altogether clear, imperial authority tended to remain strong and *shōen* proprietorships took over rather

[31] Ishii Ryōsuke, *Nihon hōseishi gaisetsu,* 230-231. Takeuchi Rizō, *Jiryō shōen no kenkyū* (Tokyo, 1942). Hereafter cited as Takeuchi, *Jiryō.*
[32] Nishioka, *Shōen,* 59.

slowly from the areas of public authority. The records of the ninth and tenth centuries have revealed the names of only a few specific *shōen,* and we can assume that for the province at large the authority of provincial officials continued to be fairly strong.

Precisely when the practice of absentee governorships began in Bizen is not clear, but at least until the end of the tenth century there is evidence that governors conscientiously took up residence in Bizen. Yet from time to time even during these years there are appointments which look suspiciously as though they were purely honorary. During the tenth century four appointments were made to members of the Fujiwara family who later rose to the post of imperial regent. Among these was the famous Michinaga, who was appointed governor in 987 when he was twenty-one years old. It is certainly unlikely that such members of the high court nobility should exercise more than a titular authority over the province.

Michinaga's appointment was made in the year following one of the most interesting and revealing episodes of the tenth century serving to illuminate the relationship between court, province, and *shōen* interests in Bizen. This is the well-known case of the conflict between Shikada-no-shō and the provincial authorities which took place between 985 and 986.[33] The trouble began when the governor of Bizen, Fujiwara-no-Masakane, took upon himself to extract certain payments which he considered due the provincial headquarters from the *shōen* of Shikada. The manager of the *shōen,* himself a Fujiwara, complained of the governor's action and the case was taken up by the head of the Fujiwara family, the imperial regent Fujiwara-no-Yoritada. (This man, by the way, had served as governor of Bizen from 964-969.) Yoritada sent an agent to Bizen to inquire into the complaint, but the governor of the province secretly made his way to the capital and reported that the investigating official was abusing his authority. The court believed the governor's accusations, deprived the agent of his rank and office, and ordered the governor to arrest the steward of Shikada-no-shō. Masakane quickly returned to Bizen, mustered several hundred men and entered the *shōen,* capturing the steward and the investigating official, who had remained in Bizen. At the same time he broke into the *shōen* granaries and appro-

<hr>

[33] Fujii Shun, "Bizen-no-kuni Shikada-no-shō ni tsuite."

priated 300 *koku* of rice. He also set fire to a large number of houses and made off with the personal property of the inhabitants of the *shōen*.

This conduct aroused the abbot of *Kōfukuji*, the temple which shared the proprietorship of the Shikada-no-shō along with the Fujiwara family, and a new appeal was made to the regent Yoritada. This time two imperial police commissioners were sent to investigate. But the commissioners, rather than settling the case, made new impositions upon the *shōen*, extracting in all over 2000 *koku* of rice. In the next year still other inspectors of higher rank were sent out from Kyoto, and it was they who finally settled the case in favor of the *shōen* and ordered the return of various ill-gotten goods. In the end Masakane was completely discredited and was returned to the capital where he was stripped of his rank and expelled from the Fujiwara house as a disgrace to the Fujiwara name.

This case throws a number of interesting sidelights upon internal conditions in Bizen during the tenth century. First of all we note that, despite the conflict of interest between the provincial governor and *shōen* manager, both individuals were members of the Fujiwara family. No doubt Masakane was pressing certain private ambitions which were incompatible with the larger interests of the family as a whole.

The incident also provides an example of an occasion when the provincial governor actually took up residence in the province. It shows that the governor was able to muster an armed guard and hence was not without some source of coercive power. Moreover, provincial affairs were far from being completely out of control from the capital. Authorities in the capital could react to trouble in the provinces, if only by sending out fact-finding agents.

Yet, despite the continued scrutiny which the capital exercised over Bizen, it is quite obvious that conditions within the province had deteriorated. For one thing the system of public recruitment of labor from the *kubunden* was now almost unheard of. Even as much as fifty years before this event, the governor of neighboring Bitchū province, the famous Miyoshi-no-Kiyoyuki, had complained that although the province had once been one of the wealthiest it was now almost impossible to recruit manpower from the province. The district from which Kibi-no-Makibi had come produced in the eighth century some 1900 recruitable males. By the middle of the ninth century the number had diminished to 70. By the time Miyoshi wrote, he claimed that there was not one single name on the registers.[34]

This is, of course, not to be taken as evidence that a complete breakdown of the provincial tax system had occurred. References to the shipment of tax rice from Bizen to the capital during the ninth century and the clear evidence that rice and goods were still being shipped as state taxes in the thirteenth century is enough to show that the *kokugaryō* functioned as a source of revenue throughout this period. But the nature of the entire tax collecting procedure had changed drastically, for it was now being collected as customary payments from *myōshu* who held hereditary occupancy to subdivisions (*myō*) of the public proprietorship. Within the administrative hierarchy, also, the penetration of hereditary practices meant that the Fujiwara family was able to dominate the province increasingly, perhaps even to the point of bringing it under its private appointment prerogative by the eleventh century. Probably during most of these years a relationship between Fujiwara interests in the capital and those of the Fujiwara governors and *shōen* managers worked in concert to the advantage of the Fujiwara family. At all levels of the provincial aristocracy in Bizen the Fujiwara name was appearing ever more frequently, and we can conclude that in the wake of the constant line of Fujiwara governors many members of the Fujiwara family had taken up residence in the province.

With the appearance of the government of the cloistered emperors the dominance of the Fujiwara house in Bizen was cut in upon. The emperor Shirakawa alone converted eight large parcels of Bizen territory to *shōen*, so that the land remaining under public proprietorship was reduced to about half of the area of the province. From the year 1113 it even seems that the emperor Shirakawa acquired proprietorship of the province, so that a different line of subordinate court officials began to move into the province. By the twelfth century, however, there were further changes affecting provincial government which require our attention. The manner in which provincial proprietorships and governorships were passed around between the cloister and the

[34] Taniguchi Sumio, *Kyōdo no rekishi*, 12.

Fujiwara indicate both a lack of cohesion at the capital and a growing separation between court and province. It is about this time that the names of Taira and Minamoto begin to figure prominently in provincial affairs—an indication that the military aristocracy was making its appearance in Bizen.

V. THE RISE OF THE BUSHI
AND THE ORIGINS OF FEUDAL AUTHORITY

THE year 931 provides the first evidence in Bizen that imperial
authority exercised through the organs of provincial administration was proving inadequate to deal with lawlessness on a
major scale. In that year, Fujiwara-no-Sumitomo, deputy governor
of the nearby province of Iyo, turned rebel and began to terrorize
the provinces of the Inland Sea region. Sumitomo ironically had
been sent to Iyo with a commission to suppress pirates who had
been interfering with tax shipments along the inland waterway.
Official reports from as early as 862 complain of the work of such
pirates. In that year the provincial officials of Bizen reported that
a vessel carrying 50 *koku* of tax rice had been attacked, the rice
stolen, and eleven peasants killed. In response the central government ordered the provincial authorities of thirteen western provinces to mobilize forces and deal with the menace. Four years
later the central government complained that pirates were still
active and that if the situation did not improve, the provincial
officials would be accused of negligence.[1] But the problem of
piracy and brigandage became endemic, spreading into the
eastern provinces as well.

Fujiwara-no-Sumitomo, dispatched from Kyoto to suppress
pirates in 931, gathered a large force and actually appeared to
be moving against the pirates when he himself revolted and assumed leadership of the most active outlaws in the area. His
depredations over the next few years drove the court in Kyoto
to exasperation, but they found themselves powerless, especially
since a simultaneous (and much more serious) threat to the peace
had been created by Taira-no-Masakado's revolt in the eastern
provinces. Perhaps the most flagrant of Sumitomo's action, other
than plundering the provincial seat of Iyo, was his killing of the
deputy governor of Bizen. The latter, Fujiwara-no-Sanetaka was
on his way to the capital in 939 to report some of the latest of
Sumitomo's mischief, when he was intercepted by the pirates and
killed. His wife, who was accompanying him, was taken captive
by Sumitomo himself.[2]

[1] *Tsūshi*, 1.601-602, quoting from the *Sandai jitsuroku*.
[2] *Ibid.*, 1.602, quoting from the *Fusō ryakki*.

In 939, the court dispatched two men of known military ability as constables (*tsuibushi*) to clean up the Inland Sea. Ono-no-Yoshifuru and Minamoto-no-Tsunemoto engaged in two years of difficult fighting against seemingly insuperable odds (Sumitomo at one point met their inadequate force of 200 ships with a fleet said to consist of 1,500 vessels). With the defection of Sumitomo's second in command, however, the constables gained the advantage. The severed heads of Sumitomo and his son were triumphantly sent to the capital, and the remnants of his followers were either captured or killed. A period of relative peace returned to the Inland Sea provinces.

The Sumitomo affair was unsettling to court and provincial officials alike, but perhaps the most significant revelation which came from it was not that the enforcement branches of provincial government were so inept, but that there was evidence of an entirely new development in provincial life. This was revealed most directly in the memorial presented by Ono-no-Yoshifuru in 946 after his successful suppression of the Sumitomo band. In the memorial Yoshifuru warned that there was a dangerous trend toward the building up of private armed forces in the provinces. As he put it, "Many make lawless use of power and authority; form confederacies; engage daily in military exercises; collect and maintain men and horses under pretext of hunting game; menace district governors; plunder the common people; violate their wives and daughters; and steal their beasts of burden and employ them for their own purposes. Thus interrupting agricultural operations. ... My appeal is that, with the exception of provincial governors' envoys, any who enter a province at the head of parties carrying bows and arrows . . . shall be recognized as common bandits and thrown into prison on apprehension."[3] What Ono reported was evidence of a return to private arms-bearing among the provincial elite, a trend which was to lead to the formation of a class of professional fighters to which the Japanese were to give the name *bushi*.

Although, in the eyes of the court aristocracy, the *bushi* presented something of a new problem, it is probably closer to fact that the provincial aristocracy was never far from the center of military activity in Japan. Families such as the Kibi and Wake

[3] Translated in F. Brinkley, *A History of the Japanese People* (New York and London, 1915), 255.

had been quite active in military commands prior to the Taika Reform. And although the adoption of a centralized conscription system had technically disarmed the provincial aristocracy, it seems that provincial families continued to play a significant role in the armed forces of the imperial government. In fact, it may well be that military service was the main career open for ambitious members of the provincial aristocracy. It is not by accident that men like Kibi-no-Makibi's father and Wake-no-Kiyomaro himself were first employed at the capital as military officers. The time was to come, with the breakdown of the conscript system, when the families of the district governor class were to be relied on more and more not only as officers but as the prime source of military manpower.

The novel feature of the return to private arms-bearing after the tenth century, however, was the leading role played by families who had only recently moved to the provinces from the capital. The increased assignment of the provincial officials to military functions resulted as much from shifts within the operations of the imperial system as from any natural propensity of the provincial landowners to take up private arms in order to settle their disputes. What historians have described as the "rise of the *bushi*" was the product of a complex process involving changes at a number of levels of society, both at the capital and in the provinces and cannot be thought of simply as a conquest of the heartland by the rough and ready men of the frontier provinces.

While it is commonly believed that the bearing of private arms came about in defiance of civil authority, in actuality in its early stages the practice was encouraged or at least condoned by the higher civil authorities who delegated military powers to provincial officials so as to give them the means of enforcing law and of maintaining the peace. Under the Taihō code, provincial officials, except for those in charge of the local garrison, were rigidly restricted to civilian functions, there being a separate military command. Members of the provincial governor's staff were also restricted from bearing arms.[4] During the ninth century, however, we hear of provincial and district governors requesting permission to arm themselves and their staffs for self-protection

[4] Takeuchi Rizō, "Zaichō kanjin," 27.

or so they might enforce decisions. This development, which began in the eastern provinces, was an indication of the decline in the ability of civilian-controlled military and police units to function effectively. As local conditions became worse, the central government granted military and police powers to provincial officials, assigning such additional titles as sheriff (*ōryōshi*) or military police (*tsuibushi*) to officers of the rank of governor. These assignments were at first emergency and temporary, providing civil officials with the necessary authority to mobilize armed forces for defense or punitive measures. But as posts at the provincial capitals became increasingly hereditary and as local emergencies extended over long periods of time, military functions became an integral part of local administration, and military titles began to overshadow civil appointments. In any case, the lower levels of the provincial officialdom were increasingly relied on for their military capacities, while the provincial governors resorted increasingly to the use of armed guards recruited, quite legitimately, from their provincial subordinates.[5]

In the *shōen*, too, the need to develop internal security obliged members of the managerial class to maintain themselves and their subordinates in readiness to take military action. While at first the *shōen* could depend for the enforcement of their legal privileges and immunities upon the administrative powers of the provincial governors, this resource became less and less reliable as civil authority weakened. When, for instance, disputes referred to the central government through the local provincial office remained undecided, or when the provincial authorities were unable to enforce decisions, then the owners of *shōen* felt obliged to resort to strong-arm methods.[6] Inevitably, as in the case of the trouble between Shikada-no-shō and the provincial governor of Bizen in 986, clashes between provincial and *shōen* interests led to armed conflict.

At the same time, the importance of the provincial aristocracy to the profession of arms was further accentuated by changes in the general nature of fighting forces throughout Japan. As the idea of a conscript army, recruited from among the peasantry and led by government-appointed officials, proved inadequate, there was a general return to reliance on the mounted archer and

[5] *Ibid.*, 29.   [6] Nishioka, "Shōensei," 60.

armored swordsman. The breakdown of the Taihō system of military organization came rapidly in the eighth century and was accelerated by the wars against the Ezo in northern Japan. The use of provincial conscript armies (*gundan*) was abandoned in 792 in favor of a militia system which depended on recruits from among young men drawn from families of the district chief class. Here was a tacit recognition that provincial families of means already provided the main source of effective fighting men. The public recruitment of such armed men on a regular basis did not long survive, but instead, with the deterioration of local administration, the bearing of arms became a privileged occupation of the provincial aristocracy of all levels who had the means to equip themselves. Within the *shōen* and *kokugaryō*, military duty (*heishi yaku*) became a regular form of service. Up and down the *shōen* hierarchy, superiors began to draft fighters from among their subordinates, forming armed guards on a regular basis and striking forces as the occasions arose.[7] In the *kokuryō* a similar process of recruitment by local officials took place. Governors, or their deputies, staffed the military guards from among their own family members and from among the lesser officials and *myōshu* on their private holdings or in the public territories, using the authority of their regular government posts or of their temporary military titles to legitimize their commands. The offices such as *tsuibushi* and *ōryōshi* created in 878 and the new capital offices of metropolitan constable (*kebiishi*) were effective simply because they could draw upon the recruitment powers of the men to whom the posts were given.

Thus as a result of the abandonment of the conscription policy and the spread of patrimonial command systems there eventually came into existence a new military system and with it a new style of life. In the provinces the authority vested in titles such as *tsuibushi* and *ōryōshi* provided legitimization for the formation of guard groups and armies. Meanwhile, members of provincial families were encouraged to acquire the technically demanding skills of archery, swordsmanship, and horsemanship, in other words the skills and equipment which were to make of them a military elite.

All of this had important implications for the performance of local government, particularly in the crucial area between civil

[7] *Ibid.*, 62.

authority and the power of enforcement. Increasingly within the provinces the capacity to assert authority rested upon the ability to apply the force of arms. Officials appointed to civil posts found it essential to acquire their own concurrent military or police powers in order to back up their civil position. At almost every level of central and local government, officials maintained bands of fighters to assure protection or to enforce authority. The regular police and military offices, no longer able to rely on conscripted manpower, turned to the recruitment of elite fighters from the *shōen* or public territories over which the commanding officers held jurisdiction. At the capital the *kurōdo-dokoro* added its own military guard after 889; the *kebiishi* of the capital were likewise permitted to draw their own recruits from the provinces; the Fujiwara attached private troops to their *samurai-dokoro* or organized family guards (*ōban-toneri*) for use by the regent or other leading members of the house; the six palace guard groups (*roku efu*) were staffed with *bushi* recruits from the provinces, and the temples and monasteries built up armed guards from their *shōen*.[8] As enforcement became dependent upon military power in hand, the subtle line between *de jure* authority vested in office or status and *de facto* authority derived from the ability to muster superior force was becoming blurred.

The conversion of the provincial aristocracy into a military elite was not immediately disruptive to the existing order, for it simply carried out the trend exemplified by the *shōen* in the fiscal areas of the government. The *bushi* were simply officials of the public (*kokuga*) or private (*shōen*) systems of local authority, who engaged professionally in military service as well. This military service was at first performed within one or another of the recognized command systems. But in the long run, the expansion of the military function of the provincial aristocracy created a problem of a new order, for it encouraged the provincial aristocracy to acquire new interests and new ties of association which ultimately cut across the power structure which centered on the court. It encouraged the formation, in other words, of bands or cliques based on regional interests quite independent of those of the central aristocracy.

To assume that the *bushi* families were somehow unusual be-

---

[8] Kodama Kōta, ed., *Zusetsu Nihon bunkashi taikei*, 5.131.

cause of their propensity to form factions or cliques is to ignore
the long tradition of familial association which had been exemplified in the *uji* structure of pre-Taika Japan. Particularly in the
provinces it was most likely that long-ingrained social habits
would continue unchanged despite the political reforms of the
seventh century. In provincial areas rivalry for power and influence continued to take the form of competition among family
cliques. The appearance of cliques among *bushi* houses was not
so much indicative of something new as it was the outcropping
of a pattern of organization among local families which had
long lain below the surface. The so-called *bushi* bands as they
began to attract public attention in the tenth century were called
tō. Such bands were drawn together by many diverse bonds of
mutual interest or family association. Many of course derived
directly from the hierarchic authority structures of the *shōen* or
the provincial administrations. But the larger bands tended to
extend beyond the confines of a given proprietorship or provincial jurisdiction.

Most bands had at their core a network of kinship or ritual-
kinship relationships of the type which had long marked Japanese
familial structure. The branching of families and the constant
marriage and intermarriage within localities generally provided
the first and most basic set of ties upon which local interest
groups formed.[9] By this time, of course, the extended *uji* system
had begun to break up. In its stead a more tightly knit and
geographically cohesive kinship community was taking shape.
But differences with the old *uji* system were mainly terminological.
The heads of the familial group were now known as *sōryō* and
the members of his immediate family as *ichimon* or *ichizoku*.
Branch families (referred to generally as *shoshi*) were treated as
patrimonial followers (*ienoko*). Unrelated followers were called
housemen or retainers (*kenin* or *rōtō*). In characteristic fashion,
terms of kinship origin were used to cover associations which
were not at all based on consanguinity, and the head of the group
continued to function as a religious leader in ceremonies before
family patron shrines or before local protective deities.[10]

[9] Satō Saburō, "Chūsei bushi-shakai ni okeru zokuteki danketsu," *Shakaikeizaishigaku*, 8.3 (June 1938), 346-374.
[10] Okuda Shinkei, "Bushi kaikyū no seiritsu hatten" in *Shin Nihonshi kōza*
(Tokyo, 1948), 18-32.

But bonds of kinship, even when fictionally extended, had limited applicability. It was the development of systems of military alliances which served most to expand the *bushi* bands. Agreements in arms among the military aristocracy tended to be personal and enduring. Military action also drew together men from widely scattered localities, from beyond the limits of the weakening jurisdictions of civil offices or the confines of kin relationships. It was this element—identified with the European practice of vassalage—which became the identifying characteristic of the new authority system created by the *bushi*.

Large regional *bushi* bands generally resulted from periods of extended military action, and particularly as members of the court aristocracy moved into the provinces to take the lead in special military or police actions. It is no accident that the men who came to the fore during the tenth and eleventh centuries as provincial military leaders almost uniformly bore surnames which showed them to be scions of the court aristocracy. The combination of military authority and social prestige with which they moved into the provinces gave them a characteristic advantage which few purely local leaders could match. In Bizen, which reflected the developments rather slowly, we nonetheless find by the tenth century that the provincial records are full of references to members of the Fujiwara, Taira, or Minamoto families serving as members of the *shōen* managerial staffs, or as deputy governors or resident officials in the public domain. Such men, as they settled in the province, were able to gain the following of families native to the province (such as the Mino, Kaya, Shimotsumichi, and their branches) by marriage alliances and because of their superior status in the provincial government or *shōen* administrations and often because they received superior military commands. In the country at large, it was ultimately the series of outbreaks of lawlessness during the tenth and eleventh centuries which provided the conditions most conducive to the rise of a number of outstanding military leaders and to the formation of regional cliques of extended size.[11]

An early uprising, and a particularly distressing one from the viewpoint of the imperial court, was the revolt of Taira-no-Masakado in the eastern provinces. Masakado, fifth generation

[11] Shimizu Mitsuō, "Kokugaryō to bushi," in *Shirin* 27.4 (1937), 137.

descendant of the emperor Kammu, was a tempestuous leader with strong personal ambitions. In 935 he started a rebellious drive in the province of Hitachi, attacking and killing his relative Taira-no-Kunika, deputy governor of the province. In 939 Masakado captured the provincial capitals of Shimotsuke and Kōzuke, defying imperial authority in the area. At one point he even styled himself the "new emperor." He was eventually killed and his rebellion put down by Fujiwara-no-Hidesato (who held the title of Constable of Shimotsuke) and Taira-no-Sadamori, son of Kunika. Sadamori, as reward for his action, received appointment to the post of General of the Pacification Headquarters (Chinjufu-shōgun), the most prestigious military title available in eastern Japan. Hard on top of the Masakado rebellion was the affair of Fujiwara-no-Sumitomo, in which Ono-no-Yoshifuru and Minamoto-no-Tsunemoto distinguished themselves.

As a result of these incidents we find members of the Taira and Minamoto families appearing in increasingly significant positions in the provinces and even at court. Tsunemoto's son, Mitsunaka, allied himself with the *sesshō-kampaku* line of the Fujiwara house and soon had served in a variety of provincial posts and acquired a large number of *shōen* holdings in the home provinces of Settsu, Yamato, and Mino, from which bases he recruited the fighting force for the Fujiwara guards. Before long, men of Seiwa-Genji (that is, of the Seiwa-Minamoto) lineage were serving both as high court officials (including posts of ministerial rank) and as provincial officials. The Taira descendants of Sadamori (the Kammu-Heike) for the most part took up posts in the eastern provinces, but other lines of Taira surname descended from Emperor Kammu became prominent in the western provinces, especially during the eleventh century. The lengthy disturbances which called for almost continuous military action in the eastern provinces between 1051 and 1088 provided further opportunity for the Seiwa-Genji and Kammu-Heike to entrench themselves in the provinces and to extend their usefulness at court. By the end of the century the major cliques were beginning to polarize, the Minamoto under Yoshiie establishing strong bases in Musashi and Shimotsuke, while the Taira, acquiring the patronage of the cloistered ex-emperors, moved increasingly into positions of influence in the home provinces.

The story could be told at much greater length and in more

detail. But the significance of these outstanding examples is clear. A whole class of families holding provincial posts and military appointments was gaining in importance, not only as keepers of peace in the provinces but as participants in the power struggles shaping up at court. The gap between the provinces and the capital was again being bridged, but this time it was the scions of former court families who were being returned to the capital after several generations in the provinces, enriched by their provincial land holdings and backed by their ability to recruit bands of fighting men for the capital guards. This new military aristocracy could not have gained its ultimate power of interference at court, of course, had it not been for the deterioration of conditions in Kyoto, so that the formerly potent aristocratic families relied more and more upon the strong arms of their provincial followers. And this condition in turn was an outcome of the spread of patrimonialism in government and the manner in which so many areas in the bureaucracy became the private preserve of particular court families or a few individuals at court (particularly the ex-emperor and the head of the Fujiwara family) who had the power of appointment over large blocs of provincial posts. To serve the Fujiwara or the cloistered emperor was to be in line for provincial governorships or extensive *shōen* responsibilities. Conversely, to serve in the *shōen* of these families was to be in line for service in the capital.

This new intermediate position of the *bushi* scions of court families placed them in a strategic position to work both ends against the old court establishment. As increasingly such families became the wielders of forceful power in the capital, they found the means of advancing their status politically and economically. Low-ranked Taira or Minamoto moved into the provinces to take up relatively profitable positions on the land. They were able to acquire private holdings (reclaimed or carved from the public domain) which had been favorably commended to the court, and in the process they were able to retain a rather large degree of authority over the land. Frequently the major portion of the rights of proprietorship (alienation) remained in their hands owing to the ineffectiveness of court authority in distant provinces. Thus, while it is the official titles of these provincial leaders that are played up in the historical narratives, most of them served concurrently as *shōkan* or *gunji* charged with remitting rents and services to their superiors in the capital. They became, in fact, resident proprietors (*ryōshu*) engaged in what should be described as a partnership with court families.[12]

The strength of these resident proprietors within the land system constantly grew as the court families lost power. By the eleventh century, provincial leaders had sometimes gained sufficient influence and status that they could serve as *ryōke* in their own right, and as such they were looked to for protection by the smaller land owners of the provinces. Thus they became the focus of land commendation on a considerable scale. Circumstances, furthermore, frequently placed these provincial proprietors in opposition to the court-centered powers which had long stood at the apex of the *shōen* hierarchies. It is recorded, for instance, that in 1088 when Yoshiie discovered that his exploits were to go unrewarded by the court, he took out of his own holdings land with which he rewarded his followers. Such actions, together with his fame as a warrior, induced large numbers of local *bushi* to commend land to him for protection. The court in 1091 issued an order prohibiting such commendation.

Stories of this kind give evidence that an important new dimension was being added to the relationships between military leader and follower in the provinces. Authority relations based on kinship bonds, or contractual command relations (as in the *shōen* system), or upon the channels of provincial civil or military administrative commands, were essentially uni-directional. Obedience was expected as part of the requirements of the system itself. A new dimension was added to the exercise of authority when loyalty became a personal commitment rewarded by grants of land. The swearing of private oaths of loyalty and the reciprocal receipt of land grants became more common as the practices of patrimonial organization spread and particularly as military service became a prime reason for enlistment under a superior authority. The risking of life and limb was service for which tangible compensation could be expected. The reward was generally land. Military bands as they took shape created in their wake extensive interlocking systems of land holdings and *shōen* rights.

The time was coming, therefore, when a member of the new provincial aristocracy could assemble the elements of power (land,

[12] Ishimoda Shō, "Kamakura seiken no seiritsu katei ni tsuite," *Rekishigaku kenkyū*, 200 (October 1956), 15. Hereafter cited Ishimoda, "Kamakura."

titles, offices, military forces) sufficient to assert a dominant voice in court affairs. This was not to happen for yet another century, however, until the court families themselves had been further weakened by factionalism and inattention to administrative affairs and until the conflicting interests of the great religious centers, the cloistered emperors, and the Fujiwara had destroyed the unity of the court. The first provincial group to take advantage of this court weakness was the faction led by the main line of the Kammu-Taira. The story of the rise of the Taira draws our attention back to central Japan and to a limited extent to the province of Bizen itself.

The provinces of Kibi did not figure prominently as bases for any of the leading members of the military aristocracy. Perhaps one reason for this is that these provinces were traditionally more closely tied to the Fujiwara house (later the imperial house through the cloister) than those in the east. As a result the public domain appears to have retained its importance as a base for provincial administration much longer than in other provinces both closer to the capital and more distant. Bizen was probably brought under the appointment prerogative of the Fujiwara family rather early in the tenth century. Those governors who in the next century and a half left their mark on Bizen, either for good government or for bad, were uniformly of Fujiwara surname. Sanetaka, who lost his life at the hands of Sumitomo; Masakane, who precipitated the difficulty with Shikada-no-shō; Sadatsune, who gained merit as governor of Bitchū by rebuilding Kibitsu shrine in 1064; Nakazane, who traveled to Bitchū with his mistress in 1081—all were Fujiwara of modest rank. By the eleventh century appointments to the posts of provincial governor were being made as special prerogatives by the Fujiwara regents (or occasionally by one of the ex-emperors). Being Fujiwara, brought up in the capital, such appointees tended to act the courtier rather than as *bushi*. Yet it is significant that most of these men, at one time or another, traveled to their provincial posts. Nakazane even had the misfortune of being on hand when his provincial residence burned in 1104.[13]

It is into this context that the Taira began to intrude their

[13] Fujii, "Bitchū," 648; Arimoto Minoru, "Chigyō-koku to shite no Bizen-no-kuni," *Setonaikai kenkyū,* 6 (March 1954), 43. Henceforth cited as Arimoto, "Chigyō."

presence as competitive aspirants for posts in the provincial service. Their patrons at court were the cloistered emperors, and it was largely as the cloister managed to cut in upon the Fujiwara monopoly of provincial appointments that the Taira began to find opportunities in the Kibi area. The close connection of the Kammu-Taira with the cloister began in 1097 when Tairo-no-Masamori commended his holdings in the province of Iga to the ex-emperor Shirakawa.[14] Masamori subsequently performed various services for the cloister, and was named governor of Bizen and other provinces of the Inland Sea region. His appointment to Bizen, from 1113 to 1120, was the direct result of Shirakawa's acquisition of proprietary rights over the province.[15] In 1120 he exchanged provinces with Fujiwara-no-Akiyoshi, governor of Sanuki. When in 1126, Akiyoshi was shifted to Echizen, Masamori's son Taira-no-Tadamori moved to Bizen. Tadamori, who served the ex-emperors Shirakawa, Horikawa, and Toba for many years, was an outstanding example of the new military courtier who filled the ranks of the provincial governorships. Active as a military officer, he made a name by suppressing piracy in the Inland Sea. Yet he was frequently in the capital where he acquired the necessary social graces to give him entree into court society. As manager (*bettō*) of the ex-emperor Toba's cloister headquarters he supervised the far-flung interests of the imperial family. He ultimately attained the rank of senior fourth rank upper grade, not exceptionally high, but it gave him the power of imperial audience and permitted his son Kiyomori to enter court service at the fifth rank.

Tadamori in his lifetime did much to extend the position of the Kammu-Taira in central and western Japan. And it was probably at this time that the Taira acquired proprietorship of Saiki-no-shō in central Bizen. Other areas in which the Taira may have gained a foothold were in Kojima and in the vicinity of some of the main Bizen ports, for a special interest in trade and maritime affairs was to become a trade-mark of the Taira family. Tadamori, who gained some notice in the capital for his abilities as a poet, has provided us also with one of those rare bits of human evidence which links the place with the man in Bizen's history. A *waka* of

[14] Hayashiya Tatsusaburō, "Insei to bushi," in *Nihon rekeishi kōza*, 2, *Genshi-kodai* (Tokyo, 1951), 209.
[15] Arimoto, "Chigyō," 44.

his contained in the *Gyokuyōshū* expresses the following sentiment:

> Dawn along the Mushiake channel!
> To see it is to forget even the capital.

Tadamori's duties as governor of Bizen had undoubtedly taken
him quite frequently to the village of Mushiake which served
as one of the principal ports of Bizen.[16]

But Bizen was not one of the major bases of Taira strength
in the provinces in these early years. Although Tadamori served
as governor of Bizen for two terms, from 1126 to 1136, the province was subsequently brought under the proprietorship of the
Fujiwara regent Tadamichi. When later the ex-emperor Toba requested Bizen to contribute toward the construction of a lotus
pond in his palace, Tadamichi declined on the excuse that he
had only just succeeded to the governance of the province.[17]
Bizen was held until after 1160 by the Fujiwara, so that the
provincial appointments during this period again came from
among the household retainers of Tadamichi's family.

Meanwhile, Taira-no-Kiyomori, Tadamori's son, had begun his
ascension at court. By the middle of the twelfth century the court
was in a state of considerable confusion as conflicting centers of
influence—the cloister, the Fujiwara, and the great temples—
competed among themselves. The court interests, relying more
and more upon their provincial subordinates to handle local affairs
and on private military guards to maintain order at the capital,
were coming dangerously close to losing their capacity to exercise
effective control over their military appointees. The day was
fast approaching when those in command of the armed guards
would be able to take their fortunes into their own hands. It was
Taira-no-Kiyomori who first exploited this situation.

After Tadamori's death in 1153, Kiyomori succeeded to the
head of the Kammu-Heike lineage. He had previously served in
several provincial posts, the most important being governor of
Aki province. Among the aristocracy of provincial origin, he had
been the most favored at court and had risen to the highest status
of any non-courtier. In this he was conspicuously more successful
than Minamoto-no-Tameyoshi, head of the Seiwa-Genji, whose

---

[16] *Tsūshi*, 1.618.
[17] Arimoto, "Chigyō," 44.

highest appointment had been to the imperial police (*kageyushi*). In 1156 a complicated set of conflicting interests precipitated the first attempt of a court faction to gain its objectives in the capital by open military action. In the resulting Hōgen disturbance, Kiyomori, who supported the interests of Emperor Go-Shirakawa, won a decisive victory over the supporters of the cloistered emperor Sutoku. On the losing side was Minamoto-no-Tameyoshi, whose subsequent execution greatly weakened the position of the Seiwa-Minamoto at court. Kiyomori, on the other hand, improved his standing, being rewarded with the governorship of Harima and the office of deputy head of Dazaifu. More significantly, in terms of the precarious power struggle at court, Kiyomori had but one major competitor among men like himself who combined high court rank with the capacity to exercise military leadership. Minamoto-no-Yoshitomo, one of Tameyoshi's sons had sided with Go-Shirakawa in 1156 and hence remained on hand to keep alive the weakening Seiwa-Minamoto interests. In 1160 Yoshitomo joined a conspiracy to eliminate Kiyomori. He was defeated, and with his death, Kiyomori was left without military competition at court. Kiyomori's subsequent promotion to councillor (*Sangi*) holding third court rank for the first time put a man of the "provincial aristocracy" into the upper ranks of the court nobility and within the policy councils of the court. Kiyomori had gained a position from which, if he chose, he could virtually dominate the court. And this is precisely what he set out to do.[18]

The Taira mastery over the court was accomplished in much the same fashion as the Fujiwara hegemony which had preceded it. To be sure, Kiyomori's methods were unusual, for he himself was both a leader of military forces and a courtier. But the meteoric rise which he now underwent at court was not primarily achieved by his use of military force. Rather he relied on established practices of advancement at court. In the fashion of the cloistered emperor, he extended proprietary control over as many provinces as possible, eventually acquiring title to 30 of the 66 provinces of Japan. In these he was able to place his followers and family members as officials. Like the Fujiwara leaders he infiltrated the high posts of the central government and even

[18] Yasuda, "Chūsei," 1-9.

intermarried with the imperial family. He was then able to displace other courtiers, members of the Fujiwara family or supporters of the cloister, with his own appointees. He himself became prime minister (*dajōdaijin*), his son became inner minister (*naidaijin*), 16 of his relatives became high courtiers (*kugyō*), 30 became middle-rank courtiers (*tenjōbito*), and 60 became provincial governors or heads of the capital guards. In 1180 he achieved the crowning success of his life when he was able to place his three-year-old grandson on the imperial throne. Kiyomori's palace headquarters at Rokuhara had already become the prime locus of political influence within the capital.[19]

To explain Kiyomori's hegemony as simply the conquest of the court by the Taira *bushi* band, as some historians have done, is quite misleading. By 1160 Kiyomori and his family had become *kuge* and, although they were more successful in utilizing military force in the struggle for power at court, the ultimate success of the Taira was achieved by infiltration of civil posts in the imperial system. Neither the posts, the sources of wealth, nor the lines of authority utilized by Kiyomori broke precedent. He essentially outdid the Fujiwara at an old game. To the Taira, therefore, the imperial system of administration and the existing *shōen* structure became the scaffolding upon which they climbed. In the provinces the Taira proprietorships (nine held for a comparatively long period of time) and governorships (making up a total of 30 provinces) provided a network of offices into which Taira partisans could be placed.[20] In the *shōen*, some 500 of which were eventually brought under Taira proprietorship (*honke* or *ryōke* rights), the Taira were also able to place their followers. There is some evidence that Kiyomori attempted some innovations in administrative organization. In the Taira *shōen* he named stewards (*jitō*) of his own choosing and set up agents (*bugyō*) in the east and west to control the *bushi*. His drastic decision in 1182 to move the court to Fukuhara and there to create a new center of government outside of Kyoto was ill-conceived, but it reflected his recognition that the Taira must rely more fully on their provincial sources of strength.[21] But on the whole the Taira saw only dimly

[19] Yasuda, *Chūsei*, 12-20; Itō Tasaburō, *Nihon hōkenseido shi* (Tokyo, 1951), 79. Henceforth cited as Itō, *Hōken*.
[20] See the table of Taira holdings compiled in *Sekai rekishi jiten*, 22.149-162.
[21] Itō, *Hōken*, 80.

the need for a new system of government. Their hegemony was too much the making of one man whose single-handed forcefulness maintained the Taira hegemony only throughout his life.

For Bizen, the Taira ascendancy in Kyoto brought little immediate change. After the transfer of Taira-no-Tadamori from Bizen, the proprietorship of the province passed to the Fujiwara regent Tadamichi and remained in his hands for some twenty-five years. Tadamichi made appointments to the governorship of Bizen from out of his entourage. Men like Minamoto-no-Nobutoki, Fujiwara-no-Nobuyoshi, and Fujiwara-no-Kunitsuna were all patrimonial officials of the regent's house. Tadamichi eventually became one of the principals in the Hōgen disturbance, at which time something of an alliance was worked out between the Fujiwara house and Taira-no-Kiyomori. From Tadamichi the regency passed to his son Motozane, who had taken one of Kiyomori's daughters in marriage. Thus, rather slowly, Bizen was drawn under the appointment powers of courtiers friendly to the Taira. When Motozane died in 1166, his Taira widow Moriko managed to inherit his properties, including his provincial appointment rights. The proprietorship of Bizen was passed on to Fujiwara-no-Kunitsuna, a loyal supporter of the Taira in their push for power at court.[22]

This act had a deep effect upon the struggle for power at the capital, for what Kiyomori had managed to do was to drain off a large bloc of Fujiwara land holdings (which by rights should have passed to the regent Fujiwara-no-Motofusa). The seizure was legal, but not at all in the spirit of court precedent, for it had been made possible only because of the fortunate circumstance that Kiyomori's daughter Moriko had outlived her husband. Such acts helped to turn Go-Shirakawa, now the cloistered emperor, against Kiyomori, and soon the wily ex-emperor was plotting against the Taira chief. The Shishigatani affair of 1179 in which Go-Shirakawa encouraged a conspiracy against Kiyomori had as one of its immediate objects the effort to recover the Fujiwara properties. Kiyomori's strong-arm reaction in this plot resulted in the banishment of Motofusa, the regent, and the degradation of 39 high officials who had served Go-Shirakawa. All of this further accentuated the factionalism which developed in the wake of Kiyomori's rise. Interestingly, Motofusa was sent

[22] Arimoto, "Chigyō," 44-45.

to exile in Bizen, where he came under the jurisdiction of the Taira partisan, Fujiwara-no-Kunitsuna. He was pardoned in the following year and permitted to return to the capital. With Kunitsuna's death in 1181, Bizen was finally taken over completely by members of the Taira clique. The proprietor became Taira-no-Shigemori and the governor, Taira-no-Tokimoto. Shortly before this, Bitchū had also come under the appointment prerogatives of the Taira.[23]

The Taira hegemony over the court was destined to be short-lived. Kiyomori's actions continually aroused the bitter opposition of the court and priesthood. Go-Shirakawa, the cloistered emperor, became a leader of intrigue. Against Kiyomori were many counts: his dictatorial action, his use of armed force within the capital, his family's monopoly of high posts, his patronage of temples and shrines other than the traditionally powerful ones in Nara and Kyoto, and specifically his rash burning of Miidera, Tōdaiji, and Kōfukuji. Since the Taira encroached upon the standard sources of aristocratic influence and wealth, they had competed constantly with other court interests, notably the cloister and the Fujiwara regency. Each Taira gain had been a loss to their competitors, and the reaction eventually set in. In 1180, Mochihito, second son of Go-Shirakawa, entered into a conspiracy against the Taira with Minamoto-no-Yorimasa and the priests of Onjōji and Kōfukuji. The plot failed, but a call to arms, sent out in the name of Mochihito, reached other remnants of the Seiwa-Genji in the eastern provinces. Presently Yoritomo, heir to the headship of the Seiwa line, raised his standard in Izu. Yoshinaka, a more distant kinsman, rallied a following in Shinano. When Kiyomori died in 1181, the shadow of a Minamoto revival was falling across the Taira fortunes. By 1183 the Taira had been driven from the capital, and in 1185 they were destroyed at Dannoura.

In the last years of fighting between the Minamoto and Taira, Bizen finally appears to have felt the effects of what had become a full-fledged civil war. Since the Taira proprietorship of the provinces of Bizen and Bitchū had come fairly late, we must assume that the Taira ability to mobilize the *bushi* of these areas was not very complete. Yet in the years after 1181 it appears that

[23] *Ibid.*, 45-46.

Taira leaders must have entered the provinces in some numbers in order to recruit a following.

One of the few men of Kibi we hear of as a fighter in the Gempei war is Senō-no-Kaneyasu. A local *bushi* who had made a name for land reclamation and irrigation works, he was proprietor of the large *shōen* of Senō on the boundary between Bitchū and Bizen. Kaneyasu threw in his lot with the Taira, taking with him a large band of fighters. Before his military capacities were called upon, he had apparently been designated as overseer of the Taira estates in the three southern Kibi provinces. In the face of Minamoto-no-Yoshinaka's advance into western Japan in 1183, he occupied the provincial seat of Bizen and gathered a reported 2000 men-at-arms for defense of the area but was defeated.[24]

Shortly after this, in the summer of 1183, the westward momentum of the Minamoto force under Yoshinaka was blocked by a defeat at Mizushima in Bitchū in a naval battle in which the former proprietor of Bizen, Taira-no-Shigehira, served as commander. The Mizushima victory in which the Taira took "twelve hundred or more heads" was a minor turning point in the civil war, setting up the stalemate of the winter of 1183-1184 and permitting the Taira control of the Inland Sea. In Bizen the Taira established Fujito, on the narrows of Kojima, as a major strong point, putting in command Kiyomori's grandson Yukimori with a force of 20 ships and 500 horsemen. It was here that in the twelfth month of 1184 the Minamoto forces were led across the Fujito straits by Sasaki-no-Moritsuna in a surprise attack which destroyed the Taira outpost and started the withdrawal which ended at Dannoura.[25]

Since the summer of 1183, however, the Taira had already been designated rebels, the cloistered emperor Go-Shirakawa had confiscated the Taira titles and land holdings, and Bizen had been legally taken out of the hands of the Taira. For a brief period in 1183, Minamoto-no-Yukiie was appointed governor of Bizen, probably for strategic military reasons, but by 1184 Go-Shirakawa felt confident enough to put his own follower, Fujiwara-no-Norihide, into the governorship. The cloister had at long last gained control of Bizen.[26]

[24] *Okayama-ken no rekishi*, 150-156; *Tsūshi*, 1.650-654.
[25] *Tsūshi*, 1.654-667.   [26] Arimoto, "Chigyō," 46.

By the end of 1185, as the tide of battle passed from Bizen, it must have appeared that the province would again settle back under the control of the capital aristocracy as it had before the interlude of Taira ascendancy. Yet in fact the Minamoto victory was to prove even more disruptive to the imperial system. Minamoto-no-Yoritomo, whether by intent or accident, brought into being a new balance between military and civil authority which was to change fundamentally the structure of central and local government. The fact that this new dispensation was not immediately communicated to a province like Bizen was a product of the great distance which separated Kamakura from western Japan and the continuing strength of the cloistered emperor's position in the home and central provinces.

Minamoto-no-Yoritomo, claiming a mandate from Prince Mochihito, had begun in 1180 to raise forces against the Taira in the province of Izu. His original mission had been simply to revive the fortunes of the house of Minamoto and to free the eastern provinces of the Taira. He ended by forming a military hegemony over the entire country. Yoritomo himself at the outset had but one outstanding asset, he was head of the Seiwa-Genji lineage. He had no official position or titles. His ascendancy, therefore, was based upon his lineage and whatever following he could draw about him. In the latter he was fortunate, for the unpopularity of the Taira made him an ideal focus of resistance. It was of critical significance to Yoritomo's final success that he began his rise as a rebel in the distant Kantō, for to him the easy success of a palace revolution and the subsequent rapid promotion in court service was denied. For him, therefore, the process of gaining power was exactly reversed from that of the Taira: the organization of a military power base preceded court honors and titles.

Yet it must be credited to the cautious genius of Yoritomo (or his willingness to rely on his provincial advisers) that he recognized this fact and constantly rejected the temptation to proceed to Kyoto to gain the titles by which a more rapid rise might have been achieved. The first instance of this caution was probably the most significant, for after his first success at Fujigawa, when the Heike forces were thoroughly routed, Yoritomo might well have taken the road to Kyoto. Instead he turned to the more mundane task of consolidating his base and eliminating the Taira from the Kantō area, leaving to others the fighting in western Japan. Yoritomo therefore stayed in the Kantō, building up his following, putting his men in key positions, confirming land holdings, and in general bringing all military families of the area under his leadership and enlisting them among his "housemen" (*gokenin*). In fact by late 1180, having established headquarters in Kamakura, he undertook the task of regulating his military followers through his *samurai-dokoro* and by appointing "military governors" (*shugo*) to the provinces of the Kantō.[27]

Yoritomo's actions in his first two years of campaigning is most revealing, for he had but the narrowest of claims to legality. Relying mainly upon the uncertain (perhaps nonexistent) mandate of Prince Mochihito and upon the past positions held by the chiefs of his lineage, he asserted the right to "govern the eastern provinces." Yet in actuality he was obliged to rely primarily on his family charisma and on the "righteousness" of his cause. The claims of authority Yoritomo built up over his followers were much more of the personal variety: pledges of loyalty from the follower, pledges of support from Yoritomo. Most typical of Yoritomo's actions was the "confirmation of holdings" (*shoryō ando*) by which he pledged to protect the holdings of his followers. How much his actions required the military successes which later confirmed his own claims to prominence is illustrated by the fact that twice before 1184 he had been branded a rebel by the changeable ex-emperor Go-Shirakawa.

Yoritomo's sensitivity to court opinion is indicated by the importance he attached to the acquisition of legitimacy. Yet it was not until 1183, long after his military conquest of the Kantō, that he received from Go-Shirakawa a rather vague admission of his right to military supremacy in the eastern provinces. It may well have been that Yoritomo would have been content with this, for he is known to have sent to the cloister a plan to divide military authority in Japan between the Minamoto and Taira. But the proposal was rejected by the Taira, and shortly thereafter Minamoto-no-Yoshinaka had entered the capital. Soon the Minamoto were extending their operations beyond Kyoto, and the court increasingly began to look to Yoritomo as the future stabilizer of the country.[28]

[27] Ishimoda, "Kamakura," 2-7; Kuroda Toshio, "Buke seiken no seiritsu," in *Nihon rekishi kōza 2, Kōdai-Chūsei* (Tokyo, 1959), 171.

[28] Ishimoda, *op.cit.*, 12-16; Kuroda, *op.cit.*, 166.

Yoritomo's final victory over the Taira in 1185 gave him the opportunity to claim powers which were national in scope. While these were powers confined chiefly to the military and police functions of the state, they also included important fiscal rights. By taking the titles of *sō-shugo* (chief of military governors) and *sō-jito* (chief of military land stewards) Yoritomo gained the authority to make military appointments in every province in the country and the responsibility to keep the *shōen* rents and services flowing. In 1190 Yoritomo received the posts of general of the right imperial guard (*u-konnoe-taishō*), acting great councillor (*gon-dainagon*), and chief of military police (*sō-tsuibushi*), and then in 1192 he secured the title of shogun (*sei-i tai-shōgun*). These titles were accompanied by the grant of high court rank. His merit at Dannoura had raised him to second rank junior grade. And in the following year he attained second rank senior grade. These, then, constituted the elements of Yoritomo's legitimacy.[29]

As has been suggested, Yoritomo's final ascendancy was the outcome of a process which was the reverse of that utilized by the Taira. For while the Taira had built up a nationwide following by acquiring strategic titles and commissions from the court, the Minamoto had first built up their following through military successes in the provinces and then had clothed their hegemony with legitimacy. To Yoritomo, his band of adherents was consequently the foundation of his power. The power structure created by Yoritomo and assembled at Kamakura was first of all based on the military band of which he was chief. The band was eventually extended to include the majority of important *bushi* families in the Kantō and then spread out more thinly to the rest of the provinces. The members of Yoritomo's band were of various capacities. Some were resident proprietors or *shōen* officials of considerable importance with lands and authority stretching over several districts. To the largest and most powerful of these, and to those who gave closest support to his cause, Yoritomo gave special status within his band. Families such as the Hōjō, Wada, and Chiba were treated as "elders" and given positions of responsibility in the Minamoto organization. Beyond these were the

[29] Ishii Susumu, "Kamakura bakufu ron," in *Iwanami kōza, Nihon rekishi, 5, Chūsei, 1* (Tokyo, 1962), 102-114.

rank and file of adherents who were enlisted as housemen (*gokenin*).

It was the particular advantage of the Minamoto band over which Yoritomo presided that it constituted a group of men instantly responsive to his authority and will. And this was particularly significant in an age when other systems of command were breaking down. Yoritomo was assured of loyal compliance to his commands because of the bonds which existed between him and his subordinates. These bonds were personal and intimate and did not need to rely on the channels of public authority utilized by provincial administration or the patrimonial ties of the *shōen* system. The ties between Yoritomo and his housemen were to this extent "feudal," that is they involved acknowledgment of vassalage on the part of the houseman and a ceremonial certification of the obligation of loyal service. In return, housemen were confirmed in their holdings or were given additional lands, after which they were assigned posts within Yoritomo's military or administrative organization. In other words the personal bond preceded official appointment and provided the main inducement to the acceptance of the authority relationship between Yoritomo and his subordinates. For its age the Kamakura authority system simply worked better and more effectively than that over which the civil authorities presided. And though there is no clear evidence that Yoritomo sought to control the whole country, he was induced to extend its jurisdiction and his powers in the process of eliminating the Taira and protecting his own position.

Yoritomo first claimed authority to interfere with provincial administration and *shōen* rights on the basis of a rather free interpretation of Mochihito's mandate that he assume supreme military command in a time of national crisis. From this point on his legal status remained closely related to his acquisition of real military influence, the two processes of conquest of legitimization working in close accord. For instance, the military conquest of each Taira partisan put the lands of the defeated at Yoritomo's disposal. Meanwhile, the title of *so-tsuibushi* gave him the rights of prosecution over major crimes, the power to recruit guards for palace duty in Kyoto, and the authority to supervise the affairs of the shrines and temples and to regulate the post-stations throughout the whole country. His appointment to the post of *so-jito* placed upon him the responsibility to assure the smooth flow of taxes from the provinces, and this, at least by implication, gave him authority to interfere in the affairs of all *shōen* and all public domains. As he further ascended the ladder of court ranks and took the titles of chief of military governors, general of the right imperial guard, and finally commander-in-chief (*shōgun*), he gained both legal and actual power.[30]

By the time Yoritomo became shogun, a situation of the following order had developed. The shogun as chief (*chōja*) of the Seiwa-Minamoto line, *ason*, and senior second court rank, held directly a large agglomeration of *shōen* (perhaps 120 pieces in 39 provinces) confiscated from the Taira and confirmed to him by the cloister. He was also proprietor of many other *shōen* which had been commended to him directly. This made him a power within the *shōen* system comparable to other factions within the high aristocracy and the great temples. Yoritomo, though he resided in Kamakura, functioned as *honke* and *ryōke* for a significant number of *shōen*. In still other territories he held more limited rights of appointment over specific functions. Furthermore, as shogun he was the "proprietor" (*kokushu*) of nine provinces in the Kantō and proprietor in all but name in seven others. This meant that practically the entire administration of the Tōkai and Tōzan provinces were subject to his direction. Throughout these areas of Japan, then, he had the authority to appoint governors, civil officials, and even certain *shōen* officials. And since he was able to enforce this authority, he was for all intents and purposes, "the government" of eastern Japan. In most of central Japan his authority was more limited and rested on his rights to set up two new types of officials: military governors (*shugo*) and military land stewards (*jitō*). Yet again in western Japan, on the island of Kyushu, Yoritomo was given nearly complete powers of governance through the office of Dazaifu.[31]

Other than the fact that Yoritomo established his headquarters at Kamakura and placed his reliance on monopoly of military powers, the Minamoto hegemony would not have differed markedly from that of the Fujiwara and Taira were it not for the new posts of *shugo* and *jitō*. Justified originally in 1185 be-

[30] Satō Shin'ichi, "Bakufu ron," in *Shin Nihonshi kōza* (Tokyo, 1951), 13.
[31] Ishii Susumu, "Kamakura bakufu ron," 115-124; Kuroda Toshio, "Buke seiken no seiritsu," 183; Watanabe Nobuo, "Kōbu kenryoku to shōensei," in *Iwanami kōza, Nihon rekishi, 5, Chūsei 1* (Tokyo, 1962), 208-219; Yasuda, *Chūsei*, 85-97.

cause of the need to clean up the remnants of military resistance and to bring order to the provinces, Yoritomo secured the right to set *shugo* over all provinces, where they would exercise control over provincial military and police affairs, and to appoint *jitō* over all land, so as to assure regular remission of land dues and the collection of an emergency military tax for the prosecution of the war. The *shugo-jitō* appointments, while not displacing provincial civil administration, gave to the shogun a network of provincial connections which extended over the entire country. It was this network which converted Yoritomo's Kamakura headquarters into more than a mere power among powers and gave it its special nationwide authority. As Yoritomo appointed his housemen to posts of *shugo* and *jitō* in distant provinces, he built his band of followers into the elements of a national administration which touched governmental affairs at two sensitive points, tax collection and law enforcement.[32]

The relationship of this new authority to the entire structure of government in twelfth century Japan must be clearly understood. Yoritomo had acquired powers which operated alongside of, and only incidentally in competition with, that exercised by the court. In reality, the shogun's position was not a usurpation but a growth within the old system. It was based upon a legal division of powers made by the court itself. And Yoritomo's careful maintenance of legality, his claim to be protector, not destroyer, of the imperial regime must therefore be taken seriously.[33] But in the final analysis the shogunal system created a mechanism capable of assuming the entire burden of local government. Furthermore the mechanism was vastly more effective than the weakening system of authority upon which the court nobility relied. Under the *gokenin* system the bond between superior and inferior was personal and military, and existed irrespective of the inferior's position in the administrative organization. The *gokenin* system introduced a new type of authority relationship which would eventually displace (or absorb) the civil government derived from the Taihō code. Feudal relations had long existed in Japan, but with the establishment of the Kamakura headquarters

<hr>

[32] Satō Shin'ichi, "Bakufu ron," 14-17; Watanabe, *op.cit.*, 218-226; Ishii Ryōsuke, "Kamakura bakufu no seiritsu," in *Rekishi kyōiku*, 8.7 (1960), 1-8.

[33] Kuroda Toshio, "Chūsei no kokka to tennō," 283; Minoru Shinoda, *The Founding of the Kamakura Shogunate 1180-1185* (New York, 1960), 130-144.

an incipient government based on feudal authority gained national recognition. The new system was still immature and was in a sense still contained within the framework of the imperial order. But the Japanese of the twelfth century recognized the dawning of a new day in the contrasts they saw between Kamakura and Kyoto, between the *buke* and *kuge*. The establishment of the shogunate in Kamakura created a new focus of power associated with a new class.

VI. BIZEN DURING THE KAMAKURA PERIOD

THE end of the Gempei war and the establishment of the Kamakura shogunate brought to an end a lengthy period of disorder in Bizen. Not that the war had been particularly disruptive to the life of the province, but the constant struggle at court between the cloister and the Fujiwara regents for possession of the revenue powers of Bizen, and then the hastily extended Taira control over the province, had led to considerable confusion regarding the legality of orders emanating from Kyoto. The Taira grip on Bizen had not been demanding, yet a fair number of the province's *bushi* must have perished in the battle of Mizushima. By contrast the battle of Fujito probably claimed almost no Bizen lives, since the forces that met there were both composed of men drawn from outside the province. We do not know either how much of a turnover in personnel the provincial office and the various *shōen* headquarters must have experienced as first the Taira, then the Minamoto, and finally the cloister claimed supreme authority in the province. It seems probable, however, that because of the extent of the public domain and the large number of imperial and religious *shōen* in Bizen, the number of changes was relatively slight.

Nor does it appear that the final Minamoto victory and the establishment of the shogunate drastically changed the political configuration of Bizen and its relationship to the capital. Bizen was never to become a stronghold of Minamoto influence, but rather it continued to be closely attached to the interests of the court and the religious centers of the capital. The establishment of the Kamakura headquarters did not, of course, alter Bizen's status as a unit of administration under the imperial system. Bizen continued to receive the appointment of governors and other civil officials sent out by the provincial proprietor who resided in Kyoto. This proprietorship, having long been coveted by the cloister Go-Shirakawa, was seized by him at the earliest opportunity during the Gempei war, and from 1184 to 1192 remained in his hands. Go-Shirakawa's first two appointments as governor were men of Fujiwara lineage, men who had gained experience in the cloister's service as governors of Mino and Harima. In 1186 he put the province in the hands of Taira-no-Mitsumori, son of Yorimori, one of the few Taira to hold aloof from the warfare which had extinguished his kinsmen.[1] Mitsumori was also one of the few Taira leaders to make his peace with Yoritomo. But he was essentially Go-Shirakawa's favorite, and his appointment to Bizen was a mark of independence on the part of the cloister. Mitsumori, having acquired a large *shōen* in Bizen, apparently took up residence in the province where he served both as governor and as a *shōen* proprietor.[2]

We can imagine that by the end of the twelfth century the power of a governor such as Mitsumori, though severely limited, was still important to the residents of the province. The governor could still claim full authority over the public domains and the taxable private lands; he held certain cadastral and census rights over the province, the power to impose emergency imposts, and the right to exercise police powers over the non-immune territories. Mitsumori's signature is preserved in a scattering of documents, notably the orders confirming the immunity of certain rice lands previously commended to Kinzanji by a former governor. As the documents which passed from governor to resident officials and then to the priests of Kinzanji indicate, the procedures governing the conditions of land tenure were still a matter of official record, and the provincial office probably served as the main records center for all such documentation. Fairly abundant though fragmentary documentation remaining from this period attests to the continued existence of a provincial office (the *rusudokoro*), most likely attached to the residence of the governor's representative (*mokudai*) rather than to that of the governor himself. What the complement of personnel for this office was is not clear, but documents of the thirteenth century emanating from the office are generally signed by the representative and several (sometimes up to six) "seal bearers."[3]

With the establishment of the Kamakura *bakufu*, of course, another chain of authority was introduced into the local government of Bizen, as the new military posts of *shugo* and *jitō* were established in the province. The *shugo*, sometimes called *sō-tsuibushi*, were essentially military governors, whose functions coincided with, and in most ways supplanted, those of the *tsui-*

---

[1] Arimoto, "Chigyō," 46.

[2] *Komonjo-shū*, 2, intro. 2-6; 2-3 (Kinzanji documents. Note that I have here adopted the more generally prevalent pronunciation rather than the preferred local pronunciation, Kanayamaji).

[3] *Komonjo-shū*, 2.6-13 (Kinzanji documents).

bushi and *kebiishi* of the civil government. In a three-clause statement referred to as *taibon-sankajō*, the *shugo* were given responsibility for the mustering of guards for service in Kyoto and Kamakura as well as the active command of the shogun's housemen in time of war, for the apprehension and prosecution of major criminals, and for the supervision of roads and religious bodies.[4] Such authority buttressed but also, as we shall see later, potentially conflicted with the similar duties of the civil officials of the *kokugaryō* and the *shōen*.[5] As we shall note later it appears that few *shugo* were actually in residence in Bizen for very much of the Kamakura period. But *shugo* authority did touch the affairs of the provincial office directly through the shogun's headquarters in Kyoto. Bizen was probably close enough to Kyoto to suffer no great inconvenience by being superintended from the office of the Kyoto *tandai*.

More intimate in their involvement in the affairs of Bizen were the *jitō*, or military land stewards, who were in time to affect the life of the province profoundly. Evidence of the activity of *jitō* in Bizen appears fairly early in the Kamakura period. Yoritomo's attempt to make the *jitō* system nationwide in 1185 had been resisted by the Kyoto and Nara interests, and in 1186 certain appointments were withdrawn. Whether this happened in Bizen is not reported, but the existence of *jitō* in Bizen before 1221, when the system was extended to all territory, is certain. We can conclude that Bizen harbored at least a few of the shogun's housemen in the early years before the turn into the thirteenth century, and it was from among these that the first *jitō* were named.

The legal authority of the *jitō* extended into the lower levels of fiscal administration and land management. These included police surveillance, the collection of rents, supervision of land use, settlement of disputes over land, and the collection of a military tax (*hyōryō mai*).[6] Most *jitō* appointed before 1221 (the so-called

[4] *Goseibai shikimoku*, clause 3 (quoted and analyzed in *Sekai rekishi jiten*, 22.167-169); Satō Shin'ichi, "Shoki hōkenshakai no keisei," in *Shin Nihonshi taikei, 3, Chūsei shakai* (Tokyo, 1952), 18.

[5] Satō Shin'ichi, *Kamakura bakufu shugo-seido no kenkyū* (Tokyo, 1948), 191; hereafter cited as Satō, *Shugo-seido*; Ishii Susumu, "Kamakura bakufu to ritsuryō seido chihō gyōsei kikan to no kankei," in *Shigaku zasshi*, 66.11 (1957), 956-994; Ōyama Kyōhei, "Kokugaryō jitō no ichi keitai," *Nihon rekishi*, 158 (August 1961), 58-66.

[6] Yasuda, *Shōenshi*, 65-67; *Sekai rekishi jiten*, 22.166-169.

hompo-jitō) were *bushi* who were already functioning as *shōen* managers or as officials in the public domain, and so their appointment did not appreciably change the existing local power structure or the distribution of land income. The shogunate merely confirmed the holdings of these existing *bushi* and formalized their position of stewardship and of subordination to the shogunate. (Most *jitō* in eastern Japan were of this variety.) By contrast new *jitō* had to be intruded into the existing *shōen* or public domain structure by the shogun. Thus they inevitably displaced existing interests and competed with civil officials for the income of the proprietorships over which they were given jurisdiction. It was to this feature of the *jitō* system that the religious and court groups of Kyoto objected so strenuously when Yoritomo made his initial appointments in 1185. But after 1221 the court was powerless to resist, and *jitō* authority was pushed into all territory within the provinces. This called for a large number of new appointees, many of whom were selected and sent out from among the shogun's housemen in the Kantō area. It was at this time in particular that members of the Kantō band infiltrated the western provinces, taking up their positions as a new military elite. Bizen must have received its share of such new arrivals.[7]

PERHAPS because there were now two centers of authority over the land, with the consequent multiplication of documents and records, the Kamakura period affords for the first time in Bizen's history the possibility of reconstructing with some accuracy the internal configuration of local jurisdictions within the province. The year 1200 is, in fact, a convenient date at which to stop for a closer look at the actual conditions which existed in Bizen within the various mingled and sometimes overlapping spheres of authority.

The most striking feature of local administration in Bizen of 1200 is that, despite successive changes in the organization of power, the boundaries within which local administration was exercised tended to conform to the familiar shapes which had existed from the Nara period. In other words the district (*kōri*), the village (*gō*), and occasionally the community (*ho*) boundaries remained intact and provided the outlines of administrative

---

[7] Kawai Masaharu, "Tōgoku bushidan no saisen to sono seichō," in *Shigaku kenkyū kinen ronsō* (Kyoto, 1950), 4-13.

Bizen

Shōen and Kokugaryō
c. 1200

10 miles

Legend:
- Kokugaryō
- Imperial shōen
- Shōen of court or central temple or shrine
- Shōen of local temple or shrine
- Uncertain

1. Kibitsu-no-miya
2. Daianji-konden (Daianji)
3. Daianji-no-shō (Daianji)
4. Mino-no-shin-gō
5. Nishi Noda-no-ho (Kibitsu-no-miya)
6. Tsushima-no-gō
7. Ifuku-no-gō
8. Noda-no-ho (Tōdaiji)
9. Shin Tsutsumi-no-ho
10. Kinzanji
11. Hiraishi-no-gō
12. Mino-no-gō
13. Hirose-no-gō
14. Izushi-no-gō
15. Shikada-no-shō (Fujiwara Denka-watari-ryō)
16. Takiyama Bessho (Takiyamaji)
17. Seijitsu-no-ho
18. Kamutsumichi-no-gō
19. Uji-no-gō

20. Hata-no-gō
21. Takara-no-gō
22. Taema-no-gō
23. Kachi-no-gō
24. Iwanasu-no-gō
25. Yoshioka-no-gō
26. Kusakabe-no-gō
27. Fukuoka-no-shō (Saishōkōin)
28. Takehara-no-shō (Kamo Jinja)
29. Asagoi-no-shō
30. Kanaoka-no-shō (Hachijōin)
31. Hattōji-no-ho (Hattōji)
32. Anyōji
33. Yoshinaga-no-ho
34. Yugei-no-gō
35. Hattori-no-ho
36. Haji-no-gō
37. Mameda-no-shō (Saidaiji)
38. Yamoda-no-shō (Kamo Jinja)
39. Owari-no-ho
40. Toyohara-no-shō

41. Kanematsu-no-ho
42. Minami Hōjō-no-shō (Tōdaiji)
43. Naganuma-no-shō (Tōdaiji)
44. Kanzaki-no-shō (Tōdaiji)
45. Toyohara-no-shō (Gotoba-in)
46. Rengeji
47. Guhōji
48. Ani Jinja
49. Kataoka-no-shō (Iwashimizu Hachiman)
50. Kashino-no-shō
51. Ushimado-no-shō (Iwashimizu Hachiman)
52. Tasurashima-no-shō
53. Shionasu-no-shō (Enryakuji)
54. Hazakawa-no-shō (Shin Kumano)
55. Mochiyoshi-no-gō

jurisdiction. Of these the district had probably lost most of its importance as a unit of government (though officials who called themselves district chiefs continued to exist). The most significant subdivisions of the province were the *gō* and *ho*. Administration in both the public domain and the *shōen* tended to be defined in terms of these units. As of 1200, Bizen was divided into 88 such administrative pieces, of which 44 were public proprietorships and 44 were private. (This contrasts with 51 *gō* into which the province had been divided under the Taihō system. See page 74.)

Bizen, it appears, retained more public domain than many provinces of similar distance from the capital. It certainly had more than the far distant ones of the Kantō or of Kyushu. Satsuma, for instance, had retained only one-tenth of its territory as public domain; Ōsumi had reduced all but one-twentieth of its land to *shōen,* and in Hyūga only one-one hundred and twentieth was administered as public domain. But provinces closer to the capital showed a somewhat different balance. During the middle of the thirteenth century in the province of Awaji, one-third of the cultivated land was classed as public domain. Somewhat later in the same century, one-sixth of the rice land of Wakasa was held under public control. Iwami in 1223 showed more public than private domain. Bizen was evidently among the provinces with the largest percentage of *kokugaryō* in its total area.[8]

The location of the 44 pieces of public domain in Bizen are determinable with some accuracy. They were confined, for the most part, to central Bizen on either side of the provincial capital. Twenty-five units were *gō*, twelve were *ho*, and the remainder were islands or were called *shōen*. The best indication that these units were still responsive to superior civil authority is found in the fact that they actually provided tax returns for their court-based proprietors.

The size of the tax receipts from these public domains together with a fragmentary but extremely detailed picture of the fiscal procedures of the Bizen *kokugaryō* are revealed in a document discovered on the back of a religious manuscript known as the

[8] Itō, *Hōken*, 39; Shimizu Saburō, "Kokugaryō," 136. Watanabe, "Kōbu," 197-199, interprets the figures relied on by other writers somewhat differently. His conclusion is that at the turn of the twelfth century most provinces other than those on the frontiers retained from 25 to 29 percent of their lands as *kokugaryō*.

"The Good Works of Namuamidabutsu."[9] This rare find records the summer wheat tax for 1203 when the provincial proprietorship of Bizen, a frequent "gift province" for pious purposes during the Kamakura period, was held by Tōdaiji of Nara. The court in other words had granted the Bizen revenues from 1193 until several years beyond 1206 for the reconstruction of buildings destroyed by fire in 1181.[10]

The essence of this 1203 record is a remarkably strict accounting of the collection and disbursement of a summer wheat (or possibly barley) tax assessed at 2153.323 *koku* (a variable unit later 5.2 bu.) of which 293.159 was in default and 1653.037 available to Tōdaiji. A summary breakdown following the structure of the original closely but systematized for easier comprehension has been worked out by Mr. Kanai Madoka:[11]

1. *Income*   (*koku*)

Wheat paid directly to the *kokuga* by 2 *gō*	33.493
Payment of goods in lieu of wheat by 2 *ho*	52.362
Wheat tax handled by *jitō* of Nyūta-no-shō	198.145
Wheat tax collected by deputy-*jitō* of 6 *gō* of Ōku	340.310
Wheat tax collected by *gōji* and *hōji*	565.230
Wheat tax collected by the resident office	116.583
Wheat tax collected by tax officers (priests) from Kyoto	419.257
Wheat tax paid by the *myōshu* Kuramitsu (including amount for Kibitsu shrine)	134.779
Wheat tax in default from *gō, ho,* and cultivators	293.159
	2,153.323

2. *Allocation*

Expenses of the *kokuga* (wheat)	33.493
Expenses of the *kokuga* (produce)	52.362
Jitō's half-rent share of Nyūta-no-shō	99.072
Tōdaiji's half-rent share of Nyūta-no-shō	99.073

[9] The original is in the Historiographical Institute of Tokyo University. It is reprinted in *Dai Nihon shiryō*, 4.9.76-82. The reverse side, upon which the tax report is written is reprinted in *Dai Nihon shiryō*, 4.7.1078-1088.

[10] Arimoto, "Chigyo," 48-49.

[11] Kanai Madoka, "Kamakura jidai no Bizen kokugaryō ni tsuite," in *Nihon rekishi*, 150 (December 1960), 49. Hereafter cited as Kanai, "Bizen." Whether the actual grain collected was wheat or barley is not completely certain. At any rate it was the harvest of dry winter fields, and I have referred to it as wheat throughout.

Tōdaiji construction fund	1,553.964
For support of Kibitsu shrine	22.200
Arrears	293.159
	2,153.323

Out of the wheat tax, Tōdaiji had for its immediate use the fourth and fifth items in its list of allocations. This added up to 1653.037 *koku*. For accounting purposes by the home temple, however, this sum had to be recalculated to the standard grain measure used by Tōdaiji. This yielded the sum of 2142.731 *koku*, which then was disbursed as follows:

3. *Disbursements* (by Tōdaiji)   (*koku*)

Wheat shipped to Tōdaiji	391.376
Shipping expenses for above	110.782
Expenses for sawing lumber in Suō Province	216.550
Shipping expenses for roof tiles	907.720
For drum maker	107.000
Shipping expenses for lime	51.766
For handling of rough and cut lumber	23.910
Shipping expenses for early rice	10.322
Shipping expenses for firewood	18.840
Shipping expenses for wheat cakes	1.860
Shipping expenses for straw mats	1.957
Shipping expenses for vegetables	2.125
Shipping expenses, miscellaneous	26.175
For use by temples and shrines in Bizen	155.804
Remainder (to be used for tile shipment)	116.544
	2,142.731

This is of course only the summer wheat tax. The fall rice tax must have been several times as great, and there were in addition various other civil and military service requirements with which the document does not deal. Nonetheless the document offers proof that Bizen was regularly tied to the capital area by its rent shipments. The roughly 2000 bushels of wheat sent to Nara in 1203 was not great, but it took at least six vessels to transport this amount. The expense of grain shipment must certainly have been a factor limiting the amount of grain sent directly to Nara, for it took more than one-quarter of the value of the shipment to pay for transportation. If we consider that the figures for tax shipment given in the *Engishiki* for the tenth century would have come to only 40 *koku* rather than the above 111 *koku*, we must assume that costs had gone up or that the earlier figures were unrealistic. Rather than grain, therefore, the tendency appears to have been to ship local specialty products such as roof tiles, lumber, lime, and special craft produce. It is interesting that Bizen's tax surplus was not all expended either in Bizen or Nara. The tiles probably came from Bitchū. Mention of the sawing of lumber in Suō Province, farther to the west, is indication of a triangular movement of goods between Bizen, Suō, and Nara. Suō, also a "gift province" assigned to Tōdaiji, was a major source of heavy timbers for temple buildings.

Turning to the process of tax collection itself, we can see that a fairly complex and cumbersome division of responsibilities was in operation. In certain instances the *gō* and *ho* chiefs collected the tax; in others the tax was collected by officers of the governor's office or by the *jitō*. In still others direct payments were made by the cultivators (*myōshu*). Two particular circumstances require amplification. First, the collection by special tax agents of Tōdaiji and, second, the activity of the *jitō*.

The 1203 document lists twelve individuals, all brought in from outside the areas over which they were placed, as special tax officials under temple authority. One of these, Iga-no-Jūrō, appears to be a *bushi* from a neighboring *shōen*. Others were mostly priests who had experience as land stewards in other parts of the county. One was a special superintendent who came from Kyoto.

The manner in which Tōdaiji served as tax collector of Bizen reflects the special advantages which religious bodies had when it came to exploiting their provincial holdings. The great temples were, first of all, advantageously organized to carry on administrative and fiscal functions. Not only did such institutions have a powerful central administration but they also maintained branch temples in the provinces. Undoubtedly the temples and shrines were able to maintain better organized bureaucracies, in which the center could assert a more effective control over the personnel and activities of the provincial branches, than the court families. Branch temples provided ideal centers from which to exercise provincial supervision.

The special agents in Bizen collected more than one-fifth of the 1203 take. The need for extra coercion to produce tax payments, and the existence of a default of roughly thirteen percent of the total assessment indicates that even with these added pressures the collection of taxes did not proceed smoothly. Tōdaiji apparently had even more trouble in collecting in Suō.[12]

The thoroughness with which Tōdaiji exploited the resources of Bizen is in part attributable to the efforts of a remarkable priest by the name of Chōgen. This man, originally of Daigoji temple near Kyoto, had traveled to China in his youth and had risen rapidly in priestly service. In 1181 he was made superintendent of the reconstruction of Tōdaiji and served in that capacity until his death in 1206. Chōgen had obtained from the cloister first the public taxes of Suō province, then those of Bizen. Throughout the arduous process of organizing the resources of these provinces for the building program, he visited Suō and Bizen several times. His vigorous policies did not stop at mere exploitation of existing lands; on behalf of Tōdaiji he reclaimed 260 *chō* of new fields in Bizen alone. And it was these scattered fields which were exchanged for the consolidated piece of public domain, Noda-no-ho, in 1196. But he also diverted much energy and expense to the rehabilitation of local religious institutions, setting aside funds for Kibitsu shrine, the restoration of the provincial capital of Bizen, the building of spas, and other projects. He also presented the local temples of Bizen with statues, paintings, and other sacred objects for their religious enrichment.[13]

These allocations for local religious purposes, as shown in the 1203 document, point to the continued exercise of a few public responsibilities by the provincial office. Kibitsu shrine, the official "first shrine" was still under the superintendence of the *kokuga,* since it received part of its support from public domain. The work of temple construction and repair engaged in by Chōgen and paid for out of the receipts from the public domain may have been undertaken on Chōgen's initiative, but more probably it reflects action which any governor or provincial proprietor might have undertaken as part of his sense of public responsibility.

From the 1203 document it is clear that *jitō* did not serve as the province's main tax collectors. In only Nyūta and the six *gō* of Ōku did military stewards actually collect the rent from the public domain. Although called a *shō,* it seems most likely that

[12] Ōyama Kyōhei, *op.cit.,* 59; Kanai, "Bizen," 49-50.
[13] Fujii, "Chōgen," 25; 29.

Nyūta-gō was actually part of the public domain. The *jitō* of Nyūta-no-shō probably served as chief *jitō* for the entire *kokugaryō*. For his office income he took one-half of the tax proceeds of this unit. How this was calculated is unclear. The amount is more than would be normal if the *jitō*'s jurisdiction were limited to Nyūta alone, yet it is much less than an eleventh of the entire proceeds from the public domain, the sum to which the *shimpojitō* were entitled at a slightly later date.[14] Probably so long as Tōdaiji and its priestly bureaucracy were involved in managing the public domain of Bizen the authority of the *jitō* was curtailed. Chōgen had reported troubles over jurisdiction with the *jitō* in Suō, and it may be that he was able to resist some of their more costly services in Bizen.[15] But certainly once the strong hand of the Tōdaiji priests was withdrawn from the province, the agents of Kamakura came much more into evidence.

In 1213 the province's taxes were assigned to Enryakuji for building purposes.[16] Thereafter, while the names of governors have remained on the records (they are all drawn from the lower court aristocracy) the identity of the province's proprietors is uncertain. Clearly the last outstanding period of close fiscal association between Kyoto and Bizen came during the periods when Bizen was contributing to the rebuilding of Tōdaiji and Enryakuji. When next we learn of the *kokugaryō* (in the fourteenth century) they will have become part of the private holdings of the shogun.

TURNING from the public to the private proprietorships, we find that there were 44 private jurisdictions in Bizen at the beginning of the thirteenth century. Of these only 36 are sufficiently well documented so that their proprietorships are known. Eight of these were held by the imperial family, fourteen by temples, ten by shrines, and four by court nobility. For most of the *shōen* for which we have records, the *honke* and *ryōke* rights were held in Kyoto; only ten small areas were held by local temples or shrines functioning as local proprietors. Conspicuously absent were *shōen* under the proprietorship of powerful military families. While it is possible that one or two of the undocumented *shōen* on Kojima may have belonged to *gokenin* families, the overall picture is one of civil and religious absentee proprietorships with close ties

[14] Kanai, "Bizen," 45-51.   [15] Ōyama, *op.cit.*, 62-63.
[16] Arimoto, "Chigyō," 48-49.

drawn to Kyoto. Thus at this time in Bizen the *bushi* class was still located in the middle brackets of the private and public land systems, performing services as *shōen* managers or stewards, or as *gunji* or *gōji*, or military *jitō*. They had not yet broken out of the civil framework to become independent proprietors as in eastern Japan.

Of the many *shōen* in Bizen the majority appear to have resulted from the conversion of entire units of public domain into private proprietorships. The only exceptions, as a glance at the provincial map of 1200 shows, were two areas on either side of the mouths of the Asahi and Yoshii rivers in which clusters of small *shōen* had become intermixed, the result, no doubt, of the relative rapidity of change in political and economic conditions along with the establishment of temples, ports, and markets. Elsewhere large areas the size of *gō* or *ho* had become *shōen*. These were all large enough to provide a broad base for a manner of local administration which largely duplicated the practices that had existed under the imperial system. In some *shōen*, in fact, officials went by the same titles that they had held when the territory was still part of the public domain.[17]

While it would be unnecessary to name and describe all the *shōen* whose proprietorships are known, the history and external organization of the *shōen* of Bizen are so varied that it will be necessary to describe a number of different types to provide a rounded picture. There were four main categories of *shōen* proprietorship: religious, imperial, court nobility, and military.

The largest group of *shōen* in Bizen in 1200 consisted of proprietorships belonging to temples and shrines. These *shōen* had the longest and most completely documented history, and so we shall take up their analysis first, though their political importance was less than that of the holdings of the court aristocracy. The following list shows their distribution and their proprietary connections:

Central Temples	*Shōen*
Daianji	Daianji-no-shō
	Daianji Konden
Enryakuji	Shionasu-no-shō

[17] Egashira Tsuneharu, "Bingo-no-kuni Ōta-shō no kenkyū," *Keizaishi kenkyū*, 39 and 40 (January and February, 1933), 413.

Saidaiji	Mameda-no-shō
Tōdaiji	Kanzaki-no-shō
	Minami-Hōjō-no-shō
	Naganuma-no-shō
	Noda-no-ho

Local Temples

Anyōji	in Nyūta-no-shō
Kōhōji	in Toyohara-no-shō
Hattōji	Hattōji-no-ho
Kinzanji	Hirose-no-gō
(or Kanayamadera)	
Rengeji	in Toyohara-no-shō
Takiyamadera	Takiyama Besshō

Central Shrines

Iwashimizu Hachiman	Ushimado-no-shō
	Hida-no-shō
	Kataoka-no-shō
Kamo	Takehara-no-shō
	Yamada-no-shō

Local Shrines

Ani	in Toyohara-no-shō
Kibitsuhiko	Nishi Noda-no-ho
	Umaya-no-gō
Shin Kumanosan	Hazakawa-no-shō

There were, of course, many more sects and varieties of religious organizations which maintained temples and shrines within Bizen. The above seventeen institutions, however, are the ones which by 1200 had acquired proprietary rights over large aggregate *shōen*. That these Buddhist and Shinto institutions had been especially favored by the central government is revealed in the location of their *shōen*, generally on the most desirable lands close to the centers of provincial government and trade. Contrary to our expectation it was not the state-supported Kokubunji which was most successful in acquiring *shōen*. Outstanding among the temples in this respect were those of the officially sponsored "official great temples" (*kan-daiji*) class, which at first numbered four, including Daianji, and later seven with the addition of Tōdaiji, Kōfukuji, and Saidaiji. After the Heian period Enryakuji and Tōji also received direct government support and as a result acquired *shōen* in Bizen.

Of the great temples Tōdaiji was the most conspicuous of the proprietors, possessing four *shōen* in southern Bizen.[18] Yet Tōdaiji may be regarded as only the most impressive of many examples of the flourishing condition of the religious institutions in the provinces during the early Kamakura period. This was a great era of religious awakening, when Buddhism was touching the hearts of all classes of people and large numbers of dedicated priests and laymen were active in support of religious establishments. The great spread of the Buddhist priesthood into the villages and the growth of the priesthood as the educated class of the provinces came at about this time. While administratively the older temples such as Tōdaiji led in this religious revival, much of the spiritual drive came in time from the spread of the new faith and meditative sects. As of 1200, however, these new movements had not put down roots of any size in Bizen. Although Eisai, the founder of the Rinzai Zen sect, came from the Kaya family, keepers of the Kibitsu shrine in Bitchū, the Zen order was not active in Bizen until a century or so later. Eisai is best remembered as having resided for some time in the Bizen temple of Kinzanji.[19]

Kinzanji was probably the best known of the local temples which by 1200 had secured extensive immune lands for their support. It was the foremost Tendai sect temple in Bizen, and the entire *gō* of Hiraishi, which surrounded the temple, had been acquired as its *shōen*. Yet this area was small and mountainous and not to be compared with the *shōen* held by centrally based institutions. In the long run, however, it was local proprietorships of this sort which alone were able to weather the centuries of military strife and emerge in the seventeenth century with some land still in their possession. Established on their own holdings, such temples were better able to make the fight necessary to defend their land rights against infringement.

The Kamakura period also witnessed the spread of nationally organized Shintō institutions. The Hachiman cult received its impetus first from the sponsorship of Tōdaiji that counted the

[18] Fujii, "Chōgen," 20.
[19] Okayama-shi Shi Henshū Iinkai, *Gaikan Okayama-shi shi* (Okayama, 1958), 39. Hereafter cited by title only.

Usa Hachiman shrine as its native guardian deity. The Iwashimizu Hachiman shrine located in Kyoto in 859, became a center of court worship and was taken as the *ujigami* of the Minamoto family. Thus the Hachiman cult spread among *buke* families, Hachiman gaining the status of patron deity of the warrior class and the personification of warlike qualities.

In Bizen by 1200 four Iwashimizu Hachiman shrines had acquired sizable *shōen.* These were associated with the central shrine in Kyoto in much the same fashion as branch temples were to their parent establishments. The Kamo and Kumano shrines, also with headquarters in or near Kyoto, were favored by the court and had by 1200 received, through commendation, holdings of modest size in Bizen. The local shrine which stands out among others is, of course, the shrine of Kibitsuhiko in Bizen. This shrine, closely linked to the Kibitsu shrine of Bitchū, was the Ichi-no-miya of Bizen, and for this reason was supported with proceeds from the public domain of Umaya-no-gō.

OF GREATER political significance than the religious proprietorships were those held by members of the imperial family and the other court nobility. The imperial *shōen,* it will be noted, took up a sizable proportion of the territory of Bizen. The composition and legal apparatus surrounding these proprietorships had certain common features which distinguished them from the others. Most often the *honke-shiki* was held by the cloistered emperor, a reigning emperor, or a lady of empress rank (*nyoin*). The *ryōke-shiki,* however, was vested in a public institution, generally some especially created religious body such as a chapel within the imperial palace. This was done as a means of assuring continuity and protection within a complex inheritance system.[20] The frequent use of widowed or unmarried female members of the imperial house as holders of proprietorships also indicated a technique to prevent the breakup of holdings through divided inheritance. Apparently the imperial house was determined to avoid the experience of 1166 when the Taira wife of the Fujiwara regent managed to take with her the holdings of her deceased husband.[21]

[20] Okuno, *Kōshitsu,* 35-38.
[21] *Sekai rekishi jiten,* 17.84; Nakamura Naokatsu, *Shōen no kenkyū* (Tokyo, 1939), 598. Hereafter cited as Nakamura, *Shōen.*

Still another feature of the imperial *shōen* was the way in which a certain cluster or portfolio of holdings, having been put together under a given *honke-ryōke* arrangement, acquired the name of either the *honke* or *ryōke* and then was handed down intact to succeeding generations. Bizen gives us the example of three such portfolios, all of which came to play an important role in the finances of the imperial household over some two centuries following their creation in the twelfth century.[22]

The Chōkōdō domains, numbering 90 individual proprietorships in 42 provinces in 1191, were gathered together in 1183 by the cloistered emperor Go-Shirakawa, who established a chapel of that name in the palace to serve as *ryōke*.[23] The portfolio may eventually have expanded to 180 proprietorships. Among them was Tottori-no-shō of Bizen. Situated in the central hill country of Bizen on either side of the river Sunagawa, this *shō* occupied most of southern Akasaka district. Its boundary was practically identical to that of Tottori-no-gō of former days. Its area was roughly 25 square miles, of which just over half was forest and upland waste.[24] Although hilly, it was a productive area and as late as the fourteenth century yielded 1000 *koku* annually for the imperial family.

References in the diaries of court nobles indicate that problems of transmission, administration, and revenue derived from the Chōkōdō portfolio were of major concern in Kyoto. During the thirteenth and fourteenth centuries the holdings were passed from the ex-emperor Go-Shirakawa to his daughter and then to successive cloistered emperors. After the division of the imperial house into two branches, the Chōkōdō proprietorships became a major support of the senior or Jimyō-in branch.

Two of Bizen's *shōen* were contained in the portfolio protected by Saishōkō-in chapel. Of these, Osada-no-shō was the larger. Occupying the northwest corner of Bizen, it had an area of approximately sixty square miles. The terrain is mostly mountainous and today has less than thirty percent of its land under cultivation.[25] But the *shōen* produced a number of mountain products

---

[22] Watanabe, "Kōbu," 182-190 for a concise survey.

[23] Nakamura, *Shōen*, 559-564; Watanabe, "Kōbu," 186.

[24] *Nōchi shi*, 416-422; Okayama-ken, *Okayama-ken tōkei nempō* (Okayama, 1952), 20.

[25] *Ibid.*

such as paper, silk, cotton, cloth, vegetable oil, charcoal, fodder, lumber, fish, and fowl for shipment to Kyoto.[26]

Osada-no-shō also was probably converted from public domain to *shōen* by the cloistered emperor Go-Shirakawa. When in 1172 the Saishōkō-in chapel was established in the name of Go-Shirakawa's second wife Taira-no-Shigeko, whose retired name was Kenshunmon-in, the *honke-shiki* of the *shōen* was put in her name, while the *ryōke-shiki* and a portion of the proceeds went to the chapel.[27] When Kenshunmon-in died in 1175, the *honke-shiki* was passed to her sister and in succession to various wives and daughters of Go-Shirakawa or his successors as cloistered emperors.[28] In 1243, the retired empress Muromachi-in was granted the *ryōke-shiki* to a portion of the Saishōkō-in proprietorships, and as a result the new portfolio took on her name. Later the Muromachi-in domains were divided into two halves and distributed between the senior and junior branches of the imperial family. The junior, or Daikakuji, branch at that time received 52 *shōen* in 21 provinces.[29]

Another Saishōkō-in proprietorship, Fukuoka-no-shō, probably began as an imperial *shōen* but fell into the hands of the Taira during Kiyomori's dominance of the court. In 1183 Minamoto-no-Yoritomo confiscated the Taira holdings and presented them to the cloistered emperor Go-Shirakawa. The cloister, however, returned them to Yoritomo. Fukuoka-no-shō was briefly commended to the mortuary temple of Emperor Sutokuin, but eventually it returned to the hands of the cloistered emperor and was added to the Saishōkō-in portfolio.

Two other *shōen* in Bizen, Kagato-no-shō and Kanaoka-no-shō were included in a group of holdings brought together in 1159 under the *honke-shiki* of Hachijō-in, daughter of Emperor Toba and mother of Emperor Nijō. The Hachijō-in lands were actually made up of several packages gathered by Emperor Toba during his long reign as emperor and cloistered emperor. One of these packages, placed under the *honke* privileges of Anrakuji-in, was made up of over sixty *shōen* in thirty or more provinces. The Hachijō-in estates were briefly confiscated in 1221 as a result of

[26] Watanabe, "Kōbu," 186-187; Shimizu Masatake, comp., *Shōen shiryō* (2 vols., Tokyo, 1933), 1124. Hereafter cited as Shimizu, *Shōen*.

[27] Shimizu, *Shōen*, 1287; *Nōchi shi*, 414-415.

[28] Nakamura, *Shōen*, 605-612.

[29] Okuno, *Kōshitsu*, 39; Nakamura *Shōen*, 601-643; Watanabe, "Kōbu," 188.

the Kamakura victory over Emperor Go-Toba. They were returned to the hands of a branch of the imperial house friendly to Kamakura in 1224.[30]

Our present state of knowledge of the imperial *shōen* is too limited to permit a detailed statement on the economic worth of these *shōen* in Bizen, but cumulatively we know the imperial *shōen* provided the sovereign and his close relatives with the means of ostentatious living for yet a century or more. Ex-emperor Go-Toba, as cloister, is recorded to have held 1180 *shōen* in 59 provinces.[31] As the income of the imperial family dwindled, it came about not so much from the loss of proprietorships over estates and provincial domains as because such proprietorships were to become increasingly meaningless as sources of revenue.

Of the category of *shōen* held by important court families, the most prominent historically was Shikada-no-shō owned by the Fujiwara family. A piece of land about four miles square, probably much of it reclaimed from the delta of the Asahi River, it bordered on the bay of Kojima and the mouth of the Asahi River. While small in area it was extremely productive, for this same area was assessed at 11,300 *koku* of rice during the seventeenth century.

The first mention of the Shikada-no-shō is in the year 813 when Fujiwara-no-Fuyutsugu granted a portion of its revenue (roughly 1100 *koku*) to the Fujiwara family temple of Kōfukuji. Later on other revenues were diverted for the Fujiwara family shrine of Kasuga. During the early Heian period Shikada took its place among the four special *shōen* held in perpetuity as a portfolio belonging to the *sesshō-kampaku* line of the Fujiwara family and designated the *denka-watari-ryō*.[32] A drawing of a portion of Shikada-no-shō in about 1200 shows the domain in a prosperous state.[33] On the grounds were storehouses and market places with such names as Futsuka-ichi (second-day market), Nanoka-ichi (seventh-day market), Tōka-ichi (tenth-day market), names which are found on the present-day map of southern Okayama.

[30] Nakamura, *Shōen*, 654-657; Watanabe, "Kōbu," 187.
[31] Watanabe, "Kōbu," 188, cites Yashiro Kuniharu's *Shōen mokuroku* but thinks a smaller figure of 769 closer to the truth. Takeuchi Rizō has compiled a list of 5566 known *shōen* in his *Shōen sakuin*, so that whether we take the larger or smaller figure, the imperial holdings were still a large percentage of the whole.
[32] Fujii, "Shikada-no-shō," 131-134.
[33] Reproduced in Nishioka Toranosuke, *Shin Nihonshi zuroku* (vol. 1, Tokyo, 1952), 415.

There must have been numerous other *shōen* in Bizen which had *kuge* proprietorships, but few have left sufficient records to make identification possible. There is some evidence that Karube-no-shō was a proprietorship of the main Fujiwara lineage and that Makae-no-shō was held in concert by the Fujiwara family and Kōfukuji temple. Kayō-no-shō may have belonged to the Saionji branch of the Fujiwara family. Otherwise the only readily identified *shōen* of this type is that of Saiki, which in 1200 was in the hands of a descendant of Taira-no-Yorimori. This *shōen* is of special interest because it is one of the few Taira estates confiscated by Minamoto-no-Yoritomo which was later returned to Taira proprietorship. A *shōen* of about twenty square miles, it was in the hill region of central Bizen and consisted of some fifty percent of forest and waste. The fact that it was returned to the Taira after their defeat was due to the coincidence that it was part of a package of 33 *shōen* held by Ike-no-Zenni, the wife of Taira-no-Kiyomori, whose intercession had saved Minamoto-no-Yoritomo's life in 1159. After 1181, when the Taira were being driven from Kyoto, Yoritomo and the cloistered emperor protected Taira-no-Yorimori, Ike-no-Zenni's son. Before the final defeat of the Taira, Yoritomo had befriended Yorimori, and had guaranteed protection of his *shōen*. Yorimori died in 1186, but his sons succeeded to his lands. His eldest son, Mitsumori, who served as governor of Bizen for some time, probably used this *shōen* as one of his provincial bases.[34]

THE civil and religious estates described above, though differing in types of proprietorship, were nearly all administered in a common fashion, so that their internal affairs may be considered as a group. For all of these *shōen*, except the ten belonging to local religious bodies, the proprietors resided in Kyoto. There each individual proprietor established some sort of administrative office (*honjo*) to handle the documents and the financial and managerial affairs of the *shōen*. Contact between absentee proprietor and *shō* took a variety of forms. Since each *shōen* had its local administrative office (*mandokoro*), from a functional standpoint this relationship was one between *honjo* and *mandokoro*. In Ōta-no-shō of Bingo, to borrow an example from a neighboring province, *shōen* administration was divided into four sectors corresponding

[34] *Nōchi shi*, 425.

to the four *go* over which the *shōen* extended. The *mandokoro* served as the headquarters of the local manager (*zasshō*) below whom a hierarchy of lesser officials served.[35] In Osada-no-shō of Bizen the roster of officials included, in addition to the manager, the clerk (*kumon*), the scribe (*anju*), the constable (*sō-tsui-bushi*), the police officer (*ōryōshi*), and the shrine superintendent (*shosha-kannushi*).[36] In Ōta-no-shō, the managers of each of the four sectors alternated residence between Kyoto and the *shōen*. The local staff of each sector included a deputy manager (*zasshō-dai*), a steward (*gesu*), a clerk, and several lower officials (*kunin*). Serving over the entire *shōen* were two land officers (*sō-tado-koro*) and two constables.[37] Large aggregate domains of this type therefore included all the facilities of local civil and military government including provisions for the enforcement of law and order.[38]

Income from the *shōen* varied from proprietorship to proprietorship, yet we must presume that certain customary norms were also in evidence. The best documented *shōen* in Bizen for fiscal data is Tottori-no-shō. In 1407 when conditions had greatly deteriorated, the grain tax from this domain destined for delivery to Kyoto was 1000 *koku* of rice. Special goods and services derived annually from Tottori by the *ryōke* are listed for 1191. These included 13 bamboo curtains, 6 pieces of matting, 30 units of special sand, 10 bolts of hemp cloth, vegetables for the proprietor's table on the 19th and 20th of each month, and 30 pieces of specially colored paper. Labor service was exacted at the rate of three armed men for each of the three gates of the cloistered emperor's palace during the second month of each year.[39]

A better idea of the amount and distribution of income from a typical *shōen* of the Kibi area can be had from Ōta-no-shō of Bingo. During the early Kamakura period this imperial proprietorship had a total cultivated area of 613 *chō* (ca. 1839 acres). Of this 33 *chō* (99 acres) was exempt land of local temples and shrines, or exempt salary land of lower officials. The remaining 530 *chō* (1740 acres) produced taxes for the proprietor and provided the base upon which miscellaneous imposts were collected.

[35] Egashira, "Ōta-no-shō," 406; also Egashira Tsuneharu, *Nihon shōen keizaishi ron* (Hikone, 1955), 192. Henceforth cited as Egashira, *Shōen*.
[36] Shimizu, *Shōen*, 1122; *Nōchi shi*, 414.
[37] Egashira, "Ōta," 406-409.
[38] Takeuchi, *Jiryō*, 510.   [39] Shimizu, *Shōen*, 1106.

This land was of three types. First, an area of 12 *chō* (36 acres) comprised the proprietor's desmene (*tsukuda*) and was cultivated directly on his behalf by labor from the rest of the *shō*. Second were 236 *chō* (708 acres) of land exempt of miscellaneous services (*zōji-menden*). These fields paid the regular land rent but were exempted from labor dues because they served as salary fields for *shōen* officials. Third, the remaining 332 *chō* (996 acres) were common fields, the cultivators of which paid regular dues and all services.[40]

The distribution of rents and services from the above categories of lands is known in broad outline. The *ryōke*'s share was the largest and amounted to the following: 1838 *koku* of grain, an undetermined quantity of soy beans, 34 *koku* of sesame seed, 20 small mats (*tatami*), 10 bolts of white hemp cloth, 42 bolts of hemp cloth in lieu of mulberry, 1 post horse per 2 *chō* of land, 1 laborer per *chō* of land, 1 post runner per 20 *chō*. Out of the *ryōke* share, however, it was necessary to subtract the fees of the upper managerial staff. Thus each of the four managers received 36 *koku* of grain and a portion of soybeans. This was calculated on the basis of a flat fee of 8 *shō* per *koku* of rent rice and amounted to just under 10 percent of the whole. Managers received special labor services while on duty in the *shōen* and a maintenance stipend of rice and special products such as charcoal, vegetables, and forage for their horses. They also received prescribed gifts of cloth from the lower officials who had been appointed by them. Also from the lower officials they received payment of cloth sufficient to defray travel expenses to the capital. Managers held an unrevealed amount of salary land (*kyūden*) and received a portion of the income from judicial hearings. They also were able to use a portion of the labor service destined for the *ryōke*.[41]

The deputy managers received treatment at a level only slightly below that of the managers. They could recruit labor service; they also received gifts from officials lower than they in the *shōen* administration, a percentage of income from legal cases, and a flat fee assessed on the grain rent of the lands under their management. Interestingly enough, this fee was similar in amount to that which had been collected by the previous district chiefs

[40] Egashira, "Ōta-no-shō," 405-406.
[41] *Op.cit.*, 409-412.

(*gunji*). Stewards (*gesu*) received a surtax (*kachōmai*) of 3 *shō* per *tan* of land under their stewardship, salary land of 3 *chō* each, the privilege of holding land exempted of service dues (this amounted to from 3 to 50 *chō*), other special fees and produce payments such as hemp cloth and vegetables, and the privilege of keeping servant families exempt of other duties. The surtax amounted to 170 *koku* for the four stewards or 43 *koku* for each. Clerks were assigned a salary fee of 2 *shō* per *tan* and salary land of 2 *chō* (6 acres). The land managers (*tadokoro*) were given a fee of 5 *gō* per *tan*, and the constable received a portion of the income from legal hearings. All lower officials were entitled to certain exemptions for their lands and those of the attached houses which served them.[42]

To summarize the tax situation of Ōta-no-shō: the proprietor and managers together taxed the *shōen* at the rate of 2.9 *to* per *tan* (roughly 4 bu. per acre) which amounted to about 24 percent of the yield. The combined fees of the lesser officials was .85 *to* per *tan* and yielded 7 percent of the produce. The remaining 69 percent remained with the *myōshu* and *hyakushō* classes.[43] This may not seem like an exorbitant tax rate, and Ōta-no-shō does appear to be rather low by usual standards, but it should be remembered that in addition to the land rent, the cultivators were burdened with many other dues: produce taxes, labor and military service duties, the provision of horses, and the like. Moreover, between these requisitions and the cultivator proper stood the *myōshu*. The combined rents of the proprietor (*nengu*) and the land rent (*kajishi*) exacted by the *myōshu* might be expected to add up to a rate of 8 *to* per *tan* or over 60 percent of the yield.[44]

Although the payment of rents and services had become a matter of fairly routine practice based upon customary face-to-face contacts, there is evidence that the whole tax collection procedure was accompanied by a regular system of paper work which specified the annual quota, acknowledged receipt of taxes, and verified shipments. The following item which remains in the Tōdaiji archives from Noda-no-shō will exemplify such documents.

[42] *Op.cit.*, 413-419; Egashira, *Shōen*, 222.
[43] Egashira, *Shōen*, 237.
[44] Kodama Kōta, ed., *Zusetsu Nihon bunkashi taikei*, 6.99.

Report of the receipt at Yugura of the annual rent in rice
and cash from Noda-no-shō.

Total   rice 71.8 *koku*

                  cash 35 *kanmon* (strings). . . .

A copy of the record of payment of annual rent is forwarded
as authentication.

1305, 1, 14   Yugura[45]

In general terms we see that the income for a *shōen* was derived
in one of two ways. For each official there was a small amount of
desmene which provided a direct yield. But, for the most part,
revenue consisted of rent and service payments from the independent cultivators. Such payments were the responsibility of the
registered cultivators, or *myōshu*. These were the men whose
names, in one form or another, appeared on the cadastral records
against units of land for which payments were due. Land within
a *shōen* not reserved in some fashion was divided into *myō* upon
which specific imposts were placed. Unfortunately for Bizen we
do not have records which categorize the tax responsibilities of
individual *myō*, but a number of cadastral surveys of the following
type are in existence:

Province of Bizen, Toyohara-no-shō, Ōku village, Kōhōji of
Senjuzan, a temple of the imperial vow established by imperial order and provincial directive, has continued in this
locality from the time of its establishment to the present.
However, the place of keeping of the documents of commendation which had been received from numerous sources
was destroyed by fire unexpectedly during the night of the
15th day of the 10th month of last year. All records and evidence have been destroyed. Therefore the following record
is made of the immune wet and dry lands:

1. 1 *chō* exempted in the name of the Society for Eternal
Happiness:

Narioka-*ri*	tsubo No. 31	Matsutoki-*myō*	1 *tan*
Uno-*ri*	tsubo No. 30	Tomotatsu-*myō*	1 *tan*
Ōishi-*ri*	tsubo No. 3	Matsutoki-*myō*	1 *tan*
"	tsubo No. 15	Chikasane-*myō*	1 *tan*
"	tsubo No. 23	Narikuni-*myō*	1 *tan*

[45] Fujii, "Chōgen," 26.

Tsukimoto-*ri* tsubo No.	2	Nagayoshi-*myō*	1 *tan*
" tsubo No.	13	Yasutomi-*myō*	1 *tan*
Ikeda-*ri* tsubo No.	4	Nagayoshi-*myō*	1 *tan*.....[46]

The date of this document is somewhat late, being 1374, yet it is included at this point for want of earlier documentation. Its date does not detract from its ability to point up a number of important features of the *shōen* land practices of the Kamakura period. For instance we know from it that *myō* cultivators were named but bore no surnames, their holdings were scattered fairly widely within the village, and above all, in this portion of Bizen, the manner of field division inherited from the Nara period was still in use. Fields were still referred to by their *jōri* grid numbers, and each field was also uniformly one *tan* in size.

The size of *myō* naturally differed according to location within Bizen. In the more mountainous areas, *myōshu* may well have held parcels of land several acres in extent. In the more developed plains areas, the *myōshu* tended to be more numerous and have smaller holdings. In Kanaoka-no-shō, not too far removed from Toyohara-no-shō, referred to above, the entire holdings of 10 *myōshu* are revealed in a cadastral survey dated 1323. The most common holding was 1.3 *tan* (.4 acres) while three *myōshu* held 9.25, 6.35, and 4.0 *tan* respectively.[47]

The procedures for rent collection and distribution, though differing greatly according to locale and circumstance, can best be illustrated for the Kibi area by the example of Ōta-no-shō. Collection was made twice a year, in summer and late fall, under the supervision of the deputy managers. Rent rice destined for Kyoto was shipped to the port of Onomichi and stored in granaries to await transport by ship up the Inland Sea. Shipment was under the superintendence of the tax collector (*nassho*) who subtracted 3 *shō* per *koku* (3 percent) of rice for his services. The overland transport to Onomichi was the responsibility of the *shōen* cultivators, and the tax officials exacted a fee of 9 *go* per *tan* if done at their expense.[48] These operations fitted in to the pattern of an expanding commercial activity. The appearance of markets in the *shōen* was not uncommon, and there was some ex-

[46] *Komonjo-shū*, 3.67-68.
[47] Hoshino Tsune, comp., *Komonjo ruisan* (Tokyo, 1894), 273-279.
[48] Egashira, "Ōta-no-shō," 420-422.

change of commodities. By the end of the Kamakura period the use of copper coins for exchange purposes was beginning to transform the produce and barter system and also helped to ease the problem of tax shipment to the capital.[49]

THE real point at issue as we review the fiscal features of the civil proprietorships in Bizen is how effectively they were administered and taxed. In the early thirteenth century we must assume that civil authority was still not openly violated. But there had been a long period of unsettlement during the Gempei war and the rents had been cut off in some instances or at least had begun to dwindle. It was into this situation that the Kamakura appointees stepped. And while as *shugo* and *jitō* they were to exact a high price for their often unwanted services, they did help to return the country to peace and fiscal stability. The Kamakura *bushi* were no doubt justified in their claim that they had improved matters for the court authorities.

We have already noted that the work of the men of Kamakura in Bizen is hard to assess in the early thirteenth century. By that time a large percentage of the lower administrative staff and the *myōshu* of both the public proprietorships and the *shōen* were men of martial training. Yet to be a *bushi* was not necessarily to be a Minamoto houseman. If in Bizen there were any *shōen* of which the proprietor was a member of the Kamakura band, we have no certain record of it. The most likely location for such *shōen* was the island of Kojima. For it is on Kojima that the *shugo* headquarters of Bizen was presumably located. The Sasaki family, several times named *shugo* of Bizen, was traditionally identified with the *shōen* of Toyooka on Kojima, but we do not have any evidence that the family held the proprietorship. The only other Kamakura *bushi* who can be definitely identified were the various *jitō*. These, as we have suggested, resided within the *shōen* and public domain. They did not at this time constitute a group of *shōen* proprietors.

Administratively, of course, the *shugo* took immediate precedence in provincial military and police affairs. But it was not the intention of Kamakura to supplant civil authority through them. It does not appear that any immediate conflict arose between the

[49] Egashira, *Shōen*, 241-302; Sugiyama Hiroshi, "Shōen ni okeru shōgyō," in *Nihon rekishi kōza, 3, Chūsei, 1* (Tokyo, 1951), 200-218.

shugo and the provincial governor's staff. Certainly the legality of the new appointees within the context of the shogun's military authority was not questioned by the provincial civil officials. On the contrary, *shugo* were frequently called upon to support the civil governors in the performance of their duties.[50] Or sometimes the *shugo* assigned by Kamakura to a province were already serving as hereditary members of the civil governor's office.[51] Thus in many instances the *shugo* actually served to infuse new life into provincial administration, lending new authority to the declining office of provincial governor and making for a period of some local stability.[52] In the Kibi area, for example, the *shugo* of Bizen, Dohi Sanehira, was ordered in 1184 to investigate the wartime behavior of certain provincial officials of Bitchū. His decision, when he discovered that the officials had not actively supported the Taira, was to have them reinstated in their offices.[53] During the Kamakura period the *shugo* were from time to time ordered to draw up province-wide cadastral registers (called *ōtabumi*). Though no records of this variety exist for Bizen, those which remain from provinces in Kyushu are the product of cooperative effort between civil and military governors.[54] It should not be supposed, therefore, that the *shugo* immediately confronted the provincial officials of Bizen with a threat to their existence. Throughout the thirteenth century at least, Kamakura attempted to keep the lines of authority between civil and military officials and between military and *shōen* officials from encroaching upon one another.[55]

The history of the military governorship of Bizen is not at all well documented. It appears unlikely, in fact, that *shugo* were actually in residence in Bizen for very much of the Kamakura period,

[50] Ishii Ryōsuke, "Kamakura bakufu no seiritsu," *Rekishi kyōiku*, 8.7 (1960), 8.
[51] Matsuoka Hisato, "Ōuchi-shi no hatten to sono ryōkoku shihai," in Uozumi Sōgorō, ed., *Daimyō ryōkoku to jōkamachi* (Kyoto, 1952), 36-39. Hereafter cited as Matsuoka, "Ouchi-shi."
[52] Shimizu Mitsuo, "Kokugaryō to bushi," *Shirin*, 27.4 (1937), 148.
[53] *Azuma kagami*, 3/25/1184 (*Kokushi taikei* edition, 32.108).
[54] Asakawa Kan'ichi, tr. and ed., *The Documents of Iriki* (New Haven, 1929), 111. Henceforth cited as Asakawa, *Iriki*.
[55] Shimizu Mitsuo, "Kokugaryō to bushi," *op.cit.*, 150; Ishii Susumu, "Kamakura bakufu to ritsuryō seido chihō kikan to no kankei," *Shigaku zasshi*, 66.11 (1957), 956-994. Both interpretations emphasize the limits of Kamakura authority. Yasuda Motohisa credits the *bakufu* with considerably more power of direct command over provincial officials after the Shōkyū conflict: *Nihon zenshi, 4, Chūsei, 1,* 152-156.

but rather that the province was superintended by a resident deputy, or even directly from the shogun's military headquarters in Kyoto. We know, of course, of the first appointments of *shugo* made in 1184. At that time two men, Dohi Sanehira and Kajiwara Kagetoki, were designated military governors of the provinces of Harima, Mimasaka, Bizen, Bitchū, and Bingo.[56] Neither man remained long in any of these provinces, however, and once fighting against the Taira had ceased they were back in Kamakura. Of the two men, Dohi was more involved in the affairs of Kibi, having been called upon to investigate the claim of the resident officials of Bitchū and also, at the end of 1184, the claim of the Kibitsu shrine for return of its lands confiscated in the course of the military operations in that area.[57] After these notices on Dohi the records (as far as Bizen is concerned) contain a break until 1221 when there is word that a branch of the Sasaki family held the office of *shugo* of Bizen with headquarters near Fujito on Kojima Island.[58]

As is well known, Yoritomo had not pushed his authority in western Japan, especially in those areas where imperial influence was strong, so that this may help account for the silence about Bizen until the time of the Shōkyū disturbance in 1221. On the other hand, it is logical to find the name Sasaki connected with Kamakura interests in Bizen. For it will be recalled that it was Sasaki-no-Moritsuna who had led the attack against the Taira at Fujito in 1184, and there is a tradition that he received a grant of holdings in Kojima as a reward. At any rate, after the Shōkyū disturbance Bizen once again became a place of exile for members of the court. In 1223 Sasaki Nobuzane, "*shugo* of Bizen," was made responsible for the exiled Prince Reizei. The latter established a residence on Kojima in Toyooka-no-shō, an estate belonging either to the Sasaki or the imperial family.[59] After this incident we hear little of the *shugo* of Bizen until the end of the Kamakura period. Probably, as in the case of Suō province, the highest ranking representative of Kamakura resident in Bizen during these years was only a deputy governor. Most important matters requiring Kamakura decisions were referred directly to

---

[56] Satō, *Shugo-seido*, 118-121; *Okayama-shi shi*, 1.841. The original reference is in *Azuma kagami*, 2/18/1184.

[57] Fujii, "Bitchū no kokuga ni tsuite," 650; *Azuma kagami*, 12/16/1184.

[58] Satō, *Shugo-seido*, 120.   [59] *Tsūshi*, 1.765-769.

the Kyoto *tandai* (the deputy shogun). Thus after the middle of the thirteenth century in Bizen it is common to find documents emanating from Kyoto which give orders directly to local officials in Bizen. Among these are the series of judgments against certain local individuals who had been trespassing on Kinzanji property.[60]

How many Kamakura housemen were to be found in Bizen is not determinable; the census of *gokenin* taken early in the Kamakura period has remained for only a few provinces. Of the more than two thousand housemen estimated to have existed throughout Japan, the majority of course were clustered in the provinces of Kantō. One estimate puts an average of about thirty housemen in each province of western Japan. Yet we know that Hizen in northern Kyushu had perhaps a hundred.[61] Bizen probably had a minimum number of Kamakura vassals. *Jitō*, being selected from among the *gokenin*, numbered even fewer. Some provinces had only one, as in the case of Satsuma; others required the services of a dozen or more. In Bizen the names of only eight *jitō* appear in the records. Of those appointed before 1221, the Fujiwara of Nyūta-no-shō supervised the public domain and possibly the imperial *shōen*. The Mino family of Mino-no-gō (possibly a descendant of the original Mino line of the Kibi family), the Tanji of Makiishi-no-shō, and others were probably given smaller and more specific jurisdictions. Among the post-Shōkyū appointments (the so-called *shimpo-jitō*) the Shikibu of Osada-no-shō appear most conspicuous. The remaining *jitō* for which there is evidence were not mentioned by surname.[62]

In Bizen the best example of the way in which *jitō* took up their new duties was revealed in Osada-no-shō. Osada was an imperial *shōen* for which the emperor Go-Toba held the *honke-shiki* and Saishōkō-in Chapel held the *ryōke-shiki*. In the last decade of the twelfth century the domain was superintended by a civil manager (*zasshō*) whose given name was Kagekado. And it was alongside of this manager that Kamakura named a *jitō*, Shikibu-no-Yorichika, probably of the Iga family of the Kantō. In appointing this *jitō* Kamakura made it clear that he was given limited legal rights with respect to the *shōen* proprietor, the exist-

[60] *Komonjo-shū*, 2.10-12.

[61] Seno Seiichirō, "Hizen-no-kuni ni okeru Kamakura gokenin," *Nihon rekishi*, 117 (March 1958), 35-37.

[62] Kanai, "Bizen," 37; Shimizu, *Shōen shiryō*, 1121ff.

ing manager, and other officials and the cultivators. In Ōta-no-shō, similarly, specific regulations defining the *jitō*'s rights were issued at the time the *jitō* was appointed in 1196. In this case, the *jitō* himself did not reside in Bingo but remained in Kamakura. He therefore carried out his duties through three resident deputy-*jitō* (*daikan*) and one sub-deputy (*matadaikan*). At the time of his appointment he was placed under a ten-clause set of regulations, of which, unfortunately, only the first four have been preserved. These touched on the following matters: (1) the *jitō*'s fee (*kachōmai*) to be collected at the rates of two or three *shō* per *tan*; (2) labor service to be limited to four men each year for service to Kamakura and other local services within the *shōen*; (3) food for the table to be received in moderation; and (4) warnings against the unlawful appropriation of abandoned land.[63]

The economic impact of these appointments can be judged by the fact that each *shimpo-jitō* was theoretically entitled to the revenue produced by one-eleventh of the land over which he was assigned. In addition he was empowered to subtract a military surtax of 5 *shō* per *tan*, to receive a share of the income from the hearings on legal cases, and to absorb a portion of the produce of mountain and stream. Thus the *jitō*, as they took up their new posts, represented a sizable drain on land rent all in the name of military protection and the maintenance of order. The brunt of this drain was felt by the proprietary interests, either of the provincial public domains or of the *shōen*.[64]

Once in being, the *jitō* came to perform more and more of the administrative and fiscal functions which had formerly been the responsibility of the resident civil officials of the *shōen* and *kokugaryō*. Yet Kamakura conscientiously tried to limit the *jitō* to their proper functions as impartial guardians of the peace, and frequently reprimanded *jitō* who pushed beyond their legitimate spheres of activity.

As we can see from the documents of litigation which accumulated during the thirteenth century, the most immediate concerns of newly appointed *jitō* were to clarify the extent of their authority over the land, the *shōen* staff, and the collection of rents. In both Osada and Ōta the *jitō* received the right of *shiki* disposition for certain positions at the level of clerk or below, a privilege previ-

[63] Egashira, "Ōta-no-shō," 524–530.
[64] Asakawa, *Iriki*, 20.

ously held by the civil stewards.[65] *Jitō* normally received limited rights of land management within the *shōen* and of rent collection on behalf of the proprietor either in part or in whole. In Osada and Ōta these rights were from the outset divided equally between the new *jitō* (representing military authority) and the previously existing *shōen* officials (representing civil authority). But in both *shōen* the division of land and tax rights became a matter of frequent contention between the military and civil authorities. In some instances disputes of this nature led to violence.[66] In Osada-no-shō, the attempt of the *jitō* to increase his share caused the civil officials to complain to the *bakufu*. The complaint was lodged through the proprietor in 1224, and shortly thereafter a settlement was made by Hōjō Masako, Yoritomo's widow, in favor of the civil authorities and reaffirming the principle of equal division between civil and military officials. A subsequent decision in 1287 made this principle even clearer by laying down the following provisions:

1. Rights and responsibilities with respect to the administration of the *shōen* must be shared between the *jitō* and *shōkan*. This should follow precedent.

2. The handling of police and judicial problems must be shared.

3. The products of forest and stream must be shared on a half and half basis.

4. The *jitō* must not take over old fields (*hondembata*) as if they are newly reclaimed and assert "half rights" to them.[67]

In this case the premature attempt of the *jitō*, to assert full managerial control of a *shōen* was thwarted by the Kamakura authorities who maintained the letter of the original conditions under which the *jitō* had been appointed.

But though the documents constantly show the *bakufu* attempting to maintain the *status quo*, the *jitō* persistently expanded their spheres of operation. The balance in shares of income between civil proprietors and military stewards, originally conceived of on an 11 to 1 basis, steadily approached the half and half division as the Kamakura period wore on. Furthermore, since an

---

[65] Egashira, "Ōta-no-shō," 531.   [66] Ōyama, *op.cit.*, 62-65.
[67] *Nōchi shi*, 414-415; Shimizu, *Shōen shiryō*, 1121ff.

abstract division of rights was hard to define and to enforce, it became increasingly common for the land within a *shōen* to be physically divided between the two types of authority. This generally came about as conflicting claims between civil and military interests became so intense that the authorities ordered a land survey leading to a meeting of minds (*wayo*) over how the *shōen* should be divided. The process of land division itself was called *shitaji-chūbun*. The most common method of such division was simply to split the *shōen* half and half. But there were many variations. In Bizen in 1289 a portion of the Kinzanji holdings were divided on the *wayo* basis, 7.35 *tan* going to the temple, and 4.55 *tan* to the *myōshu*. This was not a contest between civil and military jurisdictions, but the agreement is especially interesting for the manner in which it clarifies the division of dues:

> A record of Hisanari's portion of the 1 *chō* · 2 *tan* .80 of exempt land belonging to Kinzanji.
> In Ifuku-gō, Takayama-ri, tsubo No. 14 — 9 *tan* .5
> (less 1 *tan* which is clerk's desmene)
>
> | | | |
> |---|---|---|
> | The temple's share | 5 *tan* .25 | on the south |
> | Hisanari's share | 3 *tan* .30 | on the north |
>
> In Tsushima-gō, Kusumoto, tsubo No. 36 — 3 *tan* .35
>
> | | | |
> |---|---|---|
> | The temple's share | 2 *tan* .10 | on the west |
> | Hisanari's share | 1 *tan* .25 | on the east |
>
> The above immune lands according to agreement between both parties are divided into separate parts. Moreover, Hisanari will not subtract the rice tax from the temple's lands and the temple will not expect services from Hisanari (here known as the *myōshu*). However, both parties will share the responsibility of collecting the *jitō's* desmene service, the surtax, and the commuted labor tax due on the 9 *tan* .5 in Ifuku-gō, since there has not been a settlement of the *jitō's* responsibilities towards these lands.

> This agreement is recorded for posterity and authenticated
> 1289,3,11   (signatures representing the
>   provincial administration and
>   the temple)[68]

Documents of this type are extremely common after the middle of

---

[68] *Komonjo-shū*, 2.15-16.

the Kamakura period. They illustrate the tendency for what had
been a complex system of division of shares of income from the
land to simplify itself by the actual division of the land ownership
itself.

A good example of the *wayo* compromise between civil and
military authority is illustrated in Kanaoka-no-shō in Bizen in
which a division on the basis of ⅖ to the *ryōke* and ⅗ to the
jitō was agreed upon.[69] In most instances the actual division of
land was made by drawing an appropriate line through the
shōen, as in the example of Niimi-no-shō of Bitchū where by 1271
the *shōen* had been split into two equal portions east and west.[70]
But the example of Kanaoka-no-shō previously cited illustrates
another and more complicated method of division on a plot basis
(*tsubowake*).[71] Characteristic of all such systems of division was
the fact that the *jitō* acquired proprietary rights and powers of
alienation over the portion of the *shōen* which was awarded to
him. Thus the *jitō* bit by bit became local proprietors with the
power to alienate land or give it as reward to their followers.[72]
They were, in effect, acquiring the economic means by which to
extend their own personal bonds of influence on a feudal basis.

Division of *shōen* between *jitō* and proprietor did not, of course,
withdraw the proprietor's share from the surveillance of the *jitō*.
It was generally but a short step, therefore, from the acquisition
of a part to the assertion by the *jitō* of full administrative control
over the entire *shōen*. The *jitō* in such circumstances would assume the responsibility of tax collection on behalf of the proprietor on a contract basis. This practice, referred to as *jitō-uke,* was
exemplified in Bizen's Fukuoka-no-shō. There the *jitō,* Yoshii-no-
Yosaburo took over the entire task of collecting rents and services,
remitting a fixed amount to the *shōen* owners in Kyoto.[73] While
the *jitō-uke* system had probably not proceeded too far in Bizen
by the end of the Kamakura period, it nonetheless gave evidence
of the most common manner by which the administration of *shōen*
was eventually to pass completely out of the hands of the absentee civil proprietors.

Our study of Bizen reveals it was largely at the level of the *jitō's*

[69] Hoshino, *op.cit.,* 272-279.
[70] Sugiyama Hiroshi, "Shōen ni okeru shōgyō," *op.cit.,* 200.
[71] Hoshino, *op.cit.,* 273-279.
[72] Yasuda, *Shōenshi,* 167-168; Watanabe, "Kōbu," 224-225.
[73] *Nōchi shi,* 446.

activity that the increased encroachment of Kamakura authority within the provincial life can be measured. As we progress through the Kamakura period, the location and names of an increasing number of *gokenin* families make their appearance in the records. One important addition to the Bizen scene from the Kantō was the Matsuda family, which acquired *jitō* rights to territory near Kanagawa on the Asahi River shortly after the unhappy attempt of the court to resist Kamakura in 1221.[74] This family gradually took over *jitō* rights in the territories along the Asahi River, becoming the predominant military power in western Bizen. The Hikasa family of Wakasa province settled in northern Wake district and shortly became the leading family in that area. The name of Susuki begins to stand out in Kojima. And at the beginning of the fourteenth century the Itō became prominent at Mitsuishi in eastern Wake district.[75]

That the *jitō* were coming into their own as land owners and small proprietors in Bizen is revealed chiefly through the record of land gifts made by them to various religious institutions. During the middle of the thirteenth century we find the *jitō* of Nyūtano-shō granting at one time over six *chō* (24 acres) of land to Anyōji. At other intervals he commended several smaller pieces.[76] Kinzanji also added to its holdings through grants from neighboring *jitō* or *myōshu*. The period from 1307 to 1314 was particularly active for the temple.[77]

Beyond this point the tendency of *jitō* to become a law to themselves proceeded rather slowly in Bizen, at least by comparison with what was happening in the eastern provinces. Bizen was not a battleground during the Shōkyū incident, and the Kamakura victory in 1221 did not provide many opportunities which could be turned to profit. *Shōen* confiscated by the *bakufu* from the court at this time, among them Kanaoka and Tottori, were almost immediately returned to imperial proprietorship, and the precedence of civil authority was reestablished. But in the ensuing decades, there is evidence of an increasing aggressiveness on the part of the military families of Bizen. We have already noted the long dispute between *jitō* and proprietor in Osada-no-shō in which ostensibly the Kamakura government protected the proprietor.

[74] *Tsūshi*, 1.771.
[75] Ōae Toshimasa, *Bizen Mitsuishi-jō shi no kenkyū* (Okayama, 1942), 29-39.
[76] *Komonjo-shū*, 1.1.-12. [77] *Ibid.*, 1.17-18.

But in the end the *jitō* inevitably enlarged his sphere of influence in Osada.

Complaints against the violent and illegal acts of *bushi* against *shōen* authorities became numerous after the Shōkyū disturbance. In 1221, the temple of Hattōji complained to the Kamakura authorities of the unlawful trespassing of "evil bands" (*akutō*) of hunters on its property.[78] In 1222 Kinzanji took legal action to recover lands seized by a neighboring military official.[79] In 1303 Hattōji again complained that the deputy-*jitō* of Fujino-no-ho was attempting to usurp complete authority over its lands.[80] These are but a few of the kinds of complaints which indicated the restlessness of the *bushi* in Bizen during the later Kamakura period. In each of the above instances action was taken in Kamakura to protect the civil interests. Rulings were handed down, generally from the shogunal office in Kyoto, that *shugo* or *jitō* should take appropriate action. In some instances they were ordered to proceed to the scene of the complaint in order to enforce compliance.[81]

Yet, year by year, the *jitō* class of *bushi* became more numerous, and its spread, together with the militarization of the *kokuryō* and *shōen* officials, made for a constant increase in the relative proportion of military families in Bizen. And with the spread of such families and their increasing possession of land rights, conditions were developing whereby local *bushi* could become the centers of local military bands capable of forcible encroachment upon the predominantly civil administration of Bizen. The beginnings of such *bushi* bands in Bizen is already revealed in these documents of complaint. From Bingo there was the complaint that the *jitō* of Ōta-no-shō made a practice of enlisting the *myōshu* of the *shōen* under their private command. Clearly even without reliance on reciprocal grants of land, *jitō* could call upon the men of a *shōen* to join in military alliance. In the ensuing tests between civil and military interests, the *jitō* frequently mobilized their followings against the authority of the proprietor.[82] By the end of the Kamakura period military bands organized by *jitō* had succeeded in ousting the civil officials from a number of *shōen*. The *jitō* thereby constituted themselves independent powers only

[78] *Ibid.*, 1.688.
[79] *Ibid.*, 2.8-9.
[80] Miyoshi Iheiji, *Fujino-son shi*, 50-52.
[81] *Komonjo-shū*, 2.9.
[82] Yasuda, *Shōenshi*, 176.

remotely responsible to the absentee civil proprietors in Kyoto.[83]

The increased use of the elements of feudal authority by members of the military class in central and western Japan is not well documented, but we must assume that it was a persistent factor behind the swelling volume of complaints voiced by the civil proprietors. Studies of the Ōuchi family who served as *jitō* in Suō reveal that by the thirteenth century the family had secured proprietary rights sufficient to reward followers with grants of land and immunities.[84] In Bizen, too, once the proprietary division of *shōen* took place, *jitō* were able to use land as a means of assuring the hereditary loyalty of their subordinate kinsmen or retainers.

For an area in central Japan such as Bizen, where the tradition of imperial rule through civil officials continued strong, the outstanding feature of provincial life during most of the Kamakura period was the balance between civil and military authority. The Kamakura period is noteworthy for the fact that by the twelfth century all land in the province had become *shōen*. (The *kokugaryō* was by this time only a special case of private proprietorship.) Yet local administration continued to depend heavily upon the continuation of the imperial officialdom and the legal and bureaucratic procedures of the imperial system. The same can be said about the *shugo-jitō* system. The new military officials by no means provided a complete administrative organization for Bizen. They did not, even in the fourteenth century, provide the full range of functions necessary for local government. Hence the Kamakura system, too, was dependent upon civil organization for the maintenance of those features of government over which it had no preview.

But the Kamakura system introduced a different set of authority relationships and a new method of exercising authority into the province, and this was to influence more and more of the conduct of local government as time went on. At first the feudal ties which penetrated the province were essentially vertical ones, linking the *gokenin* to the shogun in Kamakura. But it was not long before the feudal element began to spread out within the locality horizontally. As the *jitō* families proliferated and as they

---

[83] Hattori Kentarō, "Ryōshusei hatten katei no ichi kōsatsu," *Mita Gakkai zasshi*, 45.1 (January 1952), 15-18.
[84] Matsuoka, "Ōuchi-shi," 40.

gained proprietary rights over portions of the *shōen*, they began to extend their own feudal connections within the area. The *jitō* or *shugo*, in other words, became the centers of local *bushi* bands which increasingly dominated the affairs of the province. Here obviously was the beginning of a fundamental change in the pattern of local government of Bizen. The *shitaji-chūbun* land settlements began a process which started to reverse the concentration of authority in the court, where it had resided since the eighth century, giving back to the local area some of the initiative which it had lost with the establishment of the Nara imperial bureaucracy. The long period of domination by the court aristocracy was coming to an end, and a condition in which power derived from land, manpower, and military force could be assembled at the local level in sufficient quantity to challenge central authority was again at hand. Although Bizen was slow to react to this condition, the trend was clear. By the end of the Kamakura we hear less and less of the civil officialdom, fewer members of the court aristocracy appear as active administrators in the province, and in their place the military aristocracy had absorbed an increasing share of the functions of government and the rights to benefit from the land.

VII. THE ASHIKAGA HEGEMONY AND THE RISE OF THE SHUGO DAIMYO

FROM the founding of the Kamakura shogunate until the end of the thirteenth century, the balance between civil and military authority had continued to give Japan a reasonably stable government. But this precarious condition was not to last beyond the fourteenth century, by which time the evidence of political and social unrest had become irrepressible. Quarrels among the court aristocracy reflected their growing irritability over dwindling returns from the civil proprietorships. Among the upper ranks of the Kamakura housemen there was open resentment over the manner in which the Hōjō monopolized the affairs of the shogunate. In the Kantō, particularly, the families of *shugo* status had extended their proprietary holdings and regional influence so that they controlled large combinations of landed wealth and military capacity sufficient, in fact, to stand up to the Hōjō family itself. Among the general run of military families the branching of lineages had caused a division of patrimonies into dangerously slender inheritances, and this condition had been aggravated by the strain of defense against the Mongols.

Underlying all of these symptoms of instability was the fundamental problem of the deteriorating balance between civil and military power. After a century or more of operation, the *shugo-jitō* system was running into trouble. Everywhere officials in the military sector of administration were demanding larger and larger shares of the income from the land, whether from purely selfish reasons or because in reality they had taken over the major share of administrative functions in their areas. Increasingly the *jitō* had found it difficult to work within the context of *shōen* law and to behave simply as guardians of the peace.[1] And so they had pressed for the extension of their powers, first through outright acquisition of proprietary rights and then by assumption of contract privileges over entire *shōen*. And when the slightest disturbance occurred in the provinces, the court families of Kyoto complained that the military stewards failed to deliver rents of any kind or amount. The reluctance of the officials in the shogun's service to share the fruits of the land with absentee court proprie-

[1] Yasuda, *Shōen*, 181-182.

tors reflected a fundamental difference of opinion over the importance of the services being rendered by the military sector of government.

The event which broke apart the Kamakura order and provided the opportunity for the *shugo* and *jitō* to make yet further inroads upon the remnants of civil authority and proprietary rights was the so-called Kemmu Restoration. The fact that the fighting which destroyed the Kamakura shogunate began as an attempt by the emperor Go-Daigo to regain imperial control of government has placed a confusing light upon this whole episode. Once the first attack was made upon the Kamakura system the entire country rose up to destroy it, but not necessarily with the aim of supporting Go-Daigo's objectives. The occasion for the dissolution of the Kamakura shogunate was in fact anachronistic. Go-Daigo, of the Daikakuji line, ambitious to prevent the return of power to the Jimyōin line, and hopeful of recovering the imperial prerogatives of former days, began in 1331 an open attack upon the Hōjō. The result was the brief restoration of 1334 to 1336. But the disturbance which started in 1331 was not to be resolved until 1392, and in the meantime a new shogunate and a new balance of political power which inclined even more toward localism and feudal authority had been brought into existence.

The extensive warfare precipitated by Go-Daigo's aspirations for the imperial house was fought out across the length and breadth of Japan at many varying levels of interest and motivation. Go-Daigo and his followers among the court nobles sought the return of a polity in which they would again play a dominant role, and the many centrally located temples and shrines were eager for the return of land rights taken from them by the encroachments of military officials. Ostensibly all of the warfare between 1331 and 1392 was fought in support of or against the Go-Daigo cause, but for the most part the fighting involved strictly private aspirations among the military families. Great houses such as the Ashikaga and Nitta hoped to replace the Hōjō in the hierarchy of military power; many members of the military aristocracy, displeased by their status in the *gokenin* system, especially after the complication of the Mongol invasions, looked for an improvement of their private positions; while at the bottom of society a general eagerness to alleviate the burden of rents and obligations was a compelling motive to join in military action.[2]

Go-Daigo's effort at restoration was doomed from the start. Although at the outset the emperor was joined by military leaders such as Nitta Yoshisada and Ashikaga Takauji, there was a deep cleavage of interest between the *bushi* leaders and the court. For Go-Daigo was not content merely to reinstate the old organs of imperial government. He was equally intent upon bringing the new institutions of military rule under imperial control and thus to act the complete sovereign. His granting of the title of *sei-i-tai-shōgun* to his son, Prince Morinaga, his appointment of courtiers as provincial military governors, his abandonment of the private proprietorships of the imperial family so as to wipe out the difference between the imperial house and imperial government all indicated his determination to return to centralized imperial rule. To this his military supporters had no intention of acquiescing. By 1335, Ashikaga Takauji had turned against Go-Daigo and was proceeding toward the reestablishment of a new shogunate under his own control. Having captured Kyoto and driven out Go-Daigo in 1336, Takauji set up the emperor Kōmyō of the rival Jimyōin line to legitimize his position and established a new military headquarters in the imperial city. In 1338 he became shogun. But while the dream of restoration was soon forgotten, the fighting did not cease. Go-Daigo fled with his court to the hills of Yoshino, where he and his successors clung to the claim that they were the rightful sovereigns. From 1336 to 1392, therefore, two emperors contested the throne of Japan. For the country at large, the existence of two imperial causes provided the excuse for the extensive fighting referred to as the "war of the dynasties."

The Kemmu Restoration and the wars which followed from it plunged Bizen into several periods of bitter warfare. News of Go-Daigo's plot against the Kamakura shogunate in 1331 called forth some immediate though desultory fighting in Bizen, as a number of families seized the opportunity to attack local Hōjō partisans. Most of this action emanated from imperial *shōen*, such as Toyohara, in which the tradition of loyalty to Kyoto was especially strong. There were, of course, many military families not in shogunal service who were ever on the watch for ways to

[2] Nagakara Keiji, "Namboku-chō no nairan," in *Nihon rekishi kōza, 3, Chūsei-kinsei* (Tokyo, 1957), 17-44. Hereafter cited as Nagakara, "Namboku."

retaliate against the recent inroads upon their privileges. One of the first of this kind to distinguish himself was Kojima Takanori, a man of Toyohara-no-shō, who attempted to join Go-Daigo in Kyoto in 1331. Go-Daigo's first plot was a failure, and he was sent into exile to the island of Oki. Kojima Takanori is believed to have made a futile effort to free the emperor from the Hōjō guard which was leading him into exile, and failing to do so, returned to Bizen.[3]

But Go-Daigo's exile was short-lived; in 1333 he made his escape, sending out in advance of his return to the mainland a new plea for support. The response from the provinces of Kibi was immediate. In Bizen the Kojima, Ōtomi, Wada, Chima, Fujii, Nakagiri, and Ishiu; in Bitchū the Niimi, Mimura, Shō, and many others joined the command of the Akamatsu of neighboring Harima province in an attack upon the Hōjō headquarters in Kyoto. By 1334 the restoration had been achieved. In Bizen only a few loyal vassals of Kamakura put up resistance, but they were easily swept aside.

Because of the short life of the restoration it is difficult to determine what changes it brought to the Kibi provinces. A number of proprietorships obviously changed hands, and some of these changes favored court families. For instance the office of military steward of Higasa-no-shō of Bizen was transferred to a court family. In Niimi-no-shō of Bitchū the proprietorship was granted to Tōji temple of Kyoto, thus reversing the course of military encroachment.[4] But in Bizen the post of military governor remained in military hands, since Matsuda Moritomo, a former Kamakura houseman, became the first appointment after the Restoration. Before many changes could have taken effect in Bizen, however, Ashikaga Takauji had turned against Go-Daigo, and the province was plunged into a much more serious struggle of conflicting interest between those who supported or opposed the Ashikaga.

Leadership against the Ashikaga in Bizen went to Kojima Takanori. On the Ashikaga side the Hosokawa family of Sanuki prov-

---

[3] Kojima Takanori's exploits are known only through certain passages in the *Taiheiki*, and as a consequence a number of historians of the early Meiji period questioned whether such a person actually existed. The plausibility that Takanori was a military leader who emerged from one of the *shōen* of Ōku district is now fairly well established. See Fujii Shun, "Kojima Takanori no ittō taru Imaki, Ōtomi ryōshi ni tsuite," in *Shichō*, 1936, vol. 3.

[4] *Okayama no rekishi*, 186.

ince (to the south) and the Akamatsu of Harima province (to the east) rallied the men of Bizen and Bitchū for an attack upon Go-Daigo in Kyoto. But the initial Ashikaga attack on the imperial capital proved a failure. Ashikaga Takauji retreated to Kyushu, and his supporters in central Japan fell back to defensive positions. The Akamatsu fortified their castle of Shirahata. In eastern Bizen, a castle at Mitsuishi along the Harima border became a center of support for the Ashikaga cause. Its defender, a member of the Ashikaga family, was surnamed Ishibashi. The Matsuda of western Bizen strengthened their defenses at Tomiyama. Against these centers the Kojima, Imaki, Wada, Ōtomi, and others made up the local support for Go-Daigo and his champion Nitta Yoshisada. Briefly the restoration cause gained the ascendancy. The forces of Nitta's generals, driving into Bizen from Harima, where they had invested the Akamatsu, laid siege to Mitsuishi castle and set up powerful defenses at Fukuyama just over the Bizen border in Bitchū. But by this time the Ashikaga forces had regrouped and had resumed the attack. The army of Ashikaga Tadayoshi, Takauji's brother, defeated the loyalists at Fukuyama in what turned out to be a crucial battle. From this point the Ashikaga swept through Bizen, crushed Nitta Yoshisada in Harima, and successfully relieved the Akamatsu. Takauji entered Kyoto in triumph in 1336.[5]

The Ashikaga victory over Go-Daigo and the establishment of a new shogunate in 1338 did not by any means assure the same kind of stability for Bizen that the Kamakura victory had provided a century and a half earlier. The great *shugo* families who assumed control of the provinces frequently resorted to arms to settle their conflicting interests in Bizen and adjoining provinces. Yet from the point of view of the structure of government, the establishment of the Ashikaga hegemony brought into being a new and relatively stable balance between civil and military authority which persisted for roughly a century and a half. The wars of the restoration had destroyed all but the highest symbols of civil government. The system of provincial governorships was entirely superseded. And while the *shōen* system continued to serve as the basis of land law and land management, local administration was now almost completely taken over by the lines

[5] *Okayama no rekishi*, 186-190; *Okayama-shi shi*, 1061-1114.

of authority which culminated in the Ashikaga shogunate. For areas such as Bizen, nearly all the authority of local government was concentrated in the hands of the shogun's local deputies: military governors of a new and more powerful type and their private vassals.

The Ashikaga shogunate, while superficially resembling the Kamakura shogun's headquarters, rested upon a balance of power between military and civil authority which had shifted far toward the direction of complete military hegemony. Symbolic of the encroachment of military authority over the older imperial system was the fact that Kyoto itself had become the seat of the shogunate. No longer were there two primary centers of government physically separated by several hundred miles. Kyoto was now capital to both military and civil authority. And although vestiges of imperial central government were preserved, the shogun was now admittedly the only real authority and was able to issue orders in the imperial name.[6]

In external form, of course, the imperial order remained: the emperor was still looked to as sovereign, the provinces retained their identity as administrative subdivisions of the state, and *shōen* law served as the basis of land management. But though the court families might still claim the right of proprietorship over their far-flung *shōen*, they now had almost no possibility of interference in administrative affairs and were at the mercy of military land stewards for whatever income they might receive from their lands. The Ashikaga shoguns, though they coveted high court ranks and posts, no longer depended upon such appointments to provide them with the channels through which they could exercise authority. Court backing served merely to add the stamp of legitimacy to their possession of power. In contrast to the Taira, who had had to infiltrate the imperial channels of authority, or the Minamoto, who justified their position as the military and police arm of the imperial government, the Ashikaga shoguns were able to claim in their own right all but the slightest residue of sovereign rights. They constituted in themselves the main government of Japan and governed quite frankly through their own system of command, using an expanded system of *shugo* appointment in the provinces.

[6] Kuroda Toshio, "Chūsei no kokka to tennō," 313.

The final encroachment of military authority over civil administration was probably inevitable, but it was greatly, and unwittingly, accelerated by Go-Daigo's abortive restoration. For Go-Daigo, in his attempt to assert control over all government affairs, had sought to coalesce civil and military functions under his imperial authority whenever possible. After the restoration, civil governors were no longer appointed to the provinces, for instance, because *shugo* were assigned to take their places and serve both as civil and military officers. Where possible Go-Daigo made *shugo* appointments from among his court followers. But once the restoration failed, military *shugo* merely asserted themselves in the provinces with enlarged authority. In somewhat the same manner the imperial family lost its position as an independent political force in the capital. The office of the cloister had been abolished in 1321, and many of the imperial proprietorships were thrown into the central treasury by Go-Daigo, all in an effort to return to the ideal form of centralized government. Go-Daigo's failure left the imperial family weakened both politically and economically.[7] Under the Ashikaga shoguns there literally ceased to be a civil aristocratic authority capable of influencing the process of government.

Yet the Ashikaga hegemony proved unstable from start to finish. Within his lifetime Takauji never achieved a steady grip over his vassals, and he never acquired a sufficient authority other than military force upon which he could ultimately rely. His use of family ties and claims of feudal overlordship proved insufficient. Quarrels within his family and among the vassal *shugo*, now flushed with a sense of their own autonomy, constantly divided the Ashikaga forces. The Ashikaga family lacked sufficient wealth and military resources of its own to dominate the country without the support of its vassals. And so the shogunate from the beginning took the form of an uneasy alliance of powerful families over which the shogun frequently held but a precarious preeminence.

But from time to time the Ashikaga shoguns did manage to put together an alliance which held the peace for a number of decades at a time. The most notable of such periods occurred during the latter part of the rule of Yoshimitsu, the third shogun, and lasted

[7] Matsumoto Shimpachirō, "Gaisetsu," in *Nihon rekishi kōsa, 3, Chūsei, 1* (Tokyo, 1951), 34. Hereafter cited as Matsumoto, "Gaisetsu."

for nearly two decades after 1392. By that time the southern court had capitulated, Kyushu had been pacified, and recalcitrant *shugo* such as the Yamana had made their peace with the Ashikaga. Yoshimitsu, more than any Ashikaga shogun before or after, was able to act the absolute hegemon of the country. This was the high point of Ashikaga power, and it is usual in describing the Ashikaga shogunate to picture it as it appeared during these years.

Ashikaga Takauji had established his headquarters in Kyoto, at Nijō Takakura. Yoshimitsu moved the *bakufu* in 1378 to Muromachi and after 1398 to the Kitayama district. As a general rule the shogun or a member of the Ashikaga family personally attended the affairs of the *bakufu* and made the effort to prevent the kind of usurpation of power which had followed the rise of the Hōjō at Kamakura. After 1362, the office of chief administrator (*kanrei*) was created and assigned to one among the three most powerful of the shogun's vassals: the Shiba, Hatakeyama, or Hosokawa. The Ashikaga shogun, for all his later weakness, was more of a real ruler, and the *kanrei* never attained the influence of the office of *shikken* through which the Hōjō literally became all powerful in Kamakura. Taken together, the three families who held hereditary title to the post of *kanrei* represented a balance of real power among the *shugo*.[8] The heads of these three houses formed an inner council which, when they supported the shogun, gave him the necessary backing with which to act as hegemon of the country.[9]

Unlike the Kamakura shogun whose chief support came from control of administrative and proprietary rights within the imperial system, the material resources of the Ashikaga shogun derived chiefly from the private incomes and military forces drawn from the shogun's own territories. The shogun's lands included some 60 *shōen* throughout the country.[10] At the time he became shogun, Ashikaga Takauji had his main holdings in Shimōsa, Mutsu, Sagami, Mikawa, Tamba, Mimasaka, and Awa. He was also *shugo* of Kazusa and Mikawa. The Ashikaga house therefore

[8] Satō Shin'ichi, "Shugo-ryōkokusei no tenkai," in *Shin Nihonshi taikei*, 3 *Chūsei shakai* (Tokyo, 1954), 107-108. Henceforth cited as Satō, "Shugo." *Sekai rekishi jiten*, 18.213.

[9] Matsumoto, "Gaisetsu," 53.

[10] Sugiyama Hiroshi, "Muromachi bakufu," in *Nihon rekishi kōza*, 3, *Chūsei-kinsei* (Tokyo, 1957), 61. Hereafter cited as Sugiyama, "Muromachi."

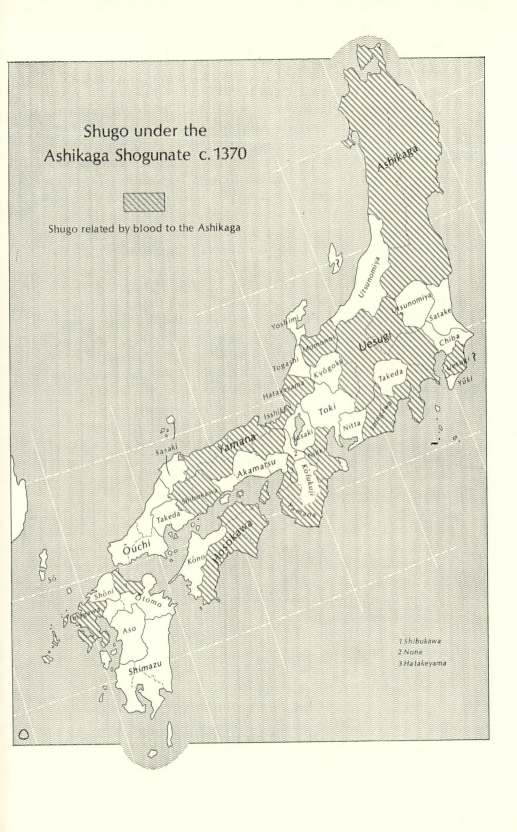

Shugo under the
Ashikaga Shogunate c. 1370

Shugo related by blood to the Ashikaga

Ashikaga

Utsunomiya

Yoshimi

Momonoi

Togashi

Hatakeyama

Isshiki

Yamana

Akamatsu

Shibukawa

Takeda

Ōuchi

Kōno

Sō

Shōni

Imagawa

Otomo

Aso

Shimazu

Hosokawa

Sasaki

Takeda

Kyōgoku

Toki

Nitta

Imagawa

Sasaki

Nikki

Kōfukuji

Yamana

Uesugi

Utsunomiya

Satake

Chiba

Uesugi?

Yūki

Sasaki

?

1 Shibukawa
2 None
3 Hatakeyama

had two prime provincial bases, one in Shimōsa and the other in Mikawa.[11] It was from these territories that the private vassals (*fudai-hikan*) of the shogun were drawn. The shogun's authority was, of course, nationwide, but outside of his own territories it was exerted indirectly through vassals of the status of *shugo*.

Under the shogun the government of the country was placed in the hands of the *shugo*. By the time of Yoshimitsu most of the *shugo* had been carefully selected by the shogun and were considered trustworthy. The majority (14 out of 21) were branches of the Ashikaga family. While they held surnames different from the Ashikaga, they were included among the cadet lines referred to as *ichimon*. The remaining seven were families, such as the Shimazu, who had been subdued to vassalage but were too powerful for elimination. They were given "outside" (*tozama*) status.[12]

The Ashikaga shoguns from the first had difficulty in retaining the loyalty of the *shugo*. To guarantee loyal service, primary reliance was placed on branch members of Ashikaga lineage, families such as the Hosokawa, Shiba, Hatakeyama, Isshiki, Yamana, and Imagawa, who had followed Takauji out of the Kantō. These families formed the core of the Ashikaga power structure and administration. Furthermore, in order to extend the hands of the shogunate to the east and west, members of the Ashikaga main line were set up in strategic spots as governors-general in the Kantō, in the far north, and in Kyushu. *Tozama shugo* were of two rather different types. Those far distant from Kyoto, such as the Shimazu and Ōtomo, were able to retain a wide area of local independence but were largely excluded from shogunal affairs. Those who held provinces close to the capital, such as the Kyōgoku, Rokkaku, Akamatsu, Toki, and Ōuchi had given voluntary support to the Ashikaga and were considered trustworthy. They were consequently assigned positions of major responsibility within the *bakufu* in later years.

From the mid-fourteenth century on, the government of Japan should be thought of in its simplest terms as a central administration (*bakufu*) under the shogun placed over numerous local administrations under the *shugo*. Legitimacy was still provided by the emperor, whose delegate the shogun was. But it was largely on the basis of feudal loyalty between shogun and vassal *shugo*

[11] Satō, "Shugo," 87.
[12] Sugiyama, "Muromachi," 58.

that the exercise of authority in the Ashikaga system was made effective. Within the Ashikaga system the *shugo* performed at both the central and local levels. *Shugo* habitually maintained residences in Kyoto as well as in the provinces. In Kyoto they took part in the operation of the *bakufu*, serving in major policy boards or functional offices, providing armed forces for the shogunal guards and armies, and attending the shogunal needs in various ways. They periodically returned to the provinces where they were charged with the administration of their territories.

Since the shogun was still legally conceived of as chief of the *shugo* (he himself was *shugo* of Kazusa and Mikawa) it is the rights and powers of the *shugo* which best reveal the extent to which military authority had expanded under the Ashikaga. By the end of the fourteenth century the *shugo* had developed into true regional rulers, having absorbed most of the governmental functions performed by officials of the earlier imperial local administration as well as many of the rights of proprietorship derived from their status in the *shōen* and *kōryō* as *jitō*.[13] In administrative terms the *shugo* of Ashikaga times can best be thought of as combining the powers of civil governor (*kokushu*), the military governor (*shugo*), and the military stewards (*jitō*), although this was never made explicit. During the brief Kemmu Restoration, it will be recalled, the same individual frequently had been appointed to both civil and military governorships.[14] After the restoration it became increasingly common to omit the appointment of civil governor, leaving to the *shugo* the ultimate authority over local affairs. *Shugo* jurisdictions were referred to as *kankoku* or *bunkoku* (reflecting the concept of proprietary governorship of the late Heian period).

The increased powers of the *shugo* were not haphazardly acquired and in most cases found legal support in the Ashikaga code. Specifically provided for in the code were the new rights of pursuit of criminals (*karita-rōzeki*) and judicial inspection and settlement of land disputes (*shisetsu-jungyō*), both of which gave the *shugo* entrance into the lands of civil and military proprietors.[15] Supervision of temples and shrines and the authority to carry out land surveys was taken over from the provincial governors. Of great importance also was a fundamental change in the duties

---

[13] *Ibid.*, 49.   [14] Itō, *Hōken*, 142.
[15] Nagahara, "Namboku," 24; *Sekai rekishi jiten*, 22.205.

exercised by the *shugo* within the shogunal system itself. Under the Kamakura system all *gokenin* throughout the country were considered direct housemen of the shogun; thus *jitō* came only indirectly under the authority of the *shugo*. By Ashikaga times the *shugo* stood between the shogun and the lesser provincial families. In the provinces, now, the *shugo* confirmed the holdings of *jitō*, or more likely had absorbed the *jitō*'s powers into their own.[16] Military service was now recruited not in the name of the shogun but by the *shugo,* who thus became the heads of regional hierarchies of military men. When the *shugo* gained the ability to distribute lands captured in war or left vacant as a result of military action their local independence was nearing complete- ness, for this was a privilege which had once adhered to the shogun alone. Finally *shugo* received various supra-*shōen* powers derived from the civil governors to recruit labor and to collect special taxes (*tansen*) within the provinces under their jurisdic- tion. Thus while their powers did not specifically include all those of the former civil and military governors, they did come more and more to comprise a full complement of the powers of government at the local level. The ascendancy of the Ashikaga *shugo* thus robbed the civil governors of their function, so that the title rapidly lost all political significance.[17] The only provinces in which governorships remained after the fifteenth century were those of Ise, Hida, and Tosa, and these were quite special cases. On the other hand, military houses of *shugo* rank freely acquired the titles of provincial governors for their own social distinction.

The new circumstances to which the military aristocracy of Ashikaga times had risen was made apparent in numerous ways. Beginning with the shogun, the great families of provincial aris- tocratic provenance took up residence in Kyoto and began to assume the cultural guise of the old nobility, building palaces, patronizing temples, dressing and behaving in courtly fashion. In their lives the *shugo* sought to exemplify the new political status they had achieved. This was particularly evident in the provinces, where the *shugo* and their great vassals now consti- tuted the only real aristocracy. The civil court families were too politically weak and too much removed from practical affairs to serve as anything more than a shadowy reminder of the days of

[16] Yasuda, *Shōen,* 274.   [17] Satō "Shugo," 106-115.

imperial grandeur. No longer did scions of the Fujiwara or the imperial family descend to the provinces, there to dominate local affairs in the name of the court. Their position was now taken by the military nobility, who by their acquisition of outstanding landed wealth, political power, and noble status fused at the local level the tokens of superiority which had previously been divided between the *bushi* and *kuge*.

Such changes in the way of life of the provincial military elite were the natural outcome of the changing capacities of the military families, as against the old court and religious bodies, to profit from the landed proprietorships which still persisted in Japan. Although it was not until the end of the fifteenth century that the *shōen* system finally came to an end and the court aristocracy was cut off entirely from its economic support, the elimination of civil authority over the land system was more or less complete by the time the Ashikaga type *shugo* had entrenched themselves. The wars of the dynasties had done much to weaken the prestige and wealth of the imperial family and the court nobility. The bitter years during which the court had been divided into two camps had left the whole structure of *shōen* proprietorships in confusion. With the defeat of the southern court, many *shōen* were lost outright to their civil proprietors. The imperial house, for instance, lost most of the *shōen* held by the junior branch, for Go-Daigo, confident of his ability to revive the imperial system of government, had actually given back to the public domain the *shōen* in his possession. These were the portfolios of Hachijōin, part of Shichijōin, and half of Muromachiin.[18] The failure of the Go-Daigo cause meant that all these lands passed into the hands of military proprietors. Remaining to the imperial house were only the estates of the senior branch of the family, among them the Chōkōdō and half of the Muromachiin proprietorships. Meanwhile the imperial family had lost its control over the public domains of the provinces. By Ashikaga times even the practice of granting provinces as proprietorships was abandoned or taken over by the shogun. In Bizen, for instance, while a few parcels of public domain remained on the books, these were held under the disposal rights of the shogun.

As for the other court families, during and after the war of

---

[18] Okuno, *Kōshitsu*, 39.

the dynasties, many of them were extinguished and their estates taken over by local interests. Many other courtiers, finding that the titles to their *shōen* were empty of economic return, moved to the country and began to live directly off their lands in a final desperate attempt to salvage a living from their inheritances. Within a generation, these families ceased to retain their identity as courtiers. Those few court families whose prestige was too great to permit their complete elimination, notably the main Fujiwara families, remained in the capital and eventually became utterly dependent upon the shogun and *shugo* to protect their absentee interests. By the middle of the fifteenth century such families were living mainly on the sufferance of the great provincial military lords who, out of a lingering sense of obligation, or because the courtiers could provide certain cultural and prestige benefits, continued to make token payments on *shōen* in the provinces under their control.[19]

Among the old non-military interests the religious bodies alone managed to improve their position somewhat under the Ashikaga regime. The reasons for this will become more apparent in the following chapter. In an age of sincere religious belief, of course, temples and shrines possessed a spiritual power which protected them from the most flagrant violation of their rights. Buddhist establishments such as the great monastic temples of Kōyasan, Tōdaiji, Kōfukuji, Tōji, and Saidaiji were generally able to take care of their local interests, however, through their branch temples and the extensive bureaucratic organizations staffed by their priesthood. In the struggle for power both at the capital and in the provinces, the great temples had certain advantages. They were able to recruit and maintain large bodies of armed monks for protection or coercion. Their considerable military power thus enhanced their status as objects of favor by competing court groups during the unsettled years before and after the Kemmu Restoration. The emperor Go-Daigo, for instance, gave liberally to Enryakuji and Tōji to curry their support, and as a result Osada-no-shō in Bizen passed to Tōji in 1326. The newly emergent military aristocracy also gave generously to the temples. Thus in most locations, including Bizen, the religious establishments increased their proprietary holdings at this time.

[19] Itō, *Hōken*, 130-132.

But the ability to retain or increase the number of proprietor-ships was to mean increasingly little as time went on. For one thing, with the establishment of the Ashikaga shogunate the entire legal superstructure of the *shōen* system was largely taken out of the hands of the civil authorities. By the time of Yoshimitsu the ultimate legal authority relating to the *shōen* now resided en-tirely with the shogun and extended to the provinces through the *shugo*. Courtiers and temples were therefore obliged to take their *shōen* problems to the *bakufu*. It was the shogun who now de-termined such important matters as the division of shares of in-come between civil and military sectors. During the fourteenth century the shogun permitted a constant encroachment of the military interests over those of civil proprietors.

By the end of the Kamakura period many *shōen* had been divided between military and civil proprietary sectors. This prac-tice had gone furthest in the peripheral provinces. In central Japan, court and religious bodies had had better success in re-taining their absentee land rights. But during the north-south dynasty wars, those local families who had involved themselves in the fighting had everywhere broken with the customary re-straint of *shōen* or *jitō* law, in many instances claiming the entire proceeds of *shōen* on the pretext of military necessity. When peace was restored, the Ashikaga shogunate saw that a return to pre-Kemmu conditions would be impossible, since the costs of maintaining military establishments had grown so drastically. As a result the shogunate legalized a practice known as *hanzei*, or half rights. Under it the *shugo* were empowered to hold back for military purposes one half of the *shōen* proceeds destined to the absentee proprietor. Although in 1368 the lands of the imperial family, the principal Fujiwara house, and the primary holdings of the great temples were exempted from the *hanzei* system, this order had little effect in limiting the further encroachments upon the non-military proprietorships.[20]

The *hanzei* provision made for important changes in the overall system of land management and local administration. Although unlike the *chūbun* procedure, *hanzei* practice did not result in an immediate division of proprietary rights over the *shōen*, it gave the *shugo* authority to hold back one-half of the

[20] *Sekai rekishi jiten,* 22.305-306.

proprietor's share at the provincial level. Before long, therefore, this was actually translated into a division of the land base, placing still further holdings under the proprietary powers of the military families.[21] For the civil aristocracy this was a heavy blow. For in those holdings in which the *shitaji-chūbun* division had not been carried out, the *hanzei* order provided the excuse for an immediate half-and-half division of land rights. Where such a division had already been made, it became the justification of a further reduction by half of the absentee proprietor's income.

The other special feature of the *hanzei* practice was that it was enforced by the *shugo*, not the *jitō*. This meant that the provincial military governors automatically acquired fiscal rights in all non-military *shōen* within the area over which they were given jurisdiction, and their rights were quickly extended through the practice of contract management on behalf of absentee proprietorships. As the *jitō* had done previously, now the *shugo* began to assume the entire responsibility of rent collection for the court or temple proprietors, setting up their agents (called *daikan*) to manage the *shōen*.

Once this had happened the authority of the civil proprietors to interfere in local affairs became minimal. The *shugo* had become the sole authorities in the provinces. And as they became increasingly independent of shogunal control, they became the real masters of the countryside. By such time, the *shugo* had converted themselves into what Japanese historians have called *shugo-daimyō*, that is, great regional hegemons with extensive territorial holdings. The provinces over which the *shugo-daimyō* held sway were referred to as their *ryō-koku* (proprietary provinces).

It is characteristic of the provinces of the Kibi area that not one of them gave rise to a local family of sufficient capacity to hold the title of *shugo* for any length of time. The Matsuda, with headquarters at Tomiyama on the lower Asahi river plain, were named *shugo* of Bizen at the time of the Kemmu wars and managed to retain the title until 1364. The Takahashi and Kō families based at Matsuyama on the Takahashi River, and the Shibukawa and Hosokawa of Kamogata were successively named *shugo* of Bitchū in these early years. But none of these families

---

[21] Shimizu Mitsuo, *Nihon chūsei no sonraku* (Tokyo, 1942), 343-344.

was in a position to do much more than hold a title that was greater than their capacity to fight off competitors, and they were eventually superseded.

More typical of the Kibi provinces during the period of *shugo-daimyō* ascendancy in Japan was the intrusion of powerful influences from adjoining provinces. Bizen generally found itself under the control of a *shugo* whose primary base lay in the province of Harima to the east. This meant that Bizen was contested by the Akamatsu and the Yamana families. Bitchū, most often assigned to a branch of the Hosokawa house, was in reality controlled by the main Hosokawa headquarters in Shikoku. Later on the Mōri, with headquarters at Hiroshima in Aki province, became paramount in Bingo and Bitchū. Mimasaka, constantly subject to the shifting balance of outside *shugo*, fell successively to the Akamatsu or Yamana from the east, or later to the Amako from the northwest.

If the area of the four provinces did not give rise to indigenous families able to warrant the title of *shugo*, it did support numerous local families of secondary importance. Among these the most powerful achieved the status of deputy governor, or *shugodai*, under one or another of the *shugo* based in the adjoining provinces. In Bizen in addition to the Matsuda, who fell to deputy status after 1364, there was the Urakami, foremost vassals of the Akamatsu. In Bitchū the base of the *shugodai* was generally Matsuyama castle at the site of the present city of Takahashi. Here the Akiba, Ueno, Shō, and Mimura successively dominated local affairs while acknowledging their subordination as deputies of the Hosokawa and later the Mōri. In Mimasaka no single center achieved local preeminence. Families such as the Gotō of Yunogō and the Miura of Katsuyama stood out, however, in the military struggle. (See page 264 below.)

The new Ashikaga order was imposed upon Bizen between the time of the Kemmu wars and the establishment of the Akamatsu hegemony over the province some time after 1364. From that time until 1484, when the Akamatsu house lost its ability to control its deputies, the Matsuda and Urakami, Bizen existed under the governance of a typical *shugo-daimyō* house. We can imagine that such control was never so systematic nor so effective as that provided by the civil governors and shogunal officials of the Kamakura period. The times were unsettled, warfare was frequent, and the pattern of land ownership was undergoing drastic change. Nonetheless a certain style of government developed during these years in which the *shugo-daimyō* played the dominant role. In local affairs Bizen was governed increasingly in a manner congenial to the military aristocracy in which authority followed the channels of vassalage and enfeoffment. But also, insofar as the *shugo* combined the function of civil and military governors, they exercised certain vestiges of imperial authority. Just as the *shugo* and *jitō* of the twelfth century were legitimate creations of the imperial system, so were the *shugo* of Ashikaga times the products of imperial law. Theirs was still to this extent a transitional form of government.

VIII. BIZEN UNDER THE HOUSE OF AKAMATSU

THE Akamatsu house of Harima province was one of the main participants in the struggle which attended the rise of Ashikaga Takauji in central Japan. The house itself was of relatively humble origin, taking its name from Akamatsu village in the *shōen* of Sayō, a large court proprietorship held by the Kujō family. During the Kamakura period the Akamatsu served as *jitō*, and by the end of the Kamakura period they had extended branches throughout Sayō district and had established marriage alliances with *jitō* families in nearby *shōen*.[1]

At the time of the Kemmu wars the Akamatsu chief, Norimura, was able to put a sufficient force into the field to call conspicuous attention to himself. Having thrown in his lot with the Ashikaga, he joined in the abortive attack on Kyoto in 1335, resisted the bitter assault of Nitta Yoshisada during 1335, and then, as Ashikaga Takauji fought his way back from the west, joined in the final campaigns which gained the capital and secured the shogunate for Takauji. Akamatsu Norimura was probably named *shugo* of Harima in 1336. From this point the Akamatsu rose rapidly under the Ashikaga patronage. In rapid succession, a branch of the Akamatsu family acquired the military governorship of Settsu province, a cadet branch acquired lands in Tamba and Harima, and still a third was given holdings in Settsu and in Bizen in Umaya-no-gō. The post of *shugo* of Bizen was entrusted to the head of the main line in 1364. And in 1392 an Akamatsu replaced the Yamana as *shugo* of Mimasaka. This brought the house to the pinnacle of its power. The family as a whole held five military governorships and occupied a leading position among the Ashikaga vassals at the capital. The special trust which the shogun had in the Akamatsu house is revealed by the appointment of the head of the family to the position of chief of the military council, a responsibility reserved to only three other trusted vassals of which all were kinsmen of the Ashikaga.

But despite the rapid rise of the Akamatsu in the councils of the Ashikaga, the family was never completely secure either in the trust of the Ashikaga or within the province of Harima. In

---

[1] Mizuno Kyōichirō, "Shugo Akamatsu-shi no ryōkoku shihai to Kakitsu no hen," in *Shirin*, 42.2 (1959), 254-281. Hereafter cited as Mizuno, "Akamatsu." Also *Okayama-shi shi*, 2.991.

Kyoto the position of the *shugo* was a precarious one, and as long as the southern court remained active, the pledged vassals of the shogun were constantly shifting their allegiances. The Akamatsu were particularly harassed by this problem because their closest rivals, the Yamana, masters of Inaba, Hōki, Mimasaka, Tamba, and Tango provinces, were so ambitious as to frequently turn against the Ashikaga. The Yamana not only surrounded the Akamatsu geographically, but were frequently at odds with them politically. In 1353 the Yamana switched to the southern side, and by 1360 the Akamatsu were everywhere on the defensive against the Yamana, losing their outposts along the Mimasaka border. In Bitchū and Bizen the Akamatsu, though reinforced by the Hosokawa of Shikoku, were unable to cope with the Yamana armies. It was even with considerable difficulty that they held on to their home province of Harima. But in 1364 the Yamana were back in the Ashikaga camp. Briefly again in 1379 the Yamana used the southern cause as a means of pressing new demands upon the shogunate. Returning later to the Ashikaga fold, the Yamana during the 1380's gained possession of the additional governorships of Izumi, Kii, Tajima, Izumo, and Iki. By this time they held twelve provinces, one-sixth of all Japan. Then suddenly, in 1391, the Yamana turned their massive forces against the shogunate in a further effort at expansion. They were thoroughly defeated and cut back to the three provinces of Tajima, Inaba, and Hōki. The governorships stripped from them at this time were divided among their rivals. It was as a result of this victory over the Yamana that the Akamatsu regained Bizen and received the governorship of Mimasaka.[2] The year 1392, which saw the capitulation of the southern court, also ushered in a period of comparative security for the Akamatsu in Harima. Yet a glance at the provincial bases of such a family helps to explain the precariousness of the support upon which it could rely. In terms of actual land and power in hand the *shugo* of the Ashikaga period had many difficult problems with which to cope.

The power relationships of the *shugo* of the early Ashikaga period to the provinces over which they were appointed was based

---

[2] Mizuno Kyōichirō, "Namboku-chō nairanki ni okeru Yamana-shi no dōkō," in *Okayama Daigaku Hōbungakubu gakujutsu kiyō*, 13 (May 1960), 57-70; Ōae, *Bizen*, 80-88. The largest number of *shugo*ships held by the Yamana is generally given as eleven. This is probably due to the fact that Yamashiro, the home province, was not considered a private holding.

on three prime factors. First, they were local proprietors of outstanding size and status. Second, they exercised certain legal
rights of administration as military governors. Third, they functioned as centers of extensive military alliances which extended
outward from their own and branch families to other *bushi* of the
province. In none of these categories was the *shugo's* capacity
comprehensive. It was characteristic of the *shugo* houses, except
for such long-established ones as the Shimazu of Satsuma, that
they had acquired comprehensive authority over only a fraction
of the territory of their home province. Rather they held a variety
of rights in a large number of widely scattered locations, both in
their home province and elsewhere. Such rights were still legally
phrased in terms of *shōen* practice and included some outright
proprietorships, but more commonly a variety of *jitō, shōkan,* or
hanzei rights which were accountable to the customary limitations of *shōen* practice.

The expansion of Akamatsu land holdings is not well enough
recorded to afford a complete picture of the family's economic
foundations, but remaining documents can give us some hints as
to their general nature. An official confirmation of Akamatsu land
holdings issued by the shogun in 1350 reveals the possessions of
the main family in Harima during the early years of its governorship over that province as follows:

> An order that Akamatsu Mimasaka-no-gon-no-kami Norisuke
> will forthwith hold as proprietor:
>> In Harima Province,
>>> Within Sayō-no-shō:
>>>> Akamatsu-kami-mura
>>>> Mikawa-mura
>>> Within Egawa-no-gō:
>>>> Ōta-kata
>>>> Hirose-kata
>>>> Hirooka-kata
>>> Motoida
>>> Shimo-Tokuhisa
>> Also in Harima,
>>> Within Goka-no-shō:
>>> Shuku-mura (including the *myō* proper to the *gesu,*
>>>> *kumon,* and *mandokoro*)

Ki-mura

Ōtsu-mura

In Harima,

Awakawa-no-shō, Shimo-mura

In Harima,

The *kannushi* rights of the Shirahata-chinju-hachiman
and the Kasuga shrines

In Hōki Province,

Yabashi-gun

Ōi-shimo-no-gō

The above are inheritances of the deceased father, Enshin,
and are asserted to be among the lands held by the various
branch families. You were directed by the document of this
year, seventh month, 28th day with their possession and
management (*ryōshō*). It is so ordered. 1350, 12th month,
5th day.[3]

This was the portion of the Akamatsu holdings which descended
through the main (*sōryō*) line of the house. From it we can see
that the family had its base in the village of Akamatsu, where by
now the fortress of Shirahata had been built. In addition the
family had acquired various rights to parts of *shōen* scattered
throughout Harima and Hōki. Branches of the Akamatsu house,
of course, had by this time acquired further rights and properties
in Harima and elsewhere.

As the Akamatsu rose to further prominence, their lands also
were increased, both within Harima and in the provinces of
Mimasaka, Bizen, and elsewhere. Lands previously held by former
shugo frequently changed hands as the result of the wars of rivalry
we have noted. Thus Akamatsu Norisuke received Nyūta-no-
shō, which was the prime *shugo* holding in Bizen in 1365.[4] His
son and successor Yoshinori received territories in Chitsu-gun in
Inaba, Asako-gun in Tajima, and Nakajima in Settsu.[5] Despite
these additions, the holdings of the main line of the Akamatsu
remained but a small percentage of the total territory of any one
province, even Harima. Moreover, the holdings were widely
dispersed. In fact, the case of the Akamatsu is rather more favorable than most, for among the *shugo* who came out of the Kantō

---

[3] Mizuno, "Akamatsu," 257.   [4] *Okayama-shi shi*, 2.1001.
[5] *Ibid.*, 2.1004.

with the Ashikaga, many still had their home territories in the east country though they were given military governorships over provinces far to the west. As will be revealed later, the Akamatsu lost their territories to the Yamana in 1441 but regained the governorships of Harima, Bizen, and Mimasaka in 1467. At the time of their second rise their lands were scattered more widely outside of Harima in Kaga, Bizen, Izumo, and Ise.[6]

Not only were the territories over which the *shugo* held land rights scattered, the rights themselves were of a wide variety and generally several degrees short of full proprietorship. Most commonly the Akamatsu held *jitō-shiki*, in other words the *jitō* salary lands or lands acquired by the *jitō* after division under the *shitaji-chūbun* system. In the *shōen* listed in the 1350 document of investiture, while the Akamatsu house was in possession of the *jitō* rights to Sayō-no-shō, the actual land over which it was proprietor was limited to five villages within the *shō*. The remaining territory was held by agreement with the civil proprietor or as hereditary grants made by previous shogun or military governors.

Endowed with a scattered and complicated handful of landed support the Akamatsu chief, having acquired the title of *shugo* and through it the legal backing of the Ashikaga shogun, asserted his prerogatives of military governorship over Harima and adjoining provinces. The legitimate powers of the *shugo*, as we have noted, were those of military command and appointment, administrative supervision, pursuit of criminals, adjudication of land disputes, and the collection of special military dues and imposts. We have no direct evidence on how the *hanzei* system was carried out in the provinces under Akamatsu jurisdiction, but there is no question that it was put into force. The Akamatsu also took over contract rights for a number of *shōen* in Harima and Bizen. Thus in Bizen, Tottori-no-shō was managed under the *shugo-uke* system sometime before 1441. From comments appearing in the court diaries of this time, it is clear that once the *shugo* took over as contract manager all internal affairs of the *shōen* passed into the hands of the *shugo*. The imperial family, absentee proprietor of Tottori-no-shō, was forced to rely entirely on the *shugo* or on the shogun for redress of grievances in its *shōen*.[7] In *shōen* held

[6] *Ibid.*, 2.1019.

[7] Arimoto Minoru, "Muromachi jidai ni okeru Bizen-no-kuni Tottori-no-shō," in *Kibi chihōshi geppō*, 1.4 (App., 1952), 4-7; *Nōchi shi*, 416-422.

by temples, the *shugo* generally had to be more careful of the interests of the proprietor. For instance, in Niimi-no-shō of Bitchu, the proprietary temple Tōji continued to send a financial overseer to represent its interests as late as 1461.[8] But the court aristocracy had no such resources. The Akamatsu probably acted as contractor or perhaps proprietor for the remaining *kokugaryō* of the provinces under their jurisdiction.

The growing authority of the Akamatsu in their capacity as local governors can ultimately be documented. We know that several attempts were made to collect province-wide taxes, *tansen* and *munebetsusen,* in Bizen.[9] And there are numerous documents revealing the Akamatsu attempt to prevent the alienation of land or the process whereby the family head granted or confirmed land rights to individuals. For the people of Bizen, therefore, the *shugo* became the prime authority, much as the provincial governors had once been.

But there was a fundamental difference in the manner of the *shugo's* exercise of authority from that of the old civil governors. We have seen that the land base controlled by the *shugo* was hardly sufficient for the exercise of local hegemony. Nor did the backing of the shogunate carry absolute weight. Rather it was in large measure the system of private control over other military families in the provinces that provided the effective element in the *shugo's* ability to impose his influence upon the local area. This system of control was partially patriarchal and partially feudal. The complex pattern of interrelationships between *shugo* and other military families in their jurisdictional territories had been built up in several stages. For the Akamatsu, for example, there was first the inner *sōryō* system of kinship organization. The main line with its preponderance of holdings in Harima acted as the center of a kinship system which included branch Akamatsu families, one of which held the governorship of Settsu with lands in Tamba and Harima, while another began with the *jitō* rights to *shōen* in Arima-gun in Settsu and Umaya-no-gō in Bizen. Once the Akamatsu attached themselves to the Ashikaga as high-ranking *shugo*, their cadet branches rapidly began to acquire positions of influence and high status in the military aristocracy. Thus, of the close kin of the Akamatsu, five gained honorary titles of provincial governorships: Izu, Kōzuke, Shimotsuke, Tōtōmi, and

[8] Sugiyama Hiroshi, *Shōen kaitai katei no kenkyū* (Tokyo, 1959), 209.
[9] *Tsūshi*, 1.950-952.

Noto.[10] The family, as an assemblage, comprised a power group considerably larger than that of the main family alone. Conversely such *shugo* families, as they expanded, maintained an inner solidarity through their kinship ties and their subordination to the main family head.

Aside from the cadet families which were held together under the concept of first kin (*ikke*), the Akamatsu main line could count on the support of a number of less closely related families which had branched off at earlier times and had assumed surnames derived from their villages of residence. This group of families was extremely large, the following being only a partial list of the names which the Akamatsu included among their extended kin: Uno, Majima, Kōzuki, Kashiwabara, Bessho, Saigusa, Ōta, Sayō, Kamauchi, Toyofuku, Nakajima, Nakayama, Tokuhira, Fukuhara, Suiden.[11] These families were incorporated into the extended organization of the Akamatsu house as kin (*ichizoku*). The villages with which their names are associated were clustered conspicuously in central Harima in and about Sayō-no-shō. Individually these families had acquired a variety of land rights in a large number of *shōen* in Harima and neighboring provinces, so that their collective holdings must have rivaled those of the main Akamatsu house. Over such kin families the Akamatsu chief could exercise several powers. First as *shugo* he claimed their military allegiance in the name of the shogun. As a superior kinsman he claimed the right of the *sōryō* over them. As the ultimate authority over certain lands and rights within the province, he was able to confirm, protect, or grant new land rights to them.[12] In other words, they were his administrative subordinates, his kinsmen, and his vassals.

In addition to the kin group, the Akamatsu sought to exert control over as many other military houses as possible in the provinces which they governed. In this case the task was more difficult. Many such families were of long-standing local prominence and were not inclined to subordinate themselves easily to Ashikaga or Akamatsu authority. Furthermore, the wars of dynasties gave constant opportunity to those who might wish to oppose the Akamatsu to justify their cause. The standard techniques used by the *shugo* to bring such families into line was military pressure, alliances of marriage, or grants of land based upon conditions of

---

[10] *Okayama-shi shi*, 2.991.   [11] *Ibid.*
[12] Mizuno, "Akamatsu," 259; *Okayama-shi shi*, 2.1220.

vassalage. Once securely enlisted as vassal housemen, the *shugo* aided these families in extending their land holdings and enlarging their spheres of influence over the *shōen* in which they resided, thus further cementing the interrelationships. The following list of the most important of the Akamatsu housemen indicates that the Akamatsu were able to enlist a sizable portion of the landed families of Harima as their non-kin vassals (*hikan*). Such were the Urakami, Kitano, Tomita, Kodera, Nakamura, Uehara, Hori, Kushibashi, Yorifuji, Akashi, Yakushiji, Ose, Kidokoro, Iwami, Gotō, and Kinugasa.[13] An important feature of the ability of any *shugo* to maintain authority over his housemen was the possibility of creating a balance between kin and non-kin families.

Whether for kin or non-kin housemen, an important link in the relationship between *shugo* and vassals derived from the practice of verification and confirmation of land rights. Numerous documents remain to reveal the activity of members of the Akamatsu family as the foremost source of cadastral authority in Harima and Bizen. To his kinsman Majima Norikiyo in 1365 the head of the Akamatsu house granted "one-third of the *jitō* rights of Iwami-no-shō in Itō-gun and the *jitō* rights entire of Noguchi-no-ho." To a non-kin vassal, Shimazu Tadakane, he granted in 1338 the *jitō* rights to Shimo-Ibo-no-shō-west and in 1349 the *jitō* rights to the eastern portion of the same *shō*. For the Asaka family he confirmed the following holdings: "In Shisō-gun, Asaka-no-ho, the rights of the civil steward and clerk; the rights of the clerk of Mikata-nishi-no-shō; and dry and wet fields in Himeji village."[14] The Asaka were a family of long residence in Harima, perhaps original *shōen* officials who had established themselves as a leading landed *bushi* family in their locale. Enlisted into the Akamatsu following, the family served as loyal non-kin vassals.

The Akamatsu capacity to act as guarantor, or grantor, of the above types of rights and holdings was, of course, the result of long years of piecemeal acquisition of scattered rights under the *shōen* system plus the extensive military powers accumulated while they served as *jitō* and *shugo*. The new authority granted by the Ashikaga shogun also added to the *shugo*'s ability to reward his vassals with land. The application of the *hanzei* system must have released considerable land to *shugo* disposition. As evidence we

---

[13] *Okayama-shi shi*, 2.991.
[14] Mizuno, "Akamatsu," 259-260.

learn that during the 1350's the Awauda family was granted the *hanzei* portion of Tanaka-no-shō.[15] Or again, in 1368, Akamatsu Masanori granted Namba Yukitoyo the fields vacated by the previous *jitō* in Bizen's Tottori-no-shō "for military provisions."[16]

Not all of the rearrangement of land rights under the *shugo* was accomplished peacefully. As the outcome of wars between opposing *shugo* the victor claimed the vacated holdings of the vanquished. At the provincial level, while the shogun had ultimate powers of disposal, there was little likelihood that the shogun would interfere beyond a certain formal involvement. Within the province, the *shugo* was able to determine the smaller dispositions as part of his prerogatives over his housemen. Such were the expectations of war, but there were other examples of the ways in which *bushi* families stretched the letter of the law in order to extend their interests. In the above-mentioned Tanaka-no-shō the former resident officials were soon complaining that the Awauda family had extended their *hanzei* rights into complete proprietorship (*shitaji*). In the Tōji estate of Yano-no-shō the temple's agent reported that the Akima family was asserting complete control under cover of the *shugo's* grant of *hanzei* rights.[17] Such complaints from the remaining civil interests were generally directed to the shogun over the head of the *shugo*. But they must have had little effect, for although the shogun might have communicated the complaints to the *shugo*, he generally did not have the power or the inclination to discipline his great vassals.

At any rate, the fourteenth and fifteenth centuries were notable for the rapid change in land tenures. Not only did the military houses constantly encroach on the absentee civil proprietors, but they also led the way in a general process of consolidation of holdings in which the rights of absentee proprietors, even including absentee military houses, were eliminated in favor of resident proprietorships. To cite but one example, the Narita family of Musashi, as was common in the Kamakura period, had acquired the land rights of the *jitō-shiki* of Sutomi in Harima. They lost these rights in 1339 when the Akamatsu granted them to one of their vassals on the grounds that the Narita family did not reside in Harima and so were unable to give them proper man-

[15] *Ibid.*
[16] *Okayama-shi shi*, 2.1222-1223.
[17] Mizuno, "Akamatsu," 261.

agement.[18] Although the *shōen* structure continued in external form, the vital authority of disposition of land rights was flowing more and more into the hands of the *shugo* or of his major vassals.

Yet the process of conversion to military rule was by no means complete, and at almost every level of activity the *shugo* of Ashikaga times confronted competitive interests. The Akamatsu of Harima were thus involved in a constant struggle for survival: at the top against other *shugo*, against the lingering authority of the old court powers, and even against the shogun; at the bottom against the independence or even treachery of "local men," the so-called *kokujin*. The success of the Akamatsu as provincial hegemons in large measure fluctuated with their ability to keep the support of the shogun and to retain the loyalty of the band of housemen through which their local influence could be exerted.

Provincial government as superintended by the *shugo-daimyō* was clearly less formal than it had been during the Kamakura period. Basically it took the form of an extension of the *shugo's* house organization in which the *shugo* relied on his closest vassals for council and on lesser housemen for functional administrative tasks. No longer was there an impersonal bureaucracy staffed by appointment from the capital or even hereditary officials who claimed to represent the central government. Most territorial functions were performed by resident magnates who undertook administrative responsibilities as the *shugo's* deputies. On the other hand the levels of responsibility and the territorial boundaries of administrative jurisdiction remained remarkably stable. Authority continued to be exercised within the boundaries of provinces, districts, villages, and *shōen*. The functional units, in other words, tended to show a considerable degree of continuity, but the types of individuals filling the units and the type of authority which kept the system together had changed greatly.

Once involved in *bakufu* affairs, the Akamatsu built a residence in Kyoto and made that their center of activity. Increasingly, the Akamatsu chief was drawn away from his provincial base into the power struggle in Kyoto. Thus his so-called castle headquarters of Shirahata was probably never developed into a large residential establishment. As a consequence, the *shugo's* home territories were left pretty much to the management of deputy

[18] *Ibid.*, 202.

governors (*shugodai*). Under the Akamatsu, the deputy governorship of Harima was held by the head of the Uno family, of Bizen by the Urakami, and of Mimasaka at first by the Abo and then successively by the Kigo, Uozumi, Shimizu, and Hirai.[19] Even these *shugodai* were frequently called to Kyoto to perform duties for the Akamatsu house, so that sub-deputies (*shugo-matadai*) were left in charge of provincial affairs.[20]

Below the *shugodai*, areas of administrative jurisdiction were probably arranged for by agreement among the lesser vassals of the *shugo*. There is evidence that the *shugo* used a fairly systematic procedure of allocation of responsibility which rested at least in part on the older boundaries of local administration. For example, under the Ōuchi of Suō province, a sub-deputy was placed over each district (*kōri*). Such representatives of the *shugo* acted as general intendants (*gundai*) and served as chief administrators of each area.[21] It was probably up to such officials to make sense out of the complex jumble of land rights and to see that rents were forthcoming to the proper authorities. Within the *kōri*, the *gō* also frequently remained as units over which designated *shugo* representatives were assigned. There is evidence, therefore, that the system of local administration which continued in actual practice did not necessarily coincide with the contours of land tenure boundaries but rested on the more abstract divisions made familiar under the imperial system. The fief had not yet developed to the point that it could serve as the sole basis of local administration. It was still necessary to rely upon the remnants of the imperial system for the more impersonal functions of the *shugo*'s provincial responsibilities: the collection of provincial taxes, the carrying out of cadastral surveys, and the collection of *shōen* dues under the contract system.

Within the province, we can imagine that the *shugo*'s residence served as the foremost center of government affairs. The old provincial capitals by now had fallen into decay. If we may judge from the example of the Ōuchi house, which may well have been better organized than that of the Akamatsu, it appears that *shugo* presided over a fairly complex system of house administration. *Shugo* were in the habit of building residences for their major vassals around their provincial military headquarters, although

19 *Ibid.*, 265.   20 Matsuoka, "Ōuchi," 69.
21 *Ibid.*, 71.

no "castle towns" were to emerge until after the turn into the six-teenth century. The administrative centers established by the *shugo* were probably modeled on the pattern of the *bakufu*. Thus the Ōuchi maintained such organs as a military council (*samurai-dokoro*), administrative board (*bugyō-shū*), judicial board (*hyō-jōshū*), finance office (*mandokoro*), and a large number of func-tional officers (*bugyō*) to take charge of such specific services as the supervision of temples and shrines, the *shugo*'s personal affairs, construction, records, and correspondence. A hierarchy of local deputies (*daikan*) handled regional land tax administration. There was also a fully developed military organization in which the main vassals were responsible for major divisions made up of their per-sonal troops, and the *shugo* himself could recruit various guard groups from his own lands or from his direct vassals.[22] Such was the organization of local government as it was brought to bear upon the province of Bizen by the house of Akamatsu.

The internal administration of Bizen under the rule of the *shugo-daimyō* clearly differed quite markedly from what it had been in Kamakura days. Gone were the officials of the imperial govern-ment, the civil governors or their agents in the provincial head-quarters. The *kokufu* had disappeared, though there is no precise record of when it fell into disuse. Provincial documents after the middle of the fourteenth century carry chiefly the signatures of the *shugo* and his deputy officials. Yet Bizen retained a basic orientation toward Kyoto. For despite the fact that absentee pro-prietors were able to exert less and less influence over their hold-ings in Bizen, still something over half of the territory of Bizen was divided into *shōen* of which the proprietors were located in Kyoto. In fact the *shōen* system itself was still much in evidence, though it was obvious that the administration of the *shōen* was in the hands of military stewards and of the *shugo*'s contract agents.

If we take the year 1440 as the high point of Akamatsu author-ity in Bizen, from a purely formal point of view the political map of Bizen showed that most of the territorial units—such as *shōen*, *gō*, and *ho*—which had existed in 1200 were still in evidence.[23] Pro-prietorships had changed hands, of course, and the internal organi-

[22] *Ibid.*, 77.
[23] I am grateful to Mr. Kanai Madoka for his effort in systematizing the informa-tion contained in the documents listed in Nagayama's *Nōchi shi*, 396-452. The tabulations which follow are my own.

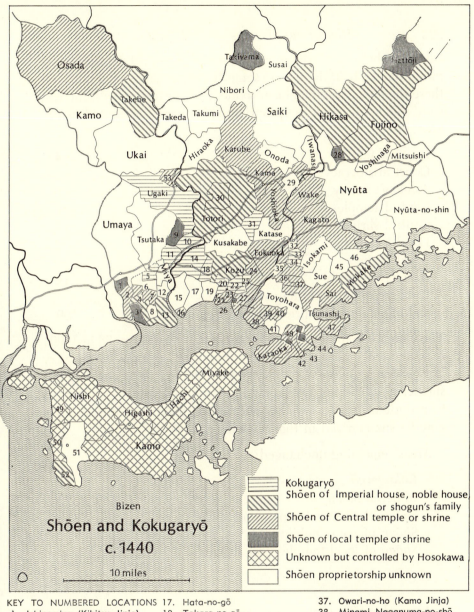

Bizen

Shōen and Kokugaryō
c. 1440

10 miles

Kokugaryō

Shōen of Imperial house, noble house,
or shogun's family

Shōen of Central temple or shrine

Shōen of local temple or shrine

Unknown but controlled by Hosokawa

Shōen proprietorship unknown

KEY TO NUMBERED LOCATIONS
1. Ichinomiya (Kibitsu Jinja)
2. Daianji-no-shō (Daianji)
3. Nishi Noda-no-shō (Kibitsu Jinja?)
4. Mino-no-shin-shō (Chōkōdō)
5. Tsushima-no-gō
6. Ifuku-no-gō
7. Higashi Noda-no-shō (Kōfukuji?)
8. Shin Tsutsumi-no-ho
9. Kinzanji
10. Hirashi-no-gō
11. Mino-no-gō
12. Izushi-no-gō
13. Shikata-no-shō (Fujiwara, Denka-watari-ryō)
14. Kamutsumichi-no-gō
15. Uji-no-gō
16. Areno-no-shō (Kasuga Jinja)
17. Hata-no-gō
18. Takara-no-gō
19. Taema-no-shō
20. Kachi-no-gō
21. Areno (Sennyūji)
22. Ōnishi-no-shō (estimated former Kanaoka Nishi-no-shō)
23. Aranuma
24. Takehara-no-shō (Kamo Jinja)
27. Kanaoka-no-sho (Gakuanji)
28. Anyōji-ryō
29. Kawada
30. Nibo-mura (Gosūkōin)
31. Motoroi-no-ho
32. Yugei-no-gō
33. Hattori-no-ho
34. Haji-no-gō
35. Mameda-no-shō
36. Yamada-no-shō (Kamo Jinja)
37. Owari-no-ho (Kamo Jinja)
38. Minami Naganuma-no-shō (Zuishin'in)
39. Naganuma-no Mikuriya (Ise Nishō Daijingū)
40. Naganuma-no-shō (Tōdaiji?)
41. Oku-no-gō
42. Ani Jinja
43. Rengeji
44. Guhōin
45. Sayama
46. Tsurumi
47. Ushimado-no-shō (Iwashimizu Hachiman)
48. Kashinō-no-shō (Miidera Onjōji)
49. Tsurashima-no-shō (Hosokawa)
50. Shionasu-no-shō (Hosokawa)
51. Kayō-no-shin-shō
52. Kayō-no-hon-shō (Saionji?)
53. Yamajo Mura (Myōkenji)

zation of these territorial units had undergone considerable transformation. In 1440 there were some 104 identifiable local units. Of
these the *kokugaryō* had been reduced to thirteen pieces; the rest
were *shōen*, of which the proprietorships were distributed as follows:

Imperial family	4
Court aristocracy	4
Ashikaga family	1
Central temples	16
Central shrines	10
Local temples	3
Local shrines	4
Hosokawa family	12
Unknown (but including *shugo* and other *bushi* proprietorships)	39

The increase in total number of units (there had been 88 in 1200)
is accounted for largely by the subdivision of some of the very
large *shōen* or pieces of public domain. In most instances the new,
smaller units did not fall below the size of *gō*, however. Changes
in proprietorship followed a number of distinct patterns. They
may be summarized in the following tables:

Areas remaining unchanged:

Kokugaryō	11
Imperial *shōen*	3
Shōen of central temples and shrines	9
Shōen of court nobility	2
Shōen of local temples and shrines	7
	—
	32

Areas changing proprietorship:

Kokugaryō to temple or shrine *shōen*	6
Kokugaryō to court *shōen*	1
Kokugaryō to *bushi shōen*	2
Kokugaryō to *shōen*, proprietor unknown	15
Imperial *shōen* to temple or shrine *shōen*	4
Temple or shrine to *bushi shōen*	4
Temple or shrine to unknown proprietor	1

Court family to another court family	1
Court family to unknown proprietor	1
	—
	35

Newly created units:

Kokugaryō	2
Temple or shrine *shōen*	7
Bushi shōen	6
Ashikaga *shōen*	1
Imperial family *shōen*	1
	—
	17

Disappeared (units recorded in 1200 for which there is no documentary evidence in 1440):

Temple or shrine *shōen*	5
Kokugaryō	6
No information:	20
	—
	104

The first observation which emerges from these figures is that the public domain had been drastically cut away. But what is not revealed in the figures is that the few lands which were still referred to as the public domain had in fact lost all their "public" character. A document of 1407 indicates that the *kokugaryō* of Bizen were now treated essentially as *shōen*. In 1407 the shogun, Ashikaga Yoshimasa, was able to devise the "public lands" of Bizen and Mino, plus other *shōen*, to his daughter, Minami-no-Gosho, the abbess of Daijiin. The grant of these lands was made to appear no different from the transfer of *shōen* proprietorships. There was no attempt to keep up a pretense of provincial jurisdiction over them.[24] Furthermore, there is little indication that the income from such domains was in any way commensurate with what it had been in 1200. Undoubtedly a farming-out procedure was used in which a military steward undertook on-the-spot tax collection, while the *shugo* accepted the responsibility of seeing to it that an agreed-upon quota of taxes was delivered to Kyoto. The Matsuda family may well have served as *jitō* of all these domains, although

[24] Takeuchi, *Jiryō*, 63-64; 77.

we can only be certain of its stewardship over Tsushima-no-go.

According to the above calculations, 24 pieces of *kokugaryō* had become *shōen*. Of these, the largest bloc with known proprietorships (six) went into the hands of temples or shrines. There were, to be sure, fifteen whose proprietorships were unknown, and most of these probably ended up in the hands of military families. We may surmise this, since the distribution of these *shōen* coincided with the known locations of some of the major *bushi* bands. All told, however, there were still a significant number of civil and religious proprietorships, and it is important to see how valuable these were as sources of income for the absentee proprietors. In the final analysis, of course, the *shōen* provided the only continuous source of income available to the court aristocracy. Their dependence upon such income was consequently desperate. So long as the *shugo* considered themselves primarily members of Kyoto society, there was some incentive for them to see to it that *shōen* rights were respected. But the actual authority of the absentee proprietor was minimal, and the income which reached Kyoto was meager and dependent almost entirely on the willingness of the military governors and their deputies to respect a weakening tradition. Income had been reduced legally by half or three-quarters, and few proprietors received even their legal dues from their holdings. In the land grant made Minami-no-gosho in 1407, for instance, it was stated that for Ōnishi-no-shō in Bizen, while the proprietor's share was 45 strings (*kan*) of cash, of late the local interests saw fit to deliver only 25 *kan*. A more common complaint was that no delivery was being made at all. The once-profitable Fujiwara holding in Bizen at Shikada-no-shō had been reduced to twenty strings of cash by 1481. When the head of the Fujiwara complained to the shogun that the Matsuda family, which acted as contract agent, had not delivered the annual rents the shogun's only reply was that the Matsuda were busy fighting their neighbors and had no surplus produce to deliver.[25]

One reason why proprietorships of religious institutions increased at this time was that the temples and shrines had the means of guarding their holdings somewhat better than court families. Moreover, by this time many of the *kuge* families, particularly the imperial family, had gained hereditary rights to cer-

[25] Fujii, "Shikada-no-shō," 137.

tain high posts in the religious hierarchy. Thus the income of the temples and shrines of the Kyoto area directly affected the well-being of the *kuge*. In the case of Osada-no-shō, the emperor Go-Daigo transferred the *shiki* of management (*shomu-daikan-shiki*) to the hands of Tōji temple in 1326. The temple consequently received one-tenth of the guardian's income but absorbed the responsibility of managing the *shōen*.[26] Within a few years Tōji held the entire guardianship rights. And then in 1353 the proprietary rights passed to Rengebuji under the seal of the Ashikaga shogun.[27] From this point on the imperial family could derive only indirect benefit from the *shōen* as members of the family entered the priesthood. In a similar manner Fukuoka-no-shō passed to the control of Tōji, and Kanaoka-no-shō to Saidaiji.

Of the court proprietorships in Bizen, Tottori-no-shō remained in imperial hands for the longest period of time. Emperors did their best to keep a hand in its affairs, appointing managing agents first from the Saionji family and later from the Hino. By Ashikaga times local supervision was farmed out to resident *jitō*-type managers. By 1420 the *shugo* contract system was in use, and the Akamatsu had named a deputy manager over the *shō*. In this way some income was assured the imperial house throughout the first half of the fifteenth century. We know, for instance, that in 1407 the income from Tottori was 1000 *koku* of rice. Although in the years which followed the emperors constantly complained to the shogunate that the *shugo* was remiss in payment of dues, the chances are that during years of peace the Akamatsu kept up their payments. In 1524 a delivery of 200 *kan* was made, and there is some indication that income reached Kyoto from Tottori-no-shō even after that.[28] In another part of Kibi, Niimi-no-shō of Bitchū, also an imperial *shōen* which had passed into the hands of Tōji, showed a record of nominal tax payment (about 20 *kan*) annually until 1458 through the auspices of the *shugo*'s deputy.[29]

While it is not always possible to determine the precise fiscal conditions of the court proprietorships of the fifteenth century, the new administrative procedures imposed by the *shugo* were quite apparent. With the maturation of the *shugo* system, we find

[26] Takeuchi, *Jiryō*, 471-472.
[27] Shimizu, *Shōen*, 1125.
[28] Arimoto Minoru, "Muromachi jidai ni okeru Bizen-no-kuni Tottori-no-shō," *op.cit.*, 5-6.
[29] Sugiyama Hiroshi, *Shōen kaitai katei no kenkyū*, 209-210.

in every instance that the *shugo*'s deputy took over the ultimate managerial powers from both the former proprietor's agents (*shōkan*) and shogun's agents (*jitō*). The chain of command between shogun, *shugo*, and *daikan* was generally short and direct. It was the propensity of the *shugo*'s agent, be he a former *jitō* or a newly intruded vassal of the *shugo,* that he collect rigorously, even ruthlessly, at the local level while passing on little to the top. It was not uncommon that, as in Niimi-no-shō during the 1460's, the inhabitants rebelled against the exactions of the *daikan,* calling for a return to conditions under the old proprietorship. But in this case even the great Tōji temple was unable to resist the intrusion of the *shugo*'s agent into their territories.

Probably what is more important to our study than a recitation of the frustrations of the civil aristocracy in Kyoto or local inhabitants in Bizen is the fact that even at this late date the *shōen* system had not altogether disappeared. It still provided the boundaries of local land organization and management. *Shōen* law, greatly modified to be sure, still provided the terminology for most of the transfers of rights and tenures as exemplified in such documents as the devise of family holdings of the Akamatsu house. Yet the system was obviously breaking down, and in large part the concept of *shiki* rights was losing its meaning. This was especially true of the large areas which had been taken over by military families: the areas on our map of Bizen about which we know comparatively little but which we assume to have passed under feudal proprietorships.

The most dramatic change between 1200 and 1440 was the expansion of proprietorships and lesser tenures belonging to military families. In the map of Bizen we can see that the Ashikaga had acquired proprietorship over the public domain and the *shōen* of Takebe. The head of the Hosokawa house held 13 *shōen,* largely on Kojima and Shōdoshima islands. These were probably part of a package which was held by virtue of the family's status as *kanrei.* It is the group of 38 units of which the proprietorship is unclear, however, which reveals the true inroads of the *bushi* into the lands of Bizen. These areas, once *shōen* or *kokugaryō,* had by now passed into that transition state in which absentee proprietorships had so little force as to have lost all meaning. Over most of these lands we can assume that local military families holding various degrees of proprietorship short of completeness were the on-the-spot masters. And it is within these territories that we must assume the *shōen* practices were most fully displaced by feudal. For Bizen as a whole we have only fragmentary evidence on the way in which local military families acquired such powers or of how they managed their lands. The rise of the Matsuda and Urakami families are the best documented, although their cases are somewhat atypical.

The early history of the Matsuda family is obscure, but there is evidence that the family was of Kantō origin and received its first grant of land in Bizen about 1221. In 1285 a member of the house, Matsuda Motoyasu, as a result of meritorious military service at the time of the first Mongol invasion, "received Ifuku-no-gō" in Bizen, although the exact nature of his tenure is not revealed. Motoyasu lived until 1310. His son, Motokuni, is said to have been rewarded with the post of *shugo* of Bizen and the additional holding of Tsushima-no-gō. Motokuni consequently moved out of the Kantō and took up residence in Bizen, building his strong point at Tomiyama.[30] The Matsuda family genealogy states at this point that Motokuni "controlled" the two districts of Mino and Tsutaka, but the nature of this control is left vague. At this same time another branch of the family appears to have been active in Bizen. Its head, Matsuda Moriyori, has already appeared in our narrative. In the wars of the Kemmu period the Matsuda supported the Ashikaga, and Moriyori (not his kinsman Moto-kuni) received the military governorship of Bizen. About the same time Motokuni acquired further lands in Tsutaka district and the additional holding of Shikada-no-gō. If we add together the holdings of the above two Matsuda families they obviously comprised a sizable portion of the four westernmost districts of Bizen. They did not, however, make possible a secure control of the province. Matsuda influence must have been particularly weak in the eastern districts.

In 1337 Matsuda Mototaka, son of Motokuni, built and entered a castle at Kanagawa, leaving his senior vassals as keepers of his previous headquarters at Tomiyama.[31] This shift of military base is of considerable significance, for it indicates that the tempo of warfare was increasing and that exposed positions, such as the one at Tomiyama, were best exchanged for less accessible moun-

[30] *Okayama-shi shi*, 2.1302-1303.
[31] *Ibid.*, 2.1305.

tain defenses. By this time most of the regional chiefs were making similar moves, and although it was still many years before castles capable of withstanding lengthy assaults were to be built, a growing emphasis was put upon internal territorial consolidation and on defense of boundaries.

Between 1345 and 1364 Matsuda Nobushige, son of Moriyori, served as military governor of Bizen.[32] But this branch of the Matsuda is not heard of after 1364, when Nobushige lost his title. On the other hand, Mototaka's succession continued to prosper at Kanagawa. There we find the next head, Motoyasu, making peace with the Akamatsu to become deputy governor of the western half of Bizen. We learn also that he took a daughter of Akamatsu Sadanori as wife, probably as an act of reconciliation. Under Motoyasu's leadership the Matsuda came to "control all of Mino-gun."[33] The next chief, Motofusa, was found fighting in the Kyoto area on behalf of the shogun Yoshimitsu. For these military services he received the additional grant of Iwanasu-no-gō. His successor, Motokata, took as wife the daughter of Mimura Shigemichi, the deputy governor of eastern Bitchū. He also improved the defenses of the family castle of Kanagawa so that it acquired the reputation of being the most formidable fortification in Bizen.[34] Thus the Matsuda constantly expanded their holdings and improved their family connections during the years they served as deputy governors for half of Bizen.

The Matsuda genealogy is too unreliable a document upon which to base an understanding of the exact nature of Matsuda holdings, for it would have us believe that the Matsuda held proprietary rights (*ryōyū*) over the entire four districts of Mino, Tsutaka, Akasaka, and Kamutsumichi. This was clearly an exaggeration. What we can believe is that Ifuku-no-gō, and probably also Iwanasu-no-gō, were held entire and complete. In these areas the Matsuda had been established the longest and so presumably possessed their fullest rights. Elsewhere within the above four districts their powers were more limited, and there is clear evidence that conflicting proprietorships existed within their boundaries. Eleven of the thirteen pieces of public domain over which the daughter of the shogun had been named proprietor were located in this area.[35] Over these the Matsuda surely could

[32] *Ibid.*, 2.1307-1308.　　[33] *Ibid.*, 2.1310.　　[34] *Ibid.*, 2.1311-1312.
[35] Kanai, "Bizen," 52-54.

have claimed only the *jitō* rights or perhaps the powers of the *shugo*'s deputy. The same was definitely true of Shikada-no-shō of which the proprietorship was still partially in the name of the Fujiwara house. As of the year 1481, it is recorded that the Matsuda served as proprietor's agent (*sōryō-ukebito*) or general deputy (*shodaikan*) for this *shōen*.[36] In Tottori-no-shō the same must have been true, since the proprietorship was clearly in the hands of the imperial family. Technically, therefore, the Matsuda position was far from comprehensive. Even as late as 1408 the Matsuda leader had this to say about his position in response to an inquiry from the *shugo*:

"I have not grasped as my personal domain half of Bizen as is sometimes said. I am only holding this territory as a source of military provisions and personnel (*hyōrō gunyaku*). If ordered to return it I will of course do so. But Ifuku-no-gō is a different matter. My family was granted this holding in Kamakura times as salary land in recognition of meritorious military service; of this there is no dispute."[37]

The Matsuda were certainly the outstanding power in western Bizen from a military point of view, and the title of deputy *shugo* gave them a legal backing to match their growing military strength. We can assume that the Matsuda headquarters at Tomiyama and Kanagawa had become the prime centers of administration, legal transaction, and tax collection for the entire four districts, and it was upon the Matsuda that the *shugo* had to depend for the execution of various contract services. Within this area as well, the Matsuda chief unquestionably was acquiring more and more land which had been granted him by confirmation from the *shugo*. Such land would be subject to no further claims of higher proprietorship and required only loyalty and military service on behalf of the *shugo*. Even such requirements were frequently nominal since the Matsuda had holdings (such as Ifuku-no-gō) which had become hereditary since Kamakura times.

In contrast to the Matsuda, the Urakami came into Bizen completely at the behest of the *shugo* and therefore started out with the narrowest of land bases. Yet within a few decades this family

---

[63] Fujii, "Shikada-no shō," 137.

[37] Dohi Tsunehira, "Bizen gunki" (Ms., 1774), modern ed. in Tanaka Seiichi comp. *Kibi gunsho shūsei* (10 vols., Tokyo, 1921), 3.26-27. Hereafter cited by title only.

also achieved a position of leadership in eastern Bizen as the *shugo's* deputy. Actually we know very little about the Urakami until after 1467 when the second phase of Akamatsu control over Bizen began. The family was originally from Harima and had become one of the chief non-kin vassals of the Akamatsu. Urakami Munetaka was assigned Mitsuishi castle after 1364 and given jurisdiction as deputy *shugo* over eastern Bizen. The Urakami position in Bizen was based on military force and the backing of the *shugo*. In other words it derived from an extension of the *shugo's* power base in Harima, not from extensive control of land or long-established connections with other local families. Upon moving into Bizen the Urakami retained their main holdings in Harima, receiving only some slender grants in the vicinity of Mitsuishi. We cannot even be sure that they acquired rights over Nyūta-no-shō (the main *jitō* proprietorship in Bizen), for the Fujiwara family was still in evidence there.[38] Not until the late fifteenth century did the Urakami expand as a major territorial power in Bizen.

The Matsuda and Urakami, two military families of very different origin and relationship to Bizen, became the major agents of the Akamatsu. It was through these deputy houses that the authority of the military governor of Bizen was exercised over the province and fashioned into something of a systematic form of government. From the period 1364 to 1441 a large number of land documents remain in which the Akamatsu, or their deputies, the Urakami and Matsuda, confirmed or guaranteed land rights in the name of shogunal law. From these documents we can visualize the manner in which the *shugo* system succeeded in supplanting the older provincial administration. In the Anyōji documents we note that the Fujiwaras of Nyūta-no-shō had been enlisted as intendants (*daikan*) under the Urakami and that the Urakami maintained a magistral office (*bugyōsho*) serving eastern Bizen.[39] Intendants appear to have been distributed in such a manner that they could act as intermediary agents between the deputy governor and the stewards of the individual proprietary units (now called *satanin* or *shishō bito*). There appears to have been a relatively systematic division of responsibility for handling the paperwork of land management.[40]

[38] *Komonjo-shū*, 1.14-15, Anyōji documents.
[39] *Ibid.*   [40] *Nōchi shi*, 436.

Beyond a statement of this sort, however, it is difficult to gain a picture of how the *shugo* exercised his provincial authority. The Akamatsu chief's powers were based primarily upon the fact of his being *shugo* and only secondarily upon his land holdings. Thus he differed from the later daimyo who had gained full proprietary rights over all territory within their domains. As the shogun's designate, the *shugo* received certain legal and administrative rights which were his to exploit. In terms of the formal action of the Ashikaga shogunate the Akamatsu had been authorized to govern all of Bizen province in both civil and military terms. Under them the deputies (Matsuda and Urakami) and below them the intendants (*daikan*) and stewards (*satanin*) constituted the recognized chain of authority within the province. But between the theoretical administrative structure and actual manner of enforcement a large area of discrepancy probably existed. The power of enforcement was not inherent in the acquisition of legitimacy from the shogun. Rather it rested upon the ability to exercise military force. This in turn depended on the ability to secure the following or at least acquiescence of indigenous landed families. In Harima, of course, the Akamatsu were supported by an extensive network of family connections and alliances within which personal bonds of vassalage served as the major binding element. In Bizen this element was not so fully developed. Over western Bizen, in fact, neither the Akamatsu nor the Yamana were able to do more than enlist the allegiance of the Matsuda. But over eastern Bizen a more personal chain of vassalage could be extended. Beginning with his long-time retainer, the Urakami, and other lesser vassal families put into the lands which came into his possession in Bizen, the Akamatsu chief extended his network of housemen into Bizen, granting new lands, confirming old holdings and in general attempting to bring the vassalage system into coincidence with the authority system.

Behind the creation of the formal Ashikaga system of authority in Bizen, then, there was the constant effort of the *shugo* to extend his band of retainers through such means as intermarriage and enfeoffment. As various land rights came into his possession, the *shugo* took every occasion to reward his followers or to gain new vassals. Copies of land grants in reward for service have been retained by a few houses that managed to survive this age of frequent local warfare. For example a document of 1467 signed by Akamatsu Masanori and addressed to Matsuda Mototaka reads as follows:

> Regarding the *hanzei* portion of Kamimura village of Ito-no-shō, although Minota Sakyō-no-suke is raising objections, these lands were assigned to Namba Jūrōbei-no-jō for military support as a result of his recent show of loyalty. This should be understood.

Again in the same year Masanori signed the following document:

> After the Katsuragi had been driven from Tottori-no-shō, Namba Jūrōbei-no-jō was assigned scattered fields for his military support. There are those who resist this disposition, claiming they are the original owners of the lands (*honshu*). But the Katsuragi were deprived of their lands because of their tardiness in joining our cause. Of this there is no doubt. Therefore quickly suppress this resistance. These lands will be managed (*sata*) by Jūrōbei-no-jō and his succession. Respectfully.[41]

In Bizen the number of military houses counted as firm Akamatsu housemen was at first small. And most were of uncertain loyalty. The Matsuda were reluctant allies at best, and it would seem that whenever the occasion presented itself they joined the enemies of the Akamatsu. Within the smaller sectors over which the deputy *shugo* had been placed, authority was no more easy to enforce. The Urakami and Matsuda, within their spheres of influence, had to contend with local chiefs who managed to preserve a good deal of independence. Thus frequently the Akamatsu were obliged to send direct commands to such families as the Iga of Osada-no-shō or the Sasaki of Kojima, for apparently the deputy *shugo* were unable to handle them. Between theory and practice in the application of authority a generous gap existed in Bizen. This is perhaps best brought out in the records of the attempt of the *shugo* to collect provincial taxes, called *munebetsu-sen*. In 1442 an attempt was made to collect such a tax for the purpose of supporting the rebuilding of Tōji. The result was far from successful. Tōji records show that fifty-six jurisdictional units were approached in Bizen in the name of the shogun and *shugo*.

[41] *Okayama-shi shi*, 2.1348-1349.

Of these, eighteen paid without resistance, six contributed under different auspices, seven resisted but were reapproached by the *shugodai,* twenty-six forcibly rejected the tax collectors. In some of these areas the local inhabitants put up barricades behind which they fought off the *shugo*'s agents.[42] Such attempts to avoid interference of the shogun or *shugo* were common during the Ashikaga period and led frequently to local uprisings or armed clashes.

It is apparent then that the authority held by the *shugo* of Bizen was at best a precarious thing and easily disturbed by conditions either at the political center of the country or at the local level. The Akamatsu fortunes, like those of so many of the *shugo* families, showed violent ups and downs. But there was a touch of romance to the Akamatsu story which has made it a favorite of Japanese historians. The downfall of the Akamatsu came at the moment of their highest success. The occasion was one of the most shocking incidents in Ashikaga history, the Kakitsu disturbance of 1441 in which Akamatsu Mitsusuke assassinated the shogun Yoshinori. The incident marked not only a turning point in Akamatsu fortunes but in the history of the Ashikaga house as well.

The shogun Yoshinori is said to have brought to a height the despotic tendencies of the Ashikaga shogunate. By 1441 several trusted *shugo* had been killed by the shogun, and the Akamatsu were being treated in a high-handed fashion. When the shogun tried to take Akamatsu Mitsusuke's lands from him to give to another member of the Akamatsu lineage, he was obviously seeking to utilize a division within the Akamatsu ranks to weaken the family. Mitsusuke invited the shogun to a theatrical performance at his residence in Kyoto and there assassinated him. Mitsusuke then returned to his castle of Kinoyama and fought to the finish against shogunal forces led by his bitter rival, the house of Yamana. In the final engagement most of the Akamatsu family were exterminated and the Yamana took over the governorships held by the family.[43] The period of Yamana ascendancy over Bizen lasted from 1441 to 1467. During this interval the Yamana extended their suzerainty over the Matsuda and, after pacifying the rest of Bizen, set up a deputy named Ogamo at the castle

[42] *Tsūshi,* 1.950-951.
[43] Mizuno, "Akamatsu," 273-277.

headquarters of Fukuoka on the eastern bank of the Yoshii River.[44]

The Yamana, it will be recalled, had been long-time rivals of the Akamatsu in central Japan and had held at one time eleven *shugo*ships. In 1392 the Yamana had been cut back to three provinces in a battle which had presaged the first period of outstanding Ashikaga stability. Now with the defeat of the Akamatsu, the Yamana held nine provinces and again stood out as one of the greatest of the *shugo*.[45] It was chiefly because of this new surge of Yamana power and the effect it had upon the military balance among the *shugo* that the Akamatsu were not obliged to remain in oblivion. The Akamatsu's loss of a strategic position in central Japan brought the Yamana face to face with the Hosokawa house, traditional recipients of the title of *kanrei*. Hosokawa Katsumoto thus advocated the revival of the Akamatsu house as a buffer against the Yamana. Several branches of the Akamatsu were encouraged to foment revolt against the Yamana in Harima, but without success. In 1458, however, some former Akamatsu vassals in a bold exploit managed to retrieve the imperial treasures which had been secreted by remnants of Go-Daigo's followers in Yoshino. For this act Akamatsu Masanori, one of the few surviving holders of the Akamatsu surname, was rewarded with the permission to revive the house of Akamatsu and was granted the *shugo*ship of half of Kaga, the *shō* of Nyūta in Bizen, and the *ho* of Takamiya in Ise.

Receipt of these grants was by no means a guarantee that a revived Akamatsu house could occupy a secure position in central Japan. The Akamatsu had recovered only Nyūta-no-shō from among their former holdings, and their position as *shugo* of half of Kaga province was largely up to them to turn into reality.[46] Harima, their former home province, was still denied them. It is understandable then that the Akamatsu should have been foremost participants in the great Ōnin war between the Hosokawa and Yamana which broke out in 1467, opposing at several crucial times the council of compromise. For the war gave the Akamatsu a chance to recover their fortunes, and in fact to regain the three

[44] *Tsūshi*, 1.942-946.

[45] *Okayama-ken no rekishi*, 200.

[46] Mizuno Kyōichirō, "Akamatsu-shi saikō o meguru ni-san no mondai," in *Kyoto Daigaku Dokushikai Sōritsu Gojūnen Kinen, Kokushi ronshū* (Kyoto, 1960), 762-778.

provinces lost in 1441. During the years of war in Kyoto, the Akamatsu managed to clear the Yamana from Harima, fight their way back into Bizen, and to defeat the Yamana agent at Fukuoka. By the termination of the war in 1477, the Akamatsu had regained possession of the title of *shugo* of Harima, Bizen, and Mimasaka. In Bizen, as before, they set up their agent, the Urakami, at Mitsuishi on the border between Harima and Bizen and subjected the Matsuda to subordination.

The high point of Akamatsu recovery in Bizen during this second stage was reached in the year 1480 when in great pomp the head of the house marched from Shirahata, along the coastal highway through Bizen, to the foremost Shinto shrine of the area, Bizen's Ichinomiya. In the course of this progress he stayed both at Mitsuishi and Tomiyama, the secondary center of Matsuda power. In this way the Akamatsu chief attempted to assure the continued allegiance of his chief vassals in Bizen, the Urakami and the Matsuda, and sought to impress his authority upon the area.[47]

But conditions in 1480 were not what they had been a century earlier. Deterioration of the powers of the Ashikaga shogunate left the *shugo* with little effective central backing, while the Ōnin war had disrupted local conditions everywhere. Local uprisings and the effect of Yamana intrusion into Harima had broken the base upon which the Akamatsu house had once built its local hegemony. This base was never rebuilt, and so within three years after the 1480 progress Akamatsu authority in Bizen was reduced to all but a nominal thing. The Matsuda, finding an opportunity to join with Yamana remnants, broke with the Akamatsu and began to contest for control of Bizen. The Urakami, remaining loyal to the Akamatsu, fortified the strategic castle of Fukuoka and with the aid of other Akamatsu supporters attempted to thwart the Matsuda. A great battle, fought in 1483 at Fukuoka, largely between the Matsuda and the Urakami forces, though inconclusive, broke the Akamatsu power over Bizen. In the years which followed, both the Matsuda and the Urakami remained firmly entrenched in their strongholds, with the Yoshii River forming the boundary between them. The major loss from the confrontation of these two houses was to the prestige of the

[47] *Okayama-shi shi*, 2.1165-1166.

Akamatsu house. Moreover, the Akamatsu were obliged to turn over to their vassals more and more of the affairs of Harima, where they were constantly beset by their traditional enemies, the Yamana, and by unrest among the local *bushi*. In a series of exhausting wars with the Yamana, the Urakami were called on frequently to do the fighting for the Akamatsu. Gradually the Urakami took over the position of leadership among the vassals of the Akamatsu until eventually rivalry among branches of the Akamatsu family gave the Urakami the opportunity to take up arms in their own cause. In 1522 Urakami Muramune killed the head of the Akamatsu house and assumed control over the former Akamatsu territories. The foremost *shugo-daimyō* which had touched the affairs of Bizen thus passed out of existence and the period of *shugo* rule in the province came to an end.

The passing of Akamatsu rule over Bizen exemplifies the problems faced by the *shugo* in their attempt to maintain control over province-size territories. Sources of *shugo* power were unavoidably mixed. *Shugo* were first of all local military powers; at the same time they were appointees of the Ashikaga shogun. But the legitimization and the backing of the Ashikaga shogunate was of insufficient benefit. Even in a *shugo*'s home province the discrepancy between authority by appointment and power in hand was dangerously great. The Akamatsu control of Bizen was particularly weak because of the limited number of kin-vassals it had in the province. Although the Akamatsu won the title of *shugo* of Bizen by military action against the Yamana, Harima remained their home province, and the base of their real power. As a military power then the Akamatsu forces and the various strong-points upon which they relied were concentrated in Harima. In Bizen they were obliged to leave matters pretty much to their agent, the Urakami, and their uncertain ally, the Matsuda. In the final analysis, therefore, the ability of the Akamatsu to influence affairs in Bizen rested on their ability to demand loyal service of the Urakami and Matsuda and through them to hold down the local families (*kokujin*) of Bizen.

The weakness of the Akamatsu grip on Bizen was further reflected in the pattern of land holding upon which it had to rely. The Akamatsu land base in Bizen was small and poorly distributed. Moreover, the major holdings of the Akamatsu were widely scattered and were by no means concentrated in Harima,

Bizen, and Mimasaka. Thus a considerable discrepancy existed between the jurisdictional area over which the family claimed authority and the lands which backed that authority. In Bizen the major portion of land was still held in various capacities by local or absentee proprietary families and by numerous temples and shrines. This complexity of land tenures made for a great diversity in the pattern of political and military allegiances within the province. We can be sure that at no time did a neat hierarchy unite all the fighting men of Bizen under the Akamatsu, but rather that conflicting claims of loyalty constantly divided them. Each time war broke out between the Akamatsu and Yamana these local families seized the opportunity to better themselves, generally by joining against the Akamatsu.

Doubtless because of the difficulty in maintaining control over the local families within the provinces, the *shugo* sought the backing of the Ashikaga shogunate whenever it could prove useful. Legitimization was essential. But the prestige conferred by the shogunal appointment was a mixed asset. For to secure it involved the *shugo* in conflicts at the center of politics which eventually hastened their decline. And as the *shugo* competed among themselves for influence within the shogunate, they weakened the very institutions upon which they hoped to rely at the same time that they neglected their provincial bases. Thus the passing of the *shugo-daimyō* was intimately related to the final decline of the Ashikaga shogunate and the collapse of the last vestiges of central authority in Japan. The Ōnin war, which briefly revived the fortunes of the Akamatsu house, was in fact the turning point in the ability of the *shugo* to serve as the primary agents of local government in the provinces.

IX. BIZEN AND THE SENGOKU DAIMYO

THE hundred years which separate the beginning of the Ōnin war in 1467 and Nobunaga's entrance into Kyoto in 1568 delimit the period in Japanese history known as Sengoku: "the country at war." The name is appropriate, for warfare wracked the entire country, and Bizen was to have its full share of battle and bloodshed. But the clash of armies was not the only activity to leave a mark upon the provinces during this tempestuous century. Momentous institutional changes were also at work across the country. Taken in its full measure of historical significance, the Sengoku period spanned a major watershed in Japanese history, when the Japan which had existed under the institutions of imperial rule gave way before a new and different state structure, the Japan which was to emerge from the full spread and maturation of feudal institutions. In most parts of Japan it was this century which brought to fullest development feudal practices of government and military organization, giving rise to the most extreme conditions of political decentralization. Political power, which during the eighth century had been drawn out of the countryside into the imperial capital, was by this time almost completely returned to the provinces, and the provinces once again became the source of initiative in national affairs. For the first time in nearly a millennium in Bizen local families with the power to enforce authority in their own right came into being. Not since the days when the Kibi and Wake families had divided the several districts of southern Bizen and Bitchū between them had the area produced indigenous rulers of such strength and capacity.

For Bizen the collapse of the house of Akamatsu ushered in the era of political decentralization which characterized the Sengoku age. For with the passing of the *shugo*, the hand of the Ashikaga shogunate was almost completely withdrawn from the province. To be sure, emperor and shogun remained in Kyoto as symbols of ultimate sovereignty, but their political roles were passive. These remnants of the old authority structure lingered on as shadowy repositories of legitimacy, but neither retained the capacity to interfere in local affairs. After the death of the shogun Yoshimasa in 1490 the shogunate possessed neither the prestige nor the power to impose upon a province a master who was not already established as the local hegemon. The last remnants of centralizing authority had been dissipated, and the country literally dissolved into autonomous territories. The fragmentation of authority which had commenced with the separation of proprietary rights from control of the state was now as complete as it could become without the division of the state itself.

It is important, of course, to reflect upon the fact that the state was not divided. The traditional locus of sovereignty and the ideal of a unified polity were not challenged. Yet the ideal was stretched to its limit. The conception of a unified central administration and of local rule as a function of central government was almost entirely abandoned, while the country fell into clusters of unitary domains which resisted all influence from Kyoto. The years after the destructive Ōnin war of 1467 to 1477 saw the rapid breakup of the former *shugo* houses and the territories over which they had been placed. In almost every part of Japan the extended jurisdictional territories split up into smaller sections, either among contending branches of the former *shugo* lines or among contending vassal houses. The new territories were smaller but they were more easily governed. Their appearance coincided with the rise of a whole new class of locally powerful military families, the so-called *sengoku-daimyō*. The process by which these new daimyo took over the provinces has been characterized as one of overturn, whereby underlings rose up to smite the powerful and the low-born emerged to appropriate the privileges of the older military aristocracy. Such indeed is what happened. But the success of the new daimyo cannot be explained simply on the basis of their treacherous conduct, as the military chronicles have done. They rose to power both as a result of certain fundamental weaknesses in the power structures over which the *shugo* presided and through their own ability to exploit new and more effective means of organizing military power and controlling territory.

Although it was not until 1521 that the Akamatsu house was eliminated as a force in the affairs of Harima, the year 1483 provided the real turning point when the Akamatsu lost their control over Bizen, and the two families, the Matsuda and the Urakami, began to assert the kind of local independence which was to convert them into successful daimyo of the Sengoku age. Beyond 1483, then, Bizen entered its period of wars. Central authority was reduced to absolute minimum and government had literally been brought down to the level of the two daimyo houses which remained as local hegemons. The maintenance of order was now a matter of local responsibility. There was no higher authority capable of enforcing a superior law or justice. The protection of life or property now depended almost wholly on armed force and stout defenses.

A record of these troubled times is extremely hard to come by, for there were few established centers which survived these years to carry their documents into succeeding ages. What we have, other than records of religious organizations, are chiefly genea-logical tables and war chronicles of the main military houses. These rather uncertain writings are limited in their content to the intrigues and battles which occupied the attention of the warring houses. Perhaps they exaggerate the incidence of war-fare. Yet it would be futile to deny the desperate struggles into which the province was plunged once the Ashikaga shogunate lost its influence. Evidence of the degree to which war and de-fense became the chief business of the landed aristocracy is seen in the dramatic growth of armed strong-points throughout the countryside. As the chronicler of the Matsuda house wrote, "The landed houses of each village and district now build fortifications and erect castles. Day and night they must exercise constant vigilance."[1] A twentieth century historian has identified through document and field study the sites of 642 forts and castles in the three Kibi provinces of Bizen, Bitchū, and Mimasaka. Not all of these sites were in use at one time, but the evidence permits no doubt of the intensity of warfare in Sengoku days.[2]

The prevalence of warfare, or rather the constant need to de-fend land rights by force of arms, led to a fundamental change in the local basis of political life in Bizen after 1483. While at the beginning of the fifteenth century Bizen had retained most of the external administrative features which had existed in the thirteenth century, by the beginning of the sixteenth century the entire political topography of the province was taking on a new and different appearance. Most of the *shōen* had entirely dis-appeared, and the boundaries of the province and of the old

[1] Sanuki Matsuda keifu, ms., quoted in *Okayama-shi shi*, 2.1351.
[2] *Tsūshi*, 1.987-1011. The count is based on Nagayama Usaburo's indefatigable investigation.

districts and villages (*gō*) held increasingly little meaning as administrative units. The contours of real power no longer coincided either with the boundaries of the *shōen* or the old administrative jurisdictions. In Bizen of the early sixteenth century the basic units out of which new combinations of political and military power were built consisted of armed men, their castles, and their lands held in fief. Such units were more intimately related to the geographical, or defense, topography of the region than to the traditional patterns of proprietorship. For this reason we are obliged to turn our attention again to the inner topographical features of Bizen to study the configuration of rivers, hills, and valleys which became the base upon which the *sengoku-daimyō* were to build their domains. Such a study must include Bizen's neighboring provinces as well, for the daimyo of Bizen fought out their lives in a military arena which embraced most of the Kibi area, in particular the provinces of Bitchū, Mimasaka, and Bizen.

This return to the raw topography of this region did not mean that the old administrative provinces and districts were necessarily forgotten. They remained as convenient terms of general geographical reference, and the areas over which daimyo held their sway were generally couched in such terms. But from a functional point of view it was the geography, particularly the river systems, which influenced the configuration of military power. The lower Yoshii valley with its wide floor and open terrain formed a rich agricultural region stretching eastward from the banks of the river toward the borders of Harima. It provided the economic base upon which control of eastern Bizen generally rested. The Asahi River valley, separated from that of the Yoshii by low-lying hills, constituted a separate region dominating western Bizen. Oriented roughly in a north-south direction, the Asahi valley contained two major economic centers: the coastal plain region controlled first by Tomiyama castle, later the great city of Okayama, and the interior valley around the present city of Kanagawa. The Takahashi River of Bitchū passed through more rugged terrain than that of Bizen and hence was not endowed with plains of comparable size. The lower coastal plain of Bitchū, where the *kokufu* had been established, remained narrow and fragmented. Within the river valley itself, north-south communication was extremely difficult, and there was no adequate base from which the entire river system could be dominated. There was an upper valley of some size with its center at the present city of Takahashi. There were also a number of tributary valleys running into the river from the west, notably those of the Oda and Nariwa, but these were of small size. The province of Mimasaka was even more fragmented. The entire region was mountainous and was much less favorably provided with agricultural land. Except for an interior plateau, dominated by the present city of Tsuyama, most of the area was split into narrow valleys which gave rise to isolated pockets of military power but never of great size.

If valleys formed the major bases of economic support for military power, they also served as the main avenues of communication within the Kibi region, providing the corridors through which armies circulated, as local forces moved against each other or as those from outside invaded the area. Thus Bizen communicated with the province of Harima, its neighbor to the east, over the watershed beyond the eastern tributary of the Yoshii River, and of course by sea. Bitchū communicated with Bingo across the watersheds of the western tributaries of the Takahashi River and also by sea. Mimasaka, though ringed by mountains to the north, was accessible from the south through the valleys of the Yoshii, Asahi, and Takahashi Rivers, and from east and west through low passes. Eastern Mimasaka was geographically more closely tied to Harima than to Bizen.

This then was the stage upon which the drama of military rivalry was played out in Bizen. The area of the three provinces contained several natural centers capable of nourishing military powers of some size. The open country to the east of the Yoshii River could support and in turn could be held by strongholds in the low hills surrounding the plain. Such were the castles of Fukuoka, Mitsuishi, and Tenjinyama. Mitsuishi was particularly important strategically, since it guarded the entrance to Bizen from Harima. The lower valley of the Asahi formed two natural focal points of military power, one located at Tomiyama, the other at Kanagawa. In the tributary valleys of the Takahashi, castles at Niimi, Matsuyama, Nariwa, Sarukake, Ashimori, and Kamogata each dominated a small but well-defined portion of Bitchū. Military centers in Mimasaka were less capable of offensive action but their defensive strength was enhanced by the rugged topography.

Castles at Toyokuni, Katsumada, Tsuyama, Kuse, Katsuyama, and Mitsuboshi were the scenes of numerous bitter attacks during the sixteenth century.

In Bizen the Sengoku period opened with the Urakami family, controlling eastern Bizen from its castle at Mitsuishi, opposed to the Matsuda family of Kanagawa who dominated western Bizen. Akamatsu influence was nearly gone. The Hosokawa (based primarily in Shikoku) still maintained a foothold at Kamogata on the coastal plain west of the mouth of the Takahashi River, but not for much longer. The sub-valleys of the Takahashi River, each giving rise to a separate family hegemony, were finally brought under a single command by the Shō, who during the 1530's conquered the three strong-points of Sarukake, Nariwa, and Matsuyama. (See page 265.)

The chronicles of the major houses of Bitchū and Bizen are filled with intimate details of how the daimyo organized their forces and contested for local supremacy. The first of the houses of Kibi to mature was the Matsuda of the Asahi valley. This family, it will be recalled, had been a power to contend with since the early years of the Ashikaga era. In 1483, on the eve of the great battle of Fukuoka, the Matsuda military organization was described by an early chronicler in the following terms: "The mountain on which the [Matsuda] castle stands is in an area of deep valleys and precipitous slopes. To the east is a great river and thick pine forests, providing an impregnable location for the castle. On top of the mountain is a tower and protective walls. In addition, garrison houses have been built, and in these the fighting men of half Bizen have been assembled."[3] A roster of the major vassals of the Matsuda listed approximately 350 horsemen (*ki*) drawn from six of the eight districts of Bizen province. Altogether it was claimed that Matsuda mustered over 5000 men-in-arms. The hierarchy of vassals consisted of four members of the Matsuda family and the important vassal families of Iga, Yokoi, Ōmura, Ugaki, Hashimoto, Izumi, Nagaoka, Ōmiya, Nakajima, Namba, and Takaoka.[4] These families represented not only commitment of manpower but the availability of an entire network of garrisoned castles, numbering over twenty in all. From the roster of vassals we can determine that the Matsuda did control

[3] "Bizen gunki," 27.
[4] *Okayama-shi shi*, 2.1325. Based on Sanuki Matsuda keifu.

by this time the five districts of Mino, Tsutaka, Akasaka, Iwanasu, and Kamutsumichi. The Matsuda castles whose sites can still be identified, were so distributed that they thoroughly covered the major agricultural areas held by the Matsuda and their vassals. Radiating outward from the central castle at Kanagawa they controlled the middle and lower valleys of the Asahi River and much of the intermediate territory stretching eastward to the Yoshii River.[5]

The Matsuda family's ambitions for the control of all Bizen were of long duration, and it will be recalled that the family briefly held the post of *shugo* of Bizen. Yet because of the Akamatsu and Yamana who managed to dominate Bizen from the east, this ambition was never fulfilled. When in 1480 Matsuda Motonari expanded his castle at Kanagawa, he aroused the suspicions of the Akamatsu Masanori who accused him of usurping authority and ordered the Urakami to attack him. The result was the great battle of Fukuoka in 1483. The battle conclusively ended the possibility that the Matsuda might have acquired control of all Bizen, but it did lay the foundation for the establishment of an independent territory stretching to the shores of the Yoshii River. In 1497 the Urakami attacked the Matsuda castle of Tomiyama with 1000 mounted men. The Matsuda successfully drove off the attack, but lost the part of Kamutsumichi which bordered on the Yoshii. Again in 1502 and 1503 Urakami forces defeated the Matsuda near Tomiyama, but did not follow up their victories due to the pressure of events in Harima. Thus the Matsuda were kept on the defensive toward the Urakami while they strengthened themselves in the less accessible portion of the middle Asahi valley.

The Urakami, after their return to Bizen in 1467, utilized their position as deputy *shugo* to infiltrate eastern Bizen. Keeping the Matsuda on the defensive, they built up a solid military alliance stretching from the Yoshii River to the border of Harima. Then when in 1521 Urakami Muramune killed the head of the Akamatsu family, he secured the western half of the Akamatsu domain for his own. The Urakami momentarily had within their grasp the ability to succeed the Akamatsu as masters of Harima and Bizen. But at the crucial moment Muramune was killed and

[5] *Okayama-shi shi*, 2.1343-1344. A list of castles for 1532 is taken from "Bizen gunki."

the Urakami house split into competing branches. Muramune's three sons, falling back upon Harima after the campaign in which their father was killed, quarreled. Masamune took the castle of Murotsu in Harima, Kunihide took Todamatsu castle near the port of Katakami in Bizen, while Munekage entered Bizen and established himself at Tenjinyama castle in the mountains of the middle Yoshii valley. He was followed into Bizen by many of the chief Urakami vassals: Ōtabara, Higasa, Nobuhara, Akashi, Okamoto, Hattori, Ukita, and some hundred others.

Having established himself at Tenjinyama, Munekage was able to extend his control over an area referred to in the chronicles as three districts of Harima, two of Mimasaka, and half of Bizen.[6] This area formed a contiguous land mass with a hard core of holdings centering on three key castles: Tenjinyama on the central Yoshii River, Mitsuishi on the frontier of Harima, and Todamatsu near Katakami on the sea frontier. Urakami power based on these strong-points fanned out but with diminishing authority to the borders of the Matsuda territory across the Yoshii River, to the rival Urakami of Murotsu in Harima, and into Mimasaka. The military chronicle *Bizen gunki* reports the following castle supporters of the Bizen Urakami in addition to their main castles:[7]

Castle	Holder
Takatoriyama	Shimamura
Toishi	Ukita Yamato-no-kami
Sone	Akashi Kageyuki
Aoyama	Higasa Yorifusa
Kidourayama	Higasa Jinzaemon
Iwōyama	Takatori Bizen
Ōnakayama	Nakayama Gorozaemon
Kasegi	Akashi Hida
Susaimura	Sasabe Kanjirō
Yamatori	Hiraga Daishin
Sakodani	Nukada Kisuke
Kumano-hogi	Akashi Genzaburō
Sakane	Akashi Ukyō
Katase	Oka Buzen
Tawara	Ukita Tosa
Tonodani	Onoda Sama-no-shin

[6] "Bizen gunki," 41. [7] *Ibid.*, 46.

Mushiage	Mushiage Kurōdo
Nishi Sue	Toriyama Sama
Oku-no-gō	Ukita Gorozaemon
Owari	Sumi Etchū

A glance at the map shows that these castles covered most of Bizen east of the Yoshii River. Here was a powerful base from which to strive for mastery of the Kibi provinces. And, as we shall see, the Urakami nearly succeeded in this venture.

To the west of the Matsuda and Urakami, the first family to emerge into prominence in Bitchū was the Shō. In 1533 the Shō, who had been based on Sarukake castle, added Matsuyama to their possession. The following description coming from the Shō family genealogy describes the position of the family as of 1533. "The Shō had for generations been masters of Sarukake castle, strategically located on the Oda River. In 1533 the Shō extended their influence to Matsuyama castle and thereby controlled half of the province of Bitchū. The head of the Shō family consequently took the title of Bitchū-no-kami. It was also at this time that the Shō built the castle of Saita and placed in it their branch family, the Ueki. As a result the head of the Shō family became the locus of military alliances (*hatagashira*) of the entire province. Branch families consisted of the Ueki, Tsutsu, and Fukui. Related to the Shō by marriage were the Mimura, Ishikawa, Narazaki, Kudō, and Noyama. Also closely related were the Tanaka, Ōtsuki, Date, and Ishiga. Besides these the small landholders of the area were all his stipendiaries (*kyūnin*)."[8]

THESE descriptions give us a general idea of the geographical distribution of the newly emergent *sengoku-daimyō*, but what of the institutional foundations upon which these domains rested? How, first of all, did houses such as the Urakami or Matsuda justify their exercise of local hegemony? Was it purely on military grounds? It would seem not. Despite their ability to fight for their domains, the *sengoku-daimyō* were concerned with problems of legitimacy and were eager to obtain some sort of recognized status. The Urakami and Matsuda, both having been deputies of the former *shugo*, could continue to lay claim to authority which had been vested in their lines by the Akamatsu. Whether the Matsuda

---

[8] *Komonjo-shū*, 1.190. Shō House documents.

tried for more ambitious titles is not revealed. The Urakami definitely did. After destruction of the Akamatsu house Urakami Muramune turned his attention to Kyoto and the politics of the Ashikaga house. He died, in fact, fighting for Hosokawa Takakuni, the Kyoto *kanrei*. But probably as important to Muramune's status as any court titles he may have acquired was the fact that he controlled as puppet the last head of the Akamatsu house and claimed to act in his name. Among the *sengoku-daimyō*, then, the concern for legitimacy was ever present. But for most the acquisition of official status was an ex-post addition to local power in hand, or else was grossly unrelated to the effective exercise of such power, as in the case of Amako Haruhisa, who received in 1552 fictional governorships over seven provinces, including Bizen and Mimasaka.[9] Kyoto thus remained the source of legitimacy and the focus of attention of those provincial daimyo who had a desire for honorary titles or court ranks. Until 1573, when the last Ashikaga shogun was deposed, legitimacy was generally couched in terms of shogunal appointments.

Behind such hollow claims to territorial jurisdiction, how did the *sengoku-daimyō* conceive of the limits of the domains over which they actually exercised control? Here the jurisdictional boundaries of titles such as *shugo* or *shugodai* could hold little meaning. In actual practice, therefore, the domains of the Sengoku lords formed from the inside out, not as administratively defined subdivisions of the state. Their shape conformed, in other words, to the territorial limits of the combined holdings of the vassals over which they exercised control, not to the abstract boundaries of provinces or districts. The true daimyo domain, therefore, was simply a composite of separate fiefs held either directly by the daimyo or by his vassals. This shift from assigned jurisdiction to command jurisdiction became one of the distinguishing features of the new daimyo domains.

If the *sengoku-daimyō* domains took shape as regionally integrated systems of military proprietorships, the essential cores of such domains were the hierarchies of military alliances which united the band of vassals around the central figure of the domain. Such vassal bands had been a long time in the making, for their origins date back to the early years of the Ashikaga pe-

---

[9] *Okayama-ken no rekishi*, 260.

rio d when such families as the Matsuda and Urakami began to
extend themselves as the agents of the *shugo*. The organizational
structure of such bands was the familiar one which placed primary
reliance upon kinsmen, but with ever increasing reliance upon
vassalage as a primary cohesive force. These networks of alliances
obviously represented several generations of effort by the main
family along two distinct lines: the gradual outward spread of
family branches to strategic positions within the locality, and the
subjugation and conversion to vassalage of other houses indigenous to the area. One of the most distinctive features of the
sengoku-daimyō vassal bands was the prevalence of identity between family names and place names. In other words within
such bands were many families which had occupied a locality for
a sufficient length of time either to take on the name of the locale
or to impart a name to it. In both the Matsuda and Shō vassal
bands, between twenty and thirty percent of the vassal families
bore the same surname as the name of the location of their castle.
The Urakami, perhaps because they had come into Bizen from
neighboring Harima, had fewer vassals of this type.

The size of the elementary vassal units of which the daimyo
domains were comprised naturally varied considerably, but the
composition of each was quite standard. Each consisted of a leading family, its castle, and its lands and workers. In Bizen alone
there is evidence of the construction of over 200 fortified spots
during the Sengoku period.[10] As we have already noted, not all of
these were active at one time, but perhaps a half of them were
in use as defense points by the major vassals of either the Urakami
or the Matsuda. Of course, most of these fortifications were small-
scale affairs, offering protection only to the proprietary family
and perhaps a handful of immediate followers.

A typical castle of these times was built upon the ridge of a
steep hill overlooking the cultivated valley floor where the castle
owner lived off his lands. Since warfare was still a matter of bows
and arrows, spears, and swords, fortifications were not extensive.
Castles generally depended upon natural features to discourage
the approach of the enemy. Ramparts were mainly earthen or
stone walls mounted by wood or plaster fences. Because of their
location on mountain ridges, such castles generally consisted of a

[10] *Tsūshi*, 1.988-1001.

number of circular protected encampments, called *maru,* which communicated with one another. Commonly only the major encampment, the *hommaru,* contained a tower erected to permit the castle chief to secure a broader view of the countryside and to give him a position from which to direct his men.

The residence of the lord of the castle was located below the hill and was not protected by the castle itself. (In time of emergency the master of the castle and his men escaped up the hill to the fortification.) The lord's residence provided for his family and perhaps for certain of his vassals who might make up a rotating military guard in times of peace. Clustered around the houses of the lord's residence were buildings for storage of grain and, of course, military supplies. Nearby was generally the Buddhist temple patronized by the owner of the castle and the local shrine which frequently was dedicated to the family's ancestral *kami.* Finally beyond the scattering of *bushi* residences and closer to the rice fields were the clustered huts of the peasants. Such combinations of fighting manpower and agricultural production making up the basic units of the daimyo's organization may indeed have had something of a minimum size. And it is probably more than coincidence that the two daimyo who rose to power in Bizen after the middle of the sixteenth century both started out as minimal vassals, enfeoffed as minor castle holders each with the command of thirty men.

Of course the main castle of a daimyo was a matter of some size and importance, permitting the continuous garrisoning of a large number of men-at-arms. The size of the castle at Tenjinyama which served the Urakami family is a good example of an early mountain fortress. A modern survey shows the string of defenses which made up Tenjinyama castle to number sixteen walled enclosures covering a long narrow mountain crest and extending roughly 1000 feet from end to end. The internal areas of the main enclosures are listed as follows:[11]

Name	Area (acres)	
Hommaru	6.00 *se*	(ca. .17)
Ni-no-maru	1.33 "	(ca. .04)

[11] Shiritsu Wake-gun Kyōikukai, *Wake-gun shi* (Okayama, 1909), 90-91; "Bizen kojō ezu," in *Kibi gunsho shūsei,* vol. 3.

Nagaya-no-dan	3.20 "	(ca. .09)
Sakura-no-baba	8.33 "	(ca. .20)
San-no-maru	4.33 "	(ca. .12)
Hiro-no-dan	2.00 "	(ca. .06)
Minami-no-dan	1.66 "	(ca. .05)
Hida-no-maru	2.66 "	(ca. .07)

While the actual functional use to which the several enclosures were put is uncertain, we may surmise that the Nagaya-no-dan contained barracks for garrison troops. Like so many similar Sengoku establishments, Tenjinyama proved adequate to withstand the kind of attack which neighboring daimyo were capable of mounting. And like other such castles it succumbed only to the unexpected appearance of superior firearms (acquired from the Portuguese) and treachery among the Urakami vassals.

As for the residential establishment built by the Urakami, which also served as the administrative center of their domain, we know next to nothing. From the point of view of topography the territory around Tenjinyama was not suitable for a large establishment, and certainly no town or cultural center emerged under the Urakami auspices. (We know little about their activity in Harima.) The Urakami domain in Bizen undoubtedly exemplified the extreme form of decentralization. Some of the other daimyo houses of longer pedigree managed to combine military strength and the patronage of arts and letters within the environs of their residential castles. The Matsuda were probably the most conspicuous in this respect. The town of Kanagawa which grew up around the Matsuda residence became a flourishing center of the Nichiren sect of Buddhism. But it was not until after the middle of the sixteenth century, when the castle city of Okayama was founded, that a major concentration of military power, and economic and cultural activity was assembled in Bizen. The province remained culturally decentralized during most of the Sengoku period.

The internal organizations of the domains of the *sengoku-daimyō* of Bizen, as would be expected, were based upon a typical lord-vassal system starting with the daimyo's household organization. The terms *kamon, ichizoku,* or *shōke* continued to be used to designate the blood-related vassals of various types.[12] The *sōryō* system of divided patrimony, however, was increasingly aban-

---

[12] Sanuki Matsuda keifu, quoted in *Okayama-shi shi,* 2.1331.

doned. Though there is no specific evidence of this with respect to the families of Bizen, there is ample data from adjoining areas. The Mōri house of Aki province to the west provides us with an excellent illustration. This family, which moved to western Japan from the Kantō in 1336, served as sub-*shugo* agents for the Hosokawa during the Ashikaga period. The Mōri power structure was based upon the *sōryō* system until about the beginning of the fifteenth century. After a crisis in which the main family was attacked by one of its branch houses, the rule of undivided inheritance was adopted. The head of the family, succeeding to the main inheritance, built up a close following of vassals irrespective of family connection. Branch families were treated strictly as vassals (*ienoko*). In other words, vassalage was considered a more trustworthy bond than kinship. By 1532 the head of the Mōri house had created a band based entirely on the submission of oaths of allegiance (*kishōmon*) and the reciprocal confirmation of land holdings.[13]

Beyond the circle of blood-related families, the daimyo's corps of vassals consisted of a wide range of allied families who had accepted the superior power of the daimyo and had become his enfeoffed vassals. The terminology by which such vassals were designated had already been widely in use, but the terms were becoming more specific in application. The general body of retainers was still called housemen (*kenin*) or retainers (*kashin*) or hereditary retainers (*fudai*). The smaller enfeoffed or stipended vassals of the main house were now quite frequently referred to as stipendiaries (*kyūnin*). It is also at this time that the term elder (*karō* or *rōshin*) came into general use to refer to the senior vassals. Thus the head of the daimyo house generally relied for his administration and the formation of military policy upon a group of elders selected from among the ablest and most experienced of his vassals. Most often the group of elders was drawn from members of the daimyo's branch families and the most powerful of his vassals. The designation *tozama* (outsider) was now frequently used for vassals who had accepted the daimyo's leadership after a particular turning point in his rise to power. Generally these were families with long-established local ties which resisted submission by playing off one emergent daimyo against another.

[13] Fukui Sakuji, "Mōri-shi no daimyō ryōshusei no hatten," *Geibi chihōshi kenkyū*, 5.6 (1954), 19-22.

Such families frequently declared their vassalage only after it was certain that the daimyo house was well on its way to local hegemony. Since by this time the main body of the daimyo's band had taken shape, these late adherents were treated as "outsiders."

Not much is known about the administrative techniques used by the *sengoku-daimyō* in their territories. Probably there were several styles of organization, one in which the main house depended upon a rather small number of extremely large branch families or vassals who among them would divide up the bulk of the smaller vassals into regional groups or commands, another in which the daimyo maintained direct, personal command over all vassals whether large or small. The choice between such patterns depended somewhat upon topography and the length of time the daimyo family had been in residence a given locality. It seems most likely that the Matsuda command was divided into a number of sub-groups each identified with a distinct section of the Asahi River valley. The Urakami appear to have maintained a more unitary command. The exercise of local administration obviously followed the pattern of enfeoffment, and the daimyo would have little cause to interfere directly into the affairs of the individual fiefs. On the other hand, since the lands of the daimyo were scattered and since there were certain domain-wide problems, such as the control of religious institutions, the daimyo also must have established some sort of administrative organization with specified duties. The most common variety of official to appear in the documents is the local agent, or deputy (*daikan*). The following set of documents provides an example of the way in which tax problems were handled between the Urakami chief and his local agent, in this case a member of the Ukita family:[14]

1. Concerning the market place established by Saidaiji in the clerk's section of Kanaoka-no-shō, [the income from] this is positively commended for building purposes. In accordance with this our deputy's impost is discontinued. Thus ordered

1492, 7, 25   Urakami Saburōshirō
                                                     Munesuke (his cipher)

    To Saidaiji,
       the temple agent

[14] *Komonjo-shū*, 3.9. Saidaiji documents.

2. Concerning the market place established by Saidaiji in the clerk's section of Kanaoka-no-shō, since [the income from] this is commended for building purposes, you will discontinue collection of imposts. Thus ordered

1492, 7, 25   Munesuke (his cipher)

   To Ukita Jirōsaburō *dono*

When organized for military purposes the daimyo's band of vassals was of course divided under various commands. Vassals selected to lead military operations or large divisions of the daimyo's command were generally called commanders (*taishō* or *shō*). Most frequently such commanders were also major castellans within the daimyo's territory. The general run of the warrior elite were termed knights (*ki*). Each knight entered battle with his own group of followers (*yoriki*) drawn from his fief.

While the use of the oath of allegiance was not new to the Sengoku period, by this time almost exclusive reliance was placed upon the oath as the mechanism for maintaining loyalty and compliance to authority. Furthermore, while the grant of land in compensation for military service had become increasingly common within the military sector of the society since Kamakura days, by now nearly all lands were held as fiefs from an immediate military superior. The most common binding element in Sengoku society then was the oath of allegiance and the grant of investiture or confirmation of land holdings. Unfortunately, examples of feudal documents of this period are scarce for the Bizen area, at least for the territories of the Urakami and Matsuda. On the other hand, since such documents are quite common elsewhere and followed a stereotyped form, the following examples taken from the Iriki domain of Kyushu will serve the purpose:

Oath (*seimon*)

That in the three provinces, whatever changes may take place, I will serve my lord singly and without reservations as in the past,

That my sentiments have been reported to Murata *dono* several times in the past, and there remains nothing else.

That in the event of any slander or evil report, the lord will inform me of it and that he will request me to state my mind.

If the above statements are false

Names of *kami* (*jimmei*)

Bummei 13, 6, 23 (1481)

Shimotsuke-no-kami   Shigetoyo[15]

In the above document the reference to "names of *kami*" was an abbreviated version of the oath taken in the names of Buddhist and Shinto deities (selected for both national and local importance) as follows:

> If these statements be false, let the punishments of
> The Tenshō Daijingū of Ise,
> The Daigongen of the three Kumano,
> The Daibosatsu of Nitta Hachiman,
> The Temman Daijizai Tenjin, and
> The Daimyōjin of Upper and Lower Suwa
> be visited upon me.[16]

The land grant naturally varied greatly according to circumstance, but the following example is fairly typical:

> The west part of Yamato-in, and Arakawa and Hashima in Satsuma-no-kōri, Satsuma-no-kuni are presented to you for the present since you would render loyal service. You shall hold (*chigyō*) them according to precedents.

Ōei 10, 12, 7 (1404)   Motohisa

To Shibuya Danjō Shōhitsu *dono*[17]

Not only was authority within the military sector of Bizen's society held together by such documents, the loyalty of the peasantry and performance of specific duties of all types was guaranteed by sworn oaths. Documents of this sort in which members of the military aristocracy swore to protect religious establishments or to observe various prohibitions are quite common among the remaining records of Bizen. A statement of the following type is illustrative.[18]

A regulation [regarding]
Kinzan-kannonji

[15] Asakawa, *Iriki*, 295 (Japanese text p. 73).
[16] *Ibid.*, 294 (Japanese p. 8).   [17] *Ibid.*, 287 (Japanese p. 9).
[18] *Komonjo-shū*, 2.22-23. Kinzanji documents.

The above temple has been a place of worship for the shogun's house and that of the *shugo*. Previously we the undersigned agreed to protect the hills, forests and wood-lots of the temple. Accordingly our household (*ichizoku*), all of the samurai within the village, all peasants and those of lesser status will be firmly prohibited from entering the hills, forests and woodlots of the temple. If anyone should violate this, he shall be punished. If by any chance there should be a failure to enforce this provision:

An Oath
Let the punishments of Honzon Senju Kannon,
Chinju Sannō Gongen,
Yumiya Hachiman Daibosatsu, and
the great and small deities be visited upon us. . .
in token of which we place our joint signatures.

Susuki Chū Yukikage (his cipher)
(and seven others)
1489

Under the *sengoku-daimyō* the transformation of the *shōen* system of proprietorship and land management into one based on enfeoffment was now complete. At the various levels of proprietorship and management a process of consolidation of the *shiki* rights had long been at work. Among the practices which now governed the exercise of land rights the position of the daimyo was in most respects identical to that of the old *shōen* proprietors. By this time the many separate levels of proprietorship (as revealed in the terms *honke, ryōke,* or *ryōshu*) and the various managerial functions (such as *nasshō, kumon,* or *jitō*) had been eliminated, and in their place there appeared a simple, uniform practice of overlordship defined by the concepts of proprietary authority (*ryō*) and the rights of management (*chigyō*).

To say that the rights of proprietorship had become uniform is not to imply that there was no distinction in the degree of independent exercise of seignorial authority. The possession of land rights, even during the Sengoku period, was conditioned by precedents and admitted to the existence of transcendental authority. Land was never held "absolutely" as though in a vacuum. There was always the superior authority which confirmed or granted rights of proprietorship. In the eyes of the superior such land was held as the fief (*chigyōchi*) of the inferior. Even the daimyo in theory held their domains at the pleasure of the shogun. It was characteristic of the fief-holder that he held comprehensive rights of use and profit from the fief on condition that he give loyal service to his superior. Gone was the intricate division of inferior managerial functions. The differences between one *chigyō* holder and another was now merely a matter of size rather than function. The situation has been admirably described by Asakawa:

> In the meantime, these "dark ages" of anarchy saw the final stages of feudalization of Japan, both socially and politically, or, in both private and public law. . . . The *shō* . . . *rapidly* disintegrated into fragments; in these the old distinction of *shiki* and the division of control between the domainal lord and the *kuni* governor were obliterated, and were superseded by a new relationship frankly based upon vassalage. . . . All domains tended to become fiefs held of lords above and divided among vassals below. Likewise, *shugo, jitō,* and *myōshu,* as well as *gokenin,* had become empty terms. The complicated arrangement which they had once expressed having now been replaced by a new organization in the *kuni.* Civil and religious lords having all but vanished, and the shogun's authority having been almost forgotten, the old *shugo* had become the overlord under whom the other lords and warriors were vassals and rear-vassals holding fiefs in a descending gradation in a scheme of hierarchical feudal relationships.[19]

We should not assume, of course, that a statement of this kind fully described all of the political life of Bizen during the sixteenth century. Conditions were not so simple, and no single neat system of authority embraced all of the land within the two daimyo domains into which Bizen had become divided. There were, for instance, a number of territories which did not come under the daimyo's powers of enfeoffment, notably the holdings of temples and shrines, many of which still maintained connections with headquarter organizations in Kyoto or Nara. There were still a few absentee proprietorships, especially of the imperial family, which were occasionally recognized by a shipment of annual

[19] Asakawa, *op.cit.*, 29.

dues. And there were communities of merchants and artisans who existed outside the daimyo's system of vassalage. But all of these groups depended increasingly upon the pleasure of the daimyo, finding it useful or necessary to secure confirmation from the daimyo of their traditional land holdings or their charters of protection for commercial or craft activities.

While within the ruling sector of Japanese society the rights of governance were undergoing consolidation into a simple form of feudal proprietorship, a similar process of consolidation and simplification of rights and responsibilities was affecting the condition of the cultivator class. Concentration of authority into the hands of a feudal elite tended to lift the level of direct participation by the managerial class in rural affairs, releasing an increasing number of the peasantry to work out their own self-management. Within the *shōen*, the large farm family, the *myō*, had been the basic unit of organization. While cultivators had lived together in communities, these groups had not served as units of administration or tax collection. Individual large families continued to serve as the objects of cooperative labor and taxation under the ubiquitous *shōen* officials.[20] But the unsettled conditions in the countryside after the wars of the dynasties, the decay of the *shōen* system, together with an expansion of the farming sector both in numbers and productivity, encouraged the formation of self-sufficient village communities. As peasant families separated more and more into individual nuclear households, extended family connections were weakened in favor of neighborhood ties. With the development of irrigation systems, regional programs for land reclamation, and the specialization of handicrafts, communal units of larger size became necessary. By the middle of the Ashikaga period, daimyo were depending more and more on the ability of peasant communities to manage their own affairs and to pay taxes on a quota basis. The local populace, in such instances, was held accountable for purposes of administration, taxation, labor and military service according to village-size units. Such village units developed their own organs of self-government and even of self-defense during the years of intense civil war which were to follow. In some localities the old administrative village units, the *gō*, came to take on new meaning as the villagers

[20] Itō, *Hōken*, 181-183.

within the *gō* organized themselves for a more stable self-government.[21] Below the *gō* the smaller community, called *mura* or *son*,
became the primary unit of local organization. Increasingly, also,
the daimyo enfeoffed his vassals in terms of units of income derived from such villages.

While the origins of the *gō-son* system of peasant organization,
as this new combination has been called, go back to the mid-
Ashikaga period, its full recognition in the land laws of the
country did not come about until the last decades of the sixteenth
century. In Bizen, in particular, the new village structure appears
to have been slow in making its appearance in documents of
land transfer. Thus the old provincial and *shōen* terminology continued in use until well beyond the middle of the sixteenth century. We have already seen this in the 1492 documents concerning
the market place established by Saidaiji in Kanaoka-no-shō. Even
in the grant of fiefs to military vassals the old terms were still used
by the Urakami. For example:

In Bizen, Katase-*gō*:
   Koshika-*myō*, the proprietor's regular-tax portion, and
In Yoshioka-no-shō-south:
   Fujino's holding, and
In Kanematsu-*gō*:
   The one-third land-rent portion

You shall surely hold the above and will render loyal service
   without equivocation. Thus ordered,

1572, 2, 23   Munekage (his cipher)

To Baba Genshō[22]

In such a land document, of course, we may assume that each
named parcel was a simple holding which could be kept in fief.
There were no superior obligations upon the land. The old terminology merely persisted as a customary means of naming particular units of land.

OUR description of the conditions of local administration and
land management in Bizen during the Sengoku period has em-

[21] Shimizu, *Chūsei no sonraku*, 121-166.
[22] *Okayama-shi shi*, 2.1261.

phasized the increasingly feudal nature of local government and hence the increasingly private nature of the exercise of authority. The conversion of what had once been a rationally organized, bureaucratic system of local administration to one based primarily upon personal agreements between lord and vassal, together with the stories of constant disorder and violence in the provinces, would lead us to suppose that conditions had greatly deteriorated for the inhabitants of the province of Bizen even by comparison with the Kamakura period. To some extent of course this is true. Life was indeed more insecure and the incidence of warfare far greater than in any previous time in Bizen's remembrance. Yet there were other aspects to life in Bizen of the sixteenth century which lead to different conclusions. If the age was more turbulent, it was also filled with greater opportunity. By comparison with Bizen of the early Kamakura period, when we last took stock of the economic and cultural assets of the province, conditions during the Sengoku period showed many signs of growth. Most obvious was the dramatic increase in agricultural production. Production of handicraft goods, the circulation of commodities, and even the adoption of monetary currency were greatly expanded in comparison with what they had been three centuries earlier. The number and variety of religious institutions had also increased, and the richness of cultural life which went on in the temples and shrines is attested to by numerous buildings and artifacts which remain from this period. While it would be impossible to describe in any great detail the economic and cultural achievements of the Ashikaga and the Sengoku ages, we would create an erroneous picture of sixteenth century life in the provinces were we to neglect developments in these fields entirely.

An outstanding characteristic of the *bushi* families was their constant and generous patronage of religious institutions. Decentralization of political power first through the spread of the *shōen* system and then as military families gained large independent holdings throughout the province meant that the sources of patronage were also multiplied and extended. Whereas the religious establishments of the Heian period had represented a limited number of sects and had been concentrated heavily in the southern portion of the province around the political center, conditions had now changed greatly. New sects had gained a footing in Bizen, a few old sects, particularly Tendai and Shingon, had staged revivals, and above all, with the breakdown of the *shōen* proprietorships, temples and shrines became dependent upon direct patronage from the province itself. Many of the religious centers which had stood since the Heian period disappeared entirely as court support diminished, while new institutions patronized by the new military leaders flourished. Among the long-established temples to retain local patronage was the Tendai monastery of Anyōji. As the foremost temple in Nyūta-no-shō it received the support of the military stewards in the Kamakura age and of the deputy *shugo* of the Ashikaga period. Its records contain pledges of protection and grants of land from the Ashikaga, Akamatsu, and Urakami families and from their retainers.[23] Kinzanji, a Tendai temple located in the area now occupied by the city of Okayama, was also patronized by members of the Urakami family and prominent military houses of southern Bizen.

More important to the Urakami house was the great temple of Saidaiji on the banks of the Yoshii River. It served both as a religious center and as an important market place. Saidaiji was a Shingon temple with origins going back to an establishment of different sectarian affiliations in the Nara period. Saidaiji grew to become one of the largest of the local temples in Bizen during the Sengoku period. Some ten branches were founded in the southern portion of eastern Bizen, all of which received support from Urakami retainers. The burning of Saidaiji in 1507 has been commemorated in a painted scroll still retained by the temple. (See figure 22.) The occasion was a wild raid into the province by Yamane Shimbei, a retainer of the Yamana house. As the scroll exclaims, Yamane earned the wrath of the Buddhist deities by setting fire to the Kannon chapel of Saidaiji. But there had been worse fires, one in 1495 and again in 1532 when a local peasant uprising set off conflagrations which burned down the entire temple complex.[24]

Several *bushi* families in Bizen became strong converts to Nichiren and aggressively patronized temples of this sect throughout the province. Honrenji, located at Ushimado, served as a guardian temple for the flourishing port town. It was actively patronized by the local castle chief, surnamed Ishihara, a family

<hr>

[23] *Komonjo-shū*, 1.3-5. Anyōji documents.
[24] *Ibid.*, 3.1-3. Saidaiji documents.

which had a record of dominance over the Ushimado area from the Kamakura period on. The foremost patrons of Nichiren in Bizen, however, were the Matsuda.[25] The conversion of the Matsuda family to this militant sect went back at least to the beginning of the Ashikaga period when we hear of the head of the Matsuda family traveling to Kyoto in order to present funds to the priest Nichizō. From this time the Matsuda headquarters of Kanagawa became a major center of Nichiren activity; by the sixteenth century heads of the Matsuda family had become fanatically attached to the sect and even attempted to forcibly extend its influence. There is a record that in the 1550's the head of the Matsuda family attempted to convert Kinzanji to a Nichiren temple, and failing to do so, burned down the temple.[26] The following entry in *Bizen gunki* (*Military Chronicles of Bizen*) describes the incident:

> Of late the Matsuda have gone to extremes in their Nichiren beliefs. Determined to convert all temples in their domain to this sect, they burn down those which refuse. Kinzan Kannonji, and Kibitsu-no-miya were burned down at this time. A Nichiren chapel has been established within the castle at Kanagawa.[27]

Apparently Matsuda religious fanaticism increased as the pressure of rival military houses upon Kanagawa mounted. But of more lasting importance than the violent conduct of the Matsuda house was the large number of Nichiren priests who went out from Bizen as a result of Matsuda patronage. Many of these were members of the Matsuda family itself or of its foremost vassal families. Their dedication to the Nichiren priesthood indicates how deeply Buddhism had penetrated into the fabric of provincial life at this time.

Bizen for some reason did not develop into a particularly strong center of Zen activity. In the province of Bitchū, however, located in the foothills above the present town of Sōja, the monastery of Hōfukuji grew into one of the largest Zen establishments in western Japan. This monastery at one time could claim land holdings extending over eleven *gō*. The monastic establishment itself is said to have contained over thirty buildings.

[25] *Ibid.*, 2.4-7. Kinzanji documents.   [26] *Ibid.*, 2. intro. 3.
[27] Quoted in *Okayama-ken no rekishi*, 232-233.

Sesshū, the great priestly artist of the fifteenth century, was born in the vicinity of this temple and received his early religious instruction in Bitchū before entering the priesthood in Kyoto.

Patronage of Shinto shrines was not neglected, though again the institutions which had enjoyed court support in previous years tended to decline in importance. Among provincial shrines the two dedicated to Kibitsu Hiko continued to be outstanding. Of the two the Bitchū shrine had greater local prestige and was consequently the more richly endowed. Records indicate that during the sixteenth century the shrine controlled lands that extended over three *gō* in the vicinity of the shrine. Keepers of Kibitsu shrine were still drawn from the Kayō family which traced its lineage back to one of the branches of the Kibi line. This family remained local land holders of some importance, and the family headquarters is said to have been fortified for protection like that of other *bushi* houses.[28] The example of the Kayō family is rather uncommon in the Kibi area, and we must imagine that most religious establishments remained undefended and strictly religious in their orientation. Bizen does not seem to have given rise to the kind of religious center which controlled large proprietary domains or which set up military defenses to protect itself from daimyo authority. Most of the temples and shrines in Bizen remained small in scale and rather fully dependent upon the patronage of local *bushi* families.

Evidence of increased economic productivity in Bizen during the Sengoku period is necessarily impressionistic, but it is nonetheless quite abundant. In agriculture, as we have noted from the mention of wheat in the tax document of 1203, Bizen must have begun at a very early age to adopt the practice of year-round cultivation. Documents found in Honrenji temple of Ushimado indicate that the practice of double cropping had expanded and that even triple cropping was practiced in some locations by the Sengoku period.[29] Bizen remained one of the highly productive agricultural regions of Japan. In the field of crafts and manufactures Bizen and Bitchū were also outstanding. Local mines produced copper and iron, the Inland Sea produced fish and salt, and local artisans were famous for tiles, pottery, paper, and especially

[28] *Komonjo-shū*, 2. intro. 13-23.
[29] *Ibid.*, 2.66. Honrenji documents.

swords. The swords of Osafune were among the most prized blades of all Japan.

Markets and port towns also flourished in the Bizen area. The famous illustrated scroll depicting the life of Ippen Shōnin in the late thirteenth century provides a glimpse of the market at Fukuoka. (See figure 21.) Here stalls were set up for sale of rice, fabrics, wine, foodstuffs, and metal goods. The market established on the grounds of Saidaiji has already made its appearance in the document of exemption granted by Urakami Munesuke. Port towns such as Ushimado, Katakami, Saidaiji, Kōri, and Shimotsui communicated not only with the capital but also with Korea and occasionally the continent of China. Unfortunately, we have less evidence on how this commercial activity related to the existing political structure. As in other parts of Japan we can assume that merchant and craft communities gained patronage and protection from both the religious institutions and the military proprietors. As the sixteenth century progressed, local *bushi* became increasingly active in the working of mines, the patronage of manufactures (especially swords and armor), and in coastal trade.

A final measure of changing economic conditions in Bizen during the Sengoku period is visible in the practices of financial transaction and tax calculation. In the Nara period we noted that tax procedures relied heavily on manpower as a basic ingredient of payment. By the Heian and Kamakura periods the tax base had shifted largely to produce, with manpower being relegated to a relatively minor role in the form of corvée and special military duties. By the sixteenth century, especially with the spread of the system of taxation by village units, payment tended to take the form of commodity and even monetary units. The use of copper coins either in actual cash transaction or as units of value for sale of land or payment of taxes is revealed in numerous documents surviving from this period. While land documents of the thirteenth century uniformly rely on measures of rice as the unit of calculation, by the fourteenth century the use of strings of cash (*kammon*) had come into general use. By the sixteenth century there are documents in which the tax value of lands granted in fief is expressed in units of cash rather than measures of rice. This practice was rather slow to develop in the Urakami domain.[30]

[30] *Okayama-ken no rekishi*, 211-213.

But documents from Bitchū, particularly those of the Fukutake house, show a definite conversion to cash units of tax calculation by 1576.[31]

SUCH were some of the important cultural developments which form a counterpoint to the dominant theme of military struggle. By the 1550's the scene was set in the Kibi provinces for another round of military activity to which we must now direct our attention. During the next few decades the area reacted to two parallel developments. First, within the region itself, the major *sengoku-daimyō* began to expand from their castle headquarters and to engage each other in a struggle for local hegemony. On top of this was added a new wave of penetration into the area by aggressive military forces from adjoining provinces. Thus to the local military competition between the Urakami of Tenjinyama, the Matsuda of Kanagawa, and the Shō of Matsuyama was intruded the counterforces of outside pressures: the Mōri of Aki pushing into Bitchū from the west, the Amako of Izumo pushing into Mimasaka from the northwest, the Yamana of Bingo and the Hosokawa of Shikoku pushing in from the southwest. In some areas of Japan the *sengoku-daimyō* rose to these new challenges, consolidated their forces and emerged to join the band of leaders who formed the victorious coalition under the great unifiers of the late sixteenth century, Oda Nobunaga and Toyotomi Hideyoshi. But in Bizen the Urakami, Matsuda, and Shō were ultimately displaced by new and more energetic fighters: daimyo more capable of weathering the climactic battles of the wars of unification.

Our story begins with the chronicles of the Urakami house of Bizen. Urakami Munekage was obliged to meet the attack of his brother of Murotsu almost immediately after entering Bizen and establishing Tenjinyama castle. In 1532 the Murotsu forces loading some 2000 horsemen in 200 boats made a surprise landing on Bizen's shores, and successfully assaulted the castle of Mitsuishi from the water side.[32] The same force reduced Todamatsu castle where Munekage's brother Kunihide was in command. Munekage himself sortied from Tenjinyama and drove off the Murotsu forces, recapturing Todamatsu but failing to regain Mitsuishi. The

[31] *Komonjo-shū*, 3.260. Fukutake House documents.
[32] "Bizen-gunki," 41.

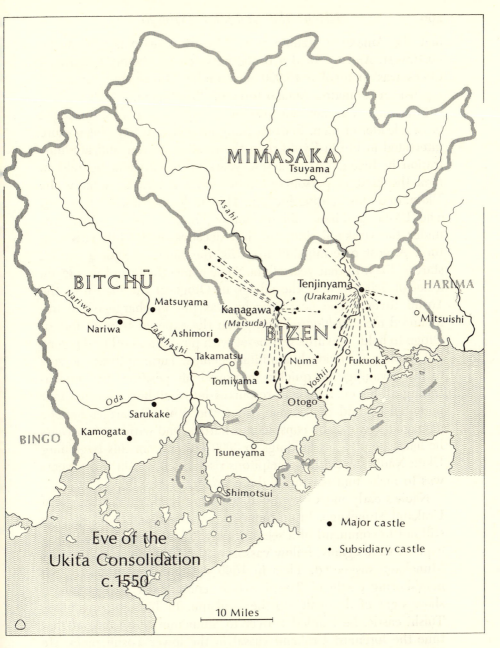

MIMASAKA
Tsuyama

BITCHŪ

Matsuyama
Nariwa
Ashimori
Takamatsu
Tomiyama

Kanagawa
(Matsuda)

BIZEN

Tenjinyama
(Urakami)

HARIMA

Mitsuishi

Numa
Fukuoka

Otogo

Sarukake

Kamogata

BINGO

Tsuneyama

Shimotsui

Asahi

Nariwa

Takahashi

Oda

Yoshii

● Major castle

• Subsidiary castle

Eve of the
Ukita Consolidation
c. 1550

10 Miles

chronicles say nothing further about Mitsuishi. These attacks
effectively split the Urakami territories into two parts, one centered on Harima and the other on Bizen. Also from this point
the Bizen branch turned its attention almost exclusively toward
Bizen and Mimasaka, leaving the affairs of Harima behind it. In

fact the Amako of Izumo were already threatening from the northwest. And by 1553 a battle between the Izumo and Bizen forces was to involve 15,000 men under Munekage's command against an estimated Amako force of 28,000 men.

Munekage was not the best of daimyo either as a strategist or as a leader of men. For one thing he seems to have been more interested in life in Kyoto than the realities of war and administration in Bizen.[33] After a few years in Tenjinyama he seldom took the field in person but relied on his vassals, notably the Ukita, to do his fighting for him. This in the end was his undoing. The Ukita, a minor military family, had a history of service under the Urakami since the last decades of the fifteenth century. Almost exterminated in 1523, the family began a second start in 1544. In that year Ukita Naoie came of age and was given a fief of 300 *kan* near the village of Otogo at the mouth of the Yoshii River.[34] The next year he was put in charge of 30 unmounted men (*ashigaru*) and given the exposed frontier fort of Otogo to hold. The area was beset with pirates and other dangers, but Naoie was obviously a military genius. Turning these dangers to his advantage he quickly improved his position. By concentrating all his energies and resources into building up a military potential beyond the normal expectations of his meager fief, he managed to win some conspicuous battles, and within a few years he had extended his holdings to 3000 *koku*. From this beginning Ukita Naoie started his precipitous rise which within thirty years was to make him master of three provinces of Kibi.

Naoie's early moves within Bizen were made at the behest of Urakami Munekage. From them we can see that Munekage was still not in command of a secure following. Most of Naoie's early exploits were against fellow vassals of the Urakami whose loyalty Munekage suspected. Thus in 1545 we find him attacking the neighboring castle of Toishi, whose commander had begun to show signs of disloyalty to the Urakami. In 1549, having taken Toishi castle, he handed it over to Shimamura Kan'ami, at that time the foremost Urakami vassal in the lower Yoshii plain. He himself moved to Narabe castle in the midst of new lands given

---

[33] "Wakeginu," *Kibi gunsho shūsei* edn., 3.40.

[34] *Okayama-shi shi*, 2.1427. Information on the rise of the Ukita family and the decline of the Urakami is given in great detail in chapters 55 to 61 (pp. 1194-1494) of the *Okayama-shi shi*. I have not documented specific data in the following paragraphs.

him for his meritorious service. In 1551 Naoie, at Urakami request, took in marriage the daughter of Nakayama Bitchū, lord of Kameyama castle, thus submitting to a strategic marriage calculated to cement relations between two Urakami vassals.

In 1559, Urakami Munekage, suspecting his vassals Nakayama and Shimamura of treachery, turned to Ukita Naoie for aid. Naoie, through a stratagem, destroyed both of these men and captured Kameyama castle. For this feat he was given "over half" of the lands vacated by his victims and the castle of Kameyama (hereafter more frequently called Numa). Naoie was by this time the prime power in the lower Yoshii plain. Holding Numa castle, strategically placed to command the plain and richly supported by the excellent agricultural land of the vicinity, he was able to put his own followers into his former castles. In fact, Naoie was now in a position rivaling that of his own overlord in power and wealth. He had become the foremost vassal upon whom Munekage relied, and he and his officers were constantly used to lead Urakami forces in Mimasaka or Bitchū. As it later developed, the sense of comradeship in arms which developed at this time between Ukita Naoie and Munekage's other vassals was eventually to make them more ready to follow Naoie than their ostensible overlord.

In 1562 on Munekage's order Naoie gave daughters in marriage to the Matsuda house of Kanagawa and the Gotō house of Mitsuboshi in Mimasaka. It was clearly the Urakami hope to stabilize the entire eastern Bizen-Mimasaka region under his command by these alliances. Momentarily, at any rate, the Matsuda house appears to have joined forces with the Urakami of Tenjinyama so as to permit the Urakami to assume leadership of all of Bizen. This act shifted the Urakami frontier westward into Bitchū and the valley of the Takahashi River. And it was this development which precipitated the bitter contest for hegemony over Kibi between the Urakami and Mimura of Bitchū.

By this time control of the Takahashi valley had shifted from the Shō to the Mimura, who were based at Nariwa and Matsuyama castles. The Mimura, in league with the Mōri forces farther to the west, had recently driven the Amako out of western Mimasaka and were in a position to contemplate expansion into Bizen and Mimasaka, just as the Urakami looked toward Bitchū. The Mimura made their move first into Bizen, taking the castles of

Funayama and Okayama. Their stratagem was to bottle up the Matsuda and Ukita, preventing their entry into Bitchū. They then turned to Mimasaka and attacked the Gotō of Mitsuboshi. Although the Bizen forces were blocked from moving westward, the northern route was open. Ukita Naoie sent support to Mimasaka, and in 1566 the Mimura leader was killed before the Gotō stronghold. Unsuccessful in Mimasaka, the Mimura remnants turned to direct attack upon the Ukita. In 1567 the Mimura sent two forces totaling 7000 men against Numa castle. Naoie met and utterly destroyed the Mimura forces and went on to send a force of 9000 men into Bitchū to attack Saita castle. In these campaigns a number of southern Bizen castles hostile to the Ukita were destroyed, notably Tsuri and Funayama. The commander of Okayama castle, Kanamitsu Munetaka, a respected military leader of the area, gave his allegiance to Naoie. Thus Naoie emerged stronger than before; in fact, his successes began to rouse the suspicions of the Urakami.

From this point, Ukita Naoie, no doubt realizing that he was not trusted by Urakami Munekage, showed more caution in his relationship to his overlord. Perhaps he had already begun to aspire to eventual supremacy in Bizen. At any rate, we find him beginning to cultivate military alliances on his own outside of the Urakami band. In the course of the next years Naoie appears to have made strategic alliances with such families as the Amako of Izumo and the Kobayakawa of Bingo, distant daimyo who might be counted on to support a play for power inside Bizen. Armed with these alliances Naoie attacked and destroyed the Matsuda of Kanagawa in 1568. In this campaign, in which the Ukita forces resorted to their usual daring and strategy, we hear of the use of firearms for the first time. By now it is obvious that Naoie was his own master as he campaigned almost yearly along the borders of the Urakami territories in an effort to extend his influence. In 1570 his forces were in Bitchū clashing with the Mōri and Mimura. At the same time he campaigned actively in Mimasaka. During the next few years the major castles of Mimasaka fell to either the Ukita or the Mōri.

Prior to this, Ukita Naoie had taken Okayama castle from the Kanemitsu. In 1573 he selected this castle as a new headquarters and proceeded to build a much greater establishment for himself and his armed forces. In the next three years Naoie was occupied primarily in Bitchū. Here he eventually joined forces with the Mōri family, which had expanded into the province from Aki, two provinces to the west. This alliance made possible the eventual elimination of the Mimura. With the fall of Matsuyama castle Bitchū went to the Mōri and Ukita and was divided between them at the Takahashi River, the Mōri occupying the western portion and the Ukita the east.

Having resolved the danger from the direction of Bitchū, Naoie was now poised for an attack upon his feudal superior, Urakami Munekage. The moment came in 1577. Seizing upon a succession issue, Naoie plotted with Munekage's vassals. The majority had by now become more attached to Naoie than to the Urakami house. Naoie marched upon Tenjinyama castle and destroyed it, eliminating the Bizen Urakami line forever. Flushed with a sense of victory, and still in alliance with the Mōri, Naoie pushed into Harima and began to take over other Urakami castles to the east. His farthest advance was to Kōzuki castle, where in 1578 a new destiny confronted him. It was at Kōzuki that Naoie first faced the massive forces of Oda Nobunaga moving in from the east and was forced to choose between retaining his Mōri alliance or submitting to Nobunaga.

As of 1578 a choice between the Mōri and Oda was not one to be lightly taken. Both confronted Naoie with overwhelming might against which he could not hold aloof. But which side held the superior potential? To be sure, Nobunaga controlled the capital, but the Mōri were nearly his match in terms of territory and manpower. And for Naoie, the Mōri must have seemed an attractive alliance, for he had already joined them in many a difficult campaign. And he was aware, too, of the forceful momentum with which the Mōri had pushed to the borders of Bizen. As of 1500 the Mōri house had been only a minor castle holder at Kōriyama in Aki province, vassal to the Amako. Mōri Motonari, the head of the house at that time, in a crucial battle at Itsukushima in 1555 won control of Aki and Bingo. Shortly thereafter, he succeeded to the Ōuchi domains of Nagato and Suō provinces. In 1566 he eliminated the Amako from Izumo and Inaba and stood on the boundaries of Bitchū. Already the Hosokawa of Kamogata had capitulated to the Mōri. Shortly thereafter the Mimura, kinsmen of the Shō, sided with the Mōri and began to fight against the Shō. Despite their many commitments elsewhere, the Mōri establishment, now stretching over fourteen provinces, maintained an active interest in the penetration of Bitchū. After Motonari's death in 1571, his successor Terumoto campaigned actively in Bitchū. Using Kasaoka as a base, he destroyed the Mimura, and placed his uncle Motokiyo into Sarukake castle. The latter took the name of Hoida. In this way Sarukake castle became the center of Mōri power in Bitchū, while the former castles of the Shō and Mimura forces became secondary military outposts. The Mōri had moved their frontier into Bitchū up to the Takahashi River where it touched the Ukita domains along a broad front.

Ukita Naoie's alliance with Mōri Terumoto technically opened up the Mōri frontier as far as the eastern border of Ukita power. The rapid push of the combined Mōri and Ukita forces into Harima after the pacification of Bitchū may have been because their leaders caught the urge toward national conquest which was then in the air. But the moment was too late. Nobunaga was already in the capital and had already thrown his ablest general, Hideyoshi, against the Mōri coalition. These were the forces that met at Kōzuki. At the historic battle, the forces led by Hideyoshi numbered 150,000 and those supporting the Mōri, 65,000. Ukita Naoie, claiming illness, provided only a token force. The ensuing battle was a draw, but the Mōri forces withdrew behind the Takahashi River, leaving the Ukita to join forces with Oda Nobunaga. When three years later in 1581 Naoie died, his son, then age eight, was confirmed in his holdings by Nobunaga, an indication that the Ukita house was now firmly in the fold of the expanding central authority based in the Kyoto area. The Mōri bid for national hegemony had been momentarily thwarted.

X. NOBUNAGA, HIDEYOSHI, AND THE
UNIFICATION OF THE DAIMYO

THE story of the consolidation of the Kibi provinces under the Mōri and Ukita houses has taken us through the Sengoku period up to the threshold of a new and dramatic era in Japanese history, when out of the turmoil of the "country at war" a national hegemony was again fashioned. Between 1568 and 1598 a powerful military force emanating out of central Japan, led by two military geniuses, Oda Nobunaga and Toyotomi Hideyoshi, hammered the daimyo into submission and imposed a rough unity upon them. The years over which Nobunaga and Hideyoshi presided, when the spirit of unification was abroad and the great daimyo were destined to fight their last battles, were dramatic not only because of the climactic struggles which shook the country but because of the far-reaching institutional reforms which swept Japan in their wake. Nobunaga, Hideyoshi, and their daimyo adherents not only forged the bonds of military unification but laid a new political and social base upon which over two hundred years of peaceful existence under the Tokugawa shogunate was built. It was during the little more than thirty years after the rise of Nobunaga that most of the fundamental policies and institutions under which the people of early modern Japan were to live came into being. With unification came not only a cessation of warfare but a new systemization of laws and procedures governing the exercise of sovereign powers, the structure of local administration, the management of land, the status of the cultivating and commercial classes, and the position of religious bodies within Japan.

The great moving force which infused the last half of the sixteenth century was the drive toward military consolidation and political unification. When precisely it was that the daimyo sensed the possibility of a national hegemony we do not know. But Nobunaga was not the first, and he fought out his life with competitors such as the Mōri, whose chances of success seemed no less potent than his. Once under way, unification proceeded by certain clearly discernible stages. The base was laid during the early sixteenth century with the appearance of the small regional hegemons to which we gave the name *sengoku-daimyō*. As these regional lords of new and militant type filled out their territories and added to their resources, they began to fall upon each other in an effort to extend their frontiers. The result, during the second quarter of the sixteenth century, had been the creation of a new group of daimyo with wider and more tightly organized domains. Such were the Mōri while still masters of Aki, the Ukita in Bizen, and the Oda in Owari. From this point another somewhat different process began. While the original domains of the daimyo remained roughly the same size and composition, expansion continued through the creation of leagues of daimyo clustered about a powerful leader. Within a given region the most powerful daimyo, reducing surrounding daimyo to submission, formed around themselves extended leagues of military houses over which they served as overlords. This is what had happened in western Japan by the time the Mōri reached Bitchū. As of 1560 this trend toward the clustering of daimyo had just begun. At that time the outstanding daimyo such as the Hōjō, Nagao, Imagawa, Hosokawa, Yamana, Amako, Ōuchi, and Shimazu, through their own domains and those of their daimyo allies, controlled about one-third of Japan. By 1572 the process had gone much further and over two-thirds of the country had been brought under the control of thirteen great houses. These were the Uesugi, Hōjō, Takeda, Tokugawa, Oda, Asakura, Asai, Yamana, Mōri, Chōsokabe, Ōtomo, Ryūzōji, and Shimazu. Among the areas still lacking regional leadership was most of central Japan from Kyoto to Bizen and the northern shores of Shikoku.

The structure of these regional leagues on the eve of unification was fairly uniform. At the center of each was the leading daimyo backed by the hereditary housemen (*fudai*) who had constituted his original vassal band. United around this power core were allied daimyo (*tozama*) who had accepted the supremacy of the regional overlord but retained considerable territorial independence. Of course not all territory gained by conquest remained in the hands of this latter type of *tozama* vassal. When possible the regional hegemon sought to eliminate competing houses and place his trusted *fudai* in the vacated territory. Regional hegemonies were extended by the reliance on both *fudai* and *tozama* type vassals, and it was this technique of expanding regional authority which was to lay the foundation for a national unity. In other words, the leading daimyo, by extending both the power of their

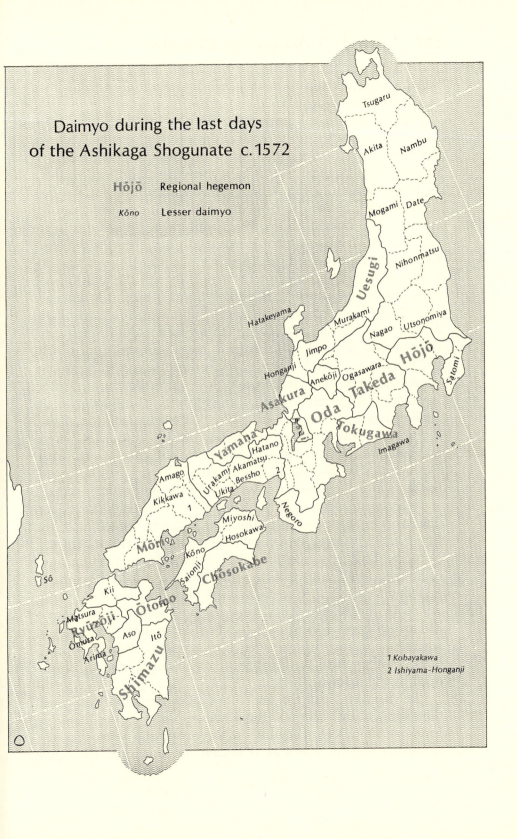

Daimyo during the last days
of the Ashikaga Shogunate c.1572

Hōjō   Regional hegemon

Kōno   Lesser daimyo

Tsugaru

Akita   Nambu

Mogami   Date

Nihonmatsu

Uesugi

Hatakeyama

Murakami   Utsonomiya

Jimpo   Nagao

Honganji   Anekōji   Ogasawara   Hōjō

Asakura   Oda   Takeda   Satomi

Tokugawa

Yamana   Hatano   Imagawa

Amago   Urakami Akamatsu

Ukita   Bessho   2

Kikkawa   1

Miyoshi   Negoro

Mōri   Hosokawa

Kōno

Saionji   Chōsokabe

Sō

Kii

Matsura   Ōtomo

Onmsa   Ryūzōji   Aso   Itō

Arinta   Shimazu

1 Kobayakawa
2 Ishiyama-Honganji

own housemen and bringing into alliance more distant *tozama* daimyo, were able to hold down increasingly large areas, and eventually to contemplate national unification.

While there is no disputing the fact that the fashioning of a national hegemony was the result of the ascendancy of one daimyo coalition over the entire nation, historians have questioned whether unification on these terms was in any way inevitable or desirable. In sixteenth century Japan, political and military power was not the monopoly of the daimyo alone. Nor did it appear inevitable that the kind of social and political institutions which the daimyo created in their domains should necessarily have become the base for a new national structure. There were in sixteenth century Japan groups opposed to the territorial lords and the political institutions they represented. Historians have debated at length and heatedly over the question of how significant these groups were to the future of Japan at that time. There were in the first instance the Buddhist monastic organizations and lay communities which had managed to hold their own against the attacks of daimyo who would have incorporated them into their territories. Among these, the monks of the great Tendai order covered the mountain of Hiei, converting it into an armed bastion on the outskirts of the capital city. The Honganji community of Ishiyama near Osaka had built itself into a fortress of impressive strength. The monkish communities of Negoro in Kii maintained over 20,000 armed monks, and having mastered quite early the production and use of firearms, managed to fight off the interference of surrounding daimyo. The Ikkō branch of the Honganji sect, establishing lay communities north of Kyoto, had driven the daimyo from Echizen, Noto, and Kaga provinces in 1488. These religious establishments, combining priestly leadership with monastic and lay following, provided an alternative to the type of feudal organization represented by the daimyo. They were able to muster the manpower and material resources of their communities to defend themselves against the daimyo who coveted their territory. Were they, perhaps, an alternative to the style of regional government developed by the daimyo?

Elsewhere in Japan the non-elite classes sporadically showed their strength by rising up against the authority of local daimyo. From the late fifteenth century on, the countryside witnessed frequent uprisings in which local inhabitants, organized spontaneously at the level of farmers and small land holders, attempted to grasp and defend territory on a corporate basis. One of the first notable uprisings of this sort took place in 1429 in Harima province under the governorship of the Akamatsu. In this incident the peasants and other non-samurai villagers joined together and attempted to eliminate "samurai," meaning Ashikaga, authority from the entire province.[1] The *shugo*, because of his connection with the *bakufu*, was a principal object of attack, and only with great difficulty did the Akamatsu suppress the uprising. In 1485 peasants and local landed families of Yamashiro, the home province, organized themselves into a corporate body for administration and defense. Driving out the shogun's agents, they maintained for ten years a local self-government independent of Kyoto. The free communities led by the Ikkō sect in Echizen and Kaga also took on the character of revolts against the *shugo-daimyō* and the Ashikaga polity.[2] Historians have suggested that here too was evidence of a political force capable of creating a different type of territorial administration from that of the daimyo domain.

Then finally there was the newly emerging merchant class. Stimulated by new demands for consumer goods and military supplies, Japan's internal and foreign trade had increased enormously during the sixteenth century. Merchant communities of many types sprang up to meet these needs. Jesuit missionaries from Europe found, to their surprise, cities such as Sakai and Hakata where merchant houses had won exemption from daimyo interference in the style of the "free cities" with which they were familiar. Was not this evidence of a rise in the merchants' social status and political and economic influence to the point that they too might have offered an alternative or at least competitive leadership to Japan in the sixteenth century?[3]

Many modern scholars have asked whether it was possible that these phenomena revealed the existence of groups or forces in Japanese society which, as in Europe, were capable of destroying the particular form of land-based military government represented by the daimyo. But the analogy of Europe on the eve of the appearance of the national states is too strained. Those who hold

---

[1] Ōishi Shinzaburō, "Sengoku jidai," in *Nihon rekishi kōza, 3, Chūsei-kinsei* (Tokyo, 1957), 167. Hereafter cited as Ōishi, "Sengoku."

[2] Suzuki Ryōichi, "Doikki ron," in *Shin Nihonshi kōza* (Tokyo, 1948), 33-40.

[3] Toyoda Takeshi, *Sakai* (Tokyo, 1957), 51-72.

to the "refeudalization" theory of the sixteenth century, claiming that the peasantry and merchants were engaged in "anti-feudal" activities which were forcibly suppressed by daimyo-based military power, have done so from a deep-set prejudice against feudalism as a system and have thus tended to upgrade the capabilities of these other social groups. Even admitting the existence of interests in Japan which might have competed against the daimyo for control of the state, there is little likelihood that any could have acquired the necessary institutions of legitimacy to comprise a national polity.[4] More recently, in fact, despite the continued prejudice of historians against the daimyo for what they consider a disregard of the aspirations of the non-military classes, there is a willingness to admit the existence of dynamic factors in the actions of the daimyo as they created their regional hegemonies, an admission that the great daimyo as they rode to power and established new social and economic policies to some extent fulfilled the aspirations of the peasant and merchant communities.[5]

In the competition for the nation's future as it lay before the Japanese people in the sixteenth century, there is little denying that the daimyo possessed the winning combination of motivation, organizational experience, military resources, and above all the claim to legitimacy. The great daimyo of 1560 had in their capacity the ability to harness the manpower and economic resources of their domains on a massive scale. Out of the process of military and administrative consolidation they had devised methods of more efficient local rule and military organization. In their domains new advances in agricultural technology, efforts to expand the land base and to promote mining and manufacturing gave evidence of their vigorous economic policies. New techniques of warfare such as the adoption of the musket and cannon and the improvement of fortifications and army organization made their armies capable of warfare on a grand scale. Within their domains, furthermore, new policies of manpower recruitment, new reliance on goods and supplies, utilized increasingly the energies

[4] Nakamura Kichiji, *Nihon hōkensei saihenseishi* (Tokyo, 1939), 243-244.
[5] The discussion of this in Kimura Motoi, *Nihon hōken-shakai kenkyū shi* (Tokyo, 1956), 142-198, is not conclusive. See, however, the writings of Nakamura Kichiji, most recently his "Sengoku-daimyō ron" in *Iwanami kōza, Nihon rekishi,* 8, *Chūsei, 4* (Tokyo, 1963), 189-237. Nakamura's thesis, with which I am in accord, is that within their domains the daimyo pursued policies which were more bureaucratic than feudal.

of the restive peasantry and ambitious merchants. Finally, the daimyo were in actual fact the successors of the provincial governors of the imperial age. To them belonged the traditional sources of legitimacy over the powers of government. To this extent, then, the great daimyo as they struggled for national hegemony were the inheritors of Japan's political future.[6]

Toward the end of the 1550's the possibility of achieving a national hegemony had occurred to more than one of the contending leaders of daimyo clusters. Indeed there seems to have been a sensing of the imminence of such unification among the great daimyo who began to move restlessly in the direction of Kyoto. The requisites for victory in the struggle which loomed ahead were not limited to brute force. Despite the political confusion of the time and the dilapidation into which the institutions of the Ashikaga shogunate and the imperial court had fallen, the new hegemony was destined to rest upon a legitimacy provided by the traditional organs of imperial and shogunal government. The first steps in the contest for hegemony were frequently purely ceremonial: for instance, Uesugi Kenshin's entrance into Kyoto in 1558 to secure the long empty title of *Kantō-kanrei*, or Oda Nobunaga's visit to Kyoto for an interview with the shogun Yoshiteru. The opening round of military action aimed to secure control of Kyoto was precipitated by Imagawa Yoshimoto. In 1560, at the head of some 25,000 men, he sought to cut his way to Kyoto across the territory of Oda Nobunaga.

The ensuing turn of events produced the first major turning point in the unification struggle. Oda Nobunaga with only 2000 men but with superior cunning routed the great Imagawa army. With this one battle Nobunaga vaulted into the ranks of the major contenders for power. But mindful of the presence of powerful enemies at his back, he bided his time till he could improve his position. Alliances with the Tokugawa and Takeda eventually secured his rear. His expanding domains permitted him to move his castled headquarters first to Komaki-yama, then in 1567 to Gifu. In 1562 and again in 1567 Nobunaga had received overtures from the emperor Ōgimachi suggesting that he provide military aid for protection of the capital. Increasingly Nobunaga felt the hand of destiny upon him. Gifu had been named in memory of the

6 J. W. Hall, "The Castle Town and Japan's Modern Urbanization," in *Far Eastern Quarterly*, 15.1 (November 1955), 42.

location from which China's great emperor Shih Huang Ti had begun his conquest of the warring states. Nobunaga had adopted at the time of his entrance into Gifu castle a seal reading *tenka fubu*, meaning "the entire land under one military power."[7] In 1568 he made his move. Entering the capital at the head of 30,000 men, he posed as the champion of Ashikaga Yoshiaki, rival claimant to the Ashikaga shogunate. Grasping military control of the capital, he installed Yoshiaki as shogun, exacting from him a sworn statement that he would refer all political decisions to Nobunaga alone. Thus he laid the foundation for what he planned to be his eventual conquest of Japan. In possession of a vast domain in the heart of Japan, controlling the capital with its wealth and social prestige, possessing a despotic hold over a puppet shogun who provided legitimacy, Nobunaga was now the most potent political power in the land.

But there were as yet numerous obstacles in the way to national hegemony. In the immediate capital area the monks of Hieizan refused to accept passively a hostile presence in the city they had so long dominated. Across Lake Biwa Asakura Yoshikage and Asai Nagamasa joined with the Hieizan forces to oppose Nobunaga. To the west Sakai remained hostile and the Ishiyama fortress, manned by the fanatical Ikkō adherents, was strategically placed to thwart his expansion in that direction. Ishiyama and Sakai were both aided against Nobunaga by the rival daimyo of Shikoku and the priests of Negoro. And behind these visible enemies were the menacing shadows of the distant forces of the Takeda, Uesugi, and Hōjō to the east and the Mōri and Shimazu to the west.

Between 1570 and 1574 Nobunaga broke down the first ring of resistance to his expansion. In 1571 the priests of Negoro were severely defeated by armed force backed by trickery. The next year the Ikkō communities of Echizen and Kaga were brought to their knees. In 1573 Nobunaga crushed the Asai and Asakura, adding their territories to his domains, and in 1574 he performed the most terrifying act of his career when he brushed aside all religious scruples to put the torch to the monasteries of Hieizan. His armies, sometimes numbering 60,000 men, had encircled Ishiyama castle in an investment which, though ten years before completion, was

---

[7] Nishida Naojirō, *Nihon bunkashi josetsu* (Tokyo, 1932), 490-496 for a discussion of the spirit of unification.

to end for all time the power of the Ikkō sect. By 1573 he had already driven the shogun Yoshiaki out of Kyoto and stood as *de facto* hegemon of the country.

From 1575 to 1582 Nobunaga put his effort into developing the resources of his new territory and in eliminating the ring of more distant rivals. When between 1576 and 1579 he built the great castle of Azuchi on the shores of Lake Biwa, a new chapter in Japanese military history was opened. Knowledge of the musket and cannon had reached Japan through the Portuguese. Nobunaga, the ceaseless innovator, had grasped the significance of these new weapons and had revolutionized the art of warfare in Japan through his use of large bands of musketeers, beginning with the campaign against the Takeda in 1575. Azuchi castle was built to sustain the force of firearms. A massive citadel with central keep surrounded by stone walls and defensive strong-points, this structure, as the Jesuit fathers recognized, was the symbol of a new age. Around his new castle Nobunaga organized his conquered territories, holding the choicest lands for his own direct support and enfeoffing his *fudai* generals as castellans in the fortresses of his conquered rivals. Daimyo who submitted to him without resistance were accepted as allies and their forces were successively placed in the vanguard of his armies in the field.

This newly created military organization Nobunaga now put to work against his more distant enemies. In 1577 he sent his most trusted general Hideyoshi into the territories west of the capital with the final objective of crushing the Mōri. Hideyoshi rapidly swept through Tamba, Tango, Tajima, Inaba, and Harima. With the capitulation of the Ukita house in 1578 Hideyoshi's armies stood facing those of the Mōri and their allies which had withdrawn into Bitchū behind the Takahashi River. Both sides brought up reinforcements and by 1582 two massive armies stood poised against each other at the castle of Takamatsu in Bitchū, the pivotal fortress on the easterly frontier of the Mōri territories.

By this time Nobunaga was master of all or part of eighteen provinces and had a potential military capacity of over 134,000 men. The Mōri had secured twelve provinces of western Japan with a military potential of some 46,000 men. Nobunaga's general Hideyoshi, placing the troops of the Ukita in the van and adding his own units, brought some 30,000 men to bear on Takamatsu castle. The western forces are said to have numbered 40,000 men.

While these huge armies held each other at bay the investment of Takamatsu castle and its 4,000 defenders began. Hideyoshi broke through the outer line of frontier forts, encircled the castle, and maneuvered the Mōri forces into the defensive.[8] It was at this juncture, when victory seemed in his hands, that Hideyoshi sent word to Nobunaga to join the battle with reinforcements. Nobunaga heeding the call, set out from Azuchi with 30,000 troops. But on the way he and his eldest son were slain by a treacherous general, Akechi Mitsuhide, in the temple of Honnōji in Kyoto.

On receiving the news of Nobunaga's death, Hideyoshi brought the Takamatsu engagement to a quick close. The castle was reduced; the Mōri leaders, ignorant of Nobunaga's death, accepted an alliance with the eastern faction, and withdrew to a line west of the Takahashi River.[9] In a few short days Hideyoshi had marched his picked troops to the capital and had killed Akechi.

Nobunaga died at the age of 49, well on his way to securing mastery of all Japan. Before his death he had gained control of one-third of Japan's sixty-six provinces. This block of territory, stretching out on either side of the capital, was held by his housemen and vassal generals: Shibata in Echizen, Maeda in Noto, Sassa in Echigo, Takigawa in Yamato, Kinoshita (later Hashiba, then Toyotomi) in Ōmi, Ikeda in Settsu, and numerous others. Though he failed to achieve his ultimate ambition, Nobunaga had laid a foundation from which his successor, Hideyoshi, could complete the task. In a variety of ways he also set the institutional pattern for the unity which was to follow him.

Oda Nobunaga had carried out on a national scale the destruction of the entrenched political and religious centers which had been brought under attack by the *sengoku-daimyō* in their more limited domains. His authority for doing so was never fully apparent. For Nobunaga received few of the signs of public support, the titles and ranks which might have provided him with legitimacy. For him, his championing of the imperial house and the Ashikaga shogun were sufficient foils behind which he could exercise his commanding military power. As a national hegemon, either of the kind exemplified by Taira-no-Kiyomori or the various shoguns, Nobunaga's position was truncated. Driving up from out of the provinces with only the status claims of a minor daimyo whose

---

[8] *Tsūshi*, 2.50-71.   [9] *Ibid.*, 2.72.

family held the title of deputy *shugo* of half of Owari, Nobunaga had won his territory by conquest, and the enfeoffment of his vassals at his pleasure was justified on the basis of such conquest. To Nobunaga belonged the practice of universalizing the granting of fiefs or the confirmation of holdings under his vermilion seal (*shuin*). The extension of the "*shuin* grant" system by Nobunaga was a sign of the final mastery of the feudal system of government over the older imperial-*shōen* system. Nobunaga's assertion of the right to confirm under his seal the powers of governance (*chigyō ken*) to his vassals indicated that he and other daimyo had now won complete possession of the rights of tenure and administration. The daimyo now clearly were complete (*isshiki*) proprietors and governors within their domains, and Oda Nobunaga as chief of the daimyo of his league asserted the right of confirmation under his protection. For most of Japan the ultimate acknowledgment of Nobunaga's superior rights to confirm land grants came as his armies swept through province after province, but more technically with the final passing of the Ashikaga shogunate in 1574. As late as 1555 Mōri Motokiyo justified his acquisition of the provinces of Suō and Nagato by receiving investiture as *shugo* by the Ashikaga shogun. Contrast this with Nobunaga's grant to his vassal Shibata Katsuie of the province of Echizen: "The entire province is entrusted to you" (*daikoku wo azuke-oku*). In Bizen when in 1578 Ukita Naoie died and his son sought confirmation of succession, it was to Nobunaga that he turned. Nobunaga's red seal had become a token of sufficient value to be worth a thousand pieces of gold.[10]

Had Nobunaga lived longer, there is little question but that he would have sought to legitimize his position under the imperial system. His interest in Confucianism and the concepts of statecraft was intense, and his concern over the imperial symbol of sovereignty is reflected in his attempt to secure court favor and his attention to the rebuilding of the imperial palace. Though a destroyer of so much of the past, Nobunaga continued the fiction that military rule should be subservient to the emperor.[11] His early death left the final adjustment of military authority into the imperial system to Hideyoshi and Tokugawa Ieyasu.

[10] Okuno Takahiro, *Nobunaga to Hideyoshi* (Tokyo, 1955), 76-78; *Okayama-shi shi*, 2.1504.

[11] Okuno, *Nobunaga to Hideyoshi*, 61-63.

Within his domains Nobunaga fostered a number of reforms which were to set the pattern for later institutional change. A new and more systematic method of village organization and tax collection, new techniques of warfare (using the long spear, musket, and ironclad ships), new castle construction, and the maintenance of large standing garrisons in these castles were all carried forward by him. In 1576 and 1578 Nobunaga began to disarm the peasantry in some of his territories, thus presaging the more complete separation of peasant and warrior which occurred under Hideyoshi. From 1571 he required the submission of cadastral registers from the new territories acquired by him, and in 1574 he started his own resurvey (*kenchi*) of Yamashiro, the home province. At this time he began, or at least confirmed, the use of the terms and units which were to become standard under Hideyoshi and the Tokugawa: a new and smaller unit of linear measure, the *kokudaka* system of assessing land productivity, and the local administrative units of *kōri* (district) and *mura* (village).[12] In his well-known commercial policies Nobunaga aimed at a unification of weights and measures and the abolition of guilds and other barriers to free circulation of goods. He began the patronage of merchant groups which within a few decades was to bring the entire class under the walls of the daimyo castles as a service corps for the military establishment.[13] And finally Nobunaga had undertaken a vigorous attack on the religious establishment of Japan which was to bring to conclusive end their once formidable political and military power. By confiscating the largest part of their territory and asserting the rights of supervision over their affairs, he brought both Buddhism and Shinto into the service of military government.

AFTER his death in 1582, Nobunaga's chief vassals and family members met at Kiyosu to determine the Oda succession. Since the first-generation heir had died at Honnōji, Nobunaga's child-grandson, Hidenobu, was selected. One of Nobunaga's sons was

[12] Kodama Kōta, ed., *Zusetsu Nihon bunkashi taikei*, 8.60-61, for a concise treatment of this complex subject. The most prolific authority on the subject is Miyagawa Mitsuru, *Taikō kenchi ron* (2 vols., Tokyo, 1957 and 1959). Still useful for clarity is Takayanagi Mitsutoshi, "Toyotomi Hideyoshi no kenchi," *Iwanami kōza Nihon rekishi* (Tokyo, 1935), 42 pp.

[13] Miyamoto Mataji, *Nihon h ōken shugi no saishuppatsu* (Koyto, 1948), 189-220; Harada Tomohiko, "Sengoku daimyō to toshi minshū," in *Nihonshi kenkyū*, 15 (March 1952), 2-16.

named guardian, and four outstanding vassal generals, Shibata Katsuie, Niwa Nagahide, Ikeda Nobuteru, and Kinoshita Hide-yoshi, were given the task of alternately administrating the capital city of Kyoto. This was a most unstable arrangement and one easily destroyed by Hideyoshi, who within the Oda league held the preponderance of military force. Moreover, he was first among the four generals to become governor of Kyoto.

During 1583 Hideyoshi moved to put on the mantle of Nobu-naga's succession, refusing to relinquish his control of Kyoto, building a new and formidable castle at Osaka, and asserting the right to determine policy for the Oda league. An open breach among Nobunaga's succession soon followed. Hideyoshi brushed Shibata aside in 1583 and during 1584 fought to a standstill with Tokugawa Ieyasu who briefly took up the cause of one of Nobu-naga's remaining sons. By 1585 Hideyoshi had concluded alliances with the Tokugawa and Uesugi and had secured the fealty of all Nobunaga's vassals and allies. He had gained supremacy within twenty provinces of central Japan.[14] Furthermore, he had dignified his position by gaining entrance into the Fujiwara lineage and taking the high court title of *kampaku.* He was now ready to take up the task of unification where Nobunaga had left off.

In 1585 the major daimyo clusters besides the one led by Hide-yoshi were nine in number, headed by the Hōjō, Takeda, Uesugi, Tokugawa, Mōri, Chōsokabe, Ōtomo, Ryūzōji, and Shimazu. With the Uesugi, Tokugawa, and Mōri safely enlisted as allies, the task confronting Hideyoshi was the reduction of the remainder. In 1585 he invaded Shikoku and eliminated the Chōsokabe. In 1587 he and his allies converged upon Kyūshū with 280,000 men. The Ōtomo and Ryūzōji were destroyed and the Shimazu reduced to submission. By 1590 Hideyoshi was ready to subdue the last re-maining opposition in the Kantō. With 200,000 men he invaded the Hōjō domains and invested their stronghold at Odawara. The final capitulation of the Hōjō, which came five months later, marked the completion of Hideyoshi's internal unification of Japan. All territory now either belonged to Hideyoshi or was held in the form of red seal grants to daimyo who had sworn fealty to him.

The "unification" achieved in 1590 had brought Japan under the control of a single daimyo cluster in which Hideyoshi as the

---

[14] Okuno, *Nobunaga to Hideyoshi,* 23.

great overlord had received the pledge of submission from all others. This was the political structure under which Japan was destined to live for another two and three-quarters centuries. The question is sometimes asked why Hideyoshi made no attempt to extend the process of unification so as to eliminate the daimyo and make himself a monarch over a united country. The answer should be obvious. From the outset the forces which had contended for supremacy of Japan had consisted of groups of daimyo held together by feudal bonds. Each successive victory, each expansion, had extended the pattern of dividing territory into the lord's domain and those of enfeoffed vassals. The constant pressure of civil war, the rivalries which surrounded each aspirant to national hegemony, induced each to extend the pattern of alliances and vassalage, consciously or unconsciously, to avoid the necessity of full extermination. Moreover, when extermination of rival daimyo was found necessary, as in the case of the Chōsokabe or Hōjō, it was won by the force of a winning alliance, not by the leader's own personal army. Such an alliance was held together in large part by the lure of reward in territory which awaited the successful campaign. Nobunaga, Hideyoshi, and later Ieyasu each achieved national leadership on a step-by-step basis, growing from small daimyo into large, and from large into still larger regional leaders of daimyo clusters. Only after they had reached the zenith of their power were they in a position to eliminate the daimyo throughout the country, yet the patterns of alliances had been so firmly set that even then they did not possess a basis of power outside the alliance system from which to destroy their vassals, had they so wanted. To such men as Hideyoshi and Ieyasu an abolition of the daimyo was unthinkable and impractical.

Let us return then to the viewpoint that Hideyoshi's victory represented not a true unification but the conquest of Japan by one daimyo league over the entire country. What shape did the new hegemony take? At the base of the new power structure was the disposition of lands and territories. Of these there were two distinct categories: Hideyoshi's granary territories (*kurai-richi*) and domains held in fief by his vassal daimyo. Hideyoshi had claimed to represent a direct continuity from Nobunaga. He therefore inherited the lands acquired by Nobunaga, to which he added his own holdings and numerous territories acquired after 1582. The heart of these holdings were the lands taken from the

Ashikaga in the capital area and the early Oda territories in Owari and Ōmi. Hideyoshi's personal domains in 1598 occupied land assessed at 2,000,000 *koku* out of the national total of about 18,500,-000 *koku*. The strategic location of these lands, together with the fact that they gave Hideyoshi control of the rich agricultural lands of Ōmi and key cities of Kyoto, Sakai, Hakata, and Nagasaki, added immeasurably to their importance.

Aside from a few estates of the imperial court and the now drastically reduced lands of the central temples and shrines, the bulk of Japanese territory was held in fief by Hideyoshi's vassals. The number of daimyo holding direct fealty to Hideyoshi was approximately 181 in 1598.[15] The territorial lords, each holding lands assessed at 10,000 *koku* or more in agricultural production, controlled somewhat over 16,000,000 *koku* in all. Hideyoshi does not appear to have devised a rigorous classification of daimyo, as the Tokugawa shoguns were to do upon their assumption to power. Nonetheless certain clear distinctions existed in the way in which Hideyoshi regarded his vassals, and this stemmed from the history of their submission to him. In the course of the unification conquests, a large corps of fighters followed first Nobunaga and then Hideyoshi through the major campaigns. Many of these men, starting as commanders of small military units, rose to become daimyo. Such men formed the hard core of close vassals which Hideyoshi counted as his housemen (*kashin*). This group, in turn, was divided between those who became daimyo in Nobunaga's time and those raised to daimyo status by Hideyoshi. Most of these men were from the province of Owari from which Nobunaga's effort at unification had begun. And so the new hegemony fostered the spread of numerous men of Owari to the far corners of Japan as first Nobunaga and then Hideyoshi enfeoffed trusted retainers with the confiscated lands of defeated rivals.[16] A few of the daimyo created out of the Oda military band had reached a size which put them among the foremost territorial lords. The most conspicuous was Maeda Toshiie whose domain was assessed at 810,000 *koku* in 1598. But Maeda had begun his rise under Nobunaga and had in fact become an "outside" daimyo to Hideyoshi. The foremost of Hideyoshi's strictly *fudai* daimyo were such men

---

[15] Fujino Tamotsu, *Bakuhan taiseishi no kenkyū* (Tokyo, 1961), see table between pages 120-121.

[16] Itō, *Hōken*, 215-216.

as Katō (250,000 *koku*), Asano (218,000), Kōnishi (200,000), Mashita (200,000), and Ishida (194,000). The great bulk of his more dependent vassals were men of from 10,000 to 50,000 *koku* rank.

In the course of military expansion the Oda-Toyotomi coalition met and conquered or coalesced with other daimyo or daimyo clusters. When, as in the case of the Hōjō, the confrontation reached the proportions of an all-out struggle, victory made possible the extermination of the rival and the full confiscation of his territory. When victory was gained through negotiation or compromise, as in the case of the Ukita and Mōri, the rival was incorporated into the winning coalition, usually with some reduction of territory. Hideyoshi's hegemony was extended over a large number of such *tozama* daimyo who in fact retained the bulk of territory in Japan. Such were the Tokugawa (2,557,000 *koku*), Mōri (1,205,000), Uesugi (1,200,000), Date (580,000), Ukita (574,000), Satake (529,000), and Shimazu (559,000), daimyo whose relationship to Hideyoshi was more that of ally than dependent vassal. Their territories consisted of daimyo clusters in which rear vassals to Hideyoshi were frequently of daimyo size. Among the *tozama*, distinctions naturally existed regarding the history of their allegiance, i.e. whether they had first submitted to Nobunaga or were first conquered by Hideyoshi. All of these factors affected the trustworthiness of the bond of submission or alliance upon which Hideyoshi could count.

Hideyoshi's genius at military strategy and in leading men did not carry over into the more prosaic fields of administration. Having achieved a national hegemony, he was less successful in his efforts to protect it. Control of the daimyo rested too much on his own personal magnetism and his despotic hand. Throughout his later years Hideyoshi attempted strenuously and sometimes desperately to maintain the coalition around him and to assure the continuance of his hegemony through some sort of balance of power. As was common practice, Hideyoshi transferred his vassal daimyo from domain to domain, cutting them away from their locales of major strength, and creating as he did so an increasingly loyal and dependent relationship to himself.[17] One of his most dramatic moves of this kind was his transfer of Tokugawa Ieyasu from Mikawa and Tōtōmi to the Kantō, where he was surrounded

[17] Asao Naohiro, "Hōshi seiken ron," in *Iwanami kōza, Nihon rekishi*, 9, *kinsei, 1* (Tokyo, 1963), 189, has an excellent map showing Hideyoshi's territorial strength.

by more dependent daimyo such as Katō, Gamō, Date, Mogami, Nakamura, Yamanouchi, and Ikeda. Hideyoshi's most trusted *fudai* generals were enfeoffed in central Japan, while his heir, Hidetsugu, was placed in Owari. Among the original band of commanders who had become daimyo in Hideyoshi's service, Kinoshita was placed in Harima to guard the approaches from the west and Katō, Konishi, and Kuroda were set in Kyūshū as a balance to the Shimazu and Nabeshima. Hideyoshi lavishly cultivated the loyalty of Ukita Hideie as a screen between himself and the Mōri.

Between himself and his daimyo adherents, Hideyoshi used with great skill the entire range of devices for securing political loyalty. All daimyo were required to swear oaths of fealty, and such written pledges were frequently sealed by taking hostages. Osaka castle first served as a residence for hostages, and here the daimyo sent wives, heirs, or principal vassals as tokens of their sincerity. Later, daimyo were obliged to build residences around Hideyoshi's palace at Fushimi where they were within reach of his call and where wives and children were kept on a semi-hostage basis. Marriage alliances and the giving or adopting of children was a favorite device for drawing vassals into a kinship relationship. The bestowal of parts of his name was a token of favoritism with which Hideyoshi rewarded his most trusted vassals, or those whose loyalty he particularly needed. Thus many daimyo received the honorary surnames of Hashiba or Toyotomi or a character out of Hideyoshi's given name. Most distinctive of Hideyoshi's behavior toward his vassals was the manner in which he distributed largess on a grand scale in order to encourage a sense of indebtedness in them.

Before his final campaign against the Hōjō forces in the Kantō Hideyoshi had succeeded in gaining imperial recognition as the legitimate hegemon of Japan. Able to proceed much farther than Nobunaga in this respect, Hideyoshi successfully created a new political structure which integrated the hierarchy of vassal daimyo into the old imperial system. Unable himself to lay claim to the status of shogun because of his failure to gain entrance into the Minamoto lineage, Hideyoshi secured adoption into the Fujiwara family and then successively took the highest civil posts in the old court officialdom: those of regent (*kampaku*) and prime minister (*dajōdaijin*). Thus as imperial regent he laid claim to ultimate civil and military powers as delegated by the emperor.

Hideyoshi's most obvious use of the symbolic sanction of the emperor occurred in 1588 on the occasion of his magnificent entertainment at his new mansion in Fushimi. All of his vassals were invited and the emperor Go-Yōzei attended in state. In the midst of the second day of celebrations the assembled daimyo were presented with the following oath for their signatures:

With respect　　　　　　　　　　　An oath

1. We shed tears of gratitude that His Majesty has honored us with his presence at Jurakudai.

2. If any evil person should interfere with the estates and lands of the Imperial House or with the fiefs of the Court Nobles, we will take firm action. Without equivocation we commit not only ourselves but our children and grandchildren.

3. We will obey the commands of the Regent down to the smallest detail.

   If any of the above provisions should be violated even in the slightest, then . . . (names of deities)[18]

Thus Hideyoshi inserted into the fabric of the lord-vassal relationship which daimyo held to him personally the traditional sanction of the Japanese throne. Shortly thereafter, in 1590, when Hideyoshi moved against the Hōjō, he was able to brand his adversary an "enemy of the throne."

Throughout most of Hideyoshi's career simple oaths and direct commands sufficed for what we might call "the laws of the land." In 1585, however, Hideyoshi devised a series of regulations for the control of daimyo and other groups in the country. The *On okite jūyon-ka-jō*, sometimes called the "wall writings of Osaka castle," contain only fourteen meager provisions but are important because they set the pattern of the political codes of the Tokugawa regime. Provisions in Hideyoshi's "wall writings" dealt with the regulation of daimyo marriages, clarification of status relations among daimyo, and the prohibition of alliances and intrigues. They enjoined courtiers and priests to keep to their traditional paths of life, and laid down rules concerning drinking, concubines, palanquins, family insignia, and like aspects of aristocratic life.

---

[18] *Sekai rekishi jiten*, 22.266.

The code also briefly established procedures for tax collection and judicial process in the daimyo domains.[19] Generally speaking, the code sought to harden the political and social structure of the country as it then existed and to minimize the causes of friction or desire for change.

Hideyoshi was slow to create political institutions to back up the hegemony which he had gained by conquest. He depended quite frankly upon the daimyo to hold down the territory within their domains, and conceived of a bare minimum of administration for holding the daimyo together. Between 1590 and 1598, however, Hideyoshi created a loosely designed organization which converted his own private administration into a mechanism for the maintenance of the national hegemony. Hideyoshi's house administration had taken shape along the same lines as those of the other great daimyo. In such domains military affairs naturally predominated, but civil functions had also begun to receive separate attention through the appointment of commissioners (*bugyō*) from among the band of vassals. Hideyoshi's appointments of this type were systematized in 1585 when Asano Nagamasa was named commissioner of lands and housemen. Maeda Gen'i, set up in Kyoto as deputy military governor (*shoshidai*), administered the city and controlled the courtiers and priests. Natsuka Masaie was made *bugyō* in charge of finances and the domestic affairs of Hideyoshi's domain. Other designated retainers handled such affairs as housing for vassals, construction, communications, military organization, supplies and procurement, and ships.[20]

In 1598, just before his death, Hideyoshi further attempted to systematize his administration, creating three bodies of daimyo which he hoped would stabilize the balance of power among his vassals. First he named Five Great Elders (*go-tairō*) consisting of Tokugawa Ieyasu, Maeda Toshiie, Uesugi Kagekatsu, Mōri Terumoto, and Ukita Hideie. This group, which was made up of the largest *tozama* daimyo, was bound by a special oath to keep the peace and support the Toyotomi cause, which would shortly be vested precariously in a child heir. Murdoch's translation of the title of this group as the Board of Regency is particularly apt.[21]

[19] Quoted and analyzed in *Okayama-shi shi*, 2.1528-1529.

[20] Jingū Shichō, *Koji ruien* (60 vols., Tokyo 1932-1936), *Kan'i-bu*, 3.527. Henceforth cited by title only.

[21] James Murdoch, *History of Japan* (vol. 2, London, 1925), 574.

At the same time a board of Five Commissioners (*go-bugyō*) was named to handle routine policy and administrative affairs of the realm. In it were Maeda Gen'i, Asano, Ishida Mitsunari, Mashita Nagamori, and Natsuka. Between these two five-man boards Hideyoshi named a group of three Middle Elders (*chūrō*) with the intent that they should mediate differences over policy, hence Murdoch's translation "Board of Mediators." This system, as we now know, never worked effectively beyond Hideyoshi's death in 1598.[22]

While Hideyoshi failed to create a lasting political structure, many of his domestic policies were profoundly important for later centuries.[23] He codified and extended the system of cadastral organization begun by Nobunaga and completed the transfer of all land under the system of proprietorship legalized by his grant in the capacity of overlord. In 1585 he began in earnest to carry out new systematic cadastral practices by ordering a complete re-survey (*kenchi*) of the country. The new survey aimed at regularizing the units of measurement and exposing land which had been hidden from taxation. By adopting a new unit of area measurement which differed from the one in use from Nara days he literally forced the entire nation to reassess its land base. Hideyoshi's system (which was not new to him but had been pioneered by Nobunaga and a few other daimyo) called for a new *tan* measurement of 300 *bu* rather than the old *tan* of 360 *bu*. In actual area, the new *tan* measured about .25 acre rather than the previous .3 acre. The new cadastral system also went far in extending the political authority of the daimyo over the land and the peasantry. In the new land registers each field plot was not only recorded as to area and ownership but was also classified by amount of production (*den'i*) and assessed for tax purposes. The system of assessment adopted the unit of rice measure known as *koku* (5.2 *bu*) rather than the cash equivalent system which was gaining popularity in parts of central Japan. Thus the system of *koku* measure (*kokumori*) was introduced throughout Japan as standard practice and with it came a standardization of the whole method of land management and tax collection.

[22] *Koji ruien, Kan'i-bu*, 3.428-531.
[23] See Asao Naohiro, *op.cit.*, 162-210; Toyoda Takeshi, "Shokuhō seiken," in *Nihon rekishi kōza, 3, Chūsei-kinsei* (Tokyo, 1957), 185-208; Suzuki Ryōichi, "Shokuhō seiken ron," in *Nihon rekishi kōza, 4, Chūsei, 2* (Tokyo, 1952), 86-102.

Hideyoshi's authority to impose this cadastral reassessment derived from his assertion of supreme proprietary overlordship. Throughout the realm all land was considered subject to his right of allocation, to be held as his private domain (*chokkatsu*) or as fiefs (*chigyō*) granted under his red seal. Though this was never spelled out by law or by any specific document, the assumption was there by virtue of Hideyoshi's conquests and his possession of high court office. The *bushi* class as a whole, directly through Hideyoshi or indirectly through the several daimyo, now held the rights of feudal proprietorship (i.e., the right to administer and tax) for approximately 99 percent of all land in Japan. (The remaining 1 percent was held by court families and religious institutions.) Since proprietorship was a unitary matter involving a uniform product from the land, the units of proprietorship were now measured in terms of assessed tax base (*kokudaka*). Fiefs were defined as being so many *koku* in size. It was at this time, then, that the strict definition of daimyo as a territorial lord with lands assessed at 10,000 *koku* came into being.

Hideyoshi's cadastral survey carried forward yet another important institutional change in the countryside by providing a new basis of village organization. We have already noted that in the previous century the large family units under the *myōshu* were tending to break up and that village communities consisting of nuclear families were becoming the common form of rural organization. Under the new land survey fields were recorded not according to the *myō* (as in the *shōen*) but in the name of the free cultivators (*hyakushō*) who headed the smaller individual families. These families, furthermore, were grouped into villages (*mura*) which now became the standard administrative unit in the countryside. Naturally this system was not enforced with equal rigor in all parts of Japan. Hideyoshi's policies embodied the practices of rural organization and cadastral management which had grown up in the more advanced regions of Japan, notably in the province of Ōmi, which was Hideyoshi's main land base. Their suitability to some of the remoter regions was questionable, and certainly efforts at enforcement were sometimes imperfect. Even in Bizen we shall see that they were not fully carried out until after Hideyoshi's death.

The land reforms of the late sixteenth century, together with the changing nature of warfare, were major factors which affected the relative roles of the warrior and cultivator in Japan at this time. Up to the time of Hideyoshi, the *bushi* class had lived close to the land and had had a direct hand in land management and tax collection. During the struggle for unification, as warfare became more intense, as the musket and long spear changed the nature of armed bodies, and as daimyo required their fighters to remain in constant military readiness close to their castle strongholds, more and more *bushi* left the land to reside permanently with their daimyo in his castle headquarters. In most localities the *kenchi* served to hasten this process by forcing an arbitrary division between cultivators and fighters. The *kenchi* was essentially a survey of cultivated land and of the individuals responsible for the payment of dues on the land. The cadastral registers said nothing about the superior proprietary rights. These were vested in the daimyo. Thus almost by definition a division was drawn within Japanese society between the farming and non-farming populace. Those listed in the cadastral registers along with the assessed pieces of land, their families and other attached personnel, these were the *hyakushō*. Those who were listed on the rolls of the daimyo as fief holders or stipendiaries were *bushi*. In most domains the *bushi* literally had been withdrawn from the countryside by the time the *kenchi* fixed the status and identity of the *hyakushō*.

This process of class separation was given its final impetus, however, by the conscious effort of individual daimyo and eventually of Hideyoshi to restrict the bearing of arms by any but the *bushi* class. Sword hunts (*katana-gari*), meant to disarm the rural and urban populace, occurred sporadically during the 1580's.[24] Hideyoshi embarked upon such a program in earnest after 1590, when defeat of the Hōjō gave him authority over all Japan. In that year Hideyoshi issued the famous three-clause edict which solidified social status: proscribing the movement of former *bushi* into the villages, restricting farmers (*hyakushō*) to their calling and prohibiting their entering the trades or commerce, and prohibiting *bushi* from leaving one master for another. In 1591 Hideyoshi also ordered a national population census (*hitobarai*) which set the pattern for the later census records (*nimbetsu-chō*) compiled by the daimyo.

[24] Kuwata Tadachika, "Toyotomi Hideyoshi no katana gari," in *Shigaku zasshi*, 54.1 (January 1943), 57-89.

Hideyoshi presided over the adoption of momentous institutional and legal changes in Japan. In him, for the first time, the feudal hegemon of Japan combined the rights and powers under the emperor to act the complete ruler. In this sense the country was reunited, and at its head stood an authority capable of issuing and enforcing decisions across the country. Hideyoshi had risen to the challenge of his new position as *de facto* head of the Japanese state by carrying forward the recodification of basic laws by which the status, functions, and interrelationships of the major segments of the populace were defined. His legislation gave form to a new legal structure based on the fundamental conception of the division of the Japanese people into classes, or estates. To be sure the Japanese state still took the form of a decentralized coalition of semi-autonomous domains. Yet the members of this coalition had begun to accept a large degree of direction from the hegemon. And within the country at large there was general acceptance of certain basic premises and practices. The position of the emperor as repository of sovereignty, the court aristocracy as guardians of social prestige and the aristocratic way of life, the *bushi* as the proprietary and governing class professionally committed to the bearing of arms, the *hyakushō* who bore the responsibility for land cultivation and production of taxes, and the groups considered peripheral, the merchants, tradesmen, artisans, and priests were each given a place and provided with their own laws and regulations.[25]

It is significant that when power based on feudal institutions of political and military organization gained control of the Japanese state, the means adopted by that power to administer the state moved away from the extreme forms of decentralization and reliance on personal bonds of authority which were most characteristic of feudal behavior. While the organization of the power structure (the coalition of daimyo) depended in large measure upon the personal compacts between Hideyoshi and his vassals, yet below this level, in the methods used to govern the non-*bushi* elements of society, Hideyoshi and his daimyo vassals adopted techniques of a more strictly bureaucratic nature.

[25] For an intimate account of the efforts of one of Hideyoshi's daimyo to codify the new political system and regulate domain practices, see Marius B. Jansen, "Tosa in the Sixteenth Century: The 100 Article Code of Chōsokabe Motochika," *Oriens Extremus*, 10.1 (April 1963), 83-108.

The vitality of Hideyoshi's domestic reforms was matched by the vigor of his external policies. The sixteenth century opened upon the scene of intense Japanese overseas activity when free-booters plundered the China coast and probed the seas beyond Indochina. The arrival of the Portuguese after 1542 further intensified the search for profits from trade. From Kyushu to Osaka new ports were opened to foreign ships, and daimyo vied for the patronage of European traders or themselves commissioned trading ships. Hideyoshi, ever open to new ways of improving his finances, sought to channel this trade to his own advantage. Osaka became a new center of domestic commerce, drawing on the silk imports from China through the Kyushu ports. Nagasaki in 1587 was placed under Hideyoshi's direct control. Hideyoshi eventually attempted to establish a national trade policy in which he sought to regulate Japanese ships under a system of charters (*shuin*) at the same time that he exerted his own influence internationally to secure expanded opportunities for Japanese traders. Hideyoshi's leniency toward the Christian missionary movement and his childlike fascination with Western objects of apparel and mechanical gadgetry reflected the temper of the times when even daimyo turned Christian and thousands of their subjects blindly took up the new religion.

The climax of Hideyoshi's foreign adventure was his grandiose scheme for the conquest of China which called forth two huge invasions of Korea. Hideyoshi inherited from Nobunaga a dream of world dominion. Having unified Japan he found the restless spirit among his daimyo unquieted. Who could doubt that the Japanese fighters were the most formidable in the East? Hideyoshi boldly drew upon his expanded fan a plan to destroy the armies of Korea and Ming China and to divide their conquered territories into fiefs for his vassals. The first invasion force of some 200,000 men quickly overran the Korean peninsula in 1592 and struck to the Yalu River. But the Japanese generals were obliged to agree to a negotiated "victory" over the Chinese at Pingyang. Hideyoshi demanded a Chinese princess as consort for the Japanese emperor, the equal division of Korea between Chinese and Japanese sectors, the establishment of a Japanese governor in Korea, and free trade between Japan and China. The Chinese refusal of these demands occasioned the second invasion of 1597-1598, which was abandoned at the time of Hideyoshi's death.

The Korean campaigns because of their futility and costliness did much to dampen the Japanese enthusiasm for overseas adventure after Hideyoshi's death. Edicts against Christian missionaries had already been issued, and foreign contacts were being considered with suspicion. Hideyoshi's successors continued for a while the patronage of foreign trade, but the dream of world conquest was forgotten. The Tokugawa preferred to close the doors of their country in order to preserve domestic tranquility. The general structure of government and the institutions of social control initiated by Hideyoshi remained the foundation upon which the long Tokugawa hegemony came to rest.

XI. BIZEN UNDER THE HOUSE OF UKITA

Hideyoshi's unification of Japan caught up the leading daimyo and their locales within the larger context of national affairs. In eastern Kibi, Ukita Naoie, at the moment of his rise to local supremacy, was confronted with the urgent necessity of choosing between the Oda-Toyotomi and Mōri forces which pressed upon him from east and west. By casting in his lot with Nobunaga in 1578, Naoie put his house and his domain into the main current of the unification movement. Naoie's son and successor, treated as adopted son and favorite by Hideyoshi, was to become one of the foremost members of the colorful band of territorial lords who composed the new hegemony. Along with the Ukita house, Bizen was drawn into a new stream of events which was to carry its fighting men to distant battlefields in Japan and even to the shores of Korea.

When in 1577 Ukita Naoie destroyed his overlord Urakami Munekage, master of Tenjinyama, he succeeded to the position of the paramount power of Bizen and Mimasaka. The Ukita by now were the most powerful leaders yet to emerge in Bizen, the first indigenous daimyo of unquestioned national importance. Naoie, and after him his son Hideie, held the great domain centered on Okayama until 1600, when defeat in the battle of Sekigahara brought their house to ruin and its leader to melancholy exile. The years between 1577 and 1600, when Bizen was held under the grip of the Ukita house and its retainers, were a turbulent era which vibrated to the climactic domestic campaigns and the grandiose foreign exploits of Toyotomi Hideyoshi.

The Ukita chiefs did not merely replace the Urakami as masters of Bizen; they gave the region a new type of leadership and government. Naoie and Hideie were daimyo of a new and more powerful type than their *sengoku* predecessors. Utilizing the techniques of military and territorial organization so successfully mastered by the great unifiers like Nobunaga, Hideyoshi, or Mōri Terumoto, these daimyo of the last half of the sixteenth century increased manyfold their capacity to draw upon the material resources of their domains. Symbolic of the new won power of these daimyo were the massive castles which guarded the centers of their domains. The turning point in the military fortunes of Bizen came, in fact, in 1573 with the selection of Okayama as the site for the main Ukita stronghold. It was from Okayama castle that Naoie won Bizen and developed the techniques of manpower recruitment and taxation which gave him resources unattainable to the Urakami or Matsuda. Between the mammoth Okayama fortress and the smaller local fortifications which had once served as local strongpoints there could no longer be any comparison. The new castle stood superior over the entire area of eastern Kibi, and in it sat a new local authority whose powers were also unchallenged. Not even in the heyday of imperial rule in Japan had Bizen been so comprehensively administered.

Ukita Naoie himself represented a new variety of leader. Self-made in the extreme, with little family background or prestige upon which to rely, he had succeeded by means of his own ability, superior courage, and military skill. His life from beginning to end was spent in battle, sharing the field with his men. To him warfare was serious business, the means to advantage, the necessity of his age. Naoie's success was compounded from his resourcefulness and strategic brilliance. Where others faltered he gambled on his courage and the loyalty of his men. He began his career by volunteering to defend the least tenable outpost in the Urakami frontier. That he succeeded where others failed showed him master of the requirements of his age of warfare. He used his armies and his battles as opportunities; he took his chances and won. What sense of destiny was it that urged Naoie to expand toward the exposed terrain of the lower Kibi delta while the Matsuda and Urakami clung to their mountain fortresses to end in oblivion? Yet throughout Japan men similarly touched by destiny were leading their forces out of the mountain valleys into the plains to take hold of the productive centers from which they could build the great consolidated domains which alone could survive the age of unification.

The twenty-three years of Ukita rule in Bizen have many elements of mystery about them. As with so many of the daimyo houses extinguished at the battle of Sekigahara, official and private papers seem almost to have been systematically obliterated. Only a barest scattering of documents remain to offer tantalizing but inconclusive hints about the conditions and events of Bizen under the Ukita house. Yet the contours are clearly visible. The Ukita gave to Bizen one of its most dynamic quarter centuries.

At the time of its farthest extension, the Ukita domain embraced the region from the Takahashi River in Bitchū on the west to the Chigusa River in Harima on the east. From the waters of the Inland Sea it stretched to the borders of Inaba province to the north. The domain confirmed by Nobunaga to Hideie in 1580 was described as follows: "The provinces of Bizen and Mimasaka, two districts of Harima and a portion of Bitchū."[1] Its total assessed tax base appears variously as 574,000, 474,000, and 472,000 *koku*.[2] While there is no firm evidence for selecting one or another of these figures, the weakness of the Ukita hold in the provinces outside of Bizen would favor the lesser totals for the early years of the Ukita hegemony with the possibility that the larger size was achieved toward the end.

This was the domain, won by Naoie's sword and confirmed to Hideie under the vermilion seals of Nobunaga and Hideyoshi. Theoretically, once the Bizen chieftain had submitted to Hideyoshi, his lands were held at the pleasure of the overlord, under conditions of loyal service. But in actuality Hideie was master of his domain, endowed with complete authority over its military and civil affairs. The people of the domain were essentially his subjects and he their ruler. The size of Hideie's domain ranked him eighth among the vassal daimyo of Hideyoshi. Hideie himself listed a group of over 1480 enfeoffed housemen in his private band (*kashindan*). Of these, seven had holdings assessed at 10,000 *koku* or more and so were of daimyo size, though not treated as such because they were rear vassals with respect to Hideyoshi. This band of retainers served Hideie as military officers and civil officials, making possible the regular mobilization of armies of from ten to twenty thousand as well as the public administration of the territory. The domain at this time was dedicated mainly to warfare, its resources being funneled into the great central citadel of Okayama or to the ten or more subsidiary castles maintained strategically throughout the territory. But the Ukita were also confronted increasingly by the problems of civil administration. And it is here that the militant daimyo who fought under Hideyoshi discovered some of their most difficult problems.

Certain aspects of the organization of the Ukita domain are

---

[1] *Okayama-shi shi*, 2.1504.

[2] *Okayama-shi shi*, 2.1633; Taniguchi Sumio, "Bizen-hansei no kakuritsu katei," in *Okayama Daigaku Kyōikugakubu kenkyū shūroku*, 2 (1956), 2 (hereafter cited as Taniguchi, "Bizen-hansei"); Fujino Tamotsu, *Bakuhan taisei no kenkyū*, between pages 120-121.

revealed in the rolls of vassals and fiefs (*bugen-chō* or *chigyō-chō*) which were drawn up by the Ukita house. Unfortunately these rolls, all of which date from around 1598, are limited to the enfeoffed housemen and so tell us little or nothing about the stipended retainers. But they help to explain the way in which the daimyo apportioned his land and controlled his retainers. Basically the land of the Ukita domain was divided into three types: the daimyo's private lands (*chokkatsuchi, kurairichi,* or *daidokoro-chi*), the fiefs of his vassals (*chigyōchi*), and the lands of local temples and shrines (*jisha-ryō*).[3] A calculation from one of the rolls reveals that the enfeoffed vassals held land assessed at 349,689 *koku.*[4] The religious estates of Bizen had been reduced to only 3000 *koku* by the time of Hideie.[5] Those in the remaining Ukita lands may have doubled this figure. Thus assuming that the overall assessment of the Ukita domain was 474,000 *koku,* we can calculate that the daimyo's private lands would come to something over 121,000 *koku,* roughly 25 percent of the whole. Vassals held as fiefs just under 74 percent of the whole. This balance between daimyo's land and vassals' fiefs is roughly what one would find in other domains of the time. For instance in the neighboring Mōri territory, out of 1,120,000 *koku* about 230,000 *koku* (20 percent) belonged to the lord and the remainder was allotted to the vassals.[6] As we shall discover later, this balance between lord and vassal was not particularly stable, and it was redressed in favor of the daimyo in later generations.

The measures taken by the Ukita to organize their territory and systematize the enfeoffment of their vassals reveal many advances in the handling of land rights, in the procedures of cadastral registration, and in the organized control of large numbers of vassals. Since in most parts of their territory, daimyo of the Sengoku period such as the Matsuda and Urakami had carried forward the process of simplifying land tenures, the Ukita acquired a domain which was relatively devoid of the claims of absentee proprietors, a territory over which they alone could assert the authority of proprietary lord. Yet within the domain

[3] Okuno Takahiro, *Nobunaga to Hideyoshi,* 72; Asao Naohiro, "Hōshi seiken ron," *loc.cit.,* 176-196.

[4] Ukita Chūnagon Hideie kyō kashi chigyō chō, ms. in *Ōoka-ke monjo,* Okayama Kenritsu Toshokan, 092.8/132.

[5] *Komonjo-shū,* 2.40. Kinzanji documents.

[6] Okuno Takahiro, *Nobunaga to Hideyoshi,* 72.

at two levels the process of unification of proprietary control was still less than complete. At the level of the individual cultivator and his plots of farm land, the *myō* style of organization had not yet been fully replaced by that of *hyakushō* organized into administrative villages. Thus the customary private relationship between local proprietor and land cultivator persisted. At a higher level, among the enfeoffed vassals, many were sufficiently entrenched in their hereditary holdings so that the power of the daimyo over them, at least in their local administration, was limited by customary restraints. In the first instance, the Ukita were unable or too preoccupied to follow Hideyoshi in implementing a complete land survey with its accompanying institutional reforms. In the second, the Ukita domain was still too close to the conditions of military strife among rival *bushi* families to permit a thorough-going separation of the daimyo's housemen from their hereditary lands and privileges. The Ukita, along with most of the daimyo of their age, exhibited in the institutions of political control over their domain certain transitional features between decentralization and centralization which distinguished them from the daimyo of the Tokugawa period. The smallness of the daimyo's personal holdings, the continued existence of semi-independent outlying castles, the excessively military orientation of the domain, and the immaturity of its civil organs of government were all features awaiting change under the Tokugawa regime.

A copy of an Ukita roll of vassals preserved in the Ōoka family documents, probably compiled during the first part of Hideie's rule (but perhaps reworked as late as 1600), reveals the following arrangement of Ukita housemen:[7]

Name of Vassal	Size of Fief (*koku*)
Togawa Higo-no-kami	25,600
his 40 musketeers	800
his 90 officers (*yoriki*)	21,746.5
	48,146.5
castle support lands contributed	2,000
Total	46,146.5

[7] See note no. 4. Other rolls are to be found in *Zoku gunsho ruiju* (see *Okayama-shi shi*, 2.1652-1670); in *Dai Nihon shiryō* (see *Tsūshi*, 2.96-102); in *Kibi shūi* (see *Kibi-gun shi*, 2.2103-2125); also Ukita-ke bugenchō, ms., *Ōoka-ke monjo*, Okayama Kenritsu Toshokan, 092.8/44.

	(*koku*)
Ukita (Miyake) Genzabei	22,400
his 33 officers	7,565
castle support lands	2,000
Total	31,969
Oka Echizen-no-kami	23,300
his 40 musketeers	800
his 123 officers	18,675
castle support lands	2,000
Total	44,805
Ukita Sakyō-no-suke	24,079.1
his 40 musketeers	800
his 26 officers	1,949
Total	26,828.1
Osafune Kichibei-no-jō	24,084
his 40 musketeers	800
his 91 officers	11,845
Total	36,729
Akashi Kamon-no-kami	33,110
his 40 musketeers	800
his officers	1,800
Total	36,710
Hanabusa Yoichirō	14,860
his 17 officers	1,230
Total	16,909
Ukita Shume	4,360
his 35 officers	1,810
Total	6,170

	(*koku*)
Ukita Kambei-no-jō	4,000
his 40 musketeers	800
his 15 officers	610
Total	5,410
Ugai Tarōbei	1,210
his 8 officers	380
Total	1,590
Naomura Gonsuke	3,100
his 22 officers	745
Total	3,840
Akashi Kyūbei	2,000
his 40 musketeers	800
his 12 officers	320
Total	3,120
Ukita Kawachi-no-kami	4,500
Ukita Naiki	3,000
his 40 musketeers	800
Total	3,800
Unattached vassals (149 were enfeoffed at 3,280 to 20 *koku*)	71,231
Domestic (*daidokoro*) staff (4 officers)	160
Nishi-no-maru guard group (for the daimyo's heir) (24 officers)	1,260
Musketeers 17 captains and 584 officers	11,680
Grand Total	349,689.6

Other existing rolls offer slightly different figures, especially if compiled after Ukita Genzabei's death. In one document, dated 1598, the total fiefs amount to 345,418 *koku*, and some difference exists in the numbers of unattached vassals and musketeers.[8] But for purposes of structural analysis of the Ukita band of housemen these differences are not significant.

Of the 1483 or more vassals enfeoffed by the Ukita, seven held lands assessed at from 14,860 to 33,100 *koku*. Another 43 had fiefs of from 1000 to 4500 *koku*. Sixty-two men were enfeoffed at between 500 to 1000 *koku*. Some 156 men were of 100 to 500 *koku* rank, and the remaining 1215 were enfeoffed at from 10 to 99 *koku*. Taken together, the 268 men with fiefs of 100 *koku* or more constituted 17 percent of the enrolled vassals; the remaining 83 percent held fiefs of less than 100 *koku*. Among these, the roll reveals that only eleven were given less than 20 *koku*. Thus we can assume that the officer or knight of minimum holding at this time possessed at least 20 *koku*. This was probably the size of fief necessary to maintain and equip a mounted or armored member of the daimyo's military retinue.

Since the Ukita rolls do not tell us about the stipended vassals and other categories of footmen and supply corps recruits, we have no idea of how large the complete Ukita houseband was. We are told the daimyo of Bizen was in the habit of drawing together armies of up to 20,000 men. Such a figure probably included a large element of non-samurai recruits. Nonetheless the daimyo had lands of over 120,000 *koku*, and these must have provided support for a large number of stipended personnel. The enfeoffed vassals also went into battle followed by their own levies and stipended followers; even the poorest of the mounted officers or musketeers would have his one or two footmen. An example from the Kaga domain of a slightly later period reveals the following scale of military recruitment. For each 10,000 *koku* of fief a vassal was required to supply 7 banners, 20 mounted officers, 25 musketeers, 5 bowmen, 50 spearsmen, and an undisclosed number of supply laborers. A 500 *koku* vassal was accountable for 1 musketeer and 3 spearsmen.[9] The Mōri required 50 spearsmen, 50 musketeers, and 25 bowmen from a 10,000 koku vassal, 2 spears-

[8] Taniguchi, "Bizen-hansei," 3.
[9] Okuno Takahiro, *Nobunaga to Hideyoshi*, 72.

men, 2 musketeers, and 1 bowman from a 500 *koku* vassal.[10] The recruitment policies of the Ukita were probably comparable to these. At any rate the complete roster of men in Ukita service must have been considerably larger than the list of enfeoffed vassals.

The structure of the Ukita houseband was closely related to the turbulent conditions out of which Naoie fashioned his domain and, of course, on the pattern of consolidation which accompanied his victories. By contrast to the Urakami and other *sengoku-daimyō* bands which took the form of coalitions of locally entrenched vassals held together loosely by the daimyo, the Ukita managed to secure a tighter grip over their housemen. In this respect the Ukita band was more similar to those of the Oda and Toyotomi houses. Put together hastily during the course of one generation of fighting behind a single great leader, Naoie's corps of retainers was much more a product of his own creation and more receptive to his own commands. The close identity between family name and locale or between enfeoffed vassal and ancestral castle was now almost gone. The Ukita vassal corps was more of a military organization based on a chain of command system, although the whole was knit together by oaths of vassalage.

The Ukita household was strictly a product of Naoie's creation. Starting with only 30 men, Naoie eventually acquired a following of over 1400 enfeoffed vassals. These men were added a few at a time in the course of his conquest of the Kibi provinces. Most of these men were, like the Ukita, *bushi* of southern Bizen. A large number, in fact, came from families of long-standing local influence; families who had through the course of the Sengoku period served as vassals of the Urakami or Matsuda. This is best seen by an analysis of the middle range of Ukita vassals. The Ukita rolls list 261 men with fiefs in the range from 4500 to 100 *koku*. These men served as members of military units, group commanders, or administrative officers under the daimyo. Among these a rough check reveals that nearly one-half bore surnames of *bushi* families who had been outstanding in Bizen during the Sengoku period. The Ukita incorporated into their following members of nearly all of the major *bushi* families of Bizen who were active during the wars of consolidation. Such were the Osafune, Oka, Nagahara, Mushiage, Karita, Baba, Kanamitsu, Kunitomi, Ukai, Iwanasu, Namba, and Iga. Conspicuously lacking were members of the Mat-

[10] Okuno Takahiro, *Sengoku daimyō* (Tokyo, 1960), 109.

suda or Urakami families or of their senior vassals. Thus we can assume that Naoie's following was built up as the minor vassals of the Urakami and Matsuda swung over to his support in the course of his struggle for mastery of Bizen. No doubt the Ukita drew into their band many of the *bushi* of Bitchū and Mimasaka, but the identity of these men is more difficult to confirm. Probably not until the Ukita became vassals of Nobunaga and Hideyoshi did men from more distant provinces drift into Ukita service.

At the risk of oversimplification, we can conceive of the organization of the Ukita *kashindan* as consisting of two types of units: the military group (*kumi*) and the functional offices (*bugyōsho*). For ease of organization and command, most vassals were assigned to groups which varied in size from over 100 to around 10 men. Each such *kumi* was headed by a chief referred to literally as the parent (*yori-oya*). The men attached to the unit were called children (*yori-go* or *yoriki*). By working through a limited number of chief vassals under whom lesser retainers were grouped, the daimyo was able to maintain a command relationship over a sizable vassal band with minimum effort. Administrative and service functions were placed in charge of individual vassals (generally detached from their military group) who served as commissioners. Such officials might also receive command of a group of subordinates, thus serving as heads of functional units.

Of the seven men who acquired holdings of over 10,000 *koku* while in Naoie's service three were among the original band of thirty men assigned to Naoie in 1545. These were Togawa, Osafune, and Oka, all petty *bushi* of southern Bizen. Another, Hanabusa, joined Naoie during the late 1540's. Akashi was the most important of Urakami Munekage's vassals to throw in with the Ukita in 1577. The other two were Naoie's brothers. Each of these men eventually held in fief from Naoie lands assessed at over 10,000 *koku*. Varying in amount from 14,000 to 33,000 *koku* they totaled 168,153.1 *koku*. These seven served Naoie as his chief vassals (*karō*) and unit commanders. They were charged with the command of 381 *yoriki* who in turn were enfeoffed in lands which totaled 64,810.5 *koku*. Thus these men were in a real sense reardaimyo within a regional coalition headed by the Ukita house.

The *karō* class vassals of the Ukita were also for the most part castellans of major importance within Naoie's territory, for the Ukita domain maintained a number of castles beyond the central one at Okayama. The process of military consolidation in Kibi which took place from the 1530's to the 1580's had pitted the regionally entrenched *sengoku-daimyō* against each other until all were eliminated by the superior war machine of Ukita Naoie. In the process of Naoie's rise, one after another of the valley-centered military bands headed by such families as the Matsuda, Iga, Higasa, Katsuragi, Karita, Ugaki, and Urakami were wiped out, their main castles put to the torch or smashed beyond utility. Military consolidation had thus greatly reduced the numbers of castles and lesser fortified hills in Bizen. Naoie himself as he grew in stature moved from castle to castle, abandoning such early ones as Otogo, Narabe, and later even Numa. Within one generation the network of small castles which had blanketed Bizen was superseded (as shown on map opposite).

On the other hand it was not practical to destroy all castles in favor of the one central fortress of Okayama. For two reasons major subsidiary castles were retained within the growing domain. First for strategic purposes, such castles as Tomiyama, Tatsu-no-kuchi, and Tsuneyama were needed on the approaches to Okayama. These were enlarged and garrisoned either by the daimyo's own troops or by his closest vassals.[11] Secondly, on the domain's frontiers, in the areas newly conquered or still unsurely held, Naoie found it convenient to enfeoff his fighting generals, placing them as castellans over extensive territories. Hanabusa, enfeoffed in Bitchū and Mimasaka, Togawa in Bitchū, Akashi in Harima, and Naoie's adopted brother in Kojima, all had most difficult assignments of holding down uncertain frontier territories. On the other hand, there was always a danger for the daimyo in placing too much reliance on such castellans or in giving them too much independence. This essentially is what happened to the Urakami as they permitted Ukita Naoie to expand beyond control. Thus the Ukita maintained an ambivalence toward their castle-holding vassals, pulling them back to Okayama as soon as the need for frontier castles diminished.

It is not possible to reconstruct from existing documents, with any degree of accuracy, the disposition of castles within the Ukita domain. Aside from those mentioned above, the last to remain in use appear to have been Mitsuboshi in Mimasaka, Kajiyayama, Takayama, Takada, Daianji, Shimotsui, Tomatsu, Takamatsu, and

[11] *Kibi-gun shi*, 2.2124.

Ukita Domain, 1580–1600

MIMASAKA

Takada

Mitsuboshi

Kotsuki

BITCHŪ

Takahashū

HARIMA

Senju

Tomiyama

BIZEN

Nama 1559

Narabe 1549

Takamatsu

Tatsunokuchi

Okayama 1574

Mushiage

Otogo 1544

BINGO

Tsuneyama

Shimotsui

○ Castles occupied and abandoned
  before 1574

● Castles maintained beyond 1590
  Not all are known

∴∴∴∴ Boundaries in Harima and Bitchu
  uncertain

10 Miles

Mushiage in Bitchū and Bizen.[12] An obvious conclusion from the
various copies of the Ukita vassal rolls is that there was frequent
change in castle commands. Both Naoie and Hideie worked hard
to prevent their vassals from becoming entrenched in any one

[12] Ukita-ke bugenchō, in *Kibi-gun shi*, 2.2124.

locality, and there was a constant effort to diminish the number of active castles. By the time of the Korean wars we are safe in assuming that not more than ten subsidiary castles existed in the Ukita domain and that these were constantly being liquidated or taken over directly by the daimyo and his private stipendiaries.

Nevertheless, the major vassals under Ukita command continued to serve as castellans of daimyo proportions. It is informative to try to reconstruct how one of these castellanies was organized. After the battle of Tsuneyama in 1577, Togawa Hideyasu received Tsuneyama castle. His private holdings totaled over 25,000 *koku* by this time and his garrison command consisted of 50 officers (*yoriki*) and 3000 footmen (*hosotsu*).[13] Togawa's chief officers were used as unit commanders assigned to the various castle enclosures as follows:

Enclosure	Size		Commander
	tsubo	acre	
Hommaru	700	.6	Togawa Hideyasu
Hyōgo-no-maru	100	.08	Tokura Hyōgo
Kita-ni-no-maru	250	.2	Ikeda Toshibei
Kita-san-no-maru	220	.18	Tsushima Kurozaemon
Tenjin-maru	200	.16	Kondō Shirōzaemon
Aoki-no-maru	250	.2	Togawa Sukezaemon
Ume-no-ō	600	.5	Shindō Sakichi
Ume-ni-no-maru	500	.4	Shindō Bokkō
Higashi-ichi-no-maru	120	.1	Mushiage Sōuemon
Higashi-san-no-maru	100	.08	Tobiyama
Yatake-no-maru	200	.16	Shishido
Yatake-ni-no-maru	150	.12	Yokoi
Sōmon-ni-no-maru	150	.12	Tanaka
Sōmon-no-maru	300	.25	Kunitomi Genzaemon
(Shichi-no-maru)	—		Nakajima Kurozaemon[14]

This complex of fortifications (a comparison with the Urakami Tenjinyama castle is informative) provided for the permanent residence of a garrison of at least 3050 fighting men, some of whom were direct vassals of Naoie, others being rear vassals. Togawa retained the central keep while his second in command held the next largest enclosure. The support lands for the castle

[13] *Okayama-shi shi*, 2.1772-1779.
[14] *Ibid.*, 2.1779.

consisted of fiefs assigned directly to the castle and those of the men who manned the castle. Togawa himself had fiefs scattered widely throughout the Ukita domain. But probably a large segment of these was within easy distance of Tomiyama. The special 2000 *koku* provided for castle maintenance and the lands of the Togawa group were also probably close by. Evidence supporting such a supposition concerning the distribution of castle lands comes both from examples of other castellanies and from what we know about Tomiyama at a later date. For instance in 1575 Mōri Terumoto set up his kinsman Motokiyo in Sarukake castle in Bitchū. At the same time he granted him as fief 5000 *kan* of territory close to the castle, though not surrounding it.[15] In 1602 Kobayakawa Hideaki, who succeeded the Ukita in Bizen, assigned his vassal Iki Tōtōmi-no-kami to Tomiyama. Iki already held fiefs of 12,000 *koku* but was given an additional 4864 *koku* to support him as keeper of the castle. These new lands were distributed as follows:[16]

In Kojima district:	*Amount* (*koku*)
Hazakawa-mura	235.13
Hikozaki-mura	703.72
Kōri-mura	556.046
Kogushi-mura	437.25
Tai-mura	620.585
Tsuchigakura-mura	512.2
Hayashi-mura	1,741.5

The villages listed in this grant were all in the general area of Tomiyama.

Thus the small daimyo territories were combined to form the great Ukita domain. But castellanies which persisted after 1577 were not integrated sub-units of the domain itself. Despite the fact that the commander of the castle might have territories counted in the tens of thousands of *koku*, he was not by any means a daimyo in his own right. The Ukita castellans, except perhaps for Akashi, were strictly dependent vassals who were assigned to castle commands at the daimyo's pleasure. Nor did the castles combine with surrounding territory to make an administrative sub-unit of the

[15] *Kibi-gun shi*, 1921-1922.
[16] *Okayama-shi shi*, 2.1716-1717.

domain. They were expected to serve strictly as military outposts and as instruments for the concentration of military power under certain outstanding commanders.

As we have seen, a large part of the lesser enfeoffed housemen were organized into units, or *kumi*, headed by one or another of the major vassals. Five men of the 1000 to 5000 *koku* class are also set apart in the rolls as heads of military units. Some of these officers were used as guard group or garrison chiefs in subsidiary castles. Others headed special corps of archers and musketeers.[17] The several rolls and other records reveal names of such units as the great guard (*ōban-gumi*), the main castle guard (*jōdai-gumi*), the west-enclosure guard (*nishi-no-maru-shū*), the samurai group (*samurai-gumi*), the pages (*koshō-gumi*), the archers (*yumi-gumi*), the musketeers (*teppō-gumi*), and the domestic staff (*daidokoro-shū*).[18] There were, of course, many other varieties of units not revealed in our inadequate sources. All such units were made up by assignment from among the daimyo's retainers. Each unit was under the command of a *yorioya*, whose men were bound to him as *yorigo*.

The 149 vassals listed in the rolls as being unattached to any *kumi* were probably given special functional assignments in civil administration and in less operationally oriented military services. As *bugyō* they would be placed in charge of such tasks as tax collection, supervision of religious institutions, maintenance of public works, naval affairs, military procurement, and the like. One important category of officer was the regional administrator of the daimyo's private lands. Called deputies (*daikan*), they were generally selected from vassals of fairly low status but assigned to lands of considerable size. For instance, there is a 1597 record of such assignment in which a retainer of 300 *koku* enfeoffment was placed over lands totaling 1450 *koku*.[19]

While the civil administration of Bizen under the Ukita was rather haphazardly put together, the same was not true of the daimyo's military organization. When the Bizen chief mobilized for war his major vassals became heads of divisions, and the other units were fitted beneath them or under the daimyo's direct command. Naoie, in his most active years, used Togawa, Osafune, and

[17] See Oka's assignment to Takada castle under Togawa's command. *Kibi-gun shi*, 2.404.
[18] *Ibid.*, 2.2124.   [19] *Okayama-shi shi*, 2.1553.

Oka as his three operational commanders (*sakite*). During these
years we learn that Togawa was assigned 35,000 *koku* of *yoriki*
lands. Later this was reduced to 21,000 *koku*.[20] We may surmise
from this that Naoie at some time in his military career split up
his commands, shifting from three divisions to six. Little is known
about the forces commanded directly by the daimyo. These were
probably mostly in the nature of an elite corps of body guards
and various types of intelligence and communications officers.
Here is a partial listing of Hideie's followers at he time of the
Sekigahara battle of 1600.[21]

banners (*hata*)	47
banner spears (*hatamoto-nagae*)	100
long spears (*mochi-yari*)	30
muskets (*teppō*)	50
spears (*yari*)	50
bells, conch shells, drums (*kane, kai, taiko*)	30
inspectors of senior vassals, from the great guard (*ō-monomiyaku, ōban-gumi yori*)	
inspectors of junior vassals, from the duty guard (*ko-monomiyaku, hibangumi-yori*)	
spies (*shinobi-yaku*)	27
falcons and dogs (*taka, inu*)	20
additionally an undetermined number of attendants (*kinju*)	

Before becoming a daimyo in his own right, Ukita Naoie obviously
maintained a more powerful force under his direct command, and
it is probably only as the Ukita perfected their authority over their
karō-size vassals that they dispersed their forces more widely. The
necessity of the daimyo to have direct command over forces capable of dealing with any recalcitrant vassal was always recognized.

The Ukita house continued to use the system of direct enfeoffment of vassals. There is no remaining register of fiefs, but scattered evidence can give us some idea of the pattern of their distribution. The enfeoffment of vassals by the Ukita was not static,
as it had been under the early *sengoku-daimyō*, but was constant-

---

[20] Ukita Chūnagon Hideie kyō kashi chigyō chō, in *Ōoka-ke monjo*; Ukita Kōmon
Hideie kyō samurai chō ninzutsuke, in *Osafune-ke monjo* (see, *Ikeda-ke bunko,
zatsu*, 717).
[21] *Ibid.*

ly undergoing change. Major battles or turning points in the power struggle—such as 1568, when the Matsuda were eliminated, 1577, when the Urakami were destroyed, 1582, after the battle of Taka-matsu, and 1598, after the final withdrawal from Korea—were occasions for major redistributions. An important but incomplete document which purports to be a registry of fiefs of the Urakami vassals on the eve of the destruction of Tenjinyama should be in-troduced at this point because it reveals most clearly the distribu-tion of fiefs in what was to be the core of the Ukita domain.[22] The evidence appears to be more appropriate to the Ukita ex-perience than to the Urakami. From this document we learn that at the time Ukita Naoie's lands were assessed at 19,516 *koku*. These were held as thirteen separate grants scattered widely over southern Bizen. Akashi in the same document held a total of 17,725 *koku* made up of sixteen pieces in Bizen and Harima. Nakayoshi was given 3904 *koku* in four pieces located in Wake and Iwanashi districts. Statistically, the 58 vassals for whom data is given held fiefs on the following basis:

Size of total holdings[23]

		30,000 10,000	10,000 1,000	1,000 500	500 10	Total
Number of individual holdings	1		8	15	13	36
	2		1	1	3	5
	3		3	2		5
	4		3			3
	5		2			2
	6		1			1
	7		1			1
	8					
	9					
	10		2			2
	13	1				1
	16	1				1
	22	1				1

The obvious pattern revealed here is one in which the fiefs of large vassals were widely scattered, but contained certain large

[22] Urakami Munekage bukan, ms., *Ikeda-ke bunko,* zatsu, 717.
[23] *Ibid.*

holdings which served as base points, perhaps adjoining and supporting the castles which these vassals maintained. The fiefs of lesser vassals were not so scattered, consisting in the main of one or two parcels. Thirty-six vassals, in fact, retained single holdings, and all of these were below the level of 1500 *koku*. Such single holdings were probably the long-established ancestral lands of local *bushi* families, and it is in this category that we find the long-time residents of Bizen whose names have appeared in the previous chapters. There is little question but that the Ukita followed this pattern of enfeoffment, providing certain base holdings for each vassal family, but fragmenting and scattering other fiefs when the occasion presented.

Whether there was any such thing as a minimum-sized holding is difficult to determine. We have already noted that in the Ukita rolls there were few listings below that of 20 *koku*. Below this level the chances are that the vassal received a stipend rather than a fief. In the larger holdings, of course, a good deal of subinfeudation went on, so that the listings of grants to vassals were themselves composites of fragmented holdings. The relationship of the *bushi* class to the land and the workers of the land was still an intimate one.

Aside from the daimyo's own lands which were directly governed by him, the fiefs served as sub-units of the domain, each constituting a separate unit of rural administration and tax responsibility. The relationship of fief holders to their lands was direct and personal. In each instance the daimyo had granted or confirmed proprietary rights subject only to his overlordship. The method of granting fiefs underwent a major change under Ukita supervision. For, as we shall explain later, Ukita Hideie presided over the final abandonment of *shōen* procedures of land management in favor of the *kokudaka* system of assessment. Following the lead of Hideyoshi, Hideie ultimately undertook a complete resurvey of his domain. The change is clearly visible if we compare the language of grants made to their vassals by Naoie and Hideie. In Naoie's time the terms of land grants were still written out in the vocabulary of the *shōen* system. Take, for instance, Naoie's grants to Baba Jirōshirō in 1580:

> You are entrusted for the time being with half of the half-rights (*hanzei-hannō*) of Minami Naganuma. Remain there

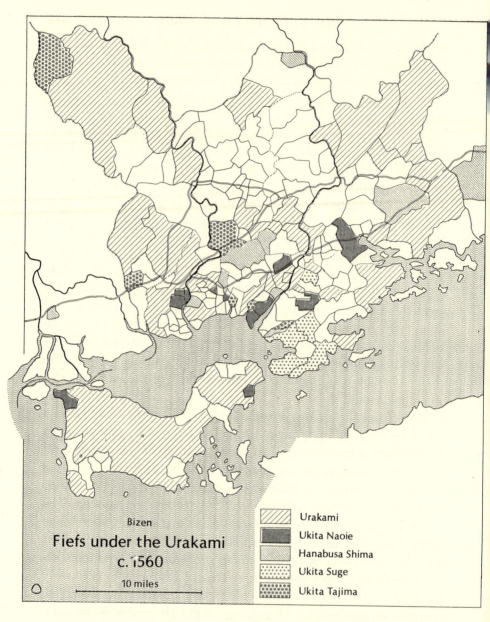

Bizen

Fiefs under the Urakami
c. 1560

10 miles

⫽⫽	Urakami
▓	Ukita Naoie
⫻	Hanabusa Shima
∴	Ukita Suge
⬤	Ukita Tajima

and apply yourself so as not to let the land rights (*gechi*) deteriorate. The land rights assigned within Tottori have been granted to another.

Respectfully.

From henceforth the three *gō* located in Toyohara and held

(*shuryō*) by us are assigned to the support of your men. You will strive to lead them in loyal service.

Respectfully.[24]

By the time of Hideie, grants were made increasingly without reference to *shōen*. Thus to Nagahara Kansaku in 1600 Hideie granted as fief (*ryōchi*) the following:

In Bitchū province, the district of Tsuu, Hachio village, 100 *koku*.[25]

Or to Ōmori Tozaemon in 1598 the following:

A listing of lands in fief (*chigyō mokuroku*)
1. 69 *koku* .577 in Bizen, Kamimichi district, Kusakabe
2. 17 *koku* .63 in Bizen, Oku district, Hattori
3. 10 *koku* .80 in Mimasaka, Aita district, Kawai

Total 100 *koku*

The above is an addition for your support. You shall administer the fiefs according to precedents and follow me in loyal service.[26]

These changes in the practices of enfeoffment reflect the process by which the Ukita sought to bring their domain under increasingly orderly control. Particularly under Hideie, once the military consolidation of the domain had been achieved, we find the attention of the domain leadership turning to the problems of internal organization: to the systemization of administrative procedures and the centralization of authority under the daimyo. The Ukita turned, in other words, to the fashioning of a new government for Bizen. A clear embodiment of the centralizing tendencies in Bizen during the period of Ukita ascendancy is evident in the story of the growth of Okayama castle.[27] The castle, which eventually became the center of the Ukita domain, was built on a small rocky knoll on the bank of the Asahi River, close to its mouth on Kojima Bay. The location had not been important until the opening of the sixteenth century when the Kanamitsu family used it as the site of their small castle. In 1573 Ukita Naoie selected Okayama as the most suitable spot for a

---

[24] *Oku-gun shi*, 1.784, based on documents of the *Baba-shi monjo*.
[25] Contained in *Okayama-shi shi*, 2.1545.
[26] *Ibid.*, 1552-1553.
[27] Taniguchi Sumio, "Jōkamachi Okayama no seiritsu" in Uozumi Sōgorō, *Daimyō ryōkoku to jōkamachi* (Kyoto, 1957), 140-151.

new and expanded citadel. Numa, his headquarters at that time, was too small to accommodate his growing band of retainers and expansion of Numa seemed out of the question because of the swampy terrain. Okayama therefore recommended itself for several reasons: it lay in the center of Ukita holdings, it commanded a wide and prosperous plain, it was protected by rocks on one side and a river on the other, and above all it was well situated from the point of view of both land and sea communications.

Having decided on Okayama as the new site for his main castle, Naoie put his chief vassal Oka in charge of construction. A great deal of heavy construction was necessary before a foundation was cleared and a moat dug to bring the water of the Asahi River around to the west of the hill. Oka laid out the plans of the fortress, which included barracks quarters for officers and troops and special facilities for a commercial sector. As construction progressed, and the daimyo was able to move into the new castle, parts of Numa castle were dismantled and used at Okayama. Within a span of three years the first stage of construction was complete.

The town which grew up in the shadow of the castle began as only a straggle of merchant houses which came into being to serve the local garrison. But the spot was a natural center of trade, as ships descended the river from Mimasaka or crossed the narrow waters from Bitchū. Moreover, as the castle grew and the daimyo began to pull more and more of his vassals off the land, large numbers of residences had to be constructed for the daimyo's retainers. Before long, artisans from all over the Kibi area and even from the capital had flocked to Okayama to engage in the construction operations, and merchants from other towns and market places in the area took up permanent quarters below the castle. By the time of Naoie's death, an imposing fortress surrounded by a sizable town had taken shape. Most of his vassals had built or acquired residences in Okayama, and even the castellans were obliged to reside in Okayama when not engaged in military operations.

Under Hideie, a number of important modifications were made in the plan of the castle and the surrounding town. The main keep was moved closer to the river on the east and heightened. The western approaches to the keep were also strengthened. At the same time the space within the ramparts was expanded to make room for more garrison quarters and officer residences, and an increasing number of vassals were moved from the countryside to the town. Outside the castle walls the merchant quarters were enlarged and beyond the commercial section, samurai residences were further extended. By 1596, one observer wrote, the town had grown 100 times its size in 1576.[28]

As the castle became the recognized political and commercial center of Bizen, the national highway was routed through it. A bridge was thrown across the Asahi River at a point just south of the castle, making it possible for through traffic to avoid the more circuitous route which crossed by ferry farther up the river. The bridge also made possible the expansion of the town at the point of its greatest congestion eastward across the river. By the 1590's Okayama had developed as a true castle city, inhabited by thousands of the daimyo's housemen and mercenaries, serviced by a flourishing commercial community, and providing facilities as a regional trading entryport. The town by now contained some twelve commercial blocks, many of them such as Katakami-chō and Saidaiji-chō bearing the names of the nearby towns from which Okayama had begun to deflect trade. Under the patronage of the daimyo, merchants from Fukuoka developed Kami-no-chō, and trading houses from the Kyoto area established Furugyō-chō. Outside the commercial sector blocks of artisans appeared in response to the demand for special services. There were streets of carpenters, sharpeners, metal workers, paperers, and many others.[29]

From 1580 to 1600 Okayama castle served Hideie as his headquarters for military operations and his own domain administration. Unfortunately we know little about the internal affairs of Bizen during these twenty years. For one thing Hideie spent little time in Okayama, for he was frequently in attendance on Hideyoshi at Fushimi or engaged in distant military campaigns. Thus the task of consolidating the Ukita domain probably did not receive the attention it deserved. Much remained to be done in 1580: the digestion of huge pieces of territory in Mimasaka and Bitchū only recently won by force of arms, the reorganization of the vassal band, the creation of an effective civil government, and the carrying out of a domain-wide land survey. Numerous

[28] *Ibid.,* 147.   [29] *Ibid.,* 149.

laws and regulations urged upon the daimyo by Hideyoshi remained to be enforced.

Two fragmentary, and at best secondary, accounts are all that
we have to tell us of the internal events of Bizen and Okayama
castle during the last twenty years of Ukita rule. In one we
learn that Nakamura Jirōbei, a samurai from the Maeda domain
of Kaga, entered Okayama as the guardian of the Maeda girl who
became Hideie's wife. This man gained the favor of the Bizen
daimyo, who permitted him to help in the setting of new domestic
policy. Nakamura appears to have been a ruthless administrator
on behalf of the daimyo. Under his direction the three leading
housemen, Osafune, Ukita Tarōzaemon, and Nobuhara, were
obliged to enforce a complete land survey according to Hideyoshi's specifications. In the process, it is said that the daimyo's
agents confiscated or readjusted the private lands of all the
daimyo's housemen, and recruited the labors of the common
people beyond endurance.[30] The other source carries on from
here to state that as a result of the land survey nearly one-half of
the lands of the housemen were confiscated and some 200,000
koku were added to the daimyo's cadastral registers.[31] These accounts are no doubt exaggerated, but there is documentary evidence to show that a start was actually made on a land resurvey
and that the holdings of vassals were scrutinized and new style
grants of fief were issued. The first group of holdings to be thoroughly investigated were those of the religious institutions. This
was carried out in 1588 and apparently was not conducted in the
manner of the later Taiko surveys. In other words, it seems
probable that the religious institutions merely presented their
own figures to the daimyo's officers rather than submitting to an
actual survey. After 1594, however, there is fairly good evidence
that rigorous cadastral surveys on the Hideyoshi model were being
made and that a considerable readjustment of land holdings was
taking place. All of this gives some credence to the possibility
that the Ukita domain did indeed expand from 474,000 to 574,000
koku in actual registry figures and that the expansion was absorbed in the main by an extension of the daimyo's private lands.

If the castle town symbolized outwardly the power and the
wealth of the Ukita house in Bizen, the national cadastral reform

---

[30] "Wake ginu," *Kibi gunsho shūsei* edn., 42-43.
[31] "Bizen gunki," *Kibi gunsho shūsei* edn., 133.

provided the inner mechanism by which power and wealth was made secure. It is surprising, therefore, that so little is known about the history of the *Taiko kenchi* in Bizen.[32] As had happened in the Nara age, so at the end of the Sengoku period, this most fundamental of reforms in land tax practice was enforced upon Bizen without leaving more than a few scraps of evidence. Yet the sheer physical task of surveying, recording, and assessing every plot of cultivated soil in the Ukita domain was no simple matter. Beyond that there were formidable social and political obstacles to be overcome. The new land tax system, though apparently only a technological reform, embodied a veritable revolution in the structure of local authority as it related to the land. The revolution struck most directly at two groups, the daimyo's enfeoffed retainers and the cultivators.

The *kenchi* did not alter the status of the daimyo's landed vassals as far as their fiefs were concerned. They still retained direct authority over the lands which they received in fief from the daimyo. But the *kenchi* did alter the nature of their exercise of authority over these fiefs. For while they had heretofore held their lands without fear of interference from the daimyo's men, the new survey exemplified the daimyo's ability to enforce uniform legal procedures throughout his domain and into his vassals' holdings. The survey represented, in fact, the physical assertion of the daimyo's claim to superior proprietary rights over his entire domain. The best example of what this meant in terms of the actual balance of power within the domain is seen in the way in which the daimyo's surveyors were able to penetrate the confines of the many individual holdings in Bizen and Mimasaka, uncovering new fields, hidden fields, or fields inadequately surveyed, and adding perhaps a hundred thousand *koku* to the daimyo's private holdings. That the work of the survey teams was not welcomed, especially by those families who had held lands for many generations without having their titles questioned, is understandable. And we shall presently see that antagonisms over the new land policies were at the root of a deep cleavage which developed between two factions in the Ukita domain

[32] See Kanai Madoka, "Shokuhō-ki ni okeru Bizen—Taikō kenchi no chiiki-sei no ichirei," *Chihōshi kenkyū*, 42 (December 1959), 9-20; Shibata Hajime, "Sengoku dogō-sō to Taikō kenchi—Ukita ryō ni okeru jirei," *Rekishi kyōiku*, 8.8 (August 1960), 52-63.

leadership. For the *bushi*, then, the *kenchi* became the beginning wedge by which the daimyo's authority encroached more and more completely upon their independence as feudal proprietors. It was, in fact, the basis of the first significant legal development reversing the trend toward dispersal of authority since the breakdown of the Taihō land system.

There is no evidence that the Ukita went beyond the enforcement of a uniform survey and the adoption of a new system of land registry and taxation in Bizen. It remained for the subsequent generations of daimyo to reduce still further the independence of the *bushi* class and to work toward an ever increasing centralization of authority within the domain. Nonetheless, the purely routine features of the new system had important implications for the status of the *bushi*. In the wake of the resurvey all patents of investiture had to be rewritten, and on a more exact basis. The shift from the inexact terminology left over from the *shōen* system to one based on the systematic assessment of production figures by individual plot meant that the definition of fiefs could be specific and standardized. Since assignments were in terms of abstract units of production (*kokudaka*), the sense of identity with particular lands or locales was weakened. And as the daimyo's men were drawn in ever greater numbers away from the villages into the castle town, the direct involvement of the fief holder in the affairs of the cultivators was also bound to diminish. It was this process which, from the time of Hideyoshi's land reform, was to lead increasingly to the centralization of the daimyo domains. In the years to come, the individual feudal proprietorships comprising the vassal's share of the daimyo's domain were to feel increasingly the authority of the daimyo, which was exercised through the domain administration. Increasingly the daimyo's proprietary rights literally came to penetrate to the village level throughout the domain.

The effect of the *kenchi* upon the cultivating class was, of course, even more immediate and drastic. Whatever areas of freedom, whatever means of avoiding authority which the cultivators had found during the confusion of the age of wars were now denied them. Over the entire countryside a rigorous and systematic procedure of land registry and taxation was enforced through the authority of the daimyo, and behind the daimyo, the national hegemon, Hideyoshi. The new cadastral registers were also directly tied to the organization of village administrative units, for the registers were compiled village (*mura*) by village.

There is today a major controversy among historians over whether the peasantry was affected favorably or adversely by the *kenchi*. That the peasantry was brought under systematic and direct supervision by the daimyo has been taken by many to mean that for the first time in Japan a "purely feudal" control was exerted over the peasantry. But the entire controversy is rather like the one concerning the status of the cultivators under the Taihō institutions. Any enforcement of a uniform system of administration upon previously disordered conditions is apt to look like the imposition of an unwanted despotism. And the question of whether the cultivators were placed under greater or lesser feudal control is too much a matter of definition of terms. To say that the capacity of the daimyo to impose his authority directly upon the peasantry was proof that the full development of feudalism had been attained is to overstress the feudal nature of the daimyo at this particular time. For the enforcement of the *kenchi* was the act of a powerful authority at work within the daimyo's domain. It signalized the end of extreme decentralization and the beginnings of a return to bureaucratic centralization in Japanese government.

With respect to the peasantry the survey necessarily introduced drastic changes. It first of all drew something of an arbitrary line between the *samurai* and *hyakushō* statuses. This meant that in many instances families which had existed on the fringes of the proprietary status (those who had both served as warriors on occasion and who continued to cultivate land) lost whatever rights of free disposal over the land they might have had. Yet the line of separation cut fairly low and the samurai class took in a large portion of the minimal land holders in the countryside. Nor were the families which remained behind in the villages uniformly reduced to the possession of only the land they directly cultivated. The "landlord peasant" status was in fact protected and recognized by the structure of village self-government which relied on the wealthy peasant for positions of responsibility within the village.

The disarming of the peasantry and the reduction of the class to a uniform condition as docile cultivators was a development which probably cut two ways. For some, for those landed peasants who were eager to join in military affairs, this was a denial of opportunity. And it should be remembered that the Sengoku age was a time of considerable social and economic mobility. But for the majority of the cultivators the harboring of arms was a matter of self-protective necessity. What can we know of the mixed sentiments with which they exchanged the symbols of an age of insecurity for one of enforced peace? But more important than the act of disarmament and the forcible scrutiny of the lands of the cultivator was the introduction of new concepts of law and authority with respect to the land and local administration.

From the time of the breakdown of the Taihō land system the cultivator had become increasingly enmeshed in a fabric of obligations involving dues and services rendered on the basis of private compacts. The essence of the status of cultivator during the Sengoku age was that he existed in a milieu of personal or familial obligations to his superiors, obligations which were often theoretically unlimited and could at any time be evoked in arbitrary fashion. The meliorating factor under such circumstances was custom alone or the ability of the cultivator to gain the strength to resist by banding together with other cultivators. The new basis of rural organization and administration brought into force by the *kenchi* made its greatest impact upon the life of the peasant by cutting away (not completely, but in large measure) the private and erratic bonds which held him to higher authority. In their place it sought to create a systematic and increasingly impersonal mechanism of local administration under the daimyo.

The process was only begun under the first round of land reforms ordered by Hideyoshi; it was to be pushed still further toward standardization and impersonalization by the Tokugawa. But a turning point was passed during the 1580's; the *hyakushō* status was defined uniformly across the country and the beginnings of class legislation toward the *hyakushō* took place. The individual *hyakushō* found himself under a new system of domain-wide law. Increasingly he was to become the "subject" of the daimyo and not the personal bondsman or serf of some *bushi* family. The implications of these changes were well understood by the daimyo's chief vassals, for the tendency of the daimyo's authority to become universalized and pervasive throughout his domain meant that the autonomy of the members of the vassal band was directly threatened. That these problems of policy strongly disturbed and divided the top domain leadership is also clear. Yet by the time of Hideie's rule over Bizen, policies of this kind were not to be determined solely at the local level. Bizen was being carried along by events of national scope. Between Bizen and the new center of the country at Osaka, Ukita Hideie was the crucial bridge. It is to the story of Hideie's life as daimyo of Bizen that we must now turn.

AT THE TIME of his father's death in 1581, Ukita Hideie was eight years old. The Ukita had only recently cast in their lot with Oda Nobunaga. In Kibi, local warfare was largely over and the more powerful forces of national centralization were at work upon the land. Upon Naoie's death, Oka, the chief Ukita retainer, hastened to Azuchi with 1000 pieces of gold to do homage and to request Nobunaga's vermilion seal in confirmation of Hideie's succession. Because of Hideie's youth, Hideyoshi took him as adopted son and vouched for him before Nobunaga. The succession was confirmed. Ukita Tadaie, the young heir's uncle, was made guardian, and Togawa, Oka, and Osafune were named domain administrators.[33] Thus the feudal relationships between the Ukita house and that of Oda were formalized. On Nobunaga's death Hideie became Hideyoshi's vassal. Hideyoshi lavished favors on Hideie, drawing him ever more tightly into his group of closest associates. From the outset, Ukita Hideie was thus caught up in the center of the unification struggle.

In 1582, at the great battle of Takamatsu, the Ukita domain was obliged to supply an army of 10,000 men for Hideyoshi's support. Bizen forces led by Ukita Tadaie, Oka, Togawa, and Osafune played a major role in defeating the Mōri. As a result, Hideyoshi gave the land in Bitchū up to the Takahashi River to Hideie and requested that Togawa be enfeoffed at Takamatsu castle.[34] From this point on, Bizen was constantly called upon by Hideyoshi in his military campaigns. Hideie is listed as having provided troops for some ten major engagements. Immediately after completion of the Takamatsu siege, Ukita troops joined in Hideyoshi's swift maneuver to defeat Akechi, Nobunaga's assassin. In 1583 these same forces joined in Hideyoshi's defeat of Shibata. In 1584 Oka, Osafune, and Hanabusa led 15,000 men under Hideyoshi's command in the war with Tokugawa Ieyasu. In 1585 Togawa and Oka joined the attack on the Negoro remnants in Kii province.

[33] *Okayama-shi shi*, 2.1494; 1504.
[34] "Bizen gunki," *Kibi gunsho shūsei* edn., 129.

Later in the same year Togawa and Osafune commanded Ukita units in Hideyoshi's conquest of Shikoku. In 1587 Hideie himself took the field for the first time at the head of 13,000 men as part of Hideyoshi's invasion of Kyushu. In 1590 Hideie spent five months with his men before Odawara castle.

The Ukita domain bore a heavy burden in the Korean campaigns. In 1591, at Hideyoshi's order, fifty seagoing transport ships were constructed in Bizen's coastal ports. The next year these ships were fitted out, and joined the Japanese invasion fleet. The Ukita forces of 10,000 men commanded by Hideie were part of a first corps of 17,200 men which constituted the second invasion wave.[35] The force was made up of units headed by Togawa, Ōoka Echizen, Osafune, Akashi Kamon, Ukita Tadaie (who acted as chief of staff), Hanabusa Shima, Ukita Shume, Ukita Kambei, Ukai Tarōbei, Naomura, Akashi Kumenojō, and Endō Kawachi. It included such military units as the *nishi-no-maru* group, the banner group, musketeers, spearsmen, and archers: the cream of Bizen fighters.[36] The Ukita force gave a creditable performance in Korea, although it appears that Hideie was most active in collecting books and art objects for return to Japan. In 1597 the Ukita domain provided another force of 10,000 men for the second Korean invasion.

What drain in men and material these expeditions made upon Bizen has gone unrecorded. Oka, the foremost Ukita general, died in Korea, but from illness and old age. Some idea of the composition of the Bizen forces can be gained by reference to the records of the Shimazu house of Satsuma. A catalogue of Satsuma forces numbering 12,433 men in 1592 shows the following:

	(*Total men*)
95 mounted knights each with 34 men	3,230
24 mounted knights each with 17 men	808
143 mounted knights each with 10 men	1,430
300 lower samurai each with 3 labor recruits	1,200
500 landless samurai each with 2 labor recruits	1,000
665 carriers	665
2,000 labor recruits from lord's land	2,000
2,000 boatmen	2,000
Grand total	12,433

[35] *Tsūshi*, 2.78-89.   [36] *Ukita-ke bugenchō, Ōoka-ke monjo, loc.cit.*

Provisions for this force for five months came to 10,522.9 *koku* of rice for the men and 616 *koku* of beans for 272 horses.[37] We can imagine while these many domestic and foreign campaigns were in progress, the internal affairs of Bizen were subordinated to the necessities of war, and that military procurement took precedence over concern for rehabilitation.

While Ukita Naoie had fought for possession of the Bizen domain, his son Hideie inherited the status of lord of Bizen to become one of the new feudal aristocracy. Hideie's rise upon the social scale, accomplished with such comparative ease, also served to draw his attention away from Bizen to the court life of Kyoto and Hideyoshi's palaces in Osaka and Fushimi. In 1585, at the age of eleven, Hideie underwent the ceremony of coming of age (*gempuku*), receiving from Hideyoshi the character "hide" for his adult name, the honorary surname Hashiba, the court rank of lower fifth junior grade, and the title of court chamberlain. The next year he rose to lower fourth rank junior grade and the title of left lieutenant of the guards (*sashōshō*). At the age of thirteen he received a further advancement to junior third rank and court councillor (*sangi*). By this time Hideie was frequently in the company of Hideyoshi, attending poetry parties where he showed a flair for genteel accomplishments. In 1589, at the age of fifteen, he was married to the third daughter of Maeda Toshiie. The girl had been previously acquired as Hideyoshi's adopted daughter, so that the marriage was technically a marriage alliance with Hideyoshi. Hideie's highest honors came by way of commendation for his efforts in Korea, for which he received the court rank of acting middle counsellor (*gon-chūnagon*). In 1595 he was named one of the five Great Elders by Hideyoshi. Of all the elders, he was the most indebted to Hideyoshi—the most loyal, the most emotionally attached.[38]

Hideie's life as a high military aristocrat was a far cry from the battlefield experiences through which his father Naoie had fought his way. With the fighting at the local level over, Hideie could live the life of an aristocrat while engaging in less dangerous campaigns in distant places. Hideie seldom had to take the field himself. And history reveals more of Hideie's predilection for

[37] Asakawa, *Iriki*, 333-334.
[38] "Bizen gunki," *Kibi gunsho shūsei* edn., 131-133.

falconry, dramatic entertainment, and poetry than of his military accomplishments.[39]

Hideie was neither by background nor temperament the forceful ruler his father had been. And since he spent much of his time away from Okayama and in the capital area, he was obliged to leave the affairs of the domain to his subordinates. Throughout most of the eighteen years from 1582 to 1600 leadership within the Ukita domain was provided by Hideie's regent and the council of advisers composed of the daimyo's senior vassals. These were all men who had fought with Naoie, veterans of the fiercest battles of the Kibi area and of Hideyoshi's final campaigns. At the time of Hideie's succession, he had been placed under guardianship of his uncle Tadaie, and Togawa, Oka, and Osafune were made chief administrators of the domain. (Later Akashi and Hanabusa also served as advisers.) Osafune was given the senior position among the *karō*. These men, because of their battle experience, their frequent use as generals in campaigns under Hideyoshi and their broad experience as castle holders and territorial administrators provided Bizen with firm guidance. They themselves became minor figures in Hideyoshi's entourage, and all were given titles by him. Togawa was named Higo-no-kami; Ukita Tadaie, Dewa-no-kami; Osafune, Etchū-no-kami; Oka, Buzen-no-kami; Akashi, Hida-no-kami; Hanabusa, Shima-no-kami. There is strong evidence that these men looked with disfavor on Hideie's character and his luxurious habits. Hanabusa Motoyuki was perhaps the most outspoken of them. He frequently remonstrated with Hideie and even incurred Hideyoshi's wrath by criticizing the display of dancing (*sarugaku*) with which Hideyoshi regaled his generals at the time of the Odawara siege.[40]

It is fairly obvious that by 1590 a deep factionalism was beginning to develop among Hideie's advisers. The sources of the split are uncertain, but they appear to have been related to differences over domain policy. In 1588 Osafune was killed by a retainer, and Oka succeeded him as head of the Ukita council. Hideie was now of an age to have a mind of his own. He found more congenial to his company and his interests not his father's old veterans but young men of a new generation. Among these was Osafune Kii-no-kami, son of Etchū-no-kami. This young

[39] *Ibid.,* 133.
[40] *Tsūshi,* 2.95.

man, the chronicles say, had a quick mind but a "mean spirit." He had been no great success as a leader of troops but apparently had ability in organization and administration. At the time of the building of Hideyoshi's palace at Fushimi he directed Hideyoshi's attention to himself and was commended to Hideie by Hideyoshi. When Nakamura entered the Ukita household from Kaga in 1589, he joined with the young Osafune to form a clique around Hideie, playing to his private weaknesses while pushing through financial policies aimed at breaking the power of the traditionally entrenched vassals and increasing the daimyo's private income.[41] When Oka died in Korea in 1592, Togawa should have become the new chief retainer. Instead, through Hideyoshi's interference, the young Osafune was given the post. It was this Osafune Kii-no-kami who headed the commission for the resurvey of lands in the Ukita domain.

From this point the Ukita housemen split rapidly into two factions. The land survey was probably the major issue. But soon still another issue added bitterness to the growing feud. Since the time of Naoie, the Nichiren sect of Buddhism had been favored in Bizen. Hideie, however, became dissatisfied with the Nichiren priesthood when they proved unable to cure his wife's illness. Meanwhile, Osafune, the young Akashi, Nakamura, and others had turned Christian and urged Hideie to do likewise. The old guard, threatened financially, was now confronted with a deep religious issue. Hanabusa, the most forthright, approached Hideie and cautioned him about the danger to his domain. For his concern he was repaid by a burst of Hideie's anger and a sentence of self-inflicted death for himself and his two sons. This sentence was later only partially reversed. Hideyoshi, in view of Hanabusa's services in Korea, interfered to reduce it to banishment for himself and one son in care of the Satake house in the far north of Japan.[42] His third son succeeded to the family lands in Bizen.

Now there was no controlling the feelings of Hideie's housemen as all took sides in the feud. Fortunately, in 1596 the domain was again active in preparing for the reinvasion of Korea. But after Hideyoshi's death and the return from Korea, the old wound was opened. In 1598 Togawa joined by the young Hanabusa, Oka, and Ukita formed a cabal and poisoned Osafune Kii-no-kami. This

[41] "Wake ginu," *Kibi gunsho shūsei* edn., 42-43.
[42] "Bizen gunki," 133-136.

gave the conservative Togawa his chance to become chief retainer. But Nakamura remained in a position from which he could
continue the agitation against the old guard and, moreover, he had
Hideie's confidence. Finally, things reached the point that Togawa, Ukita, Hanabusa, and Oka went to Osaka, where Hideie was
residing, to request Nakamura's dismissal. Nakamura fled to Kaga,
but Hideie in anger hired an assassin to kill Togawa. The petition-
ing group learned of the plot, rescued Togawa from an ambush,
and barricaded themselves in their quarters with some 250 followers. There open fighting broke out, which was quieted only by
the interference of Tokugawa Ieyasu.

The final solution to this distressing feud in the Ukita house
came with Ieyasu's decision that Togawa be sent in exile to Hitachi
province and Hanabusa to the house of Mashita in Yamato. The
rest were permitted to return to Okayama and Akashi Kamon of
the Christian party was made chief retainer.[43] The lands of the
exiled vassals this time were confiscated and their men reassigned.
At this time some forty of Hideie's vassals left with Togawa and
Hanabusa.[44]

On the eve of Sekigahara the Ukita house was in a most precarious state. Hideie, intensely loyal to Hideyoshi's memory, could
see perhaps the coming clash with Tokugawa Ieyasu, but could
not or would not change his allegiance. Akashi, his chief adviser,
was a Christian, also fully committed to Hideyoshi and Hideie.
Among the Ukita councils the sound military judgment of Naoie's
days had vanished. When, just before the clash with Ieyasu, Togawa, from his exile in the Kantō, wrote Akashi urging him to
throw Bizen in with the Tokugawa, Akashi did not even com-
municate the thought to Hideie. The Ukita house had been committed to a lost cause.

The fall of the Ukita came suddenly at the battle of Sekigahara.
Ukita Hideie, the most steadfast in support of Hideyoshi's memory, bore the brunt of the Tokugawa attack and went down in
defeat, betrayed by the confederates on whom he had counted.
Of all the band of fighting men reared by Naoie only those who
had been expelled from Bizen by Hideie survived. Hideie paid
the price of his too close reliance on Hideyoshi. But there were
other factors of weakness in his position. He himself had broken

---

[43] *Ibid.*, 151.
[44] See the evidence of this in the rolls, *Tsūshi*, 2.96-102.

the continuity of leadership needed in a new age of political consolidation. Hideie played the courtier while he should have learned
to administer his inheritance. As with so many of the daimyo who
rose to prominence under Hideyoshi, the conversion from war to
peace proved too difficult.

Nonetheless, the Ukita provided an important legacy for Bizen.
The province had been consolidated and cleared of extreme decentralization. The small valley-centered powers had been unified and all internal fighting put to an end. The beginnings of
effective administrative centralization at the castle of Okayama
had been made. Much of the *bushi* class had been withdrawn from
the countryside and brought to live in the garrison town. The
shōen system had been swept away in its entirety, and new
cadastral practices had been put into effect. The countryside, now
organized into units of village administration, was placed under
a method of control more systematic and impartial than any since
the heyday of imperial rule.

XII. THE ESTABLISHMENT OF THE TOKUGAWA HEGEMONY

HIDEYOSHI's death immediately threw into jeopardy the balance of power upon which his hegemony had been built. The Toyotomi alliance of daimyo, brought together under Hideyoshi's powerful grip and magnetic personality, now rested on a legacy of oaths and agreements surrounding a memory and an infant heir. In his final hours Hideyoshi had extracted from his chief vassals new pledges of support for his son Hideyori, and he had organized the councils of elders, mediators, and administrators which he hoped would perpetuate the balance of power until his heir was of age. Among the five *tairō*, Tokugawa Ieyasu was assigned custody of Fushimi castle and administration of the affairs of the realm; Maeda Toshiie became Hideyori's guardian and keeper of Osaka castle. But as Hideyoshi must have feared, this arrangement was potentially unstable, easily subject to the play of ambitions, easily thrown off by the death of key individuals or the development of factional differences among the daimyo.

Fundamentally the stability of the Toyotomi league depended upon a dynamic balance of power between the great *tozama* daimyo and the hard core of house daimyo, Hideyoshi's most dependent vassals. Hideyoshi had worked to create both an equilibrium between these groups of daimyo and a stability within each group. In the months after his death conflicts began to show up both within the groups themselves and at the points of juncture between them. Among the great lords, private ambitions to succeed Hideyoshi as national hegemon led to mistrust and friction between the Tokugawa, Maeda, Mōri, and Uesugi. Among Hideyoshi's house daimyo, differences of opinion over basic national policy had been growing from the time of the termination of the Korean invasion. This factionalism among Hideyoshi's housemen had a long and deep history and followed a similar pattern to that which had divided the Ukita retainers. Among the men who had risen with Hideyoshi some had made their way primarily as administrators. Such were Ishida, Mashita, and Natsuka, men who were appointed to the board of administrators. Others had served primarily in a military capacity and had made their fame as Hide-

30. Ukita Yoshiie was active in the Bizen Plain until his defeat and death in 1534.

31. Ukita Naoie (1529-1581), Yoshiie's son, led the Ukita house to its mastery of Bizen.

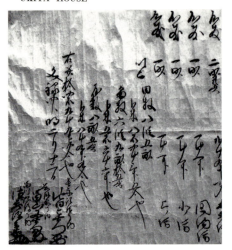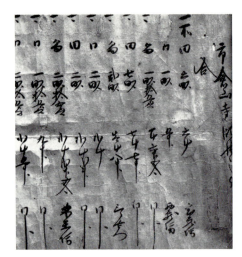

32. This example of the Taiko cadastral survey lists and grades land held by Kinzanji.

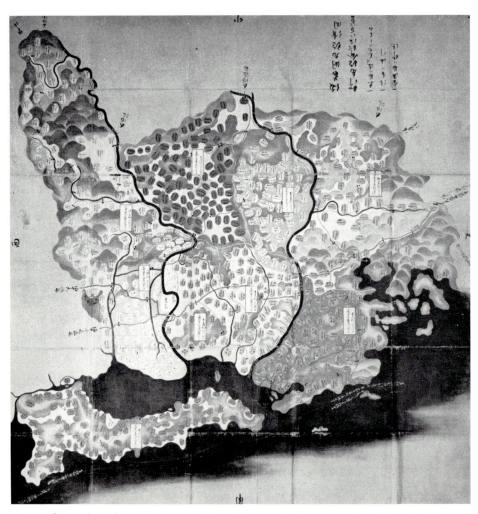

33. This early Tokugawa map (c. 7′ x 7′) records the name of each legal village and its tax assessment.

34. Yōtokuin, mother of Nobuteru (1536-1584), was wet nurse to Oda Nobunaga.

35. Terumasa (1564-1613) carried the fortunes of the Ikeda house to their height.

36. Nobuteru's grandson Mitsumasa (1609-1682) inherited and consolidated the Bizen domain.

37. The Raven castle (Ujō) of Okayama served as headquarters for the Ikeda hou

38. Not far from the castle was the Ikeda family temple Sōgenji.

39. Behind Sōgenji are the graves of the Ikeda daimyo and their wives.

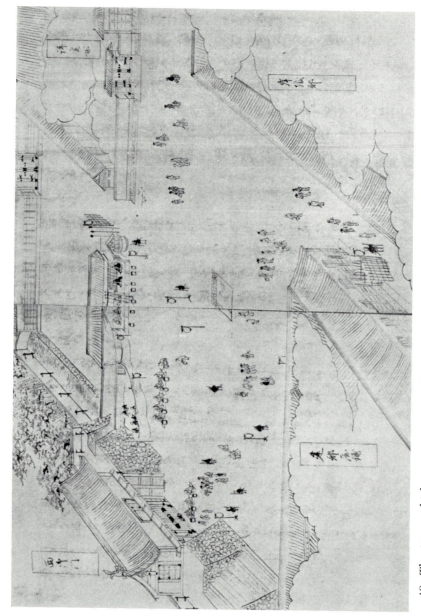

40. The town which grew up around the castle was divided between its military administration sector (above) and its commercial wards (below). This scene depicts the western castle gate, with its numerous guards and attendants.

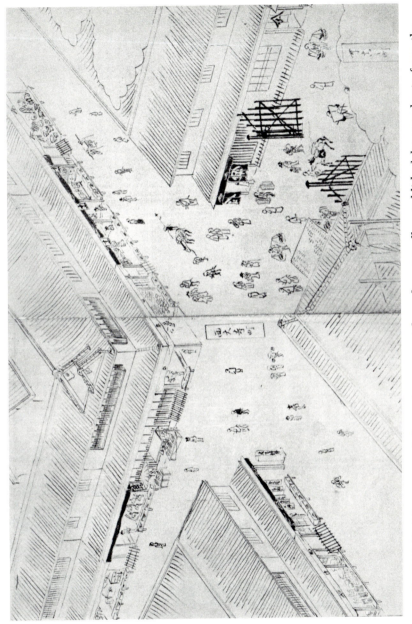

41. Saidaiji-chō was one of the main commercial wards, originally established by merchants from the town of Saidaiji.

42, 43. Shimotsui today (above) has been bypassed by the more rapid development of the modern ports of Uno and Mizushima. It retains features remarkably reminiscent of the Tokugawa period as seen in the illustration of another Bizen port, Ushimado (below).

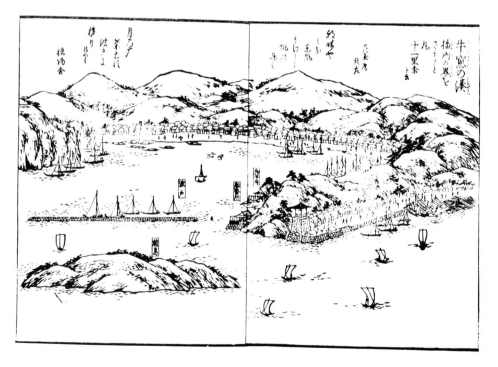

yoshi's leading generals at home and in Korea. Chief among these were Katō, Kuroda, Hosokawa, Fukushima, and Asano. Of the two groups, the first had been closest to Hideyoshi in his domestic policies; while he was alive they had depended greatly upon Hideyoshi's favor and backing; after his death they, above all others, had a stake in maintaining the Toyotomi regime in which they continued to play such a vital role. The daimyo of the second group were less dependent on the continuation of the organs of government left by Hideyoshi. They themselves had settled down as independently enfeoffed daimyo with sizable domains, so that their chief concern was to protect their own territories. This group, known as "the generals," was consequently more keenly aware of the precariousness of the Toyotomi legacy and rather quickly saw the inevitability of the Tokugawa succession to the national hegemony. While loyal to Hideyori they nonetheless favored compromise with Tokugawa Ieyasu. The other group, known as "the administrators," sought the perpetuation of Hideyoshi's cause at any cost.

Among the administrative group Ishida Mitsunari turned out to be the master of diplomacy and intrigue. Distrustful of Tokugawa Ieyasu, he worked ceaselessly to maintain a coalition against him. His first efforts were directed toward driving a wedge between Maeda Toshiie and Tokugawa Ieyasu. Opposed in this strategy by a league of seven "generals" who felt it wiser to stay on the side of the Tokugawa, Ishida was momentarily obliged to give up his office and take refuge in his home castle. When Maeda Toshiie died in 1599, the power balance upon which Hideyoshi had counted was destroyed of its own accord. Ieyasu was now the obvious great power in Japan. He had already begun to build up a faction around himself by making strategic marriage alliances; the "general" faction among the Toyotomi house daimyo had already shown where their sentiments lay, and now the Maeda faction hastily sent hostages and made overtures of support. In the fall of 1599 Ieyasu entered Osaka castle and became in the contemporary parlance "lord of the land." By the end of the year nearly half of the daimyo of the Toyotomi league had paid homage to Ieyasu and had submitted written pledges of allegiance; many, in fact, had sent hostages. Among these were Asano, Kuroda, and Hosokawa, key members of Hideyoshi's private vassal band.

During the early months of 1600 Tokugawa Ieyasu suddenly shifted the bulk of his forces along with contingents from his allies into the Kantō to meet a threatened attack from the Uesugi. To Ishida this was the supreme opportunity for a move against Ieyasu. Plunging again into the center of the Toyotomi affairs he gathered the forces of Mōri, Ukita, Shimazu, Nabeshima, Chōsokabe, Ikoma, and others of western Japan at Osaka and laid plans for an attack which would eliminate the Tokugawa threat. Potentially the alliance which Ishida led had the chance of success, but it is hard to believe it had the heart. Ishida's personal ambitions were too dominant. Mōri undoubtedly had in mind his own eventual succession to national power, but he was playing safe. Ukita followed out of loyalty. The known defections of the "band of generals" and the still secret defection of Mōri's two kinsmen Kikkawa and Kobayakawa had already weakened the cause. In the summer of 1600 when Togawa Higo-no-kami, the expelled Ukita vassal, wrote to Ukita Hideie's chief retainer Akashi, his words were prophetic. Storm clouds are gathering, he said, and both he and Ukita Sakyō had been incorporated into the advance troops of the Tokugawa. The final outcome could be foreseen, and he begged Akashi to bring his master over to the eastern side while there was yet time.[1] But this was wishful thinking. Ukita Hideie had already taken the lead in exhorting the Toyotomi alliance against Ieyasu and Akashi could not even discuss Togawa's plan with him.

On the fifteenth day of the ninth month (October 21, 1600) the final meeting between the opposing forces took place at the now historic battlefield of Sekigahara. It is estimated that the eastern league brought 70,000 men into action; the western group comprised 80,000 men, of whom only 40,000 entered the final engagement. The outcome was at first in doubt, but large segments of the western forces never committed themselves, and at the critical moment Kobayakawa made good his defection. The western cause collapsed with great slaughter. Ukita Hideie barely escaped with his life, fleeing the battle and eventually taking refuge in the distant domain of Satsuma. His men were left upon the field. Sekigahara proved the decisive turning point. Ten days later Tokugawa Ieyasu was in Osaka, the military master of the country.

[1] Quoted in *Okayama-shi shi*, 2.1610-1612.

The aftermath of Sekigahara was not completely told until 1602 when Shimazu made his peace with Ieyasu, thereby obliging Ukita Hideie to give himself up. Hideie was sent into exile to the island of Hachijōjima far to the south, where he lived out another fifty-two years, dying at the age of 92. Of the others in the western faction, Konishi, Ishida, and Ankokuji were executed in public after being paraded through the streets of Osaka and Sakai. Mashida was put in house imprisonment. Mōri was cut in his holdings from nine provinces to two. Uesugi was reduced from 1,200,000 *koku* to 300,000. Only the Shimazu, because of their isolation, were left untouched. But the Toyotomi house was not extinguished. Hideyoshi's memory was still fresh and the young Hideyori had many supporters in the imperial court and among the daimyo. Ieyasu found it inappropriate to go to the extreme of destroying Hideyoshi's legacy. Thus Hideyori was permitted to retain Osaka castle and a 650,000 *koku* domain in the surrounding provinces of Settsu, Kawachi, and Izumi. There were still several years before he would come of age, and in the meanwhile Ieyasu would have to devise a way to erase the Toyotomi memory.

Around Ieyasu a new *de facto* hegemony was quickly created. In all, eighty-seven daimyo houses had been extinguished and three drastically reduced in their holdings. A total of over 7,572,-000 *koku* had been confiscated, and this was added to Ieyasu's private lands or redistributed to his loyal followers.[2] The result was a far-reaching reorganization of the political map of Japan which gave the Tokugawa an overwhelming preponderance in the balance of military power. In the first place, since Ieyasu reallotted some 6,700,000 *koku* as rewards for fighting on his side, nearly every daimyo in the land was freshly indebted to him. Furthermore, in absolute terms the territories controlled by Ieyasu, either as his private domain or through daimyo who were his kinsmen or housemen, had been enormously expanded. Together they totaled over 6,000,000 *koku* as against the 13,000,000 *koku* held by the remaining daimyo. Moreover, among the remaining daimyo the number and size of those with large holdings which could compete with those of Ieyasu had been significantly reduced. Maeda, now the largest of the daimyo, commanded territory assessed at only 1,195,000 *koku*. The next largest domains such as

[2] Kodama Kōta, ed., *Zusetsu Nihon bunkashi taikei*, 9.54; Fujino, *Bakuhan taisei*, 150.

those of the Shimazu, Mogami, Gamō, and Date, though measured in the 600,000's, were all on the extreme fringes of the realm.[3] The Tokugawa, on the other hand, controlled the strategically important territories of central and eastern Japan including some of the largest cities.

Nonetheless, the hegemony was not completely secure; nor was it legitimized. West of Osaka, Ieyasu's influence fell off sharply. The Tokugawa had not been able to place their house daimyo into the lands of western Japan where the fabric of oaths to the Toyotomi house was still strong. Ieyasu was obliged publicly to act out his continued submission to the pledge he had sworn to Hideyoshi, and hence he continued to acknowledge a vague subordination to Hideyori. Indeed, the Tokugawa hegemony was not to be consummated until another prolonged and bloody war had been fought to eliminate the Toyotomi house finally and completely.

While outwardly honoring Hideyori, Tokugawa Ieyasu step by step acquired the power and legitimacy from which he could replace Hideyoshi as the rightful hegemon of Japan. In 1603, on the basis of his victory at Sekigahara, he assumed the position of shogun and the high court title of minister of the right (*udaijin*). As shogun he accepted the submission of all daimyo and began to gather at Edo, his home castle, an imposing collection of hostages. By now, both in terms of court and feudal rank, he stood above Hideyori. When he garrisoned Fushimi castle and placed his deputy (*shoshidai*) in Kyoto in the newly built Nijō castle, his military domination of the capital area was also secure.

In 1605 Ieyasu passed the post of shogun to his son Hidetada and established himself as the Ōgosho (retired shogun) at his family castle of Sumpu. The unsolved Toyotomi problem was pointed up when, in the same year, Hideyori gained the rank of minister of the right. Six years later, in 1611, Ieyasu's fears were roused by his interview with Hideyori. The young boy, now able to know his mind and giving obvious indications of potential ability, could no longer be trifled with. Ieyasu was now in a considerably more advantageous position than in 1600. The interview with Hideyori had been conducted in Ieyasu's Nijō castle, a public

[3] Kurita Motoji, *Edojidai shi, jō,* 1 (*Sōgō Nihonshi taikei* edn.) (Tokyo, 1926), 65-73. Hereafter cited as Kurita, *Edo.* Kurita's long-accepted figures are carefully revised by Fujino, *Bakuhan taisei,* 148-152.

admission that the Osaka party recognized the superior position of the shogun.[4] Between 1611 and 1612 the most prominent old daimyo who had fought with Hideyoshi—men like Asano, Horio, Katō, and Ikeda—died, leaving Ieyasu with few allies who would openly criticize him for a breach of his vow to Hideyoshi. From here to open war against Hideyori was but a brief step. On the pretext that the inscription on a new bell cast by Hideyori contained in the phrase "in the east the moon, in the west the sun" an implied comparison between Ieyasu and Hideyori, Osaka castle was attacked.

On the Toyotomi side there were the retainers of Hideyori and their forces drawn from the 650,000 *koku* Toyotomi territory. No other daimyo joined the cause. But Osaka became a rallying point for great numbers of ex-daimyo and samurai who had fallen and been dispossessed at Sekigahara. Out of hiding came such men as Chōsokabe, Sanada, Gotō, and, from Bizen, Akashi, the Christian general, who was to distinguish himself as one of the heroes of the coming siege. Altogether some 90,000 fighters flocked into Osaka. Ieyasu brought together the combined divisions of his house daimyo and those of his allies, 180,000 men in all. The issue seemed foredoomed, yet the first assault on the castle, the so-called winter campaign of 1614, failed—at the cost of 35,000 lives. Further defeat could have turned the entire balance of voluntary support which the daimyo tendered Ieyasu against him. Ieyasu himself realized his most critical moment had come and resorted to trickery. Calling a truce during which he filled in the outer moat of Osaka castle he prepared the way to the summer campaign of 1615 and the final destruction of the castle, its defenders, and the Toyotomi line. From Osaka there was no possible rally. The Toyotomi memory had been wiped away and the Tokugawa house stood master of Japan.

To UNDERSTAND the nature of the new Tokugawa hegemony requires that we retrace our steps briefly for a more careful study of the Tokugawa house and its history. The Tokugawa family, though of uncertain origin, claimed descent from the Minamoto line through Nitta Yoshisada, one of the foremost housemen of the Kamakura shogun.[5] The name Tokugawa came from a village

[4] Kurita, *Edo*, 24.
[5] Nakamura Kōya, *Tokugawa-ke—Ieyasu o chūshin ni* (Tokyo, 1961), 5ff. (here-

in Kōzuke where the family was first enfeoffed. At a later date, when the family moved to the province of Mikawa, it took the name of Matsudaira from the village in which its new lands were located. From this meager start the Matsudaira family became a *sengoku-daimyō* of some size and by the time of Ieyasu's father, Matsudaira Hirotada, the family controlled about half of Mikawa from the castle of Okazaki. At that time the family acknowledged the nominal suzerainty of Imagawa Yoshimoto, *shugo* of Suruga, Tōtōmi, and Mikawa. Matsudaira Hirotada found as his neighbor and rival in Owari the house of Oda, with which he carried on a continuous feud. When in 1547, at the age of six, Ieyasu was being sent to the Imagawa as a hostage, he was captured by the Oda forces and held for two years. Later in an exchange of captives he was handed over to the Imagawa, who kept him at Suruga as a hostage to guarantee the loyalty of the Matsudaira house.

In 1559 Ieyasu was returned to Okazaki castle to fight for Imagawa Yoshimoto. But when in 1560 Nobunaga defeated the Imagawa, Ieyasu threw in with his former enemy. In 1561 he cemented an alliance with Nobunaga and shortly thereafter changed his given name to Ieyasu. It was this alliance which permitted Nobunaga to move westward and Ieyasu to expand eastward. By 1565 Ieyasu held all of Mikawa. In 1566 he changed his surname back to the original Tokugawa. By 1570 he had taken Tōtōmi from the Imagawa and had moved his headquarters to Hamamatsu. From this point he was in the thick of the unification struggle. During the next ten years, Ieyasu in league with Nobunaga fought out a protracted rivalry with the Takeda. Not until 1582 did Ieyasu beat back the Takeda and take control of Suruga province, moving his headquarters to Sumpu.

Upon Nobunaga's death Ieyasu rushed to the attack against Akechi Mitsuhide, but lost the initiative to Hideyoshi. Ieyasu therefore turned his forces and invaded the provinces of Kai and Shinano, successfully wresting a portion of each from the Hōjō. In 1583 Ieyasu took up the cause of Nobunaga's second son, Nobuo, against Hideyoshi. But after an inconclusive war he pledged himself to Hideyoshi, sending his mother as hostage and accepting Hideyoshi's daughter as wife. In the next years Ieyasu played a

---

after cited as Nakamura, *Tokugawa-ke*); Itō Tasaburō, "Edo bakufu no seiritsu to buke seiji-kan," *Rekishigaku kenkyū*, 131 and 132 (1948), 132.32. Hereafter cited as Itō, "Buke seiji-kan."

comparatively passive role in Hideyoshi's battle for national consolidation, choosing to put his energy into organizing the internal administration of the domain which now embraced Mikawa, Tōtōmi, Suruga, Kai, and Shinano. In the campaign against the Hōjō in 1590, however, the men of Mikawa played a foremost role. Thus after the fall of Odawara castle, Hideyoshi, both as a token of commendation and as a means of putting the Tokugawa out of dangerous proximity to central Japan, enfeoffed Ieyasu in the "eight Kantō provinces" vacated by the Hōjō. His lands were now assessed at 2,557,000 *koku*, a domain larger than that of Hideyoshi himself.[6]

Ieyasu's rise to become the foremost daimyo in the Toyotomi league had been accomplished in several phases and had resulted in the stage-by-stage growth of his own band of followers. As with the other expanding daimyo of the time, such as the Oda or Ukita, we can identify a regular pattern of development in the internal house organs of his domain. Many of the policies and institutions of governmental organization which characterized the Tokugawa after their rise to national hegemony are directly related to practices developed by Ieyasu during the years when he was still an aspiring daimyo.[7]

As master of Okazaki castle and half of Mikawa, the Matsudaira were daimyo of medium rank to be compared perhaps with the Urakami of Bizen. At this time in the affairs of the Matsudaira domain we learn that the foremost housemen were Abe Sadayoshi and Ishikawa Yasumasa, keepers of Okazaki castle, and Torii Iga and Matsudaira Jirouemon, who were given administrative responsibility as *bugyō*. By 1560 the list of *karō* and divisional commanders engaged at Okazaki included the following: Sakai, Ishikawa, Honda, Uemura, Naruse, Yonezu, Sakakibara, Matsui, Hiraiwa, Aoyama, Doi, and Amano. These were all men whose ties as housemen to the Matsudaira had been most strong and so were by now in possession of lands of probably 5000 *koku* or more.[8]

By 1567 the beginnings of a formal military and civil organization of the Tokugawa domain had begun to take shape. Sakai and

---

[6] Matsudaira Tarō, *Edo jidai seido no kenkyū* (Tokyo, 1919), 506. Hereafter cited as Matsudaira, *Seido*.

[7] Nakamura, *Tokugawa-ke*, 1-43.

[8] *Ibid.*, 44-57; Fujino, *Bakuhan-taisei*, 21-31; Shibata Genshō, *Tokugawa Ieyasu to sono shūi* (3 vols., Hamamatsu, 1934), 1.390-391. Hereafter cited as Shibata, *Ieyasu*.

Ishikawa were set up as field generals in command of two major divisions of the Tokugawa house band. There were two advance and rearguard divisions under the daimyo's direct command, and a permanent castle guard. Individual vassals were placed over groups in charge of military communications, ships, transportation, and foot soldier recruits. Civil administration was in the hands of three chief administrators (*san-bugyō*): Ōsuka, Uemura, and Kōriki. Under them officials were placed in charge of the daimyo's finances, his land stewards, the secretariat, the corps of physicians, the kitchen, and inspectors of weights and measures.[9]

As the Tokugawa domains increased, Ieyasu's foremost housemen and generals grew in numbers and size in commensurate fashion. At the time of the Odawara campaign, for instance, Tokugawa troops were organized under the following divisional commanders, each of whom was set over a band of subordinates roughly the equivalent of one of Ukita's six divisional commands.[10]

First army: Sakurai, Honda, Sakakibara, Torii, Ōkubo, Ii
Second army: Matsudaira, Sakai, Honda, Naitō, Shibata, Ōgyū, Ishikawa

Some of these men had already attained the castellan status and all held lands over 10,000 *koku*. After Odawara, with the increase in Tokugawa domain, the number of castellans also greatly multiplied. The move to Kantō served to push the Tokugawa out of the center of political affairs, and this was in some measure hard on Ieyasu's aspirations. But the move into new territory was also a blessing, for it gave him the opportunity to rationalize the organization of his domain and to centralize authority over the vassal band which was growing so rapidly.[11]

When Ieyasu was moved to the former Hōjō domains in 1590 he received a territory larger than his previous holdings and calculated at 2,557,000 *koku*. Establishing Edo as the site of his new castle, he set to work to apportion fiefs among his vassals within the new territory. Appointing Sakakibara Yasumasa in charge of the distribution of fiefs, Ina Tadatsugu and Aoyama Tadanari as commissioners, and the dependable stewards (*daikan*) and financial officers (*kanjōkata*) of his previous lands as agents, he set down the following policy:

[9] Fujino, *Bakuhan-taisei*, 29.   [10] Shibata, *Ieyasu*, 3.354.
[11] Kitajima Masamoto, "Tokugawa-shi no shoki kenryoku kōzō," *Shigaku zasshi*, 64.9 (September 1955), 800-837. Hereafter cited as Kitajima, "Kenryoku kōzō."

1. That the daimyo's private lands (*chokkatsu*) be located close to Edo.
2. That the small fief holders be located close enough to reach Edo with only one night's stopover en route.
3. That large castellans be placed at a greater distance.

The result was a pattern of distribution which placed the daimyo's holdings primarily in Musashi, Izu, and Sagami. In Musashi, for instance, out of 660,000 *koku*, all but 120,000 was given over to small fief holders and the daimyo. In Izu and Sagami one-half to one-third of the land was retained as *chokkatsu*. Within the entire domain some 1,000,000 *koku*, or 39 percent, was *chokkatsu* and administered by Ina as the daimyo's deputy (*gundai*) and by stewards under him.[12] The remaining 61 percent of the domain was distributed as follows:[13]

> Ii Naomasa at Takasaki: 120,000 *koku*
> Sakakibara Yasumasa at Tatebayashi: 100,000 *koku*
> Honda Tadakatsu at Ōtaki: 100,000 *koku*
> Ōkubo Tadayo at Odawara: 45,000 *koku*
> Torii Mototada at Yatsukuri: 40,000 *koku*
> Hiraiwa, Okudaira, Ogasawara,
>   Matsudaira (Yoda), Sakai, and
>   Matsudaira (Ōsuka): 30,000 *koku*
> Ishikawa, Honda, Makino, Suganuma,
>   Matsudaira (Matsui) (Hisamatsu),
>   Naitō, and Kōriki: 20,000 *koku*
> Okabe Suō: 12,000 *koku*
> Seventeen families: 10,000 *koku*
> Twenty-four families: 5,000 *koku*
> Six families: 3,000 *koku*
> Two families: 2,000 *koku*

Tokugawa Ieyasu thus numbered some thirty-eight housemen with holdings of 10,000 *koku* or over. Their total lands accounted for 984,500 *koku*, or 38 percent, of the Tokugawa domain. Another 142,000 *koku* was distributed between thirty-two vassals whose holdings ranged from 2000 to 5000 *koku* each, and the remaining 426,000 *koku* was divided among the many hundred of lesser en-

---

[12] *Ibid.*, 802.
[13] Matsudaira, *Seido*, 506; Shibata, *Ieyasu*, 3.644ff.; Fujino, *Bakuhan-taisei*, 124-125; Nakamura, *Tokugawa-ke*, 107-134.

feoffed vassals. In enfeoffing the daimyo-sized vassals, most were placed in castles vacated by the Hōjō and hence were established as castellans. Yet as of 1598 these men were housemen of the Tokugawa and were not listed as daimyo within the Toyotomi league. Just as with the elders of the Ukita, these great vassals of the Tokugawa were rear-vassals to Hideyoshi and so were not tied by oath to him. Only after 1600, when the Tokugawa house acquired the capacity of supreme feudal hegemon did these retainers appear on the rolls as full-fledged daimyo. This was the origin of the category of *fudai* daimyo.

Ieyasu's transfer into the Kantō provided a further essential opportunity to carry out basic territorial reforms that were part of the procedures by which the great daimyo under Hideyoshi were reorganizing their domains under more centralized control. By being forced to pull up his retinue from their hereditary lands in Mikawa, Ieyasu found it possible to refashion the relationship between himself and his men on a more dependent basis. In the Kantō, the attachment of Ieyasu's housemen to specific localities or hereditary family holdings was broken. His men were assigned to entirely new fiefs in which they had no hereditary connections with the indigenous cultivators. They came in primarily as an "administrative" superstructure to rural government. Entering the Kantō with a clean slate, Ieyasu was able to standardize rural administration, putting it where possible under his own intendants. The concentration of power at the castle headquarters at Edo was unquestioned. And before long Ieyasu was able to push through a new land survey and to impose a uniform system of village organization. In essence the Kantō provided Ieyasu with a much more effective territorial base from which to grasp control of the country than if he had remained in Mikawa.[14]

The feudal map of Japan in 1598 reveals the Tokugawa and their housemen holding seven provinces of the Kantō interspersed by a few holdovers from the Hōjō era. Daimyo created by Nobunaga were concentrated in Kaga, Echizen, Mikawa, Tōtōmi, and Bizen. The daimyo created by Hideyoshi held Kai, Suruga, all of central Japan, northern Shikoku, and Higo in Kyushu. On the fringes of Japan there remained a few "original" daimyo, those whose lines had originated before the rise of Nobunaga and who had managed to hold on to their territories since the beginning of

14 Kitajima, "Kenryoku kōzō," 802-806.

the Sengoku period. This was the rough distribution of daimyo at the time of Hideyoshi's death.[15]

Soon after Hideyoshi's death, and notably with the mobilization against Uesugi, Tokugawa Ieyasu began to receive pledges of allegiance and sworn oaths from daimyo of the Toyotomi league, who recognized the Tokugawa as the coming power. Such daimyo, being outside the Tokugawa inner circle of housemen, were treated by Ieyasu as allies (*tozama*), while the original housemen were considered *fudai*. At the same time samurai of lesser capacity were constantly being recruited as enfeoffed (*hatamoto*) and stipended retainers (*gokenin*).[16] By 1600 the Tokugawa alliance had swelled to include nearly half of the weakening Toyotomi league, and large numbers of daimyo were waiting to see which way to move. Sekigahara proved the turning point in this whole system of alliances, for he was now able to eliminate all but the daimyo who accepted his overlordship. Moreover, he now had nearly half of the territory of all Japan to dispose of as part of the spoils of war.

At Sekigahara 6,222,000 *koku* were confiscated from the daimyo who had opposed Ieyasu and another 1,350,000 *koku* from the Toyotomi house. The lands vacated in this way permitted the Tokugawa to take back much of their old territories in central Japan and to acquire sizable pieces to the west beyond their old domains. In the reassignment of lands which followed, Ieyasu approximately doubled to 2,000,000 *koku* his *chokkatsu* lands. This still permitted him to divide among his housemen and allied daimyo the huge sum of 6,710,000 *koku*. The first major innovation after Sekigahara was the setting out of Ieyasu's former senior housemen as independent daimyo (*fudai*). This brought into being 68 new daimyo. Ieyasu's policy was to move his *fudai* out of the Kantō back into his former territory of Mikawa, Tōtōmi, Suruga, and Kai and into the heart of Hideyoshi's old area of control, Mino, Ōmi, and Owari. As he did so he rewarded his *fudai* by modest increases in territory: roughly one-half or one-third of their former holdings. Thus the largest of his *fudai*, the Ii of Hakone, was raised to 180,000 *koku* from 120,000 *koku*. Also after Sekigahara Ieyasu established two cadet houses (*shimpan*) placing them over important domains in Echizen and Owari.[17]

[15] Kodama Kōta, ed., *Zusetsu Nihon bunkashi taikei*, 8.372-373.
[16] Examples are cited in *Tsūshi*, 2.374. [17] Fujino, *Bakuhan-taisei*, 152-156.

Toward his new allies Ieyasu was especially generous. The *tozama* were mostly moved into the confiscated territories of western Japan. Despite what Ieyasu may have wished, the need to pay off his allies and the limited supply of *fudai* available to him precluded putting more than one *fudai* of importance into territories west of Osaka. This was Matsudaira Yasushige in Harima. Thus between 1600 and 1615 the strategic balance of daimyo loyalties in Japan was still precarious in the eyes of the Tokugawa. Since the *tozama* nearly all had made previous oaths of allegiance to Hideyoshi, and since the Toyotomi house was still in existence, it was conceivable that they could turn against the Tokugawa at a critical time. Acquisition of the title of shogun was helpful in providing Ieyasu with a case for his legitimacy, but it was not unchallengeable.

The elimination of the Toyotomi house at Osaka relieved Ieyasu from fear of competing loyalty and provided the occasion for further confiscation and redistribution of territory: after 1615 he was able to push his *fudai* and *chokkatsu* holdings into areas west of Harima as far as Kyushu. The *shimpan* were increased in numbers and the three branch houses of Kii, Owari, and Mito were established to protect the Tokugawa line.[18] The shift of the feudal map in favor of the Tokugawa did not end here, however. During the times of the second and third shogun, on various pretexts, the Tokugawa managed to confiscate and redistribute territory or move about daimyo so as to rearrange the distribution of the daimyo and further shift the balance of power toward them. From 1600 to 1651, besides the confiscations which came as a result of military action, the following changes were made:[19]

For lack of succession:

Confiscated and redistributed, 46 houses

involving 4,570,000 *koku*

Reduced, 12 houses

involving 160,000 *koku*

For disciplinary purposes:

Confiscated and redistributed, 59 houses

involving 6,480,000 *koku*

Reduced, 14 houses

involving 140,000 *koku*

[18] *Ibid.*, 171-218.   [19] Kurita, *Edo*, 64-65.

In the redistribution of these confiscated lands the Tokugawa made every effort to push the balance toward the *fudai,* so that between 1616 to 1651 some 3,000,000 *koku* was lost to the *tozama.* Between these dates, of the twenty-four great outside daimyo, nine had been dispossessed, one reduced, and four transferred. Furthermore, during the next century when the total area of Japan's cultivated land was undergoing tremendous expansion, while the *chokkatsu* lands of the shogun were growing from two to seven million *koku,* the lands of the daimyo remained nearly static at just over 19,000,000 *koku.*[20] By the beginning of the eighteenth century the Tokugawa land distribution had become stabilized as follows:[21]

	(*koku*)	(percent)
Imperial family lands	141,151	.5
The shogun's granary lands	4,213,171	
Lands of vassals enfeoffed at		25.8
less than 10,000 *koku*	2,606,545	
Domains of cadet and *fudai* daimyo	9,325,300	72.5
Domains of *tozama* daimyo	9,834,700	
Temple and shrine land	316,230	1.2
Total	26,437,097	

Of the above divisions, the greater part of the granary lands were administered directly by the shogun's intendants. Somewhat over 930,000 *koku* was administered by *fudai* daimyo on behalf of the shogun, and by the keepers of Osaka, Nijō, and Sumpu castles. From the granary lands the shogun financed his administration and provided salaries for his stipended housemen (*gokenin*). These numbered an estimated 17,399.[22] But when mustered together with their private retainers, they were expected to come up to a body of some 60,000 men.[23] The enfeoffed vassals or bannermen (*hatamoto*) generally numbered just over 5000 men.[24] These were enfeoffed in the following grades:[25]

[20] Kodama Kōta, ed., *Zusitsu Nihon bunkashi taikei,* 9.54.
[21] Calculated by Kanai Madoka, "Kyōtsū rondai 'hansei kakuritsu-ki no shomondai' o toriageru ni atte," *Shakai keizai shigaku,* 24.2 (1958), 134.
[22] Suzuki Hisashi, "Hatamoto-ryō no kōzō," *Rekishigaku kenkyū* 208 (June 1957) 14. Henceforth cited as Suzuki, "Hatamoto."
[23] Matsudaira, *Seido,* 382.
[24] Suzuki, "Hatamoto," 14.
[25] Itō Tasaburo in *Sekai rekishi jiten,* 15.190-191.

Above 1000 *koku*	676
from 500 to 1000 *koku*	626
from 100 to 500 *koku*	3,097
below 100 *koku*	766
unknown	4
Total	5,169

Under muster the *hatamoto* accounted for approximately 20,000 men. Together the *gokenin* and *hatamoto* provided the basis of the shogun's house troops, a body traditionally called the "eighty thousand" but which may have consisted of considerably less than half that number. In peacetime these housemen were congregated at the headquarters castle of Edo or the other shogunal castles at Sumpu, Osaka, and Nijō. There they were supported by salary (*hōroku*) payments from the shogun's granary. Enfeoffed bannermen were expected to maintain direct supervision over these fiefs, establishing administrative and tax collecting offices at the center of their lands. This relationship became less direct as time went on, however, as contract merchants took over tax collection, and as the shogun's intendants in adjoining territory set administration policy over the lands.

The extension of the Tokugawa *fudai* holdings and granary lands over all Japan meant that the shogun obtained bases of direct rule in every corner of the country. As in the case of the other shogunal regimes, the rise of the Tokugawa brought about the spread of men of the Mikawa area over the entire country. Except for those few *sengoku-daimyō* on the fringes of the islands who managed to keep their territories under the Tokugawa, the rest of the entire top bracket of the military aristocracy in Japan now traced its origins to that narrow sector of central Japan which had been the home of the Oda and Tokugawa houses. This undoubtedly had much to do with the homogeneity of institutions which characterized the rule of the daimyo under Tokugawa Ieyasu. It also helps to account for the problem of manpower scarcity which constantly plagued the Tokugawa administration.

During their rise from the status of daimyo of Mikawa, the Tokugawa constantly absorbed manpower from their conquered rivals or from the bands of unattached samurai set adrift by the wars and conflicts in other parts of the land. The example of the absorption of Togawa and Hanabusa, the former Ukita housemen, has been referred to already. After Sekigahara, Ieyasu adopted as his housemen or bannermen many of the able vassals of his rival daimyo. Nonetheless, the Tokugawa lands appeared to increase at a rate greater than the manpower resources at his command. Lack of experienced *fudai* seems to have been a constant problem, and certainly by contrast with the lands of the daimyo, the Tokugawa granary lands were thinly manned. Fortunately during the next two hundred years this was not a handicap. So long as an active balance between *fudai* and *tozama* daimyo immobilized opposition to the shogun, the Tokugawa ready forces of *gokenin* and *hatamoto* was in fact the dominant power in all Japan. The Tokugawa power structure showed no signs of cracking until the middle of the nineteenth century and then only as the coalition broke up under unexpected foreign pressure and the balance of military power was negated by the impact of a new technology of warfare.[26]

THE regime established by Tokugawa Ieyasu and carried on by his successors brought to completion a new political organization based on the mastery of one daimyo coalition over the lands and the fighting forces of the entire country. The Tokugawa house carried the process of national unification much further than either the Oda and Toyotomi houses had done. Its achievements were particularly noteworthy in the acquisition of legitimacy, in the manner of control exerted over the daimyo, and in the legal institutions of social control which it gave to the country as a whole. Since the Tokugawa house assumed the title of shogun, it adopted the manner of legitimacy and the style of government begun by the previous *bakufu* of Kamakura and Ashikaga times. During the period of Tokugawa hegemony Japan was governed under the broad unifying capacity of the shogun, but actual administration was partially decentralized under the regional authorities of the various daimyo. This was a system which had no ready counterpart to the national structures of other societies, and hence any attempt to characterize it by such terms as late feudalism, centralized feudalism, or military absolutism is apt to be misleading. The Tokugawa regime must be understood in its own terms as a political organism in which the daimyo set the basic pattern of local

[26] See the excellent analysis by Albert Craig, *Chōshū in the Meiji Restoration* (Cambridge, Mass., 1961), 13-17.

government, accepting a unity under the shogun which precluded further warfare but which left them a considerable degree of autonomy. Japan during the Tokugawa period had both its centralized and decentralized aspects, although the forces of centralization constantly expanded.

The Tokugawa system was put together slowly as the Tokugawa house rose to its position of national hegemony and as it inherited from the regimes of Nobunaga and Hideyoshi. By the time of Ieyasu's death the basic power arrangement had been set, though changes in its balance were still found necessary until the turn of the mid-seventeenth century. Likewise the legal and political institutions of the regime were not perfected until the time of Iemitsu, the third shogun. By Iemitsu's death in 1651, however, a sufficient stabilization had been achieved, so that a description of the enduring features of the Tokugawa system may be made.

The capstone of the Tokugawa hegemony was, of course, the shogun. The head of the Tokugawa house was supported in his position as hegemon by certain legal and customary prerogatives, based both on the imperial system and on the practices of vassalage which had grown up among the military houses. As shogun, the Tokugawa head was technically an appointive official of the emperor, holding delegated powers which had grown in number since the Kamakura period. By Tokugawa times these powers, in fact, covered the bulk of civil and military functions of government. But the exact legal definition of the shogun's powers had by no means been specified even at this time. It was sufficient that the Tokugawa house had the power, the title, and the Kamakura and Ashikaga precedents. The importance of the post of shogun as a custom-backed justification of national hegemony is evident in the length to which Ieyasu went to acquire the title and to conform to the tradition of its tenure. Ieyasu seriously considered seeking the title only after Hideyoshi's death when the possibility of gaining national supremacy was within his grasp. Up to this time he had claimed descent from the Fujiwara house. But after Sekigahara, his genealogists "discovered" his descent from the Seiwa Genji through the line of Nitta Yoshisada, and Ieyasu laid claim to the headship of the Minamoto house.[27] From this point Ieyasu carefully fitted into all customary requirements surrounding the office, and on receipt of the title followed the

[27] Itō, "Buke seiji-kan," 132.32-33.

precedents established by Yoritomo in his relationships with the imperial court. The three-clause oath extracted by him from the daimyo in 1611 began with the statement, "We will obey with respect the laws and practices of the shogun (*kubō*) as has been done generation after generation since the time of Yoritomo."[28]

What then was the authority to which Ieyasu was laying claim? The title of shogun from its original use by Yoritomo was a grant from the emperor, and remained so in the Tokugawa period, being renewed ceremonially for each successive generation. In its original usage the title was not particularly high on the scale of court posts, being used by the early emperors to designate supreme commanders in the campaigns against the Ainu of northern Japan. But as employed by Yoritomo it came to acquire a number of customary prerogatives as well as correlative titles and ranks which gave it outstanding political significance. By Tokugawa times the post of shogun carried with it concurrent appointment to a set of ranks and titles which put the head of the Tokugawa house high in the prestige hierarchy which centered on the court. Officially Ieyasu was named by the emperor in 1603: minister of the right (*udaijin*), barbarian-quelling generalissimo (*sei-i-tai-shōgun*), chief of the Minamoto house (*Genji-no-chōja*), rector of the Junna and Shōgaku colleges (Junna, Shōgaku ryōin bettō), and given the second court rank, the genealogical status of *ason*, and the privilege of riding in an ox-drawn carriage. He had previously received such titles as acting great counsellor, captain of the left imperial guards (*sa-konoe-taishō*), and inspector of the left imperial stables (*sa-meryō-nō-gogen*), which were also traditionally linked to the office of shogun.[29]

These imposing titles gave to the shogun a commanding position within three prestige systems of long duration. First, as acknowledged head of the Minamoto lineage, Ieyasu and his successors could claim genealogical identity with the aristocracy and ultimate connection with the imperial family. Both the civil and military aristocracy in Japan continued its deep respect for genealogical tradition, keeping intact the prestige hierarchy of lineages which had become set during the early Heian period. By the time of the Ashikaga shogunate, it had become a matter of acceptance

[28] Naitō Chisō, *Tokugawa jūgodai-shi* (12 vols., Tokyo, 1892) 1.133. Hereafter cited as Naitō, *Jūgodai-shi*.

[29] Itō, "Buke seiji-kan," 132.31.

that the shogun must be of Minamoto stock. Furthermore, a certain aura of expectancy surrounded the head of the Minamoto lineage; he was by tradition the legitimate successor to leadership among the military houses. The ability of Tokugawa Ieyasu to claim, however deviously, the position of head of the Minamoto house was immensely valuable to him and differentiated him from Hideyoshi, who failed to secure appointment as shogun. Finally, the status of *ason* reached back into the deepest sentiments of aristocratic tradition, placing the Tokugawa among the few families closest to the imperial line. These many aspects of the aristocratic social tradition were kept alive by the Tokugawa, reinforced and formalized after 1600 as new peerages were drawn up and the daimyo houses fitted into the hierarchy of lineages. Ieyasu from the first laid great stress on this aspect of his hegemony, and his successors, by requiring the submission of genealogies from the various houses (*Kan'ei shoka keizu den* and *Jōkyō shoka kakiage*), endeavored to establish for their age the official ordering of military peerages.[30]

The title of shogun and its attendant ranks and honors, though not the highest in the land, was sufficient to give the shogun respectable standing at court and a status far above that of the other military houses. At court the shogun held first or second rank and ministerial status, meaning that only a select few courtiers of imperial or Fujiwara blood could equal or supersede him. Although during his life Hideyori rivaled Ieyasu in court rank, after 1616 the shogun stood safely above his nearest competitor among the military houses, and stringent steps were taken to make sure that this difference would be a permanent thing. By maintaining the empty but still prestigious system of court ranks, the shogun was able to add still another dimension to his status. By paying honors to a small powerless court nobility, he kept alive a prestige system which provided additional sanction to the hierarchy of military houses as it became set under the Tokugawa house.

Of more direct political meaning was the fact that the title of shogun gave to its bearer acknowledged supremacy over the military forces of the country. As shogun Tokugawa Ieyasu was the recognized chief (*tōryō*) of the military houses and the foremost military official of the realm.[31] By the time of Yoritomo the post

---

[30] *Ibid.*, 132.34.

[31] For late Tokugawa clarifications of these points see, Osatake Takeshi, *Meiji*

of *sei-i-tai-shōgun* was admittedly the highest in the military hierarchy under the court. But since military service had become a matter of class distinction and hereditary privilege, the post of shogun acquired powers beyond those of supreme command of troops in the field. It gave to its bearer a commanding position within the land system as well and within the system of allegiances among the military houses. With respect to land rights, it was Yoritomo's concurrent possession of the powers of chief of the *shugo* and *jitō* which gave him the authority upon which the shogunate based its widespread fiscal and administrative rights. Then as all proprietorships passed into the hands of the military houses, as the various land tenures were consolidated into the single inclusive right of feudal proprietorship, there fell to the head of the military houses, as in the case of Hideyoshi, the authority to grant, confirm, or withdraw over his vermilion seal the exercise of proprietorship (*chigyō*) over all territory within the realm. Tokugawa Ieyasu, by conquest and as chief of the *buke*, succeeded to this privilege. Thus in an ultimate sense, the shogun's authority over the lands of the realm stemmed from *shōen* law; he was the supreme proprietor. On the other hand, it was backed by feudal practice, for the shogun, as head of the military houses, was also head of the pyramid of allegiances and fealties which linked all military personnel together under him. As head of the hierarchy of vassals and allies, the shogun held the oaths of fealty of the daimyo, his *hatamoto* and *gokenin*. Reciprocating these oaths, the shogun conferred investitures of land and rights of governance (*chigyō-ken*) to his vassals. So fully had the military houses acquired ascendancy over the land that even the estates of the emperor were assigned as largess from out of the shogunal holdings over the shogun's red seal. The lands of temples and shrines likewise were reassessed by the shogun or the daimyo and granted in new patents.

It was from these facts that the theories of shogunal prerogative in the area of political authority stemmed. From the time of Yoritomo various shogunal apologists or political essayists added to the body of theory concerning the rights of the military houses to govern the country. These concepts were most favorably set

---

Ishin (4 vols., Tokyo, 1942-1949), 1.27 (hereafter cited as Osatake, *Meiji*); Ishii Ryōsuke, *Meiji bunkashi, hōsei-hen* (Tokyo, 1954), 47 (hereafter cited as Ishii, *Meiji*).

forth during the Tokugawa period in the works of the Hayashi school of shogunal historians and Confucian scholars. The most important work which brought the lessons of the past to the support of the Tokugawa house was *Honchō tsugan* (Mirror of Japanese History) begun by Hayashi Razan and completed by his successors in 1650. The essential contribution of this work was the theory of delegation of powers by the emperor. Drawing on Chinese political theory, it explained the ritualistic position of the emperor and the practice of delegation. The *buke*, far from constituting a usurpation, were the saviors of the country and the emperor from the misgovernment of the Fujiwara. Yoritomo and his successors were protectors of the state, keepers of the peace, and loyal subjects of the emperor.[32]

During the Tokugawa period three lines of effort were made to elaborate or clarify the shogun's legitimacy. First a number of legal or epistemological sources were drawn on to strengthen the concept of delegation and to clarify the shogun's powers. From a negative point of view, the 1611 code of conduct for emperor and court, which defined the tasks of the emperor as primarily ritualistic and literary, by implication reserved the function of government to the shogun.[33] From the middle of the Tokugawa regime an effort was made to spell out more definitely the concept of delegation, perhaps as a result of the increasingly legal and bureaucratic nature of government. In 1788 a shogunal document claimed that "the sixty provinces are entrusted (*azukari*) to the shogun by the emperor. . . ."[34] In the controversy over foreign affairs in 1858 the emperor acknowledged in correspondence that "at present, government (*seimu*) is delegated (*inin*) to Kantō (the shogun). . . ."[35] The following quotation from a shogunal document expresses the official *bakufu* view of the shogun's position at the end of the regime:

> The emperors have not concerned themselves in government already for more than six hundred and eighty years. However, as they have been, since the foundation of the state, the supreme sovereigns following in a single line of divine succession and forever unalterable, and as they are revered by the nation like heavenly deities, likewise the successive *tai-kun*

[32] Itō, "Buke seiji-kan," 132.36-37.
[33] Matsudaira, *Seido*, 478.
[34] Ishii, *Meiji*, 45.
[35] Osatake, *Meiji*, 1.30.

on occasions lead *daimyo* and pay them court. The emperor entrusts to the *taikun* all political powers and awaits his decisions in silence; the *taikun*, holding all the political powers of the country, maintains the virtue of humility, and upholds the emperor with the utmost respect.[36]

Another line pursued by Tokugawa theorists concerned the terminology with which the shogun should be designated in official papers. In the diplomatic correspondence of the early Tokugawa period the shogunate under Hayashi Razan's direction seems to have used most frequently the designation of *koku-ō* (king) or *koku-shu* (sovereign) for shogun. In 1635, negotiation with Korea caused Hayashi Razan and other shogunal advisers to argue for abandonment of these phrases in favor of *taikun* (great ruler). It was their argument that this would carry more prestige than the former term which also had been adopted by the king of Korea.[37] Thereafter the Hayashi house in both external and internal documents switched to the use of *taikun*. Nearly a hundred years later this issue was heatedly debated by the Confucian-trained scholars of Edo and the scholarly advisers to the shogun. Arai Hakuseki, among others at the turn of the eighteenth century, recognizing the vagueness of the title *taikun*, argued for return to *koku-ō* in an effort to make the powers of the shogun more specific.[38] Ogyū Sorai observed in his *Seidan* that the "daimyo are the retainers (*kerai*) of the shogun but they receive their ranks and titles from the emperor. Thus in their hearts there are some who consider the emperor their lord (*kunshu*). They are submissive to the shogun for the time being merely because they fear his strength. If this attitude is not remedied it would be hard to suppose that disturbances might not result in later years."[39] So saying he argued for a frankly despotic political structure centered in the shogun. The sentiment in favor of a return of the phrase *koku-ō* and a greater assertion of the shogun's claim to sovereignty was widespread until the eighth shogun Yoshimune put the issue to rest for the remainder of the Tokugawa period by coming down in favor of the designation *taikun*.[40]

[36] Asakawa, *Iriki*, 374.

[37] Itō Tasaburō, "Shugō-mondai to shōgun no ken'i," *Nihon rekishi*, 67 (December 1953), 2-13.

[38] Matsudaira, *Seido*, 484.

[39] Itō, "Shugō-mondai," 12.   [40] *Ibid.*, 13.

The difficulties of the theorists in settling upon a suitable title for the shogun pointed up the general weakness inherent in the attempt to rationalize a political structure in which sovereignty resided in a figurehead and actual power in a military hegemon. The efforts of Tokugawa Ieyasu, through his patronage of Hayashi Razan, to achieve a rational and ethical basis for his rule clearly had this in mind. The Tokugawa were reasonably successful in eliciting from their Confucian advisers arguments on the virtue of the shogun's rule and the historical inevitability and desirability of the shogunate. The *Honchō tsugan*, and even *Dai Nihonshi* (History of Great Japan) laid the hands of Confucian sanction on military rule and on Tokugawa Ieyasu as a preserver of the state and the loyal minister of the emperor.[41] This fusion of Confucian thought and the political realities of Tokugawa hegemony became the most potent combination of ideological support for the shogun.

But there were other sources of ideological backing as well. The Tokugawa house did not neglect the wellsprings of religious tradition which had so long nourished the reverence by which the aristocracy was regarded in Japan. Tokugawa patronage of Buddhist and Shinto establishments put the house in the tradition of the aristocracy of the past. But more directly supportive of the Tokugawa house was the development of the cult of Ieyasu centered on the great shrine of Nikkō. Upon Ieyasu's death, the shogunate, "leading all the daimyo of the land, deified and established his spirit on Mt. Nikkō; the whole nation followed them and gave tributes; the emperor, also, praising his virtue, sent envoys bearing offerings, and conferred the religious title Tō-shō-gū."[42] This was the beginning of the establishment of shrines to Ieyasu throughout the country and the practice of conducting annual ceremonies of reverence to Ieyasu's memory.

Such were the many traditional sources of legitimacy plumbed by the Tokugawa shoguns. Yet despite all that has been said, the legal precariousness of the Tokugawa shogunate is obvious, and was obvious to the men of the Tokugawa period as well. Sovereignty continued to rest in the emperor, and the chief justification of the shogunate was that it was best qualified to rule in the name of the emperor. That this laid the shogunate open to attacks of

[41] Itō, "Buke seiji-kan," 132.41-43.
[42] Asakawa, *Iriki*, 374.

usurpation and that it became a fatal weakness when once its power had failed is well known. Throughout the Tokugawa period it was the existence of *real power* together with the symbols which combined to support the shogun in his position as hegemon. This in turn rested largely on the effective power base upon which the shogunate was built.

In a rough way this power base was equatable to the balance of land holdings touched upon in the previous part of this chapter. The balance, as we saw, was made up of four main divisions: the shogun's land (or *tenryō*), land held by the Tokugawa kinsmen (*shimpan* and *renshi*), by the *fudai*, and by the *tozama*. The balance in this structure in gross terms was between the Tokugawa inner coalition, which now possessed over 16,000,000 *koku*, and the *tozama*, whose lands were assessed at just under 10,000,000 *koku*. But there was a great deal more to this balance than such a rough comparison can suggest.

The subtle arrangements within the coalition of daimyo headed by the Tokugawa shogun bear analysis from a number of points of view. The most obvious comparison of the size of domains provides only a rough estimate of the relative strength of various daimyo in relation to the shogunate. As of about 1670, 45 domains were assessed at 100,000 *koku* or larger, 54 were assessed at from 50,000 to 100,000 *koku*, and 141 were smaller than 50,000 *koku* in assessment. By comparison with the distribution of daimyo within the Toyotomi alliance, the Tokugawa had achieved a much greater stability by the elimination of the extremely large competitive daimyo. The largest daimyo domain next to the shogun's private 6,000,000 *koku* was the Maeda family's 1,200,000 *koku*. Furthermore, of the thirteen so-called great daimyo whose domains were listed at over 300,000 *koku*, four were Tokugawa collaterals and *fudai*. The remainder, although *tozama*, were in most cases strongly committed to the Tokugawa house. Most of these had declared their allegiance before Sekigahara and had fought effectively for the Tokugawa in that decisive battle. Such were the Date, Maeda, Ikeda, Asano, Kuroda, and Hosakawa. Of the great daimyo only the Shimazu, Mōri, and Nabeshima had been among the western daimyo who opposed Ieyasu at Sekigahara. The importance of this distinction among the *tozama* is obvious. For in the final years of its existence it was from among the subjugated daimyo that the main attack upon the shogunate came.

One of the most effective means of drawing the Tokugawa daimyo coalition together was through the spread of family ties with the shogun's house. Ieyasu had been especially fortunate in the size and vitality of his family and was able to leave behind a group of cadet families which managed to play a major role in the power balance. Ultimately five cadet (*shimpan* or *kamon*) houses were established. These were the three Tokugawa branches (*sanke*) of Owari, Kii, and Mito and the two Matsudaira houses of Echizen and Aizu. Branches of the *sanke* were called *renshi* and numbered two. Other houses of near cadet status, either by virtue of earlier relationship to the Tokugawa or by adoption, were the Hisamatsu of Matsuyama and Kuwana, the Okudaira, and the Ikeda of Tottori. These daimyo together held 2,679,000 *koku* of territory.[43]

Ieyasu and his successors used successfully the techniques of marriage alliance and adoption to cement family relations and to buttress the system of military alliances. Daughters and grand-daughters of Ieyasu and daughters of Hidetada and Iemitsu were married, among others, to the houses of Kuroda, Koide, Katō, Okudaira, Ikeda, Asano, Arima, Maeda, Kyōgoku, Date, and Mōri.[44] Naturally such marriage alliances were not of lasting effectiveness in linking these daimyo houses to the Tokugawa, but the process was continued generation after generation; and the Tokugawa alone were free to make whatever politically valuable marriages they might wish. The practice of adoption, so liberally practical in Japan, also aided the Tokugawa cause, making it possible for the shogun to acquire through adoption extra "daughters" or "sons" who could be pressed upon daimyo in marriage or as adoptive heirs. In all such marriages and adoptions the shogun, because of his superior status, stood to benefit by the added sense of obligation and loyalty from the inferior house.

Still another technique freely used by the shogun to add the sanction of family connection to superior-inferior relations was the honorary granting of the surname Matsudaira. In all, eighteen *tozama* were honored by receiving the Matsudaira surname as a sign of the shogun's favor toward them. Among these were the Maeda, Shimazu, Date, Mōri, Hachisuka, Ikeda, Kuroda, Asano,

---

[43] Calculated in *Sekai rekishi jiten*, 12.58.
[44] Mikami Sanji, *Edo-jidai shi* (2 vols., Tokyo, 1943-1944), 1.139.

Yamauchi, and Nabeshima.[45] The granting of a character from the shogun's given name was also a mark of special honor and was bestowed in a special ceremony which served to tie the receiver more closely to the shogun.

While the *tozama* and *kamon* were treated with respect and provided special honors, the *fudai*, because of their status as house daimyo, were handled less differentially. Most *fudai* ranked far below the *tozama* in terms of land holdings and external honors such as court titles, but as house daimyo they were given positions of foremost responsibility within the shogun's service. The resulting balance between the individually powerful and independent *tozama* and the individually weak but strongly united and politically influential band of *fudai* was one of the major stabilizing features of the daimyo coalition. The *fudai* daimyo eventually numbered some 140 and held an aggregate of 9,834,700 *koku*, thus balancing nearly to the *koku* the *tozama* holdings. Their deep dependence upon the shogun for their status as daimyo made them particularly supportive and trustworthy. Within the *fudai* internal balances were also achieved among various groups classified according to the history of their relationship to the Tokugawa house. Some six or seven were especially honored because their connection to the Tokugawa house antedated its entrance into Okazaki castle. Another fifteen dated from the Okazaki period, and thirty-seven from the Sumpu era. The majority, of no special distinction, came into service after 1590.

Much has been written about the strategic disposition of *tenryō* lands and the lands of the *fudai* and *tozama* daimyo upon the political map. The Tokugawa shoguns, especially the first three, were constantly at work to improve to their advantage the arrangement of daimyo across the land. Victories at Sekigahara and Osaka, and the constant attrition through confiscation made possible a continual turnover in daimyo houses and in the disposition of their domains. By the time that the system had matured in the mid-seventeenth century, only some ten or fifteen daimyo, among them notably the Maeda, Nambu, Tsugaru, Nabeshima, and Shimazu, remained in their original lands. All others had been shifted with their retainers at least once, sometimes more often, to new locales. This not only broke local ties, making less possible the perpetua-

---

[45] Takigawa Masajirō, *Nihon shakaishi* (Tokyo, 1938), 259.

tion of local grudges or secret intrigues against the Tokugawa but also permitted the more advantageous balancing of groups on the political map. The Tokugawa, of course, never had a completely free hand in shifting daimyo, for they were constrained by precedent which made it inadvisable to advance daimyo too rapidly in terms of territory or official rank and which made arbitrary confiscation inexpedient. Thus the shogunate was obliged to bide its time and wait patiently for advantageous opportunities.

The resulting "strategic disposition" of daimyo appears rather haphazard, but contained certain distinctive features. *Tenryō* embraced important cities such as Kyoto, Osaka, Nagasaki, Fushimi, Nara, Sumpu, Sakai, and Yamada. *Tenryō* and *fudai* territories provided a solid belt of control which made communication between Edo and Kyoto or Osaka secure in peace and war. *Tozama* for the most part had been moved to Japan west of Osaka, or left on the extreme fringes of the islands. When possible, *fudai* were placed to block *tozama* from military access to strategic locales or from making alliances with each other.

Some of the most obvious strategic placements were the cadet houses of Aizu and Mito and the *fudai* house at Utsunomiya which served to protect the northern access to Edo. In Echizen and Echigo, cadet and *fudai* houses were placed to check the great Maeda of Kaga. In Ōmi, the Ii house of Hikone, the largest of the *fudai*, was set to guard the capital. Osaka was kept as a shogunal castle garrisoned on rotation by *fudai* daimyo. The cadet houses in Wakayama, Nagoya, and Kōfu all held down pivotal spots on the feudal map.

To the west of Osaka, Himeji, considered the gateway from the west, was held until 1616 by the Ikeda. Thereafter it passed to one after another of the major *fudai* houses. Okayama and Tottori, both important strategically because they guarded the roads which led to the capital from the west, were given to two divisions of the Ikeda house. The Ikeda were *tozama* but of near *fudai* or *kamon* status and justifiably considered trustworthy. Nevertheless, checks were put upon them by closely set *fudai* at Matsue, Tsuyama, and Fukuyama. On Shikoku the Tokugawa placed house daimyo at Takamatsu and Matsuyama. These, in combination with the Tokugawa branch house at Wakayama, balanced the *tozama* of Kōchi, Tokushima, and Uwajima. From this point westward, however, the Tokugawa began to run out of available *fudai*. Between the Asano of Hiroshima and Shimazu of Kagoshima (*tozama* both) only three major *fudai* could be placed. These were the Matsudaira of Funai and Shimabara and the Ōkubo of Karatsu. Otherwise the Tokugawa were obliged to depend upon old rivalries and the distinction between pre and post Sekigahara alliances in the hope that the many *tozama* of western Japan would remain disunited.[46]

Any assessment of the effective balance of military power represented by the strategic disposition of shogunal and daimyo territories must be based on an analysis of the manpower and economic resources which these territories made available to the competing groups within the political system. For this purpose the official *koku* figures, while providing a rough basis of calculation, must be further interpreted. In the first place the *koku* assessments of shogunal territories were much more apt to be exact, while those of *tozama* were generally underestimated. Furthermore, the *tenryō* was uniformly more thinly held than the lands of the *fudai* daimyo, and these in turn were less well provided with military manpower than those of the *tozama*. This was a result of the fact that throughout the formative period of the Tokugawa regime the Tokugawa inner forces were constantly expanding into new and larger territory and were spreading their resources, while the *tozama* were contracting. The sparsity of military manpower in the *tenryō* was further accentuated by the fact that such territory was administered by officials of the fiscal branch of the *bakufu*. The *tenryō* intendants (*daikan*) were officials of only minor rank, yet they administered areas of from 50,000 to 150,000 *koku*. Unlike daimyo, they had no military forces under their command. For enforcement purposes, or to meet military emergencies, they were expected to call upon the central pool of shogunal vassals or upon neighboring *fudai* daimyo.[47]

So long as the shogun could count on the availability of his own troops and those of the *fudai* he was, of course, capable of mustering a force unmatched by any potential *tozama* coalition. Added to this was a considerable dimension of superiority in the disposition and size of fortifications. Tokugawa policy restricted the number and size of the daimyos' castles while building up the shogun's own military establishments. By conscripting labor and

[46] Mikami, *Edo-jidai shi*, 1.145-146.
[47] Albert Craig, *op.cit.*, 16-17.

matériel from the *tozama,* the first three shogun erected the magnificent Edo, Osaka, Nagoya, Sumpu, and Nijō castles, all outstanding for their size and impregnability. These castles, garrisoned in rotation by *fudai* units or the shogun's guard groups, held down essential points on the strategic map. But it is significant that their locations were all east of the terminus of the Inland Sea, leaving western Japan with no major shogunal stronghold.

If Tokugawa manpower was rather thinly and irregularly distributed across the Japanese islands, the shogun's lands were outstanding in terms of their economic potential. It is generally assumed that the shogun attempted to reserve for himself land which was of highest quality and productiveness. In addition, the shogun's lands embraced most of the important commercial cities and the major gold, silver, and copper mines of the country. Edo, the great capital of the Tokugawa shogunate, became in time the largest consuming center in Japan. Osaka, Kyoto, Fushimi, Sumpu, Ōtsu, Sakai, Nagasaki, Yamada, Niigata, and many other important cities and towns were all under direct Tokugawa administration. The economic worth of these cities to the shogun is rather difficult to determine, since urban and commercial taxation was not highly developed. After the middle of the eighteenth century, however, monopoly and produce taxes and the frequent exaction of unrepaid "loans" provided a valuable but uncertain source of revenue for the shogunate. *Bakufu* administrative dominance of the major commercial centers could mean that the shogun had access to the largest supplies of loan capital, and through the great cities of Edo and Osaka the shogunate could pretty well control monetary and commercial policy in Japan.

Ownership of the important mines of Sado, Izu, Iwami, and Ashio gave the Tokugawa a near monopoly over the production of precious metals and effectively backed the shogun's authority to regulate currency. Both the treasure which came from these mines and the later profits from currency debasement contributed to the finances of the shogunate. Finally the shogun was able to assume monopoly control over foreign imports and certain internal commodities, the profits from which accrued to the shogunate. Among these were silk, imported from China through Nagasaki, copper, dried marine products, and domestic vegetable oils. So long as the economic and technological level of the country remained relatively unchanged, the Tokugawa could thus claim certain economic advantages which made possible their domination of national economic policy and the nationwide organs of exchange and transportation.

BASED upon these and many other sources of real power the Tokugawa shogunate was able to organize a system of controls which institutionalized the supremacy of the shogun in government and over the major sectors of national life. The control system was ingenious and far-reaching, and in its day was certainly far more effective than anything devised by previous military governments. Evolved in the main by Ieyasu, and after his death by his first two successors, it had reached maturity by the time of the death of the third shogun, Ieymitsu. Following the main contours of the power base, it joined these into a fabric of regulations and precedents which assured the hegemony of the shogun over the emperor and his court, over the daimyo, and over the religious orders.

The unification movement had refocused attention on the emperor as the source of legitimacy, and both Nobunaga and Hideyoshi did much to add to the public reverence paid the *tennō*. Tokugawa policy toward the emperor embraced the dual objectives of heightening the prestige of the sovereign while seeking to control him and isolate him from the daimyo. The Tokugawa treated the emperor and his court with great outward respect. Tokugawa Ieyasu himself allotted land assessed at 10,139 *koku* for the emperor's support. In 1625 another 10,075 *koku* was added by the shogunate, and in 1705 another 10,000 *koku*. Beyond this, lands were set aside for the empress and various imperial princes and courtiers.[48] By the end of the Tokugawa period the emperor, his courtiers, and certain court-related religious establishments had acquired 187,316 *koku* in support lands.[49] The *bakufu* also provided funds and donated labor (generally requisitioned from the daimyo) for the rebuilding of palaces and the shrine to the imperial ancestors at Ise. Imperial ceremonial was kept alive on a modest basis.

By virtue of their residential and genealogical isolation the imperial family, its branches, and the courtiers (mostly branches of

[48] Takekoshi Yosaburō, *Nihon keizaishi* (8 vols., Tokyo, 1920), 4.323-325.
[49] Andō Hiroshi, *Tokugawa bakufu kenchi yōryaku* (Tokyo, 1915), 69.

the Fujiwara) were considered a special group apart from the military aristocracy. To them went a continuing monopoly of highest court ranks and a sentimental respect for having maintained the classical cultural accomplishments of the Heian period. But political influence and freedom of political expression was jealously denied them. Tokugawa control over the court was exercised through the military governor (*shoshidai*) of Kyoto backed up by the military garrisons at Nijō castle and Fushimi. The military governor worked through two court officials who acted as transmitters of the shogunal will to the court. Through them the *bakufu* was able to screen all matters brought before the emperor, control the making of appointments or the granting of honors, and restrict the free association of the courtiers with the daimyo houses. This pattern of shogunal interference in court affairs was begun by Ieyasu in 1615 when he imposed upon the Kyoto nobility a seventeen-clause code which rigidly prescribed the functions and duties of the emperor and the various court officials. It limited the emperor to traditional literary and ceremonial pursuits, made mandatory prior *bakufu* consent to high official appointments, regulated the relationship between the imperial family and the great temples, set the pattern of compulsory monasticism for certain of the imperial princes, and specified procedures for adoption and succession.[50]

There is some indication that the court did not passively acquiesce to these restrictions. But the emperor was powerless to resist the shogun, and the skillful technique of melioration and infiltration practiced by the Tokugawa numbed the resistance of the nobility. In the early years the distribution of shogunal largess to the emperor was lavish, and involved not only the dramatic gift of support lands but rice, silver, and gold for the courtiers and for the merchants of Kyoto.[51] In 1619 a granddaughter of Ieyasu was made imperial consort, thereby putting into the inner confines of the palace a group of Tokugawa men, ostensibly advisers and guards to the girl, who could function as agents for the shogun. Before long this Tokugawa girl conveniently provided children who could be put on the throne. In 1630 the Tokugawa accomplished the remarkable feat of oblig-

[50] See *Sekai rekishi jiten*, 22.219-220.
[51] Kurita, *Edo*, 257.

ing the abdication of a mature emperor in favor of a seven-year-old girl who was in fact Ieyasu's great-granddaughter.

Control of the daimyo by the shogun began with the oaths of allegiance and the grant of investiture. The oath (*seishi*, sometimes referred to as *kishō*) was a sworn pledge of loyalty prepared on special paper which had been inscribed with the names of Shinto and Buddhist divinities. The form followed closely the practice developed in the days of the Sengoku wars when personal oaths of loyalty were presented to territorial lords by their vassals. In building up his military coalition, Tokugawa Ieyasu had accumulated a large collection of oaths binding his housemen and his allied daimyo to him. Once the alliance was stabilized, the requirement of periodic renewal became standardized and to an extent routinized. Oaths were of two types, the basic pledge of loyalty which applied to all daimyo and housemen, and the office oath (*yakunin-seishi*) sworn by those taking office under the shogun. The loyalty oath was sworn by all daimyo toward each shogun, either as a group upon the assumption of a new shogun or privately upon the succession of a new daimyo. It contained three basic provisions: a pledge to obey the shogun's regulations, not to enter into anti-shogunal cliques or activity, and to serve the shogun with absolute loyalty. Oaths were signed in blood and presented through the shogun's senior councillors. Vassals of less than daimyo rank presented oaths through the administrative council (*hyōjōsho*). The shogun's officials, upon appointment, sent their office oaths either through the council or other appropriate senior officers. The *seishi* thus did not involve a personal confrontation between lord and vassal but was handled bureaucratically.[52]

This procedure was more strictly worked out with respect to the *fudai* in the early years of the shogunate. At first *tozama* were given especially courteous treatment as allies rather than vassals. By the time of Iemitsu, however, any distinction which may have existed between vassal and ally was publicly swept aside. In 1632, upon the death of Hidetada, Iemitsu called together the *tozama* and announced, "With the passing of the previous shogun, I henceforth am the sole master of the land; if any of you should desire [to make an issue of it], take up weapons and make your attempt."[53] From this point on the *tozama* were treated as vassals

[52] Matsudaira, *Seido*, 264-276.   [53] Naitō, *Jūgodai-shi*, 3.121.

and much of the ceremony which had attended their treatment was dropped.

In return for the oath, the daimyo received at the shogun's pleasure an investiture of lands. This was the *ryōchi jisho* which granted a territory defined in terms of provinces, districts, villages, and their *koku* assessment. It bore the shogun's seal or signature. Such documents were referred to variously according to the type of signature. The *hammotsu* bore the shogun's written signature and was used for the great daimyo above 100,000 *koku*, the vermilion seal (*shuin*) was used for investitures below this rank. For still lesser purposes the black seal (*kokuin*) could be used.[54] Further classification of the contents of each domain was specified in the domain index (*ryōchi-mokuroku*) under the signature of the appropriate officials of the shogunal finance office.

Although the swearing of oaths and granting of investitures did not involve close personal contact between shogun and daimyo there were numerous occasions upon which the daimyo faced the shogun in ceremonial token of submission. In the New Year's ceremonies, when leaving or returning to Edo, at the time of Ieyasu's memorial service, and on a host of other occasions the assembled daimyo paid their respects to the shogun and received his benefices. In the course of his career each daimyo also passed through several important ceremonial steps, such as his first introduction to the shogun (*omemie*), his coming of age, or his receipt of a character from the shogun's name. All of these brought the daimyo into close ceremonial relationship to the shogun and reiterated the subordinate status of the daimyo with respect to the shogun.

While it was expected that daimyo held their territories as hereditary grants, in actuality their tenure was precarious and at the pleasure of each shogun. Confiscation or transfer from one locality to another was quite frequent, especially at the outset of the regime. Changes of domain, known as *kaieki*, were ordered by the shogun under a number of circumstances but primarily for lack of heir, mismanagement, infringement of the basic regulations of the shogunate, or, of course, as a sign of favor. Inheritance procedures for daimyo houses were particularly restrictive during the early years of the Tokugawa shogunate. Succession had to be approved by the shogun, and hasty adoption and in-

---

[54] Matsudaira, *Seido*, 247-253.

heritance by minors was strictly prohibited. The regulation which precluded inheritance (without special approval) of an heir unable because of age or health to carry on the affairs of the house was itself the cause of some forty-six confiscations of domain totaling 4,570,000 *koku* during the years of the first three shogun.[55] Only after 1651 when the Tokugawa felt securely in control of the country did the *bakufu* relax inheritance regulations and permit last minute adoptions by heads of *buke* families who died suddenly before the age of 50.[56]

The fundamental code of regulations for the daimyo was the *buke-sho-hatto*. This document first presented to the daimyo by Ieyasu in 1615 contained thirteen provisions which by 1635 had been augmented to twenty-one. Ieyasu's code, following the lines of Hideyoshi's "wall writings," sought to regulate the private conduct, marriages, and dress of the daimyo, to prevent them from forming cliques or altering their military establishments, and to oblige them to adhere to the hostage system. To this was added in later years a more specific regulation for attendance upon the shogun at Edo and the maintenance of hostages, the prohibition against building ocean-going ships and against Christianity, and the stipulation that the regulations of the shogun must be adhered to above all others. Through the *buke-sho-hatto*, the daimyo were obliged to submit to a continuous interference in the internal affairs of their domains and to accept the *bakufu* laws as the supreme law of the land.

Probably of all the control measures contained in the daimyo code that of alternate attendance (*sankinkōtai*) was the most far-reaching in its influence upon the relationship of daimyo to shogun. The practice of attendance upon one's lord and the giving of hostages to guarantee pledges had been common in the Sengoku period. Maeda Toshinaga was the first of the great daimyo to pay court to Ieyasu in Edo after Sekigahara. Thereafter the custom developed among the daimyo, at first voluntarily, and then after 1633 as a shogunal requirement. All daimyo were obliged to build residences in Edo where they kept their wives and children and an appropriate retinue. They themselves alternated residence between Edo and their domain headquarters. Up to 1665 the shogun set the requirements for types of hostages and maintained a superintendent of hostages (*shōnin bugyō*) to en-

[55] Kurita, *Edo*, 64.   [56] Naitō, *Jūgodai-shi*, 4,133.

sure compliance. Generally, one of the daimyo's chief vassals was required to remain in Edo in addition to members of the daimyo's family.[57]

As a consequence of the provisions of the *buke* code, but essentially as a privilege of overlordship, the shogun placed demands upon the daimyo and subjected them to various forms of scrutiny. While the shogun did not tax the daimyo directly, various exactions and contributions were required of them, often on a fairly regular basis. The constant giving of "gifts" of a prescribed nature—on occasions such as New Year's, on succession to a domain, coming of age, and the like—put in the hands of the shogun various precious commodities only partially returned as beneficences. The right to demand military and logistic assistance from vassals was commonly accepted as the privilege of the lord toward his vassal. In time of emergency such as at Osaka in 1614-1615 or Shimabara in 1636-1637 the shogun freely commanded his daimyo to fight on his behalf. The requisitioning of economic aid, particularly for the building of castles, roads, bridges, and palaces, was also a prerogative used by the shogun for his own advantage. This form of requisition known as *kokuyaku* was frequently used to weaken the more economically prosperous *tozama*. On top of this, it made possible the gigantic fortifications which put the shogunal castles far ahead of those of their rival daimyo in size and military capacity.

Inspection of the daimyo domains, both openly and through an intelligence system, was common. In 1633 Iemitsu began the practice of dispatching inspectors (*junkenshi*) to the domains of the daimyo to check on local conditions. They asked questions concerning the productivity of the domains, their financial and military resources, population, methods of administration, the standard of living of the people, and the like. Other *bakufu* officials known as auditors (*kansatsushi*) entered a domain at times when an heir sought to secure inheritance. The auditor's report was awaited before the shogun confirmed the inheritance. In addition to such direct inspection, the shogunate required various occasional and periodic reports from the daimyo such as the domain map (*kuni-ezu*), the village roll (*gōchō*), and the annual guarantee of religious orthodoxy (*shūmon-aratame*).

Shogunal control of the sources of preferment and of social

[57] Matsudaira, *Seido*, 672-709; Mikami, *Edo-jidai shi*, 1.123-137.

titles and honors provided an important means of maintaining order among the daimyo. Relying both upon the old imperial system of court ranks and official posts (now completely honorary) and upon various tokens of military status, the shogun presided over an elaborate system of classes, ranks, grades, and titles which defined a closed social hierarchy. Once the hierarchy had become set, each daimyo family came to occupy a specific hereditary status (*kakaku*) which served to define the standing of the family with respect to the whole and to limit the function of the family within the *bakufu* system.

Daimyo were first of all ranked in a rough way according to the assessed rice yield of their domains (*kokudaka*), and further according to the type of their holding. Daimyo who controlled one or more provinces were called lords of a province (*kunimochi*). Below these were the lords of castles (*jōshu*), and below them lords without castles (*mujō*). Another status scale derived from the daimyo's position within the ceremonial hierarchy of the shogun's court. Attendance upon the shogun at various ceremonial occasions took place according to prescribed precedents which were calculated to accentuate the relative standing of each participant. Each daimyo, in accordance with his rank within the Tokugawa hierarchy, was assigned to certain rooms within Edo castle. These room names, of which there were seven, eventually became appellations of rank among the daimyo.

Added to these precedents which originated from the traditions of military houses was the system of court titles and ranks administered through the imperial court. Actually, though there was an indefinite number of titles within the court hierarchy to which daimyo could aspire, the system was handled in a fairly uncomplicated fashion. Court ranks and titles given to the military families were relatively few in number and assigned on the basis of status within the military hierarchy. The shogun himself, for example, always received a ministerial (*daijin*) appointment and the second, occasionally the first, court rank. His court status was always several steps above his nearest competitor. Next in importance were the heads of the cadet houses of Owari and Kii, who at the height of their careers could expect to receive the post of great counsellor (*dainagon*) and the junior second rank. The head of the Mito house was entitled to become middle counsellor (*chūnagon*) at junior third rank. Of the remaining daimyo some of the *tozama* were privileged to reach middle commander of the guards (*chūjō*). Most lords of castles carried the title of lesser commander of the guards (*shōshō*), and the most outstanding *fudai* could attain the post of court chamberlain (*jijū*). The majority of daimyo remained on the two levels of junior fourth rank lower grade and junior fifth rank lower grade. They were assigned an assortment of honorary titles from among posts in the central court officialdom or in the provincial bureaucracy. The use of provincial governorships was particularly common at this level. Since all court appointments were initiated by the shogun, they were received essentially in recognition of service to the shogun. Through such means, then, the shogun could keep the daimyo under orderly control, assured of the fact that the hierarchy of precedence and access to positions of influence could not change unexpectedly.

Control over the lands and affairs of religious establishments presented few difficulties by the time of Tokugawa Ieyasu. The independent political and military status of these institutions had been broken by Nobunaga, and Hideyoshi had denied them a separate economic existence. As the great land survey swept across the country the ability of the temples or shrines to retain land on the basis of previous *shōen* titles was destroyed, and they too were put under the jurisdiction of the vermilion seals of the military powers. By the beginning of the Tokugawa period, therefore, the holdings of religious establishments had been drastically reduced. The official shogunal record (*Kan'ei shuin chō*) lists a total of 260,000 *koku* granted to temples and shrines under the shogun's seal. Another 101,000 *koku* may have been held by institutions less clearly identifiable in sectarian terms.[58] In addition, there were the lands of many tens of thousands of smaller temples and shrines which received confirmation of their holdings from the daimyo. In all, the holdings of religious institutions may have totaled 613,900 *koku,* a sizable figure in itself but infinitesimal when considered in relation to the number of institutions supported by these lands. The number of red seal temples themselves numbered 3490.[59] Only a few temples held territories equivalent to those of the smallest daimyo. These were Kōfukuji (15,030

---

[58] Irimajiri Yoshinaga, "Edojidai jiryō to sono shobun," in *Nihon nōmin keizaishi kenkyū* (Tokyo, 1949), 108-109.
[59] *Ibid.*, 109-110.

koku), Hieizan (12,000 *koku*), and Kōyasan (11,600 *koku*).
Tōdaiji of Nara, the greatest of the temples of the past, received
only 2137 *koku*, and the average holding of the red seal temples
was less than 100 *koku*.

Along with the rewriting of the land grants, the shogun pressed
regulatory controls of various kinds upon the religious institutions
either singly or as a whole. The seven-clause regulations issued
to Hieizan in 1608 was the beginning of an effort which by 1615
had given shape to an integrated system of control. By sponsoring
certain sects and temples in the Kantō, the shogunate managed
to depress the influence of the established temples of the old capital area. For example, Tokugawa patronage was lavished upon
Tōeizan Kan'eiji of Edo and Nikkōzan Rinnōji at Nikkō. Also
through various regulatory codes the *bakufu* interfered with the
priestly orders, restricting the relationship of the imperial family
to the priesthood, enforcing a complete centralization between
home temple and provincial branches, and in general imposing
a rigid formality upon priestly activities. With the establishment
of the superintendent of temples and shrines (*jisha bugyō*) in
1635, the entire religious establishment was brought under direct
Tokugawa supervision.

THE Tokugawa institutions of legitimacy and control provided
a remarkably stable base from which to exercise political mastery
of the country. The *baku-han* system, the term by which Japanese
historians refer to the coalition of daimyo presided over by the
Tokugawa shoguns, was fundamentally no different in its conception than the previous hegemony created by Hideyoshi, but
the power of the shogun was many times greater than that
achieved by the Taikō. It would, of course, be an exaggeration to
conceive of the shogunate as a true central government. In the
baku-han system, the shogun governed directly only his own
tenryō. The rest of the country remained under the decentralized
rule of the daimyo. Moreover the authority relationship between
shogun and territorial lords was essentially feudal, and the participation of the daimyo in national affairs, that is, in government
above the level of the domain, was done as a result of obligations
inherent in the feudal bond between daimyo and shogun. There
was no uniformly imposed national tax, no national conscript
army. Yet the centralizing capacities of the shogunate were also

remarkably strong. The preponderance of shogunal power was so great, the shogunal lands were so widespread, so many of the important towns and cities were under direct shogunal control, and so many of the daimyo (particularly the *fudai*) were so completely integrated into the *bakufu* machinery, that the shogunate did in most senses constitute a central authority. The *bakufu* bureaucracy provided for much more than simply the administration of the *tenryō*; in fact, it bore responsibility for national policy at many levels. The pledge of the daimyo to administer their territories according to *bakufu* law was by no means empty.

Where Hideyoshi had failed to organize a stable administrative structure, the Tokugawa more than succeeded. Few countries have been as "heavily administered" as Japan under the Tokugawa shogunate. The administrative machinery and concepts of government utilized by the shogunate, though remarkably similar in some respects to those of the early imperial bureaucracy, were essentially pragmatic creations which evolved gradually along with the expansion of the Tokugawa power base. The origins of *bakufu* administration are found therefore in the *karō-bugyō* style of command which had typified the daimyo houses of the late sixteenth century. When Tokugawa Ieyasu rose from the status of daimyo to that of shogun, his administrative organization expanded from one of purely local responsibility to one with national significance. At the same time his chief vassals were elevated from the status of housemen to that of *fudai* daimyo with greatly expanded responsibilities. The houses which in Okazaki had been of less than daimyo rank but had served as elders or commissioners in the Tokugawa house administration rose both in territorial rank and administrative powers. They gained status both as independent daimyo and as the foremost officials of the shogunal government.

For his administration the former daimyo of Mikawa, now become shogun, relied exclusively on his housemen for his corps of officials. Not all of the families which had served Ieyasu at Okazaki managed to survive the explosive growth of the Tokugawa house, and many new families were added. But despite certain changes in personnel, the Tokugawa based their entire administration upon the personnel provided by the private house band, that is upon the *fudai, hatamoto,* and *gokenin.* These vassals

could be treated as direct subordinates in a command relationship much more absolute than that which united the *tozama* lords
under the shogun. The *hatamoto* and *gokenin* were assigned to
the petty and private affairs of the shogun's own territories, while
the *fudai,* in the upper levels of *bakufu* administration, took on
an increasing degree of responsibility for affairs involving the
daimyo domains. *Kamon* and *tozama* daimyo were held accountable for the governance of their domains but were given no part
in *bakufu* policy formation or administration except on a con-
sultative basis.

The shogunate eventually took shape as a complex and far-
reaching functional bureaucracy. At the apex of the structure
were two policy councils. Five or six of the highest ranking
fudai were appointed senior councillors (*rōjū*) and given the
responsibility to shape overall shogunal policy and to superintend
the affairs of the daimyo. Six junior councillors (*wakadoshiyori*)
selected from among lesser *fudai* supervised the shogun's private
affairs and controlled the *hatamoto* and *gokenin.* Specific administrative functions of the *bakufu* were distributed between these
councils and assigned to individual commissioners or special
boards. Under the senior councillors were such officers as the
keepers of Edo and Osaka castles, chamberlains, inspectors-
general, magistrates of the shogun's cities (Edo, Osaka, Kyoto,
Nagasaki), magistrates of religious affairs, finance officers, engi-
neers, secretaries, and house scholars. The junior councillors were
in charge of organizing the shogun's military guards, maintaining castle garrisons, and administrating the police service.

Although the *bakufu* was most directly concerned with the private affairs of the Tokugawa territories, it unavoidably set the
pattern of administration and legislation for the entire country.
The basic policies of the Tokugawa shogunate in most instances
continued the lead begun by Nobunaga and Hideyoshi. Tokugawa
government rested on the fundamental conception that society
was composed of statuses, or estates, each with its particular function. The polity itself, consisting of the emperor, shogun, daimyo,
and samurai, was by definition placed in the hands of the military
aristocracy who held the authority to govern and to lead in war.
The "common people" (*tami*), consisting of the peasantry, artisans, and merchants, were the wards of the governing class. The
priesthood stood apart at a level somewhere between the aris-

tocracy and the people. The samurai class, being everywhere organized into military units and bound by oaths to their superiors, were expected to live by the codes of loyalty and duty which were their heritage. The people were confined to their units of registration: the village (*mura*) organization in the countryside and the block (*machi*) in the cities. Regulations assumed social stratification between the estates and assumed the desirability of controlling social and occupational mobility. The prime ingredient in all such social legislation (other than expansion or refinement) which the Tokugawa added to the earlier codes of Hideyoshi was the ideological sanction of Confucianism. Tokugawa shoguns and their daimyo subordinates made extensive use of Confucian principles of social theory and value in order to rationalize the social system of their day and add the sanctity of doctrine to the status-based legislation in which they indulged.

The vast stream of laws and regulations which flowed from the *bakufu* is beyond the scope of our concern at this point. But certain key laws of the Tokugawa shogunate, since they were particularly influential in setting the legal framework of the country as a whole, need at least to be cited. The 1615 code for emperor and courtiers (*kinchū narabi ni kuge-shū sho-hatto*) and the code for the military houses (*buke sho-hatto*) have already been referred to and their provisions need not be repeated. The *buke* code applied at first only to the daimyo, and so the shogun in 1632 drew up another similar code for samurai of less than daimyo rank. This was the *shoshi hatto* which urged the *hatamoto* and *gokenin* to loyal service, filial conduct, attention to military accomplishments, and various more specific duties. After 1680 the *buke sho-hatto* was made to serve as a general code applicable to all ranks of samurai.[60]

Serving as repositories of guiding principles and policies for the *bakufu* were two Tokugawa house codes. Both were considered "legacies" from the time of Ieyasu (one spuriously so). The hundred clause code (*hyakkajō*) and the legacy (*seiken-kōi*) both contained a mixture of administrative wisdom, precedent regarding status of *fudai* and *tozama* daimyo, and philosophy with respect to the governing of the country.[61] These codes were

[60] Kikuchi Shunsuke, ed., *Tokugawa kinrei kō* (6 vols., Tokyo, 1931-1932), 1.90-103.

[61] *Ibid.*, 1.78-89; 221-245.

not made public but were kept within the *bakufu* inner circle as general guides to policy.

Basic to the regulation of the military establishments of the daimyo were two *bakufu* pronouncements. The 1615 order restricting "one castle to a province" (*ikkoku-ichijō-rei*) prevented the daimyo from building or maintaining multiple military establishments.[62] The 1649 regulation on military service (*gunyaku ninzuwari*) set a limit to the number of troops the daimyo could keep in training of the following order:[63]

For a domain of 100,000 *koku*—2155 men including

horsemen	170
firearms	350
bows	60
spears	150
banners	20

For a domain of 10,000 *koku*—235 men including

horsemen	10
firearms	20
bows	10
spears	3
banners	3

For a domain of 1000 *koku*—21 men including

spears	2
bow	1
firearm	1

For a domain of 200 *koku*—5 men made up of

samurai	1
armor bearer	1
spear bearer	1
horse leader	1
porter	1

Buddhist and Shinto religious bodies were regulated by the code governing sects and temples (*shoshū jiin hatto*) and the code governing shrines and priests (*shosha negi kannushi hatto*), both issued in 1665.[64] The 1722 code for Buddhist sects and priests (*shoshū sōryo hatto*) completed the body of rules governing the

---

[62] Takayanagi Mitsutoshi, "Genna ikkoku-ichijō rei," *Shigaku zasshi*, 33.11 (1922), 863-888.

[63] *Tokugawa kinrei kō*, 1.129.   [64] *Ibid.*, 5.10-32.

Buddhist establishments. These documents proscribed relations between central and branch temples, and prohibited sectarian quarrels, the formation of new sects, the enunciation of new religious beliefs, or the sale of temple land. They effectively legislated the status quo in religious affairs.[65]

Anti-Christian regulations were strictly enforced beginning in 1612 with the first restrictive edict. In 1616 the death penalty for believers and other severe penalties were set. In 1633 a seventeen-clause code embodied the first provisions of national seclusion along with a strict interdiction of Christianity. In 1639 the three-clause *Kirishitan kinrei san kajō* brought to completion the anti-Christian edicts. Thereafter the *bakufu* perfected the system of religious inspection and temple registration that made any alien religion an impossibility in Japan. In 1640 the office of religious inspector (*shūmon aratame-yaku*) was established and one of the Tokugawa inspectors-general put in charge of it. In 1664 daimyo were obliged to appoint their own inspectors and adopt uniform procedures of regulation. This included the registration of all families at temples (*terauke*), the compilation of yearly religious census records (*shūmon ninbetsu chō*), the careful scrutiny of families with known Christian background, and the posting of signboards which advertised rewards for information leading to the apprehension of Christian believers.[66]

Closely related to the Tokugawa anti-Christian policy was its handling of foreign relations. The seventeen-article pronouncement of 1633, referred to above, was modified several times until in 1636 it took the form of a nineteen-clause seclusion regulation (*sakokurei*) which in addition to prohibiting Christian belief, put an end to Japanese ships going abroad, set the death penalty for Japanese returning from abroad, defined the conditions for conduct of trade at Nagasaki, and set up the *bakufu* monopoly in silk imports from China.[67] In 1685 a ban on the import of foreign books completed the fabric of seclusion.

Basic policy toward the peasantry and rural areas was most characteristically set forth in the 1649 regulations which attended the land survey of that year. The "survey regulations" (*keian kenchi jōrei*) amplified and made more specific and inclusive

65 *Ibid.*, 5.40-42.
66 *Sekai rekishi jiten*, 8.46-48, 9.189.
67 *Ibid.*, 22.242.

Hideyoshi's cadastral institutions. The "instructions of Keian" (*Keian no ofuregaki*) explained to the farmers (*hyakushō*) the basic provision of the village system, enjoined them to fear the *bakufu* laws, respect the daimyo (*ryōshu*) and shogunal deputies (*daikan*), to treat the village elders (*mura yakunin*) as parents. It established the five-family (*goningumi*) system of joint responsibility, and advocated the virtues of honesty, hard work, attention to crops, frugality, and abstention from luxuries such as wine and tobacco.[68] The 1643 prohibition against permanent alienation of land (*dembata-eitai-uri-oshioki*) attempted to stabilize the land economy of the villages.[69]

Regulations concerning the merchant and artisan classes were so numerous that it is hardly possible to single out any code or even set of codes which might constitute a basic *bakufu* policy. Perhaps the most inclusive and characteristic in this respect was the 1655 regulations for the city of Edo (*Edo machijū sadame*).

While these codes and regulations made up the most fundamental documents for the various sectors of Tokugawa government and society they by no means comprised the whole of Tokugawa legislation. In fact, the Tokugawa *bakufu* through its many judicial and administrative organs issued a constant barrage of decrees and proclamations which added constantly to the body of precedent in every field. The eighth shogun Yoshimune ordered a codification of existing law to be made which resulted in the 1742 *Osadamegaki*. The work was divided into two parts, one devoted to administrative decrees, the other to criminal injunctions. Later the contents of the *Osadamegaki* were distributed under topical headings for easier reference, giving rise to the 1767 *Kajo ruiten*. Subsequent *bakufu* decisions continued to pile up as *ofuregaki*, which were general proclamations issued by the senior councillors, *kakitsuke* or administrative notices to officials, and *tasshi* or direct orders to specific individuals or groups. Decisions of the judicial council (*hyōjōsho*) and the various *bakufu* courts also became part of a growing body of precedent. This vast body of judicial and legislative material, though primarily concerned with the affairs of the shogunal domains, applied with more or less directness to the administrative practices of the daimyo. And during the Tokugawa period the daimyo were obliged to keep

[68] Kanai Madoka, "Keian ofuregaki," *Rekishi kyōiku*, 4.10 (1956), 53-62.
[69] *Sekai rekishi jiten*, 22.336.

abreast of such *bakufu* directives and regulations, integrating them into their own administrative procedures or adopting them as laws requiring local enforcement. In this way the daimyo domains were woven ever more tightly into the fabric of a *bakufu* dominated national system, and to this extent the *bakufu* was able to establish the broad framework within which the daimyo exercised their "autonomy."

It is obvious then that the Tokugawa *baku-han* system, while built upon an authority structure which relied heavily upon feudal loyalties and a delegation of the powers of government, was nonetheless subject to strong centralizing (or at least unifying) forces emanating from the shogunate. The tendency to adopt uniform policies and procedures increased tremendously as the daimyo established their residences in Edo and themselves became part of an integrated, elite society. But while the tendency toward centralization was strong at the national level, it was even stronger within the lesser units of bureaucratic or territorial administration. The daimyo domains of which the Tokugawa system was composed, had carried the elimination of feudal decentralization much farther than had the shogun. This will become apparent as we return for a final look at the Kibi region and the province of Bizen.

XIII. BIZEN UNDER THE TOKUGAWA REGIME

THE great battle of Sekigahara which settled the fortunes of the Ukita and Tokugawa houses had an immediate and far-reaching impact upon the Kibi region. The battle ended once and for all the possibility of further civil war and the changing of the political map by force of arms. The era of the "Great Peace" was upon Japan. But the problems of adjustment to peace had only begun. The next half century was to be as unsettled a period in the affairs of Kibi as was the half century of wars which lay behind. The changes in personnel and in laws and regulations were as marked. Despite the lack of warfare the process of consolidation under the Tokugawa regime was eventful and traumatic.

The imposition of the *baku-han* political system upon Kibi was not an easy matter, and as with the fashioning of the basic elements of the Tokugawa control system, a number of decades had passed before the task was completed. After Sekigahara, for roughly a half century the Kibi area reacted under two consolidating processes. One was political and involved the intricate adjustment of the area into the Tokugawa balance of power and under shogunal administrative procedures. In the process large numbers of daimyo and Tokugawa officials moved into the area, frequently to be sent elsewhere or to be displaced by others. Bizen was obliged to live through three changes of daimyo rule before Ikeda Mitsumasa brought the province under secure control. The other problem of adjustment was administrative and involved the reorganization of local government and the institutions of popular control at the local level. Largely because of the decentralized structure of government authority under the Tokugawa shoguns, each daimyo and each *hatamoto* who held domains in the Kibi area was obliged to work out his own specific solution to the social and economic problems of his territory. The incidence of failure for one reason or another was great.

As a case study of the problems of adjustment to peaceful government after Sekigahara, and of the many different patterns which such adjustment took, the Kibi region provides a variety of insights. The three provinces of Mimasaka, Bitchū, and Bizen each fared quite differently in the years after Sekigahara and for reasons which appear to be inherent in the conditions which pertained under the Mōri and Ukita. Mimasaka, at first held in its entirety by a trusted *tozama* daimyo, eventually was divided between Tokugawa *fudai* holdings and shogunal *tenryō*. Bitchū became something of a catchall of pieces of shogunal territory, *hatamoto* domains, and small *tozama* holdings. Only Bizen remained intact under the administration of one daimyo, a *tozama* closely related to the Tokugawa house. As in most areas of western Japan, Kibi did not by any means pass completely into the hands of *fudai* or shogunal intendants. It was not for several years that direct Tokugawa control penetrated the region to any extent, and even then the penetration was spotty.

The battle of Sekigahara created a number of urgent feudal obligations which Ieyasu was obliged to pay off in grants of territory in western Japan. Thus in 1600 Ikeda Terumasa was given the entire province of Harima, while Kobayakawa Hideaki, the western turncoat, was rewarded with the bulk of the Ukita domain. The grant was specified at 510,000 *koku* and comprised all of Bizen and Mimasaka and 44,000 *koku* in Bitchū.[1] Bitchū, taken from the Mōri, was kept primarily in *tenryō* over which Kobori Shinsuke, newly established keeper of Matsuyama castle, was appointed "administrator-general" (*sōkan*).[2] Kobori, one of Hideyoshi's men, was originally from Yamato and had gained experience in administrative posts around the capital. Enlisted after Sekigahara and elevated to the status of *fudai* daimyo, with 10,000 *koku* in Bitchū and 5,000 *koku* in Yamato, he was used by Ieyasu as part of a "council of administrators" for western Japan. Besides the Kobori grant, a portion of land in Bitchū was assigned to three daimyo and a number of *hatamoto*. Togawa, former chief vassal of the Ukita, was given 30,000 *koku* at Niwase; Kinoshita, a close vassal of Hideyoshi who switched allegiances after Sekigahara, was given 25,000 *koku* at Ashimori.[3] Maida, a former petty retainer of Hideyoshi and ally of Ishida at Sekigahara, was given 10,000 *koku* at Asao.[4] Of the *hatamoto* the most important was Hanabusa, the former Ukita retainer, who received 8200 *koku* at famous Takamatsu castle. All told, the daimyo and *hatamoto* domains added up to about 130,000 *koku*, leaving some 170,000 *koku* of *tenryō* to be administered by Kobori out of Matsuyama castle.

[1] Miyake Senshū, "Edo jidai ni okern Bitchū ryōshu ni tsuite," *Setonaikai kenkyū*, 11 (1958), 47.
[2] *Tsūshi*, 2.374.   [3] *Ibid.*, 2.361.   [4] *Ibid.*, 2.352.

Most noteworthy is the fact that in all of Kibi not one assignment went to a house which had been of *fudai* or *hatamoto* standing during the Mikawa or Kantō stages in the growth of the Tokugawa house. All were late arrivals to the Tokugawa fold. Not all were ones which seemed on the surface to warrant the shogun's favor. The distribution of houses in Kibi must thus indicate the still uncertain Tokugawa hold in western Japan. And the return of former housemen of Ukita Hideie to Bitchū cannot have been accidental. They knew the area, and having been saved from the brink of oblivion at Sekigahara they could be counted on to be loyal to the Tokugawa. The new look of the feudal map in Kibi also strongly reflected the history of the local wars of consolidation which had preceded Sekigahara. The Ukita domain, which had been solidly unified, could be passed on as a unit. But Bitchū, which was on the fringe of the Mōri holdings, was still, as of 1600, divided into small castellanies. This pattern of fragmentation remained in evidence even after the ascendancy of the Tokugawa. No doubt also the looseness of Ukita control in Mimasaka had much to do with the eventual breakup of that province into small parcels of *tenryō* and *hatamoto* domains.

The assignment of Kobayakawa to Okayama turned out to be a stroke of irony which could hardly have been premeditated by Ieyasu. Hideaki, whose defection had brought on the collapse of the Ukita cause, had coveted Bizen openly. But in Okayama he found a seething opposition to his rule. He died insane in 1603, leaving no heir. This gave Ieyasu the opportunity to divide still further the former Ukita domain. Bizen (280,000 *koku*) plus 40,000 *koku* in Bitchū were given to the Ikeda of Harima. Mimasaka (186,500 *koku*) was assigned to Mori Tadamasa. Both were worthy *tozama* who had joined Ieyasu after Hideyoshi's death and before Sekigahara.[5]

The Osaka campaign and its aftermath brought on another round of changes in the distribution of military houses in Kibi. In Bitchū a number of new daimyo and *hatamoto* were created. Matsuyama castle passed into the hands of a branch of the Ikeda house of Okayama; the domain itself was increased to 65,000 *koku*. Another small *tozama* house, the Itō, was established at Okada and yet another, the Yamazaki, at Nariwa. Furthermore,

[5] *Ibid.*, 2.419.

a number of daimyo whose main domains were in other provinces received parcels of land in Bitchū to round out their total holdings. New *hatamoto* enfeoffed in Bitchū were mostly ex-vassals of the Ukita. The Hanabusa were given 5000 *koku* at Sarukake (the old headquarters of the Shō family), branches of the Togawa received Hayashima (3000 *koku*) and Obie (3000 *koku*), and a branch of the Hanabusa, taking the name to Sakakibara, received Tsudera (1000 *koku*). Most of these locations had housed castles at the time of the Takamatsu battle.[6]

Tokugawa authority in the Kibi area gained appreciably after 1641 when the *daikan* system of direct *bakufu* control over the *tenryō* was put into effect. In that year the Ikeda of Matsuyama were replaced by the Mizunoya (50,000 *koku*). At the same time management of the *tenryō* was assigned to a *daikan*, Yonekura Hiradayū, who was a minor *hatamoto*. Yonekura established an office (*daikansho*) at the port village of Kurashiki from which he administered the 90,000 *koku* or more of shogunal land which still remained in the area.[7] Thus the system whereby the shogun relied on daimyo to act as his distant representatives was superseded by a system of direct administration through an appointed officer. A few years later this system was extended to Mimasaka. The occasion was provided in 1697 when the Mori family lost the province to one of the Matsudaira line, a Tokugawa cadet house. The new keeper of Tsuyama castle was given a domain of only 97,000 *koku*. This left something over 130,000 *koku* for redistribution as minor *hatamoto* domains, *tenryō*, and one small daimyo domain, assigned to the Miura of Katsuyama (23,000 *koku*). In 1698 intendants were placed over shogunal territory in Mimasaka, but because of the mountainous topography three widely scattered *daikan* offices were required for the task.

By 1700 the three Kibi provinces had settled down to the pattern they were to maintain throughout the rest of the regime:

	(*koku*)
Bizen was held entire by the Ikeda of Okayama	280,000
Bitchū contained:	
Ikeda branch domains at Ikusaka, and	15,000
Kamogata	25,000

[6] *Ibid.*, 2.514.
[7] *Ibid.*, 2.231.

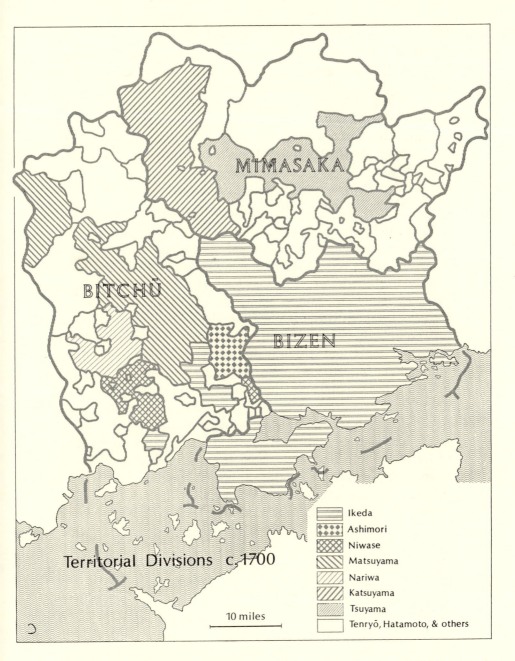

MIMASAKA

BITCHŪ

BIZEN

Territorial Divisions c. 1700

	Ikeda
	Ashimori
	Niwase
	Matsuyama
	Nariwa
	Katsuyama
	Tsuyama
	Tenryō, Hatamoto, & others

10 miles

Ikeda of Okayama holdings	35,000
daimyo located at Matsuyama, Ashimori, Niwase, and Nariwa	200,000
domain fragments, pieces held by daimyo based outside Bitchū	30,000

	koku
hatamoto domains	28,000
tenryō	50,000
Mimasaka contained:	
the Matsudaira of Tsuyama	97,000
the Miura of Katsuyama	23,000
domain fragments and *hatamoto* holdings	54,000
tenryō	28,800
lands administered by the Matsudaira or Miura for the *bakufu*	44,000

In the light of the long evolution of local rule in the Kibi area which we have followed to this point, the political map in 1700 had some rather remarkable features. Bitchū and Mimasaka, fragmented to the extreme, were divided into over thirty jurisdictions of many categories and sizes which bore little relationship to the provincial or district boundaries which had been so important up through the fifteenth century. Bizen alone retained its full territorial limits, and within it the daimyo revived the old district units (*kōri*) for administrative purposes. But this was about the limit of the retention of the former territorial boundaries. In Tokugawa times, although the geographical terminology of the imperial system was often used for purposes of identification (to locate a village or a fief), a very different concept of the limits of territorial jurisdiction persisted from Sengoku times. The domain, or *ryō*, was not defined by a specific boundary, but was conceived of as consisting of so many *koku* (generally in round figures at that). The domain was given form by putting together various pieces, big and small, of the countryside, adding here a village, subtracting there a half-district in order to make up the right number of *koku*. Even the daimyo of Bizen was given 35,000 *koku* in neighboring Bitchū to fill out his holdings.

One is struck also by the freedom with which the *bakufu* divided and redistributed territory or reassigned personnel in the Kibi area. Aside from Bizen, both Bitchū and Mimasaka had become increasingly fragmented as time went on. Was this a deterioration of the process of unification which had been carried forward by both the Ukita and Mōri, a retrogression to the days of local rivalry of the 1560's and 1570's? By 1700, daimyo or *hatamoto* had been placed at the sites of most of the major castles which had figured in the civil wars of the Sengoku period. Taka-

matsu, Sarukake, Nariwa, Matsuyama, Niimi, Katsuyama now
served as headquarters of small daimyo or *hatamoto,* though in
all instances but Matsuyama the former castles had been destroyed in the wars of consolidation. It is hard to know what was
in the minds of the *bakufu* officials who superintended the distribution of territory in this fashion. But the Tokugawa polity
did not lay much stress on the reduction of the number of administrative fragments as a desirable aim in itself. It may well
be that shatter zones like Bitchū and Mimasaka were kept as
buffers by the Tokugawa to stand between large daimyo. But it
is more likely that the areas served the more practical need of
providing repositories of small territorial units which could be
freely disposed of in order to make possible quick shifts in daimyo
holdings or to provide land for use in rewarding service to the
shogunate. The increasingly strong control exercised by the shogun's local intendants over such mixed areas meant that a counter-
current of uniform administration spread to unify these areas at
the same time that the fragmentation went on.

Bizen, however, was a different story. Whether because of the
strong foundation laid by the Ukita, or the Tokugawa concern
over the strategic importance of the area, or because of its natural
geographical homogeneity, Bizen, once unified by the Ukita, remained a single entity under the Tokugawa hegemony. As such
it found itself among some twenty or so other domains whose
borders included one or more of the traditional provinces. The
Ikeda domain as administered from Okayama consisted of all of
Bizen and 35,000 *koku* in adjoining Bitchū, a total of 315,000
koku. Its daimyo was ranked lord of a province and nineteenth
in the official scale of revenues. Bizen itself was an area of some
stature in Tokugawa Japan. Rich in agricultural produce because
of the large stretches of excellent farm land created by the delta
of its two rivers, centrally located on the Inland Sea trade route,
an important stop on the Sanyō highway, the domain figured im-
portantly both in the strategic thinking of the shogunate and in
the economic development of the country. From 1603 it came into
the hands of the Ikeda family to whose origin and rise we must
now turn.

THE Ikeda house provides one of the better examples of the
way in which *tozama* were integrated into the Tokugawa regime.

The Ikeda were also one of the more successful of the daimyo houses in perfecting the institutions of civil administration required by the years of peace which continued after Sekigahara. The Ikeda family originated in the province of Owari from which it rose to national prominence, first in the service of Nobunaga, then Hideyoshi, and finally Tokugawa Ieyasu. The head of the Ikeda house had the good fortune to shift his allegiance to Ieyasu many months in advance of Sekigahara.

Like many Tokugawa daimyo, the Ikeda managed to put together a genealogy which went back to the same Seiwa Genji as the Tokugawa house.[8] Some evidence exists to show that in Kamakura times the family resided in Ikeda-no-shō in Ikeda district of Mino province, probably serving as *jitō*. The family subsequently moved to Owari province. The first member of the family for which there is historical documentation is Tsunetoshi. Born into the Takigawa family of Ichiu castle in Ōmi province in 1509, he was adopted as heir to the Ikeda family and married to the adoptive father's daughter. Tsunetoshi served the Oda house of Owari in a minor capacity but suddenly through a twist of fortune became a vassal of particular importance. Tsunetoshi's wife, on giving birth to her first son in 1536, was able to become wet nurse to the infant Oda Nobunaga, thus setting up a strong bond between the Oda and Ikeda families.[9]

The son whose birth made possible the employment of Tsunetoshi's wife as wet nurse to Nobunaga was Ikeda Nobuteru. Born in 1536, Nobuteru became a childhood companion of Nobunaga and a favorite in the Oda house. In 1551 at the age of fifteen he "took his first head" in battle. In 1560 he was named captain (*samurai taishō*) and given command of thirty men. At this time he also received the honorific characters "nobu" from Nobunaga's name and "teru" from the shogun Yoshiteru's name and henceforth was known as Nobuteru.[10] Of the men commanded by Nobuteru at this time three were later to become Ikeda *karō* of daimyo status.[11] Throughout this period Nobuteru's mother, as the honored ex-wet-nurse of Nobunaga, continued in high regard in

[8] Ikeda-shi keifu, ms. in *Ikeda-ke bunko*. Henceforth cited as Keifu. References to photocopy, Michigan University Library, A.2-3.

[9] *Ibid.*, A.8.

[10] *Ibid.*, A.9.

[11] *Ikeda-ke rireki-ryakki*, Yoshida Tokutarō ed. (2 vols. Okayama, 1963), 1.7 (Eiroku 5). Henceforth cited as *Rireki-ryakki*.

the Oda household and was given a special fief for her support.[12]

Nobuteru rose rapidly in Nobunaga's service. In 1566 he was established as castellan at Kita castle receiving a fief of 3000 *kan* at Araodani. In 1570 he had advanced to 10,000 *kan* and the castle of Inuyama. From this point Nobuteru began to play a major part in Nobunaga's conquests, fighting against the "lawless priests" of Osaka and against the Araki of Settsu. In the capture of Hanakuma castle in 1580, one of Nobuteru's major conquests, he was joined by his two sons. As reward he was raised to a 100,000 *koku* domain in Settsu and given command of Osaka castle. Both his sons were made castle commanders as well.[13] From Osaka he joined Hideyoshi in the conquest of Awaji, and in 1581 he mobilized his forces to support Hideyoshi in the attack on the Mōri at Takamatsu. When Nobunaga was killed at Honnōji, Nobuteru joined with Hideyoshi to crush Akechi. Then with Hideyoshi, Niwa Nagahide, and Shibata Katsuie he participated in the Kiyosu conference to decide the succession to the Oda house. In 1583 he joined Hideyoshi in heading off Shibata's move for power. At this time he moved his domain to Mino, receiving 130,000 *koku* as keeper of Ōgaki castle. His eldest son now held Nobunaga's old castle of Gifu, and his second son held Ikejiri castle in Mino.[14] In 1584 Nobuteru joined Hideyoshi in the war against Oda Nobuo and Tokugawa Ieyasu. Leading a force of 12,000 men he entered the Nagakute campaign but was routed by Ieyasu. He and his eldest son were both killed and their heads taken by the Tokugawa.[15]

The unfortunate deaths of Nobuteru and his eldest son left only a minor as the surviving direct heir to the Ikeda house. Technically the house could have been extinguished at this point. But Hideyoshi permitted Terumasa (Nobuteru's second son) to succeed to the family holdings. Terumasa was an extremely able military leader and had already seen much military action. As one of Hideyoshi's most vigorous followers he received Hideyoshi's surname Hashiba in 1587 after a brilliant performance in the campaign against the Shimazu. In the next year he received the lower fourth court rank junior grade and the surname Toyotomi. For his

[12] Keifu, A.7.

[13] *Rireki-ryakki*, 1.21-24 (Tenshō 8).

[14] Tottori-han shi kōhon, ms. in Tottori Kenritsu Toshokan. References to photocopy, Michigan University Library, a.238-239.

[15] *Ibid.*, a.240-241.

services in the campaign against the Hōjō of Odawara, he was transferred to Mikawa (Ieyasu's old home province) and given 152,000 *koku* at Yoshida castle.

Terumasa was one of five daimyo not sent to Korea. His services were used instead to supervise the handling of supplies and provisions at the port of embarkation in Kyushu. He was also counted on to prevent any hostile military action in the eastland. In 1594, on Hideyoshi's order, he took as his second wife one of Tokugawa Ieyasu's daughters. Thus when Ishida Mitsunari began his intrigue against Ieyasu in 1598, Terumasa was inclined to side with the Tokugawa. Terumasa became one of a number of former Toyotomi vassals who joined Ieyasu against the Uesugi in 1600. When news came of Ishida's organization of a force against Ieyasu, Terumasa quickly swore allegiance to Ieyasu. He joined in the fighting at Sekigahara, helped to rout the Chōsokabe forces, and also guarded the Tokugawa rear against the Mōri. Following the battle, he aided in clearing Osaka castle of Mōri and Mashita forces. His services on behalf of the Tokugawa were among the most vigorous, and as reward he was given the strategically important Himeji castle and 520,000 *koku* in Harima. Among the daimyo Terumasa now stood ninth in the country. In addition his brother Nagayoshi had received 60,000 *koku* at Tottori castle in Inaba and in 1603 his second son Tadatsugu received all of Bizen's 280,000 *koku,* and his wife received 40,000 *koku* in Bitchū.[16]

Terumasa was one of the first daimyo to travel to Edo to pledge his allegiance to the new shogun. He was given the signal honor of being met at the Hakone pass by Ōkubo and Ando, two of Ieyasu's elders. In 1604 Ieyasu visited Terumasa's residence in Fushimi and presented him with 2000 pieces (*ryō*) of gold and 100 varieties of gifts. In the next few years he received other gifts —including a falconry preserve in Musashi—from Toyotomi Hideyori, from the emperor, and from the shogun. In 1610 his third son Tadao received 60,000 *koku* in Awaji. Since both his sons were yet minors Terumasa actually controlled their domains, and hence his total holdings were 860,000 *koku*. Including the lands of other family members, the total approached 1,000,000 *koku* and put the Ikeda family next to the Maeda in importance.

---

[16] Keifu, A.11; Tottori-han shi kōhon, a.245-246.

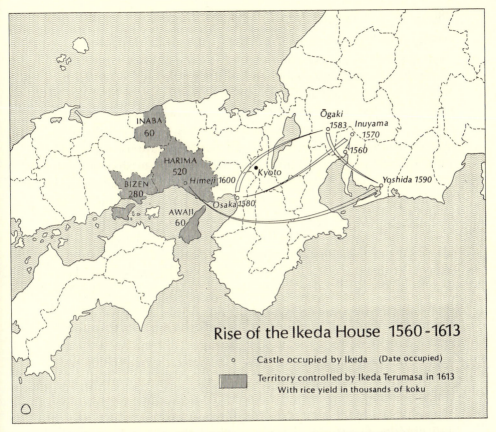

INABA
60

Ōgaki
1583 Inuyama
1570
1560

HARIMA
520

BIZEN
280

Himeji 1600

Kyoto

Yoshida 1590

AWAJI
60

Osaka 1580

Rise of the Ikeda House 1560-1613

○   Castle occupied by Ikeda   (Date occupied)

▨   Territory controlled by Ikeda Terumasa in 1613
    With rice yield in thousands of koku

He was popularly called "shogun of the west" (*saigoku-shōgun*). Treated with utmost respect by Ieyasu, he had received the honorary surname Matsudaira and the third court rank by the time of his death in 1613.[17]

The years just before 1613 brought the Ikeda house to the pinnacle of its power. Its rise had been rapid, and like that of the Ukita had been based primarily upon military prowess. For the Ikeda, victories in battle had been translated into advancement in land holdings and court ranks. Even more quickly than the Ukita, the Ikeda had been caught up in the unification movement. Constantly rising, but also constantly subject to transfer and reassignment, Nobuteru and Terumasa grew accustomed to the mobile life of the camp and the constant shifting of domains. Riding the crest of success on the winning side in the unification struggle, the Ikeda and their vassals were urged on to extend their capacities and to perform larger and larger feats of warfare and

[17] Tottori-han shi kōhon, a.246,

territorial administration. Thus after each battle the Ikeda absorbed into their corps of housemen (*kashindan*) new talent from among the military personnel cut adrift by the civil wars. In this way the Ikeda houseband both expanded and gained in practical experience, and it was this factor of growth which made possible the steady rise of the house from the status of a small daimyo's stipended retainer to become in just two generations one of the three or four most powerful among the military aristocracy.

Terumasa's castle at Himeji was one of the outstanding fortifications in Japan; today it stands as a national monument, one of the few fully preserved great castles of the Tokugawa period. Known as the White Heron Castle (*shirasagi-jō*), its white walls above the massive stone ramparts are a landmark for miles around. When Terumasa moved to Himeji a castle with three-storied keep was in existence, having been built by Hideyoshi in 1581 when he was preparing for his move against the Mōri. This castle proved completely inadequate either to hold Terumasa's large military establishment or to serve as the foremost fortress west of the capital. (Himeji was now expected to be the strong-point from which west central Japan and Kyushu could be kept under control.)[18] Terumasa recruited laborers from Harima, Bizen, and Mimasaka to build alongside the three-storied structure a new and grander five-storied keep, enlarging the entire base of the fortress. Today the keep rises 109 feet from its base and 260 feet from the level of the outer moat. Aside from the main castle and its battlements, three other large enclosures were constructed to protect samurai residences and garrison quarters. An outside moat 180 feet wide enclosed an area some two miles in diameter. Beyond this was the commercial section consisting of 88 city blocks.[19]

Like the other great daimyo houses we have studied, the Ikeda by this time were in command of a vast assemblage of retainers, many of whom were enfeoffed at more than 10,000 *koku*. The top ten vassals who served under Terumasa at Himeji had fiefs of the following size:

	(*koku*)
Igi Nagato	33,000
Ikeda Dewa	32,000

---

[18] *Ikeda Mitsumasa-kō den*, Ishizaka Zenjirō, pub. (2 vols., Tokyo, 1932), 1.186. Henceforth cited as *Mitsumasa-kō*.

[19] *Rireki-ryakki*, 1.60-61 (Keichō 6).

Ikeda Shinkichi	22,000
Hiki Buzen	14,000
Ikeda Shimōsa	14,000
Tokura Shinano	10,000
Arao Tajima	10,000
Arao Shima	7,000
Niwa Yamashiro	5,000
Dohi Suō	5,000

The total number of enfeoffed vassals was 1074, of which only a handful held less than 100 *koku*. Stipended retainers were many times more numerous. Terumasa divided his retainers into two major divisions which in turn were grouped into some 100 military units, or *kumi*.[20]

Upon his death Ikeda Terumasa left a great store of military supplies and treasure which, divided among his sons and kinsmen, amounted to 75 naval ships, 36,984 pounds of gunpowder, 1212 muskets, 513 bags of shot each containing 260 pellets, 56,378 pounds of lead, 14,772 pounds of saltpeter, 3702 pounds of sulfur, 1123 bows, 1640 arrows, 122 suits of armor, 400 pieces of gold, 100 *kan* of silver, numerous famous swords, and art objects.[21] Such were the private resources which could be amassed by the warrior daimyo of the era of consolidation.

Tokugawa policy toward Ikeda Terumasa was understandably ambivalent. As a trustworthy *tozama*, Ieyasu looked upon the Ikeda to counterbalance the still dangerous Toyotomi group at Osaka, but it was always dangerous to permit a daimyo to grow so large. Thus after Terumasa's death and with the elimination of the Osaka threat, Ieyasu was able to effect a division of the Ikeda house and a reduction of its holdings. Terumasa's death, coming just before the Osaka campaign, was most unfortunate for the Ikeda fortunes. Even more so was the series of deaths among the next generation of male members of the family which came in quick succession after 1615. It was this turn of events which eventually gave the *bakufu* the opportunity to split up the great territory left by Terumasa. By 1632 the Ikeda house had been divided into two separate branches, the combined holdings of which totaled less than 700,000 *koku*. This proved a bitter blow to

[20] *Mitsumasa-kō*, 1.196-216.
[21] *Rireki-ryakki*, 1.93-97 (Keichō 17).

the Ikeda who never really accepted the reduction of their domains. And to the end of the Tokugawa period the two divisions
of the house between them continued to support the same number of vassals as there had been in Terumasa's heyday, scaling
down the income of each houseman in proportion to the reduction in the overall size of the Ikeda holdings.

On Terumasa's death, Ieyasu made the following disposition
of the main Ikeda holdings. The eldest son, Toshitaka, received
Himeji and 420,000 *koku* in Harima; the second son, Tadatsugu,
retained Bizen and three districts of Harima for a total of 380,000
koku; and the third son, Tadao, retained Awaji. These Ikeda
brothers figured prominently in the Osaka campaigns, leading
many assaults on the castle. When Tadatsugu died in 1615, Tadao
was given Bizen, and the three districts of Harima were divided
among other members of the family. Then in 1616 Toshitaka
died suddenly, leaving a seven-year-old heir, Mitsumasa. This
boy was not permitted to retain Harima. On the pretext that
Himeji castle was too important strategically, Mitsumasa was
removed to Tottori and given a domain of 320,000 *koku* in Inaba
and Hōki. Ikeda Nagayoshi, keeper of Tottori castle, was moved
to Matsuyama in Bitchū to make room for Mitsumasa.[22] Thus the
Ikeda were deprived of Himeji, and though there was some feel-
ing that the *bakufu* had promised one day to return them to
Harima, they were never to return.

Tadao governed Bizen with distinction, working energetically
to put it on to a peacetime footing by clarifying the civil laws
and precedents. But his death in 1632 left a child, Mitsunaka, as
his heir, and again the *bakufu* intervened. This time Bizen was
considered too important to be held by a minor, and on this pretext an exchange of domains between Mitsumasa (of Tottori)
and Mitsunaka took place. In 1641 the branch of the Ikeda family
in Bitchū lost Matsuyama, and when the last of the minor lines
in Harima died out in 1678, the Ikeda had been reduced to the
two domains of Okayama and Tottori. For Bizen the modern history of the area really begins in 1632 with Mitsumasa's entry into
Okayama castle.

Fortunately for the Ikeda both Mitsumasa and Mitsunaka
proved able administrators and passed on their domains to a long

[22] *Tsūshi*, 2.377.

line of successors until the Restoration of 1868. In fact, from the low point in 1632 the Ikeda raised their overall status as daimyo somewhat. In 1672 Mitsumasa's second son, Masakoto, was given a separate domain of 25,000 *koku* at Kamogata in Bitchū, and his third son, Terutoshi, a smaller domain of 15,000 at Ikusaka in Bitchū.[23] These two branch *han* (*shihan*) served the Ikeda of Bizen in somewhat the same fashion as the three cadet houses of the Tokugawa. The Tottori Ikeda likewise created two branch domains of 25,000 *koku* and 15,000 *koku*.

With the breakup of the Ikeda domains, and in line with the new policy of more uninhibited control begun by Iemitsu, the Okayama and Tottori Ikeda came under more direct and exacting *bakufu* regulation after 1632. No longer treated as honored military allies who had fought at the side of the head of the Tokugawa house, the *tozama* were gradually handled in much the same way as the *fudai*. Toward the Ikeda the *bakufu* preserved an attitude of constant vigilance although numerous tokens of repect passed between the shogun and the Ikeda daimyo. The Tottori branch of the house, because it descended from the union of Terumasa and Tokugawa Ieyasu's second daughter, was given a status equivalent to that of *kamon*. Both Toshitaka and Mitsumasa received adoptive daughters of Tokugawa shoguns as wives. In turn, Mitsumasa's daughter was adopted by Iemitsu and given in marriage to the Ichijō family, one of the court nobility.[24] Such entwining of marriage and adoption ties was calculated to draw the Ikeda into a network of obligations toward the shogun and thus make them more answerable to Tokugawa domination. The effort was not without its results. The Okayama Ikeda remained loyal to the Tokugawa house and were notably inactive in opposing the *bakufu* in the last years of the regime. In 1863 the Bizen Ikeda had even adopted as head of the house and daimyo of Okayama a brother of Tokugawa Yoshinobu, the last shogun.

To THE house of Ikeda fell the task of pacifying Bizen and establishing a stable form of local administration under the Tokugawa regime. As of 1603 Bizen was still under wartime conditions. The confusion which had attended the destruction of the house of Ukita at Sekigahara had been little relieved by the three years

---

[23] *Ibid.*, 2.323-331. [24] Keifu, A.25.

of Kobayakawa rule. Kobayakawa Hideaki, but 21 years old in 1600, was a vain and unstable person. Adopted by Hideyoshi while still a young boy, he became adoptive heir to Kobayakawa Takakage of Chikuzen at the age of thirteen. In 1597, when he was only 18, he succeeded to the head of the Kobayakawa house and in the same year was named commander-in-chief of the second Korean expeditionary force. In Korea Hideaki's rash deeds displeased Hideyoshi; and Ishida Mitsunari accused him of endangering the success of the expedition by his erratic behavior. Before Hideyoshi's death, Hideaki was called back to Fushimi and was reprimanded. "For a senior commander to compete for exploits in battle with his troops and to fight so carelessly," the angry Hideyoshi had exclaimed, "is most unbecoming."[25] Hideaki formed a deep hatred of Ishida Mitsunari, whom he accused of setting Hideyoshi against him. And it is easy to see how his sympathy turned to Ieyasu once Hideyoshi had died. Before the battle of Sekigahara, Hideaki had already coveted the Ukita domains and had bargained his fidelity to the western cause for the prospect of replacing the Ukita at Okayama. When, after the battle, he heard that he was to receive only the 280,000 *koku* of Bizen, he complained that this would give him no more than he already held in Chikuzen. He apparently managed to persuade Ieyasu to add Mimasaka to his grant.[26]

In Okayama, Hideaki acted the moody and erratic despot. His agents were ruthless in their disciplinary measures and tax exactions, while he himself wasted his time in amusements. Under his orders his *karo* undertook a new land survey, redrawing the boundaries of cultivated plots, bringing to light new fields, increasing tax assessments, and further restricting the holdings of temples and shrines. Also in response to Tokugawa orders a large number of castles were destroyed, leaving only Kanagawa, Tsuneyama, and Kokura in active use besides the main fortress at Okayama. Demolition of Tomiyama and Numa castles made possible the further expansion of Okayama castle.[27]

But Hideaki himself after coming to Okayama took pleasure in little more than falconry and the hunt. On one occasion he arbitrarily ordered the death sentence for an innocent man. When his councillors intervened, he turned against them and plotted

[25] *Okayama-shi shi*, 2.1687.
[26] *Ibid.*, 2.1691.   [27] *Ibid.*, 2.1691-1692.

their deaths. Later he ordered his most trusted councillor killed, and then, reversing himself, sent out a messenger to call back the man who had been dispatched to perform the execution. But it was too late, for the deed had been done. News of this senseless action shook his retainers, while outside Bizen the ex-housemen of the Ukita, many of whom had been enfeoffed in Bitchū, agitated against Hideaki. The Togawa of Niwase even threw up defenses on the border between Bitchū and Bizen in anticipation of Hideaki's retaliation. By 1602 the Bizen domain was in turmoil, one *karō* had fled to Osaka, another, the keeper of Kokura castle, had abandoned his command, still another took refuge with the Togawa, and yet another fled Okayama in a woman's palanquin. A rumor that the spirit of the falsely killed *karō* haunted Okayama castle swept through the domain. Hideaki in a fit of insanity died in 1602 at the age of 23.[28]

The three years of Kobayakawa rule had thus ended in great confusion. When in 1603 Ikeda Toshitaka in the name of Tadatsugu assumed the administration of Bizen, a most difficult task confronted him. Problems of samurai discipline, economic recovery, and domain administrative organization had long been neglected. The eventual enforcement of law and order in Bizen followed in most ways the course of development which typified other parts of the country as the Tokugawa regime matured and the administrations of the daimyo were improved and adapted to peaceful conditions. Most of the daimyo who fought to hegemony under Tokugawa Ieyasu had been men of outstanding qualities of leadership. But their talents had been chiefly those of the battlefield. Able military leaders, clever strategists, effective in the exaction of matériel from their domains, vigorous in the discipline of their vassals and troops, they faced an entirely new order of problems when they entered the era of peaceful rule which followed Sekigahara. Kobayakawa Hideaki and many others like him who craved the excitement of battle succumbed. Those who succeeded in the years that followed were obliged to exercise their leadership in other fields, primarily in the areas of domestic reform involving the management of the land and the people.[29]

[28] *Ibid.*, 2.1694-1695.
[29] Itō Tasaburō, "Kinsei daimyō kenkyū josetsu," *Shigaku zasshi*, 55.9; 11 (September and November, 1944), 9.14. Henceforth cited as Itō, "Daimyō."

The foundations for daimyo rule had of course been laid in Bizen by the previous inhabitants of Okayama castle. The first land resurvey had been carried out. The castle was being converted to an administrative center, but within the domain the remnants of feudal decentralization were still strongly in evidence, and the overwhelming emphasis on military preparation distorted the flow of the economic and cultural energies of the area. In the century after Sekigahara the many tendencies toward administrative centralization which characterized the policies of the great *sengoku-daimyō* were extended and amplified. By the end of the seventeenth century nearly all daimyo had successfully withdrawn their retainers from the land and had clipped their ability to touch the peasants directly. The private fief had been absorbed into the daimyo's uniform field administration. As a consequence the peasantry and other classes as well came to acquire a more uniform public identity under the laws of the *bakufu* and daimyo. Above the villagers the daimyo and their retainers stood, not as manorial lords or patriarchal superiors, but as rulers and officials.

It is this subtle but fundamental change in the whole structure of society and the exercise of authority in Japan which marked the transition from the age of the *sengoku-daimyō* to that of the Tokugawa *baku-han* system. As the daimyo relied increasingly on the technique of organizing their housemen into functional units, as the *bushi* left the villages to congregate in the castle towns, as the cultivating class earned the legal status of *hyakushō*, and as the merchant community grew wealthy in the castle towns, the old forms of social organization through familial or feudal associations were replaced, and their function taken over by more impersonal practices. Increasingly society was administered in terms of broadly conceived groups or statuses which reflected the functional structure of domain society, that is, in terms of farmers, artisans, merchants, administrative and military officers, and priests. Throughout Japanese society the authority relationships between lord and vassal, between enfeoffed proprietor and cultivator, between patriarchal family head and attached household, these essentially vertical systems were being replaced by more generalized, horizontally defined, functional group relationships. New generalized concepts of status or estate (*mibun*) were relied on increasingly as the basis for legal and administrative practice.

But the spread of this new functional approach to social organization created yet another need, that the daimyo devise a more rational basis of authority, a new ideological foundation for his rule and the type of society it embraced. It was this requirement which put a premium upon the daimyo's ability to civilize himself and to assume the guise of the enlightened despot. And it was in this context that the Tokugawa reliance on Confucian ethical values and concepts of social structure played such important roles. The successful daimyo after 1600 was one who learned to master the ethical-rational system of beliefs which supported his right to rule as a benevolent autocrat committed to the welfare of his subjects.[30] These in most general terms were the tasks which lay before the daimyo as they took up after so many decades of warfare the "problems of peace." For the Tokugawa shogunate the task was not complete until the 1650's. For the daimyo the process took even longer. In Bizen it was not until the 1680's that the institutional foundations had been stabilized.

The first years of Ikeda rule in Bizen were turbulent and full of vigorous activity. From 1603 to 1615, it will be recalled, Bizen was administered as part of the large composite domain headed by Terumasa of Himeji. We can infer the unsettled conditions Terumasa found in his domains from the first brief pronouncements which he issued upon arriving in Harima. These read, "There shall be no indiscriminate cutting of bamboo or trees. No one shall seize empty houses or uncultivated land. There shall be no seizure of the wives or children of the previous daimyo's retainers (*kyūnin*). Collection of taxes will be based on last year's figures. If there be farmers who have been taken into service they shall return to their villages promptly. If anyone demands of farmers more than is proper, the village as a group may seize him and bring him to us for handling. . . ."[31]

Bizen, of course, was given a somewhat separate administration at this time under Terumasa's son and his regent, Ikeda Toshitaka. Okayama remained the center of the Bizen domain, and for administrative purposes a suitable body of Ikeda retainers was detached for service in Bizen. Toshitaka's rule in Bizen is revealed in general outline by a partial collection of laws issued by him

[30] *Ibid.*, 9.19.   [31] *Tsūshi*, 2.191.

and transmitted to later generations under the title *Bushū-sama hōrei*. We know thereby that his first acts upon entering Bizen were to distribute fiefs (*chigyōwari*) and assign major vassals to strategic locations. Toshitaka was particularly concerned about guarding the main entrances to Bizen from adjoining provinces and the seaport towns on the Inland Sea. The increased importance of sea communication is revealed by the fact that Toshitaka built a new castle at Shimotsui on the Inland Sea, replacing Tsuneyama which was located on Kojima Bay, as the main outpost on the sea frontier.[32]

Having seen to the defense of the domain Toshitaka was able to turn to its domestic needs. Early priority was given to the land, the peasantry, and the status of the samurai. Fief allotments and the structure of administrative control over the daimyo's lands were clarified under laws dated 1603. Free use of forest and meadow was restricted, farmers who had left their fields were ordered back to their villages, and a system of rural controls under district superintendents (*kōri bugyō*) and intendants (*daikan*) was extended over the entire domain.[33] In 1604 the most comprehensive, and probably the first complete, cadastral survey of all Bizen was undertaken. Commissioners (*kenchi bugyō*) were appointed and stringent regulations were issued to avoid corruption or bias so as to assure a completely new and impartial survey.[34] From extant copies of this survey we know that the standard system was followed under which parcels of land were registered as wet or dry; their quality was assessed as good, medium, poor; their dimensions and area were carefully recorded and the cultivator or the individual responsible for tax payment was named. This work became the foundation upon which all later Ikeda tax assessments of rural Bizen were based.[35]

A large portion of Toshitaka's injunctions dealt with the duties of farmers and the rights of fief holders over their land and its cultivators. Laws were issued to regulate the use of forced labor and domestic service by the *bushi*, and to break indentured service ties. One provision states that if farmers were used for

---

[32] Hampō Kenkyūkai, ed., *Hampōshū, 1, Okayama-han* (2 vols., Tokyo, 1959), 2.943-944 (Bushū-sama hōrei). Henceforth cited as *Hampōshū*.

[33] *Ibid.*, 2.931 (Bushū-sama hōrei).

[34] *Ibid.*, 2.933 (Bushū-sama hōrei).

[35] Taniguchi, "Bizen hansei," 6.

labor service beyond a specified term they must be recompensed at the official rate of four *shō* of rice per day.[36] The daimyo's local officials were given jurisdiction over problems arising from conflicts between fief holders and farmers. Thus while the allocation of fiefs continued, the powers of the fief holders were held in check by the daimyo.

Methods of tax collection and determination of the tax rate were also standardized. In the fiefs, tax rates were still arranged by mutual agreement between proprietor and cultivator. The domain, however, put pressure on the fief holders to adopt a uniform rate. There is some indication that an overall rate of six to the government and four to the cultivator was exacted, as evidence the statement in *Biyōki* that the total income of Bizen was 222,310 *koku* and the tax collected was 137,461 *koku,* roughly 60 percent.[37] (Comparisons with later tax yields are difficult because of the changing tax base.) In addition to the main rice tax a forage tax (*nukawara dai*) was exacted at the rate of 10 *koku* per 100 *koku* of tax paid. Taxes in lieu of labor service were set at 6 *koku* per 100 *koku* of tax. The distance over which *hyakushō* were required to transport their tax rice free of charge was set at 5 *ri* (12 miles).[38]

As a more effective means of organizing the Ikeda housemen, Toshitaka extended the system of *kumi* units whereby "group chiefs" were made accountable for the discipline and the handling of personal requests or grievances of the men assigned to them.[39] The conduct of the housemen was regulated by sumptuary edicts, curfew regulations, and other rules of behavior. When the Ikeda house was called upon to contribute to the building of Edo and Sumpu castles, the entire retinue was obliged to share the burden. Tables of income deductions were issued to the housemen. As work teams left Okayama for Edo or Sumpu, Toshitaka showered them with admonitions. The men of Bizen were warned not to fraternize or quarrel with the men of other domains, to restrict their expenditures, to be frugal in their food and lodging, and especially to refrain from visiting (the gay towns of) Kyoto or Kiyosu. For infraction of each of these provisions a scale of fines

[36] *Hampōshū,* 2.934 (Bushū-sama hōrei).
[37] Taniguchi, "Bizen hansei," 8.
[38] *Hampōshū,* 2.934 (Bushū-sama hōrei).
[39] *Ibid.,* 2.933.

was posted. Thus a visit to Kyoto was punishable at 10 pieces of silver, to Kiyosu one piece of silver for a samurai and one string of cash for his attendant or a worker.[40] The conduct of the Bizen groups in Edo was a matter of particular concern. They were warned to obey *bakufu* laws implicitly, not to walk about the streets of Edo, not to enter gaming establishments or bath houses, and to refrain from sight-seeing.[41]

Under Toshitaka the castle town of Okayama was still further enlarged, the system of canals and moats around the castle was improved, and regulations on the status and conduct of the merchant class were further elaborated. Street guards were posted and unauthorized persons were subject to inspection. The sale or purchase of city houses was made subject to approval of the daimyo's city commissioner and the city elders. Injunctions were issued against gambling, begging, streetwalking, and the playing of the *shamisen* and *shakuhachi* in the streets. Punishments for the handling of stolen property, the abuse of horses, smoking of tobacco, and a host of other acts were made public.[42]

Toshitaka thus began the process of legislation for the peace-time regulation of the various classes of people in the Bizen domain. One is struck by the rather haphazard, pragmatic nature of his injunctions. Most of them were short and were directed to specific administrative problems. The era of comprehensive codes governing whole areas of political or economic behavior had not yet arrived.

In 1615 Ikeda Tadao succeeded his brother Tadatsugu in Bizen, and Toshitaka's regency in Okayama ended. Tadao had had experience in governing the Awaji domain of 63,000 *koku* and had distinguished himself in the Osaka campaigns. In 1619 he was called upon to lead a contingent of troops to Hiroshima to handle the transfer of Hiroshima castle from the Fukushima house to the Asano house. During the seventeen years he remained in Okayama he also handled effectively Bizen's share in constructing Osaka castle and in making repairs on Edo castle. Thus there is every indication that he served with distinction among the leading daimyo under Ieyasu and Hidetada.[43] With the death of Toshitaka in 1616 and the removal of Mitsumasa to Tottori, an overall tightening up of the Ikeda establishment be-

[40] *Ibid.*, 2.935-940.　　[41] *Ibid.*, 2.941-942.　　[42] *Ibid.*, 2.931-932.
[43] *Tottori-han shi kōhon*, a.258-266.

came necessary. The great band of vassals assembled by Teru-masa was divided into two, and Bizen, no longer overshadowed by the adjoining Ikeda holdings in Harima, began to develop more fully as an independent domain.

Beginning in 1624 Tadao issued a series of codes which summarized and expanded the work of Toshitaka and clarified domain policy on a variety of issues and with respect to the major social groups. First came the code governing discipline within Okayama castle during the daimyo's absence in Edo. It assigned responsibility for command of the castle and administration of the rural areas, exhorted the inspectoral staff (*yokome*) to vigilance, and laid down rules of conduct for the housemen.[44] Another code contained rules for the behavior for housemen while on the road between Okayama and Edo. It enjoined the housemen to deport themselves as gentlemen, pay their bills promptly, and refrain from taking unauthorized side trips. A third code governed conduct of the Bizen housemen while in Edo, admonishing them to obey Tokugawa laws, not to fraternize with men from other provinces, to avoid prostitution and public bath houses, not to walk about the Edo streets, and to behave themselves as gentlemen within the quarters assigned them.[45]

In 1625 a twenty-three-clause code standardized bureaucratic procedure in the domain. It set down rules for office hours, procurement and purchase of office supplies, conduct of the private household affairs of the daimyo's retainers, the system of guard duty, and many other like subjects. This was followed in 1626 by further regulations on administrative service, the provision of extra allowances for certain duties (*tashimai*), the recruiting of domestic and official service from the villages (*hōkōnin*), purchase and sale of goods, house rentals, interest rates on loans (15 percent per year on silver, 20 percent on rice) and many other matters. A three-clause code established procedures for determining the land tax on the basis of yearly inspection. A series of lengthy regulations set the exchange rate between cash and silver (1 string to 17 *me* of silver), prohibited the setting of discriminatory rates on various types of coins, outlined exchange procedures, regulated travel and the use of post horses, and set rates for porterage (for horses 3 *bu* of silver or 17 *mon* of copper per *ri*

---

[44] *Hampōshū*, 2.951 (Tadao-sama hōrei).
[45] *Ibid.*, 2.951-952.

[2.44 mi.] and for a porter 7 *mon* per *ri*). In 1627 provisions were made for the relief of farmers who were instructed to supplement their economy by cutting and selling firewood. Further regulations touched on the sale of commodities, supervision of the Inland Sea ports, and the purchase of seed rice by farmers.[46] The collected regulations of Tadao end at this point. Whether the work of codification had been completed for the time being or whether later documents were lost is not clear. But the sum of Tadao's legislation had provided a firm foundation for the administration of Bizen.

Meanwhile the member of the Ikeda family who was to inherit the Bizen domain was gathering experience and stature in Tottori. Ikeda Mitsumasa, son of Toshitaka and grandson to both Terumasa and Ieyasu, was brought up from the start as a ruler of men. Greatly favored by Ieyasu, he was frequently in the company of the shogun or his chief ministers. Legends of Mitsumasa's youth tell of a bright and eager boy with a constant drive to prove himself the heir to a noble line of warriors and administrators. "When Mitsumasa first was presented to Ieyasu at the age of five, he received a sword from the shogun. On this occasion as he sat by Ieyasu, the shogun patted him on his boyish head and said, 'You are the grandson of Terumasa; hurry and become a man.' Mitsumasa in a twinkling drew from its scabbard the sword he had just received and in a mannish gesture showed his ability to the shogun. Ieyasu, exclaiming, 'Watch out, that's dangerous!,' took up the scabbard and slipped back the sword. After Mitsumasa had left Ieyasu turned to his companions and said, 'Did you notice the sparkle in his eyes? He will not be an ordinary man.' "[47]

Mitsumasa was but eight years old when his father died, and the *bakufu* stepped in to deprive him of Harima. This was a most unwelcome turn of events, especially for the main line of the Ikeda house. Not only did this cause a decline in the strategic importance of the house but it meant a considerable loss in size of its domain, a fall from roughly 500,000 to 320,000 *koku*. There is some indication that the Ikeda elders had been given to be-

---

[46] *Ibid.*, 2.952-962.

[47] Ōzawa Koresada, "Kibi onko hiroku, Yūhiroku," in *Kibi gunsho shūsei* (10 vols., Tokyo, 1932), 10.503. For a recent study of Mitsumasa see Taniguchi Sumio, *Ikeda Mitsumasa* (Tokyo, 1961).

lieve that once Mitsumasa reached maturity Harima and its
500,000 *koku* would be returned to him by the *bakufu*. At any
rate, as the Ikeda left Harima for Inaba and Hōki, they kept
alive the hope of returning by retaining in service the entire
retinue of housemen who had been gathered at the great Himeji
castle. Moreover, they resorted to a complicated practice of in-
flating the production figures of the new domain so as to retain
on paper the semblance of the larger domain they had just left.
According to this practice, called "adjusting the assessment"
(*naoshi daka*), Mitsumasa's advisers continued to use in a nominal
way the same fief and salary figures which had been used in
Harima, merely calculating the real income from these nominal
figures on the basis of the ratio between 320,000 to 500,000. Thus
if 100 *koku* in Harima yielded 100 bags of rice, in Tottori the
yield would be only thirty-two—fiftieths of one hundred, or 64
bags. The appearances of a 500,000 *koku* domain were de-
liberately maintained in Tottori, and later on in Bizen when
Mitsumasa moved there.[48]

Because of Mitsumasa's youth the move to Tottori had been
handled by a council of his senior retainers under the watchful
eyes of two Tokugawa inspectors. The shogun's men stayed in
Tottori for a hundred days, overseeing the transfer, inspecting
the domain, codifying and enforcing the basic laws. Since most
of Mitsumasa's senior vassals were young and inexperienced at
the time, the two elder of them, Hiki and Tokura, were named
chief ministers.[49]

Little is known about the laws and practices devised by Mitsumasa in Tottori between 1617 and 1632. Undoubtedly he carried
out a program of reorganization and codification similar to that
of Tadao in Okayama. One of the first and most pressing needs in
Tottori, however, was a castle commensurate to the size of the
domain which would be administered from Tottori. The existing
castle was much too limited in its facilities, so that the first few
years after 1617 were of necessity devoted to the task of building
walls, digging moats, and extending quarters for the housemen
and merchants.[50]

After the death of Tadao in 1632, Mitsumasa was called to Edo
and met by the Tokugawa great elder Sakai, who explained in

---

[48] Taniguchi, "Bizen hansei," 7-8.
[49] *Mitsumasa-kō*, 1.279-280.   [50] *Ibid.*, 1.304-305.

private that since Tadao's death left a child as heir to the Bizen domain, the *bakufu* was naturally concerned. "Bizen is a province of strategic importance and not to be left in the hands of a minor," he said. "I am thinking to recommend an exchange of domains between you and him. You hold two provinces at present. What would you think of the change?" The shift from two provinces to one was of course something of a come-down, but Mitsumasa must have thought also of how much more central and important Okayama was. At any rate he assented to the change and was shortly called before the shogun and publicly informed of the exchange of domains. The end of the eighth month was set for completion of the transfer; it was then already the end of the fifth month. On the tenth day of the sixth month of 1632 Mitsumasa began in earnest the task of transferring his retinue from Tottori to Okayama. The overland route between the two castle headquarters, a three-day journey, was decided upon and the necessary organizational steps were taken. The following orders were issued:

> There shall be no damage done to the samurai quarters. There will be no cutting of trees or bamboo in the domain. Roads and bridges will be inspected and repaired. Such items in the samurai quarters as *tatami* needing repair shall be reported. Temples in the town or country shall repair *shōji* and *tatami*.[51]

Thus every effort was made to leave the domain in as good shape as possible for the new tenants of Tottori castle. Loans were also given to housemen to enable them to prepare for the trip to Okayama.[52] On the thirteenth of the month, men were assigned to the following duties:

to take over Okayama castle—5 men
to oversee the "myriad small matters"—3 men
to stand guard over the area within Hommaru bridge—3 men
to guard the samurai residences and grade the condition of each house as good, medium, poor—5 men
to guard the merchant quarters and prevent property damage—3 men
to grade the town houses by quality—3 men

[51] *Rireki-ryakki*, 1.142.   [52] Tottori-han shi kōhon, a.276.

to prepare to deliver the castles of Inaba and Hōki to the new masters—3 men

Orders were issued throughout the domain that the year's taxes should be collected up through the spring tax and that the special service taxes (*komononari*) should be paid up to the month in which the exchange of domains took place; the remaining portion was to be forgotten.[53] Documents were prepared setting forth the tax and financial conditions of Inaba-Hōki. Similar documents were received from Okayama. Accordingly it was ascertained that at Tottori the annual income had been 183,054 *koku*; Okayama had the following:

Tax base (*kokudaka*)	(*koku*)
Bizen	280,200
Bitchū	35,000
In addition: reclaimed land	34,000
Total	349,200
Tax return on the above	198,000[54]

On the sixteenth day of the seventh month three of Mitsumasa's chief retainers, Igi, Ikeda Iga, and Dohi, departed from Tottori for Okayama. Already officials from Okayama had entered Tottori to take over essential posts. Mitsumasa left Edo for Osaka by palanquin and thence by boat to Okayama, arriving there on the twelfth day of the eighth month. The housemen to a man made the transfer from Tottori by the eighteenth. Thus the move had taken just two months from the time the first orders were sent out. A total of 3,873 families had left Okayama for Tottori; it is probable that even a larger number entered Okayama with Mitsumasa.[55]

In Okayama the first task was the assignment of quarters. To this day there remains in the Okayama Ikeda archives a large map of the castle town prepared during Tadao's rule for recording the occupancy of samurai residences. Over the names in this map are now pasted the new assignments made when Mitsumasa's retinue received their quarters. Mansions, houses, and side-by-side quarters, graded according to size, were carefully distributed to Mitsumasa's men according to rank.

[53] *Rireki-ryakki*, 1.142-143.   [54] *Ibid.*, 1.143-144.
[55] Tottori-han shi kōhon, a.276.

Having settled his housemen in Okayama, Mitsumasa set about organizing the administration. His first appointments were:

district administrators (*kōri-bugyō*)	10
city administrators (*machi-bugyō*)	3
inspectors (*yokome*)	10

These were followed by the creation of a committee of six officers charged with working out the assignment of fiefs. At the same time the following appointments were made:

superintendents of construction (*sakuji-bugyō*)	4
superintendent of metal work (*kaji-bugyō*)	1
superintendents of quarters (*yashiki bugyō*)	2
superintendents of works in rural areas (*gun-gun fushin bugyō*)	20

Meanwhile Mitsumasa's major vassals had been assigned the responsibility of guarding the strategic entrances into the Bizen domain and the major ports. In keeping with these assignments, the chief vassals were given the first fief allotments. These were sizable territories each of which centered upon a strategic location. Finally, on the first day of 1633, the remaining fief assignments were made known and the enfeoffment certificates presented by the daimyo.[56] With this act behind him, Mitsumasa set off to Edo to report the completion of the transfer to the shogun. This remarkable logistic feat, repeated so often by the Tokugawa daimyo in the years between 1600 and 1651, had been carried off smoothly and efficiently within seven months.

IKEDA MITSUMASA entered Okayama at the beginning of his mature career. To him the opportunity afforded by a new domain of increased importance and wealth, and perhaps the psychological change from the "shady side" of Japan to the "sunny side" bordering on the Inland Sea provided a lift which is evident in the nature of his administration of Bizen. In Bizen Mitsumasa quickly proved himself one of the great daimyo of his age, gaining a reputation as one of the "three outstanding administrators" of the Tokugawa period. The events of Mitsumasa's rule are therefore doubly important, since it was under him that the institutions of the Tokugawa Great Peace were firmly established

[56] *Rireki-ryakki*, 1.144-147.

in Bizen and since Mitsumasa provides us with one of the best examples of the successful daimyo of the Tokugawa age. Bizen was fortunate in having such a man to set the style of local government which was to last for another two hundred years.

The outstanding quality which Mitsumasa brought to Bizen was a certain style of benevolent authoritarianism based on Confucian principles of governance. Mitsumasa built upon the foundations of military organization and civil administration which had been laid by his predecessors, filling out the body of codified injunctions and bureaucratic precedents. But he went further and added to his rule the indispensable ingredient of moral rationale. Mitsumasa was not alone in this. The Tokugawa *bakufu* had led the way in drawing upon the concepts of Confucianism and seeking ideological justification for its regime in the claims of benevolent government. Mitsumasa's fame rests on the fact that he pioneered in adapting these ideas to the field of daimyo rule and that he so persistently sought to regulate his own conduct by them.

A comparison between Ikeda Mitsumasa and Ukita Naoie reveals dramatically the change which had taken place in Bizen within fifty short years, between the ruler as military hegemon and as an ethically guided leader. Under Ukita Naoie the domain was frankly considered the base for recruitment of military forces, under Mitsumasa the daimyo spoke of his responsibility to his subjects, to rule them well and to give them peace and prosperity. As he stated so forcefully, "The shogun receives authority over the people of Japan as a trust from heaven. The daimyo receives authority over the people of the province as a trust from the shogun. The daimyo's councillors and retainers should aid the daimyo in bringing peace and harmony to the people."[57]

If Mitsumasa added the quality of social responsibility to daimyo rule in Bizen, he also brought to perfection the many legal and administrative institutions which had been created by his predecessors, moving toward a more effective bureaucratic centralization and a more strict dependence on public law at the local level. Mitsumasa, along with other daimyo of his time, had begun to achieve a degree of centralized control over the houseband and the people of the domain far beyond what had been

[57] *Hampōshū*, 1.335 (Horeishū, section 36).

possible for Ukita Naoie. With regard to the housemen this condition was measurable first in the withdrawal of the samurai from
the land and secondly in the abolition of the independent fief.
In Bizen the second process was never carried to full completion.
Mitsumasa's great vassals, the *karo,* retained enfeoffments over
which they kept a measure of independent control. But all other
grants of fief became essentially salary payments. Under Mitsumasa the condition was reached whereby the daimyo's law governed all relationships between samurai and cultivator, and all
taxes (except for the *karō*) whether on the daimyo's land or that
of the enfeoffed vassals were collected by the daimyo's intendants.
Mitsumasa's housemen therefore were converted from what under
the Urakami had been a band of locally enfeoffed chiefs called to
duty as needed, into a corps of house officials domiciled in a castle
town and assigned regularly to bureaucratic or military duties.
This same trend toward centralization runs through nearly every
other aspect of domain organization in Bizen. Laws governing
the villages and city blocks were standardized and codified. Religious institutions were brought under the scrutiny of domain
officials and the most important sects obliged to move their headquarters into the castle town itself. Trade, finance, even the arts
were brought under the daimyo's direct supervision.

All of this was not accomplished overnight. The first decade
or so of Mitsumasa's life in Okayama appears relatively unevent-
ful. Mitsumasa himself was probably still unsure of his own mind
or of the problems which most needed his attention. Furthermore,
a great deal by way of routine organization and readjustment was
necessary following the move from Tottori. Mitsumasa's personal
diary begins in the year 1637, an indication perhaps of his growing sense of destiny. Then in the next few years, from 1640 to
1644, a series of basic codes and proscriptions were issued under
his direction which were to set the foundation for his entire rule
in Bizen. In 1640 the basic law on taxation and handling of tax
rice (*nengu-kō*) was issued. The next year a revised code on conduct of domain affairs during the daimyo's duty in Edo was
promulgated. In 1642 the office of domain administrator (*shioki*)
was created from among the *karō* and new regulations for conduct of village affairs (*gunchū-kō*), tax assessment (*kemi-kō*), domain finances (*kanjōsho-kō*), and control of fire (*shōbō-kō*) were
issued. In the year 1644, Mitsumasa requested and obtained per-

mission to set up in Okayama a private shrine to Ieyasu modeled on the Nikkō Tōshōgū.[58] In 1641 the first domain school (Hana-batake Kyōjō) was founded, and when in 1647 Kumazawa Banzan was hired as Mitsumasa's Confucian adviser the basic foundations of Mitsumasa's early administrative policies had become apparent.

These early moves, as we can see, were mostly of an administrative or bureaucratic nature and sought to clarify the procedures of government and the chains of administrative responsibility. Mitsumasa's selection of a limited number of *karō* for administrative and executive service was an important step in that it emphasized the importance of civil, as against military, service and that it clearly made administrative talent a criterion for selection. His request to set up a Tōshōgū in Okayama clarified the relationship between his family and that of the Tokugawa house, putting the prestige of the Tokugawa shogunate squarely behind his own position in Bizen.

In his diary Mitsumasa constantly expressed his concern over the problems of maintaining disciplinary control over his retainers and of creating a more stable and efficient machinery of government in Okayama. His opportunity to move in on these problems came after 1654, when a series of natural calamities shook Bizen and shocked Mitsumasa into a strenuous reform of domain policy. In the spring and early summer of that year there had been a prolonged drought which broke in the seventh month with a torrential storm. The Asahi River rampaged through the town of Okayama and elsewhere rivers and canals broke their dikes, inundated villages, and tore fields to pieces. The official estimate of damage read as follows:

1. Inundation of the central keep of the castle
2. 439 samurai houses swept away or damaged
3. 573 houses of lower class samurai destroyed
4. 443 houses of merchants destroyed
5. All but one bridge across the castle moats swept away
6. Moats filled with sand
7. Loss of several castle gates and guard houses
8. Four breaks in the castle ramparts
9. 2,284 farm houses and their occupants swept away
10. 11,664 *koku* of land permanently damaged

[58] *Rireki-ryakki*, 1.176ff.

11. 304,870 yards of breakage in river embankments
12. Damage to 84 irrigation ponds
13. Damage to 46 water distribution facilities
14. Damage to 242 water gates
15. 207 ships swept away
16. 20 bridges in rural areas swept away
17. 156 persons killed
18. 210 cows and horses killed[59]

Failure of the year's crop brought famine conditions in its wake, and the suffering of the peasantry during the winter of 1654 was extreme.

Mitsumasa took these events as a direct reflection on his rule, and reacted vigorously both by providing relief for the sufferers and by admonishing his housemen for lax behavior. He believed that in too many instances his enfeoffed retainers had sacrificed the welfare of the peasantry in order to squeeze taxes from their fiefs. After 1654 Mitsumasa focused his attention upon popular affairs (*minsei*). His first move was to cut his enfeoffed housemen away from any direct control over their lands, thereby bringing all domain land under the daimyo's rule. (Five *karō* were permitted to retain country residences, but they were denied any autonomy in their territories.) Administration of the rural area was placed under the daimyo's intendants who were now required to reside periodically in the countryside to keep in touch with local conditions.[60] After the flood of 1654, Mitsumasa became much more the firm authoritarian ruler of his domain, preaching frequently to his assembled housemen about the need for discipline, loyalty, and selfless service to the people of the domain.

The role of Kumazawa Banzan during his years in Okayama was a stormy one, and one not fully understood. This petulant student of the Yōmei school of Confucianism was taken into Mitsumasa's confidence after 1647 and advanced to the high post of *bangashira* with a salary of 3000 *koku*. Much of Mitsumasa's own thoughts on government and political morality were developed or reinforced by Banzan. Whether Banzan was party to the tightening of the daimyo's control over Bizen we cannot know, for there is little evidence that he had any direct contact

[59] *Ibid.*, 1.232.
[60] Taniguchi, "Bizen hansei," 10-11.

with the legal or administrative procedures of the domain. More-over, it was not until the late 1660's, after Banzan had been dis-missed from Bizen, that Mitsumasa began his major educational and ideological reforms. Yet the general effect of a vigorous resident Confucianist is evident in the tenor of Mitsumasa's actions. Emphasis on ideology was strong throughout these years and Mitsumasa's pioneer role in this emphasis is indicated by the efforts of the *bakufu* to force the Okayama daimyo to give up his unorthodox Yōmei doctrines for more acceptable ones.

A third phase of Mitsumasa's rule in Bizen is visible during the years 1665 to 1670 when he brought to completion his policies on education and organized religion. In 1665, in response to *bakufu* urging, Mitsumasa appointed an inspector of religions (*shūmon bugyō*) and asserted a vigorous anti-Christian policy. At the same time he turned his reforming zeal against the Buddhist priesthood and advocated Confucianism and Shinto as the chief spiritual foundations of his domain. In 1666 he issued the order requiring his housemen and subjects to register at Shinto shrines (*shinshoku-uke*) rather than at Buddhist temples as a sign of their freedom from Christian contamination. (The *bakufu* had left the choice open but preferred Buddhist affiliations instead of Shinto.) At the same time he pursued a vigorous purge of Buddhist temples and monasteries which he considered super-fluous and wasteful of the wealth of the domain. All told he is said to have abolished 583 temples out of the 1044 in existence in 1666. He defrocked some 847 priests and confiscated over a thousand *koku* of temple land. After the purge only 1110 Buddhist priests and nuns remained in Bizen, and temple lands accounted for only 1937 *koku*.[61]

Essentially what Mitsumasa was attempting to do was to create a new ethical orientation within his domain, placing emphasis upon the civil aspects of rulership and loyalty. He attacked Buddhism because it exalted transcendental religious beliefs above the immediate political order. His establishment of the shrine to Ieyasu in Bizen and his unusual emphasis upon Confucianism was calculated to place symbols of a more practical nature before the people of his domain. In 1666 Mitsumasa brought the remains of his father and grandfather to Bizen and enshrined them in Con-

---

[61] Mizuno Kyōichirō, "Bizen-han ni okeru shinshoku-uke seido," *Okayama Daigaku Hōbungakubu gakujutsu kiyō*, 5 (March 1956), 74.

fucian style in the mountains of remote Wake district. These monuments were to be the center of a new loyalty system centered on the daimyo's house as rulers of Bizen. His emphasis on Shinto rather than Buddhism was an effort to heighten within the domain a sense of attachment to the soil of the locality.

Meanwhile he proceeded with a vigorous educational policy. In 1660 a new domain college (*karigakkan*) based on Confucian principles was begun and in 1668 a system of elementary writing schools (*tenaraijo*) for commoners was ordered into effect. The latter proved too costly and had to be abandoned. Education for the upper levels only of the common people was eventually taken care of after 1670 with the establishment of Shizutani School (*Shizutani gakkō*) to which samurai also went. On a somewhat broader, more popular level Mitsumasa established a massive program of rewards for good conduct, honoring in 1665 a total of 1684 individuals, samurai and commoner alike, for virtuous and loyal conduct during the previous three years.[62] The categories of reward are informative: filial piety (219), loyalty (52), truthfulness (226), ability at literary and military arts (111), good performance of official duties (214). These were the values Mitsumasa was working so hard to inculcate.

Mitsumasa retired in 1672, handing over to his son Tsunamasa the reins of administration, though he himself lived for another ten years. Tsunamasa was a leader of different cut from his father. Though constantly preached to and admonished by his father to follow the moral principles of Confucianism, to rule seriously, and to eschew luxury, Tsunamasa had been brought up too much to enjoy life. His relaxed and practical attitude toward domain administration began to show through immediately after 1672. Much of the actual administration of these days was placed in the hands of an official named Tsuda Eichū (1639-1707) who served in various capacities of trust under Mitsumasa and Tsunamasa. Tsuda was known for his interest in the economics of the domain and in his desire to achieve organizational symmetry. The major accomplishments of the Bizen daimyo after 1672 were therefore along these lines. The Okayama bureaucracy was further improved in 1672 by the assignment of responsibility for administrative policy functions to a second council of officials. These were the *koshioki*, named from among the second level of

[62] *Rireki-ryakki,* 1.358.

housemen, the so-called group leaders (*bangashira*). In 1682 the office of rural affairs (*kōri kaisho*) was created. A similar office for town affairs (*machi kaisho*) had been set up in 1667. When in 1685 the basic military duty and organization regulations were codified, the finishing touches had been put on the political and military procedures of the domain.

Meanwhile a number of major public works were absorbing the attention of the daimyo's officials. Mitsumasa had constantly encouraged land reclamation, but the projects sponsored by him had all been modest. Land reclaimed from 1632 to 1672 was productive in all of just over 12,000 *koku*. Between 1673 and 1698 Tsunamasa's agents recovered, mostly from the sea, land producing over 43,000 *koku*. One project alone, that of Oki south of Okayama, added 28,000 *koku* to the domain's productive base. In 1699 a great canal was cut to lead water from upstream on the Yoshii River down across Bizen to a point on the Asahi River just below Okayama. This canal served for the transport of goods but also irrigated an extensive area of the Okayama plain, making the Oki reclamation possible. In 1686 a major engineering effort provided a diversionary channel for the Asahi River to protect Okayama from flood.[63] In 1695 the breakwater at Ushimado was completed, making the port safe and attractive to ships passing through the Inland Sea. By 1707 regulations governing shipping at Bizen's ports had become necessary. In 1679 the domain began its first issue of silver certificates, and the problem of fiscal relationship between Okayama and the Osaka market had attracted the attention of domain officials.

While Mitsumasa had emphasized the moral leadership of the daimyo, Tsunamasa built up the daimyo's prestige through his behavior as a cultural leader of aristocratic style. Famed for his interest in poetry, tea ceremony, and *nō* drama, he became a patron of the arts, building in 1687 the beautiful recreation park Kōrakuen (across the Asahi River from his castle) in which he held various spectacles. As a patron of religion, he reversed his father's fanatical emphasis on Confucianism, and returned to the patronage of Buddhism. In 1698 he built outside of Okayama the temple of Sōgenji to serve as the Ikeda ancestral temple and burial site. Tsunamasa was in no way the serious ruler that Mit-

[63] *Okayama-ken no rekishi*, 352-362.

sumasa was. Preferring to leave to his officers the details of government, he himself played the aristocrat, but in so doing, he too added to the stature of the daimyo in local affairs and to the pattern of rule by a civil officialdom.

By 1700 the foundations of civil rule under the Tokugawa regime had been laid in Bizen. Mitsumasa and Tsunamasa each in his way had added to the basic structure of daimyo administration so that for another 150 years few additions or changes were necessary. It is a curious fact that for a century or more after 1700 the Ikeda family history is almost totally devoid of important events, reporting only such matters as changes in office personnel, births, deaths, suicides, natural calamities, or entertainments. Life in Bizen had settled down to a routine in which the precedents established by the two "founding daimyo" were now sufficient.

By 1700, then, we may assume that the basic structure of government and society in Bizen under the Tokugawa system had been set. After 1700 few fundamental and noteworthy innovations were made, nor was it necessary to devise additional codes or basic policies. The now smoothly working bureaucracy was turning out legal decisions and administrative ordinances sometimes in great volume. The details of government were tidied up here and there. The economic and cultural life of the people was enriched. Yet all of this was accomplished under the more or less routine operation of the domain's bureaucracy. The position of the daimyo had become more and more that of the figurehead atop the great body of precedent which governed the domain.

THE year 1700 offers us another convenient stopping point for an overview of the way the province of Bizen looked under the Tokugawa regime. The administration of Bizen was typical of the kind which was provided by the larger daimyo of the Tokugawa period. Over Bizen stood a ruler who exercised the rights of governance, that is, of taxation, legislation, and judicial process, in full capacity, subject only to his subordination to the shogun and to the contours of shogunal practice. These rights, as in the case of the shogun, were never specified by law or document. Yet they were firmly established by custom, and toward the end of the regime certain clarifications of the content of these customary powers were attempted. Thus in 1869 when

the domains were abolished, it was said that the daimyo returned
to the emperor the *han,* or land registers, and the *seki,* or census
registers. In the words of the day this was portrayed as a return
of jurisdiction over "the land and people." Previously—in 1868,
at the time of the first attempt to rationalize the structure of local
administration under the emperor—the daimyo were admonished
to execute the laws of the land and administer according to the
principles of the imperial oath, not to interpret from one to
another body of law, not to bestow court titles under their own
authority, not to mint their own coins, not to employ private
foreign personnel, not to enter into compacts with neighboring
daimyo or foreign countries, not to override national authority
with their local authority, but to uphold the national political
structure.[64] In the same document the powers of the domain
chiefs were defined as follows: "Within his *han* to administer the
shrine and population census registers, to promote the welfare
of the samurai and people, to spread moral principles, to encourage good conduct, to collect taxes, oversee labor service, judge
rewards and punishments, administer the registration of Buddhist
priests, and command the *han* troops."[65] These late efforts at
definition of the powers of the territorial rulers reveal by implication what the powers of the daimyo had become by the end of
the Tokugawa period. Given jurisdiction over the land and people
of the territories specified in their grants from the shogun, the
daimyo were territorial rulers of a type more complete in their
authority than any Japan had seen even at the height of the
early empire.

The center of domain affairs was the castle city of Okayama.
Here the daimyo resided in his many-storied fortress, the Raven
Castle (*Ujō*) as it was called because of the charred boards which
were placed over the plastered walls as a measure of protection.
Surrounding the daimyo's central keep in concentric circles lay
the residences of the chief Ikeda retainers and the many samurai
retainers of lesser status. The houseband provided the reservoir
of manpower from which the civil government and military defense of Bizen was drawn. To the daimyo and his samurai belonged the upper levels of local administration. The daimyo
himself, symbolizing the legitimacy of local rule by delegation

---

[64] Ishii, *Meiji hōsei,* 67.   [65] *Ibid.,* 72.

from the shogun, constantly reenacted the ritual of association between local administration and the shogunate by his periodic travels made in great pomp and with a large retinue between Okayama and Edo.

The daimyo's government had by now become a most complex bureaucratic operation. His houseband, organized strictly by rank and status held together under the disciplinary controls of personnel "group heads," was by now organized into a thoroughly comprehensive machinery of local defense and administration. All told, the Ikeda daimyo could count on something under 5000 families in his personal retinue, depending on when and how the count was made. These were ranged into ten basic ranks as follows.[66]

Rank	Number of Families	Fief or Stipend Range
Elder (*karō*)	6	10,000-33,000 *koku*
Divisional Commander (*bangashira*)	14-22	500- 5,000 *koku*
Task Commander (*monogashira*)	25-28	below 500 *koku*
Attendant (*kinju-kashirabun*)	20	"
Divisional Captain (*kumigashira*)	20-30	"
Officer (*heishi*)	730-840	40 bales or more
Musketeer Officer (*samurai-deppō*)	70	4 rations
Senior Petty Officer (*kachi*)	450-490	3 rations
Junior Petty Officer (*keihai*)	550	2 rations
Footsoldier (*ashigaru*)	1,900-2,600	1 ration

From this group the daimyo drew his administrative bureaucracy and military organization.

Between the daimyo and the specific military and civil posts filled by his retainers stood the chief decision-making body of the domain, the Council (*hyōjōsho*). It was staffed by two of the daimyo's elders and by various other members of the top level

---

[66] Taniguchi Sumio, "Han kashindan no keisei to kōzō—Okayama-han no baai," *Shigaku zasshi* 66.6 (June 1957), 607.

of the administrative staff. Military organization was considerably scaled down from what it had been in the first years of the Tokugawa period. In theory, of course, all samurai were accountable for military service, and many of the civil agencies within the bureaucracy were conceived of as being instantly convertible to military service. However, due to the strict limitations placed on the size of the domain forces by the shogun, and the heavy shift of emphasis toward the civil problems of administration, by 1700 a clearly defined special military branch of service had come into being. A number of vassal families retained hereditary membership in the Guards under hereditary divisional commanders (*bangashira*). Special branches of the armed forces were headed by officials such as the superintendent of naval affairs (*funate bugyō*), superintendent of works (*fushin bugyō*), and superintendent of flags (*hata bugyō*), the last acting as a communications officer.

The civil administration was much more elaborately structured. Senior administrative responsibility rested with the three councillors (*shioki*) and three junior councillors (*ko-shioki*), who were appointed from the top two levels of the daimyo's vassals. Under them a number of service and supervisory functions were performed by such officials as chamberlains (*ō kosho gashira*), chief inspectors (*ō metsuke*), secretaries (*yūhitsu gashira*), and recorders (*tomegata*). The main executive duties were performed by the magistrates of rural affairs (*gundai*), financial affairs (*sakumaigata*), town affairs (*machi bugyō*), temple and shrine affairs (*jisha bugyō*), school affairs (*gakkō bugyō*), and numerous lesser officials. Each of the magistrates headed a staff of appropriate size to exercise the function of his office. Some of these, notably the magistrates of county, town, and financial affairs, were established in permanent office quarters either within the castle or in the town of Okayama.

So much is known about the government and economy of Bizen during the Tokugawa period that it will form the subject of a separate volume. Our purpose at this point is only to sketch in the main outlines of what the province was like in 1700, and for this we are able to draw upon a remarkable document. In 1764 when a shogunal inspection team visited Okayama as part of the official formality of passing upon the succession of Ikeda Harumasa, they requested of the domain authorities detailed information on the laws, administrative practices, and economic conditions of the domain. The answer to these questions has been retained. While the information refers to conditions of a somewhat later period than 1700, the document is still valuable in that it gives us an intimate view of the public features of the domain in the eighteenth century. In answer to the shogun's inspectors, the domain authorities, after indicating that the daimyo was in the habit of strictly enjoining his retainers to obey the laws of the shogunate and to maintain frugality in their way of life, and after explaining in detail the elaborate procedures used by the domain to assure the eradication of Christianity within the domain, set forth the following statistics:

Offices in the castle and castle town:
    In the second enclosure within the west gate—
        the council
        the finance magistrate
    In the second enclosure within the Mizuta gate—
        the office of works
    In the town—
        the magistrate of rural affairs
        the magistrate of town affairs
    Across the river from the castle—
        the office of irrigation works
    In the southern block of samurai residences—
        the office of public works
    In the western block of samurai residences—
        the office of houses and grounds
    On the river beyond Kawate ward—
        the shipyards
    To the south and west of the town—
        three storehouses
Military equipment stored in the castle:
    Communication flags—68 sets
    Spears—3,316
    Halberds—50
    Pikes—30
    Armor—2,320 sets
    Bows—1,460
    Arrows—30,000

Muskets—3,787

Cannon—14

Also at the Fukushima River mouth gun emplacement: 10 cannon

Powder depots:

One in the castle

Two outside the town

Weapons in the possession of retainers:

Armor—4,081 sets

Spears—5,010

Bows—1,755

Arrows—87,750

Firearms—4,698

Other firearms:

Licensed for private hunting—1,265

Unable to shoot—46

Confiscated and kept in the storehouse—636

Roster of daimyo's housemen and their incomes:

Enfeoffed vassals, 1,568 of which:

6—more than 10,000 *koku*

26—2,000 *koku* and above

532—100 *koku* and above (31 are physicians)

1,004—99 *koku* or less

Stipended vassals, 4,725 of which:

447—officer class (38 are physicians)

1,010—soldier

3,161—petty footsoldier or below

107—unranked

Village administration:

There are 8 districts, 634 villages, 38 branch villages

Tax rice received at the daimyo's granary for 3 years (Bizen only and excluding income of fiefs):

1762	105,386 *koku*
1763	106,994 *koku*
1764	103,715 *koku*

Note: the salaries of retainers and other hired personnel are taken from this figure.

Taxes left after payment of stipends:

In 1762 total taxes were 105,386 *koku*. Of this 56,200 *koku* went for stipends and rice delivered to Edo, Kyoto, Osaka.

There remained 49,100 *koku* for general expenses.
Commercial taxes of Bizen:

1762	silver	65.430 *kan*
	rice	231.000 *koku*
1763	silver	64.184 *kan*
	rice	274.000 *koku*
1764	silver	66.293 *kan*
	rice	197.000 *koku*

The above derived from taxes on licenses to take forest
and thicket produce, salt tax, boat tax, fishing tax, cotton
tax, water wheel tax, ferry tax, pottery tax, canal tax,
indigo tax.

Famous local product—Imbe pottery

Exchange houses in Okayama—45

Ships:
  Oared ships—195
  Sailing ships—1,675 (of which 1,013 are of 40 to 1,500
    koku burden)

Ports:
  In Kojima district—Shimotsui
  In Oku district—Ushimado
  In Wake district—Ōtabu

Checkpoints for handling ships and boats from other provinces—one in each district and in the castle town

Fishing villages—116

Ports handling large cargo ships:
  Shimotsui
  Ushimado
  Ōtabu
  Plus the following:
    Fukushima village
    Kogushi village
    Kanaoka village
    Katakami village

River guard—there is one at Fukushima village with the following table of organization:
    1 officer of the Office of Naval Affairs
    1 petty officer
    2 watchmen

There are also lightly manned river guards at Wake
village and Kawamoto village
Residences of the daimyo's retainers—1,295
Horses:
  For the daimyo's use—30
  Kept by retainers—300
City blocks—62
Residences in the city—5,065
Hot springs—none
Horse breeding grounds—none
Mines producing gold, silver, copper, iron, tin—none
Medicinal herb production—none
Forests—161 places
Bamboo forests—77 places
Population [not including samurai]:
  In rural areas—

People	306,583
Horses	671
Cows	21,624

  In the city—

People	23,385
Horses	62
Cows	2

Horse and cattle markets—several places
Descendents of Christians:
  12 among retainers
  14 in the castle town
   4 in the countryside
Silver certificates:
  In 1730 certificates were issued with a 25-year limitation
  on circulation. These were in use until 1755 when by request the certificates were extended for another 25 years.
  The present certificates will circulate for another 14. Certificates were issued in the denominations of 1 *me*, 5, 4,
  3, 2 *bu*. In all 5 denominations.
Multiple residences:
  Aside from the country residences of the *karō*, there are
  no multiple residences [among the daimyo's retainers]
Actors—there are no outstanding actors
Endowed religious establishments [and endowments]:

The Shrine of Ieyasu, located in Kadota village,
   (from the daimyo's granary)   300 *koku*
Kannonji of the Tendai sect   166 *koku*
Kokuseiji, the daimyo's house temple in the
   castle, branch of Myōshinji, Zen sect   200 *koku*
Sōgenji, the daimyo's burial temple in Maru-
   yama village, branch of Myōshinji, Zen sect   200 *koku*
Total endowed temple and shrine lands:
   Shrines—203   1,399 *koku*
   Temples—80   2,814 *koku*
   Total lands   4,213 *koku*
Unendowed temples and shrines:
   Shrines—1,525
   Temples—373
Temples in Bizen by sect:
   Tendai—107
   Jōdo—17
   Zen—35
   Shin—213
   Nichiren—63
   Ikkō—80
Schools:
   The Okayama School was founded in 1669. Students are
     limited to the children of the daimyo's retainers. The
     school has an endowment of 1,000 *koku*.
   Shizutani School is provided with 279 *koku*. It was founded
     in 1670 and is situated in Wake district. Even farmers'
     children are taught at this school.[67]

The above information is interspersed in the original document
with answers to questions regarding the procedures for keeping
the village areas under supervision and for inspecting the domain's mountains and streams, regarding methods by which
domain residents could request and obtain permission to travel
outside Bizen, could change residence at time of marriage, and
many other aspects of the security system of the domain. The
overall impression created by this document is that of a provincial
community of great economic diversity and considerable cultural
activity which nonetheless was governed tightly under severe

[67] Otazune shinajina kakiage, ms., dated 1765, *Ikeda-ke bunko*.

security measures and a meticulous control system which regulated the status, residential location, and the comings and goings of every resident. Still the domain had many outside contacts, and there was constant travel of official personnel between Okayama and the Ikeda residences in Edo, Osaka, and on the outskirts of Kyoto. Merchants also moved fairly freely between Okayama and Osaka, and the ports of the Inland Sea were thriving with business as ships from other domains anchored along the coast or vessels plied the rapid waters which descended into Bizen from Mimasaka.

Bizen in 1700 was part of a larger national community. Not a province in the sense it had once been, of course, for the fact that it retained the boundaries that had been set in the eighth century was largely fortuitous. And Bizen was not governed as a province in the strict sense but as part of a larger domain which also included territory in adjoining Bitchū. Nonetheless, it was not accidental that the boundaries of the old province remained in use. (The statistics reported to the shogun in 1764 differentiated between figures for Bizen and Bitchū.) And within the Ikeda domain not only Bizen but also the districts of which the province had been composed a thousand years previously retained their boundaries and some functional significance. Unquestionably Bizen was more thoroughly and systematically governed during the eighteenth century than at any time since the eighth. Within the province the supreme authority had its visible seat in the imposing castle of the daimyo, and the codes of law and the procedures of administration which were made public and rigidly enforced. In many ways the style of administration had come to resemble the provincial administration of the imperial period.

But the analogy should not be pushed. The great difference in the conditions of government in Bizen between the eighteenth century and the eighth is apparent not merely in the technological complexity of the political, economic, and cultural life of the later age but also in the nature of the ruling class which manned the local bureaucracy. Government in Tokugawa times was literally the result of the conversion of a military organization into a peacetime system of local administration. Granted that little by little the nature of this government, its basic orientation, policies, recruitment techniques, and legal procedures became less military. Granted also that the nature of the samurai himself changed from what was basically a military elite to more of a civil administrative type. Nonetheless the fact that the samurai was a military officer and that the badge of his social status consisted in the wearing of his two swords, gave to government of the Tokugawa age an inescapable quality. Tokugawa society remained highly military. And despite the overlay of Confucian rationale, authority could always be justified on terms of military necessity.

If an analogy is to be made with some period in Japan's past, the most useful is perhaps between the Tokugawa period and the centuries preceding the Taika Reform. For Japan in 1700 was both isolated and in need of foreign contact, both stable in its social and political institutions and yet on the verge of a fundamental transformation. The fact that in each instance the impetus for change and the model upon which reform was to be based came from abroad makes the analogy more appealing. The long years of daimyo government under the Tokugawa shoguns have seemed on the surface to constitute a period of stagnant stability, a time of massive permanence just when the Western world was making its most startling advances. But as we were able to note in the conditions of Japanese society which preceded the Taika Reform, so also in the eighteenth and early nineteenth centuries the façade of permanence masked deep-running currents of growth and dislocation which only confrontation with an alien culture was to resolve.

While our narration of the history of Bizen is terminated in this study at 1700, we cannot leave the province without a glance beyond that date and without an inquiry into some of the processes of change at work in Bizen. The political structure, of course, was not easily altered, but the political and administrative procedures, the social structure, and conditions of the economy were less permanently fixed by the Tokugawa system. Evidences of economic growth are perhaps the most easily identified, though not in such a way to be quantified. In area under cultivation, by 1854 fields productive of some 160,000 *koku* had been added to the land base inherited by Ikeda Tadao in 1615. Thus the actual productive base of the Ikeda domain rose to over 400,000 *koku*. Population appears to have been relatively stable after 1700, though we cannot be entirely sure of the census figures. What of the standard of living then if production rose and population remained relatively stable? The evidence is strong that at least the material needs of the people of Bizen were being met more fully. Certainly there was an increased diversity in the economy and in the goods produced and consumed by the people of Bizen.

The eighteenth century saw the addition of a number of new crops to Bizen agriculture. Sweet potatoes and various vegetable and fruit delicacies were grown in significant quantities in addition to the older staple cereals. Various commercial crops such as cotton, tobacco, mat rush, sugar cane took on new importance. Along the coast, fishing, gathering of edible seaweed, and production of salt provided a living for an increasingly prosperous coastal population. Bizen's hills and forests provided lumber, firewood, and charcoal. Her artisans produced swords, ironwork, tiles, and pottery for export.

Evidences of the expanding commercial activity are visible not only in the growth of Okayama city but in the development of new markets, ports, and small towns in the countryside. In the villages wealthy farmers took to making wine, soy sauce, paper, and textiles. A complex wholesaling system organized in Okayama with roots in the countryside and outlets in Osaka linked Bizen's rural production to the national market. By the mid-eighteenth century the volume of trade between Bizen and Osaka was such that currency control became necessary. Paper silver certificates became legal tender in Bizen, so that silver bullion could be retained by the domain office to balance the exchange between Okayama and Osaka.

The domain which had begun with a policy of agrarian self-sufficiency had by the eighteenth century begun to enter the field of commercial regulation and taxation. Various commercial monopolies were licensed and in the early nineteenth century a factory (*kaisha*) system was established. Under the control of this domain factory, various commercial products such as salt, cotton, or sugar were handled by monopoly arrangement between the Bizen authorities and local wholesale merchants so as to yield a profit to both the domain and the merchants.

Such indications of economic growth or at least technological improvement and increased economic complexity cannot directly be linked to a growing standard of well-being. The work on which the comparative assessment of living standards might be made is not yet available. On the one hand we have the dismal story of economic dislocation and growing poverty which has been told by Tokugawa political economists. To judge from these writings we must believe that misery was the common lot of the farmer and samurai. The former resorted to infanticide and rebellion, the latter to domestic handicrafts and sullen resignation. Bizen was not without such problems. The domain treasury, strained by numerous unusual or emergency demands such as special construction for the *bakufu*, famine relief, and reconstruction after fires, and constantly drained by the demands of travel to Edo, was periodically in a state of crisis. From the days of Mitsumasa few years saw a balanced budget, and the domain debt grew constantly bigger.

But the problems of economic imbalance did not bring the life of Bizen to a standstill. The relative prosperity of the domain is certainly told in the lack of serious peasant disturbances. On the contrary, there are signs that for many groups in Bizen the overall standard of living had greatly improved. What had been luxuries once were by the nineteenth century necessities. The city and village wealthy in particular could afford education for their children and the pursuit of cultural pastimes. Itinerant poets or artists, traveling between villages, made a profitable business of instructing the leading peasant families in their specialities. With increasing frequency villagers themselves were able to put up capital for land reclamation. In numerous ways, in clothes, pastimes, food, objects of household use, we can estimate the growing economic margin of at least an upper stratum within village and town.

Interspersed with these clear but disparate signs of economic growth and commercial activity were evidences of change in social structure and values. The growing bureaucratization of the samurai class had a profound effect upon what had once been a feudal aristocracy. Life in the garrison town dedicated to civil administration, based on the ethical teachings of Confucianism, eroded the commitment of the *bushi* to military affairs despite persisting features of a political order inherited from the era of great civil wars. The older forms of political loyalty based on personal commitment and oaths individually sworn were being displaced by more generalized political values of loyalty to domain or to country. In the countryside new conditions "freed the peasant of the goals of subsistence farming . . . at the same time . . . loosened the control of the social group over his methods and routine."[68] The strict social hierarchy which had been idealized in Mitsumasa's day was obviously being placed under strain. The economy itself had come to deny many of its premises. Despite regulations prohibiting alienation of land, for instance, landlordism and tenancy spread, to the dismay of the domain authorities. The castle-city monopoly merchants, protected by domain patents, were nevertheless forced into competition by more independent village traders. The spread of learning among the wealthier of the merchants and peasants and among the lower levels of the samurai class opened new horizons of aspiration to the traditionally underprivileged groups in the Tokugawa system.

Yet if we are looking for signs of incipient revolution against the system which had been put together by the early Tokugawa shoguns and the daimyo of the seventeenth century we shall not find it. Signs of social and economic tension there were, but none so critical that they should have led to open subversion. The picture of Bizen even in the mid-nineteenth century is one of fair stability under the Tokugawa Great Peace. It took the intrusion of a foreign menace to rouse the people of Bizen to participation in Japan's modern revolution.

[68] Thomas C. Smith, *The Agrarian Origins of Modern Japan* (Stanford, 1959), 211.

BIBLIOGRAPHY
AND INDEX

BIBLIOGRAPHY*

*The historical and institutional range of my study precludes the compilation of a complete or systematically selected bibliography. The items listed here are limited to reference works dealing specifically with the local history of Okayama and to works cited in the preceding pages.

BIBLIOGRAPHIES AND INDICES TO DOCUMENTARY COLLECTIONS IN OKAYAMA

Okayama Daigaku Fuzoku Toshokan, *Ikeda-ke Bunko kari mokuroku,* Okayama, 1952. Ditto, *tsuika,* Okayama, 1960.

Okayama Daigaku nai, Ikeda-ke Bunko Seiri Iinkai, *Okayama Daigaku shozō Ikeda-ke Bunko kaidai,* Okayama, 1953.

Okayama-ken Chihōshi Kenkyū Renraku Kyōgikai, *Kaihō,* Okayama, 1962+ (irregular). Contains: "Okayama-ken chihōshi bunken mokuroku."

————, *Okayama-ken chihōshi kenkyū nyūmon* (Special issue of *Kaihō,* November 1963).

Okayama-ken Kōhōka, Kenshi-Kenseishi Hensanshitsu, *Okayama-ken chō-son shi mokuroku,* Okayama, 1961.

Okayama-ken Sōgō Bunka Sentā, *Okayama-ken kyōdo shiryō sōgō mokuroku,* 2 vols., Okayama, 1959 and 1960.

Umehara Sueji, "Okayama kenka no kofun chōsa kiroku," *Setonaikai kenkyū* nos. 8 and 9 (March and October 1956).

SOURCES (MANUSCRIPT COLLECTIONS AND PRINTED DOCUMENTS)

Asakawa Kan-ichi, tr. and ed., *The Documents of Iriki; Illustrative of the development of the feudal institutions of Japan,* New Haven, 1929. Rev. ed., Tokyo, 1955.

Dohi Tsunehira, *Bizen gunki* (ms., 1774) in Tanaka Seiichi, comp., *Kibi gunsho shūsei,* vol. 3, pp. 19-180.

Fujii Shun, ed., *Kibitsu-jinja monjo,* Okayama, 1955.

Fujii Shun and Mizuno Kyōichirō, eds., *Okayama-ken komonjo shū,* 3 vols., Okayama, 1953-1956.

John Whitney Hall, "Materials for the Study of Local History in Japan: Pre-Miiji Daimyō Records," *Harvard Journal of Asiatic Studies,* 20.1 and 2 (June 1957), 187-212.

Hampō Kenkyūkai, ed., *Hampōshū 1, Okayama-han,* 2 vols., Tokyo, 1959. Contains: "Hōreishū"; "Bushū-sama hōrei"; "Tadao-sama hōrei."

Hoshino Tsune, comp., *Komonjo ruisan,* Tokyo, 1894.

Ikeda-ke bunko, Okayama Daigaku Fuzoku Toshokan, Okayama. Contains the following cited manuscripts: "Bizen-no-kuni kyū-gun dembata takachō" (1654); "Ikeda-ke keifu"; "Ikeda Mitsumasa nikki" (1637-1669); "Otazune shinajina kakiage" (1765); "Ukita Kōmon Hideie kyō samurai-chō ninzutsuke" (*Osafune monjo* collection, 1713 copy).

Iwatsu Masaemon, ed., *Okayama-ken ko-kenchiku zuroku*, Okayama, 1948.

Jingi Shichō, *Koji ruien*, 60 vols., Tokyo, 1932-1936.

Kikuchi Shunsuke, ed., *Tokugawa kinreikō*, 6 vols., Tokyo, 1931-1932.

Kodama Kōta *et al.*, eds., *Shiryō ni yoru Nihon no ayumi*, 4 vols., Tokyo, 1957.

Kuroita Katsumi, comp., *Shintei zōho, Kokushi taikei*, rev. ed., 60 vols., Tokyo, 1929-1958. Reference made to: vols. 1 and 2 *Nihon shoki*; vols. 32 and 33, *Azuma kagami*; vols. 53-55, *Kugyō bunin*.

Nakada Kaoru, *Shōen no kenkyū*, Hōseishi sōsho edition, 3 vols., Tokyo, 1948.

Nishioka Toranosuke, *Shin Nihonshi zuroku*, 2 vols., Tokyo, 1952.

Okayama-ken, *Okayama-ken tōkei nempō* (*Shōwa 25 nendo bun*), Okayama, 1952.

Ōoka-ke monjo, Okayama Kenritsu Toshokan. Reference to: "Ukita Chūnagon Hideie kyō kashi chigyō chō" (cat. no. 092.8 1132).

Osafune-ke monjo, in *Ikeda-ke bunko*, Okayama.

Ōzawa Koresada, "Kibi onko hiroku, Yūhiroku" in Tanaka Seiichi, ed., *Kibi gunsho shūsei*, vol. 10.

Setonaikai Sōgō Kenkyūkai, *Bitchū-no-kuni Niimi-no-shō shiryō*, Okayama, 1952.

Shimizu Masatake, comp., *Shōen shiryō*, 2 vols., Tokyo, 1933.

Tanaka Seiichi, comp., *Kibi gunsho shūsei*, 10 vols., Tokyo, 1921.

Tottori Kenritsu Toshokan, "Tottori-han shi kōkon" (mss. incomplete).

Yoshida Tokutarō, ed., *Ikeda-ke rireki-ryakki*, 2 vols., Okayama, 1963.

MAIN WORKS ON OKAYAMA HISTORY

Fujii Shun, Taniguchi Sumio, Mizuno Kyōichirō, *Okayama-ken no rekishi*, Okayama, 1962.

Iwatsu Masaemon and Kamaki Yoshimasa, *Okayama-ken jūyō bunkazai zuroku, Kōko shiryō hen*, Tokyo, 1957.

Kobayashi Kumao, ed., *Kaitei Oku-gun shi*, 2 vols., Okayama-ken, Oku-chō, 1953-1954.

Kurashiki Kōkokan, *Kibi no kofun*, Okayama, 1960.

Miyoshi Iheiji, ed., *Okayama-ken Wake-gun Fujino-son shi*, Okayama, 1953.

Nagayama Usaburō, *Ikeda Mitsumasa-kō den*, 2 vols., Tokyo, Ishizaka Zenjirō (private publication), 1932.

———, *Kibi-gun shi*, 3 vols., Okayama, 1937-1938.

———, *Okayama-ken nōchi shi*, Okayama, 1952.

———, *Okayama-ken tsūshi*, 2 vols., Okayama, 1930.

Nishitani Shinji and Kamaki Yoshimasa, *Kanakura-yama kofun*, Kurashiki, 1959.

Okayama-shi Shi Henshū Iinkai, ed., *Gaikan Okayama-shi shi*, Okayama, 1958.

Okayama Shiyakusho, ed., *Okayama-shi shi*, 6 vols., Okayama, 1938.

Shiritsu Wake-gun Kyōikukai, *Wake-gun shi*, Okayama, 1909.

Taniguchi Sumio, *Ikeda Mitsumasa*, Tokyo, 1962.

———, ed., *Kyōdo no rekishi, Chūgoku-hen*, Tokyo, 1959.

———, *Okayama-han*, Tokyo, 1964.

———, *Okayama hansei shi no kenkyū*, Tokyo, 1964.

BOOKS AND SERIES

Andō Hiroshi, *Tokugawa bakufu kenchi yōryaku*, Tokyo, 1915.

Albert Craig, *Chōshū in the Meiji Restoration*, Cambridge, Mass., 1961.

Egashira Tsuneharu, *Nihon shōen keizaishi ron*, rev. ed., Shiga-ken Hikone-shi, 1955.

Fujino Tamotsu, *Bakuhan taiseishi no kenkyū*, Tokyo, 1961.

Furushima Toshio, *Nihon nōgyō shi*, Tokyo, 1956.

Hiroshima Bunri Daigaku, Shigakka-kyōshitsu, *Shigaku Kenkyū kinen ronsō*, Kyoto, 1950.

Hiroshima Shigaku Kenkyūkai, *Shigaku Kenkyū sanjisshūnen kinen ronsō*, Hiroshima, 1960.

Hiroshima Shiyakusho, *Shinshū Hiroshima-shi shi*, 7 vols., Hiroshima, 1961.

Irimajiri Yoshinaga, *Nihon nōmin keizaishi kenkyū*, Tokyo, 1949.

Ishii Ryōsuke, *Meiji bunkashi, Hōsei-hen*, Tokyo, 1954.

———, *Nihon hōseishi gaisetsu*, Tokyo, 1948.

———, *Nihon hōsei shiyō*, Tokyo, 1949.

Itō Tasaburō, *Nihon hōkenseido shi*, Tokyo, 1951.

Iwanami kōza, Nihon rekishi, 23 vols., Tokyo, 1962-1963.

Iyanaga Teizō, *Nara jidai no kizoku to nōmin*, Tokyo, 1956.

Kanai Madoka, *Hansei*, Tokyo, 1962.

Kimura Motoi, *Nihon hōken shakai kenkyūshi*, Tokyo, 1956.

Kodama Kōta, ed., *Zusetsu Nihon bunkashi taikei*, 14 vols., Tokyo, 1956.

Kobayashi Yukio, *Kofun jidai no kenkyū*, Tokyo, 1961.

Kodaigaku Kyōkai, *Nihon kodaishi ronsō*, Tokyo, 1960.

Kokushi Kenkyūkai, ed., *Iwanami kōza, Nihon rekishi,* 18 cases, Tokyo, 1933-1935.

Kurita Motoji, *Edo jidai shi, jō,* in *Sōgō Nihonshi taikei,* 8 vols., Tokyo, 1926.

F. Joüon des Longrais, *L'est et l'ouest,* Tokyo and Paris, 1958.

Matsudaira Tarō, *Edo jidai seido no kenkyū,* Tokyo, 1919.

Mikami Sanji, *Edo jidai shi,* 2 vols., Tokyo, 1943, 1944.

Miyagawa Mitsuru, *Taikō kenchi ron,* 2 vols., Tokyo, 1957, 1959.

Miyamoto Mataji, *Hōkenshugi no saishuppatsu,* Kyoto, 1948.

Murao Jirō, *Ritsuryō zaiseishi no kenkyū,* Tokyo, 1961.

James Murdoch, *A History of Japan,* vol. 2, London, 1925.

Naitō Chisō, *Tokugawa jūgodai shi,* 12 vols., Tokyo, 1892.

Nakamura Kichiji, *Nihon hōkensei saihensei shi,* Tokyo, 1939.

————, *Nihon shakai shi,* Tokyo, 1952.

Nakamura Kōya, *Tokugawa-ke,* Tokyo, 1961.

Nakamura Naokatsu, *Shōen no kenkyū,* Tokyo, 1939.

Naoki Kōjirō, *Nihon kodai kokka no kōzō,* Tokyo, 1958.

Nihon rekishi kōza, 8 vols., Tokyo, Kawade Shobō, 1951-1952.

Nishida Naojirō, *Nihon bunkashi josetsu,* Tokyo, 1932.

Nishioka Toranosuke, *Shōenshi no kenkyū,* 3 vols., 3rd. ed., Tokyo, 1956-1957.

————, *Shin Nihonshi zuroku,* 2 vols., 1952.

Ōae Toshimasa, *Bizen Mitsuishi-jō shi no kenkyū,* Okayama, 1942.

Okuno Takahiro, *Kōshitsu gokeizaishi no kenkyū,* rev. ed., Tokyo, 1942.

————, *Nobunaga to Hideyoshi,* Tokyo, 1955.

Ōsaka Rekishigakkai, *Ritsuryō kokka no kiso kōzō,* Tokyo, 1960.

Osatake Takeshi, *Meiji Ishin,* 4 vols., Tokyo, 1942-1947.

Ōta Akira, *Zentei Nihon jōdai shakai soshiki no kenkyū,* rev. ed., Tokyo, 1955.

Rekishigaku Kenkyūkai, Nihonshi Kenkyūkai, eds., *Nihon rekishi kōza,* 8 vols., Tokyo, 1956-1958.

Sakamoto Tarō, *Nihon zenshi,* 2, *Kodai,* 1, Tokyo, 1960.

George Sansom, *A History of Japan to 1334,* Stanford, 1958.

Satō Shin'ichi, *Kamakara bakufu shugo-seido kenkyū—Shokoku shugo enkaku kōshō hen,* Tokyo, 1948.

Sawada Goichi, *Nara-chō jidai minsei keizai no sūteki kenkyū,* Tokyo, 1927.

Shakaikeizaishi Gakkai, ed., *Hōken ryōshusei no kakuritsu—Taikō kenchi o meguru shomondai,* Tokyo, 1957.

Sekai rekishi jiten, 25 vols., Tokyo, Heibonsha, 1950-1955.

Shibata Genshō, *Tokugawa Ieyasu to sono shūi,* 3 vols., Hamamatsu, 1934.

Shimizu Mitsuo, *Jōdai no tochi-kankei,* Tokyo, 1943.

———, *Nihon chūsei no sonraku*, Tokyo, 1942.

Shin Nihonshi kōza, 20 cases, Tokyo, Chūō Kōron Sha, 1948-1952.

Shin Nihonshi taikei, 6 vols., Tokyo, Asakura Shoten, 1952-1954.

Minoru Shinoda, *The Founding of the Kamakura Shogunate 1180-1185*, New York, 1960.

Thomas C. Smith, *The Agrarian Origins of Modern Japan*, Stanford, 1959.

Sonrakushakai Kenkyūkai, *Sonraku kenkyū no seika to kadai* (Tokyo, 1954).

Sugiyama Hiroshi, *Shōen kaitai katei no kenkyū*, Tokyo, 1959.

Takekoshi Yosaburō, *Nihon keizaishi*, 8 vols., Tokyo, 1920.

Takeuchi Rizō, *Jiryō shōen no kenkyū*, Tokyo, 1942.

———, ed., *Nihon hōkensei seiritsu no kenkyū*, Tokyo, 1955.

———, *Ritsuryō-sei to kizoku seiken*, Tokyo, vol. 1, 1959; vol. 2, 1958.

Takikawa Masajirō, *Nihon shakai shi*, Tokyo, 1938.

———, *Nihon dorei keizaishi*, Tokyo, 1930.

Torao Toshiya, *Handen shūju-hō no kenkyū*, Tokyo, 1961.

Toyoda Takeshi, *Sakai*, Tokyo, 1957.

Tsunoda Ryūsaku, tr., *Japan in the Chinese Dynastic Histories: Late Han through Ming Dynasties*, South Pasadena, Calif., 1951.

Uozumi Sōgorō, ed., *Daimyō ryōkoku to jōkamachi*, Tokyo, 1957.

———, ed., *Setonaikai-chiiki no shakaishiteki kenkyū*, Kyoto, 1952.

Max Weber, *The Theory of Social and Economic Organization* (Henderson and Parsons, trs.), Glencoe, Ill.

Yasuda Motohisa, *Nihon shōenshi gaisetsu*, Tokyo, 1957.

———, *Nihon zenshi, 4, Chūsei, 1*, Tokyo, 1958.

Yoshimura Shigeki, *Kokushi-seido hōkai ni kansuru kenkyū*, Tokyo, 1957.

Yamaguchi-ken Bunkashi Hensan Iinkai, ed., *Yamaguchi-ken bunkashi, Tsūshi-hen*, Yamaguchi, 1951.

ARTICLES

Abe Takehiko, "Jōdai keishisei no han-i ni tsuite," *Shigaku zasshi*, 35.2 (February 1944), 138-154.

Aoki Kazuo, "Ritsuyō zaisei," in *Iwanami kōza, Nihon rekishi, 3, Kodai, 3* (1963), 115-146.

Ariga Kizaemon, "Nihon jōdai no ie to sonraku," *Tōa shakai kenkyū, 1* (1943).

Arimoto Minoru, "Chigyō-koku to shite no Bizen-no-kuni," *Setonaikai kenkyū, 6* (March 1954), 42-56.

———, "Muromachi jidai ni okeru Bizen-no-kuni Tottori-no-shō," *Kibi chihōshi geppō, 1.4* (April 1952), 4-7.

Asao Naohiro, "Hōshi seiken ron," in *Iwanami kōza, Nihon rekishi*, 9, *kinsei, 1* (1963), 162-210.

Egashira Tsuneharu, "Bingo-no-kuni Ōta-no-shō no kenkyū," *Keizaishi kenkyū*, 39 and 40 (January and February, 1933).

Fujii Shun, "Bizen-no-kuni Shikada-no-shō ni tsuite," in Uozumi Sōgorō, ed., *Setonaikai-chiiki no shakaishiteki kenkyū*, 131-139.

———, "Bitchū no kokuga ni tsuite," Dokushi Kai sōritsu gojūnen kinen, *Kokushi ronshū*, Tokyo, 1959.

———, "Kodai-shi jō no Kibi no Kojima," Kodaigaku Kyōkai, *Nihon kodai shi ronsō*, 588-604.

———, "Kojima Takanori no ittō taru Imaki, Ōtomi ryōshi ni tsuite," *Shichō* (March 1936).

———, "Shunjōbō Chōgen to Bizen-no-kuni," *Okayama shigaku*, 1 (1955), 20-37.

Fujino Tamotsu, "Sengoku-daimyō kashindan no sonzai keitai," *Nihon rekishi*, 122 (August 1958), 58-67.

Fukuda Eijirō, "Sōmura no hatten," in *Nihon rekishi kōza*, 3 (1957), 69-94.

Fukui Sakuji, "Mōri-shi no daimyō ryōshūsei no hatten," *Geibi chihōshi kenkyū*, 5.6 (April 1954), 17-24.

John Whitney Hall, "The Castle Town and Japan's Modern Urbanization," *The Far Eastern Quarterly*, 15.1 (November 1955), 37-56.

Harada Tomohiko, "Sengoku daimyō to toshi minshū," *Nihonshi kenkyū*, 15 (March 1952), 2-16.

Hattori Kentarō, "Jitō-ryōshu to shōen taisei," *Mita Gakkai zasshi*, 45.3 (March 1950), 161-178.

———, "Ryōshusei hatten katei no ichi kōsatsu—Bingo-no-kuni Ota-no-shō ni okeru ichirei," *Mita Gakkai zasshi*, 45.1 (January 1952), 1-25.

Hayashiya Tatsusaburō, "Insei to bushi," *Nihon rekishi kōza*, 2, *Genshi-kodai* (1951).

———, "Ritsuryōsei yori shōensei e," *Rekishigaku kenkyū*, 183 (May 1955), 1-9.

Hirano Kunio, "Taika zendai no shakai kōzō," in *Iwanami kōza Nihon rekishi*, 2, *Kodai 2* (1962), 81-122.

Inoue Mitsusada, "Bemin-shi ron," in *Shin Nihonshi kōza*, case 4 (1948).

———, "Kokuzō-sei no seiritsu," *Shigaku zasshi*, 60.11 (November 1951), 964-1005.

———, "Ritsuryō taisei no seiritsu," *Iwanami kōza, Nihon rekishi*, 3, *Kodai 3* (Tokyo, 1962), 1-31.

Inoue Tatsuō, "Iwai no hanran to Nansen," *Nihon rekishi kōza, 1, Genshi-kodai* (1958), 101-131.

Irimajiri Yoshinaga, "Tokugawa jidai jiryō to sono shobun," in *Nihon nōmin keizaishi kenkyū* (Tokyo, 1949), 85-141.

Ishida Minoru, "Okayama-ken jōri no rekishi-chirigaku-teki kenkyū," *Okayama-ken Chihōshi Kenkyū Renraku Kyōgikai kaihō,* 3 (1960), 51-62.

Ishii Ryōsuke, "Kamakura bakufu no seiritsu," *Rekishi kyōiku,* 8.7 (1960), 1-8.

Ishimoda Shō, "Kamakura seiken no seiritsu katei ni tsuite—Tōgoku ni okeru 1180—83 nen no seiji katei o chūshin to shite," *Rekishigaku kenkyū,* 200 (October 1956), 2-16.

Ishii Susumu, "Kamakura bakufu ron," in *Iwanami kōza, Nihon rekishi,* 5, *Chūsei, 1* (1962), 87-134.

———, "Kamakura bakufu to ritsuryō seido chihō gyōsei kikan to no kankei—shokoku ōtabumi sakusei o chūshin to shite," *Shigaku zasshi,* 66.11 (November 1957), 956-994.

Itō Tasaburō, "Edo bakufu no seiritsu to buke seijikan," *Rekishigaku kenkyū,* nos. 131 and 132 (1948).

———, "Kinsei daimyō kenkyū josetsu," *Shigaku zasshi,* 55.9 and 11 (September and November 1944).

———, "Shugō-mondai to shōgun no ken'i," *Nihon rekishi,* 67 (December 1953), 2-13.

Iyanaga Teizō, "Ritsuryō-teki tochi shoyū," in *Iwanami kōza, Nihon rekishi, 3, Kodai, 3* (1962), 33-78.

Marius B. Jansen, "Tosa in the Sixteenth Century: The 100 Article Code of Chōsokabe Motochika," *Oriens Extremus,* 10.1 (April 1963), 83-108.

Kanai Madoka, "Kamakura jidai no Bizen kokugaryō ni tsuite," *Nihon rekishi,* 150 (December 1960), 36-54.

———, "Keian ofuregaki," *Rekishi kyōiku,* 4.10 (1956), 53-62.

———, "Kyōtsū rondai 'hansei kakuritsu-ki no shomondai' o tonageru ni atatte," *Shakai-keizaishigaku,* 24.2 (1958).

———, "Shokuhō-ki ni okeru Bizen—Taikō kenchi no chiiki-sei no ichirei," *Chihōshi kenkyū,* 42 (December 1959), 9-20.

Kawai Masaji, "Kobayakawa-shi no hatten to Setonaikai," in Uozumi Sōgorō, ed., *Setonaikai-chiiki no shakaishiteki kenkyū,* 109-129.

———, "Sengoku daimyō to shite no Mōri-shi no seikaku," *Shigaku kenkyū,* 54 (1954), 26-35.

———, "Tōgoku bushidan no seisei to sono seichō—Gei-Bi ryōkoku o chūshin to shite," *Shigaku Kenkyū kinen ronsō* (1950), 53-72.

Kikuchi Takeo, "Sengoku daimyō no kenryoku kōzō," *Rekishigaku kenkyū,* 166 (November 1953), 1-17.

Kitajima Masamoto, "Tokugawa-shi no shoki kenryoku kōzō—kenchi to waritsuke kisai yori mitaru," *Shigaku zasshi,* 64.9 (September 1955), 800-837.

Kondō Yoshirō, "Bizen Akaiwa-gun Nishiyama-son shozai no ni-san no kofun ni tsuite," *Setonaikai kenkyū,* 4.5 (March 1953), 32-38.

———, "Nihon kofun bunka," in *Nihon rekishi kōza, 1, Genshi-kodai* (1958), 61-100.

Kuroda Toshio, "Buke seiken no seiritsu," in *Nihon rekishi kōza, 2, Kodai-chūsei* (1959), 169-199.

———, "Chūsei no kokka to tennō," *Iwanami kōza, Nihon rekishi, 6, Chūsei, 2* (1963).

Kuwata Tadachika, "Toyotomi Hideyoshi no katanagari," *Shigaku zasshi,* 54.1 (January 1943), 57-89.

Matsumoto Shimpachirō, "Gaisetsu," *Nihon rekishi kōza, 3, Chūsei, 1* (1951), 2-67.

Matsuoka Hisato, "Kamakura jidai no kokugaryō—Aki Tadokoro monjo o tsūjite mitaru," *Shigaku Kenkyū kinen ronsō* (1950), 25-51.

———, "Ōuchi-shi no hatten to sono ryōkoku shihai," in Uozumi Sōgorō, ed., *Daimyō ryōkoku to jōkamachi,* 24-98.

Mayuzumi Hiromichi, "Kokushi-sei no seiritsu," in Ōsaka Rekishigakkai, *Ritsuryō kokka no kiso kōzō,* 107-146.

———, "Taika-kaishin shō to Ritsuryō to no kankei," *Rekishi kyōiku,* 9.5 (1961), 12-17.

Miyake Chiaki, "Edo jidai ni okeru Bitchū ryōshu ni tsuite," *Setonaikai kenkyū,* 11 (May 1958), 43-54.

Miyoshi Motoyuki, "Jūsan-shi-seiki Bitchū-no-kuni Niimi-no-shō ni okeru zaichi no henka ni tsuite," *Shigaku kenkyū,* 69 (May 1958), 15-28.

Mizuno Kyōichirō, "Akamatsu-shi saikō o meguru ni-san no mondai," in Kyōto Daigaku Dokushikai Sōritsu Gojūnen Kinen, *Kokushi ronshū* (Kyoto, 1959), 763-776.

———, "Bizen-han ni okeru shinshoku-uke seido ni tsuite," *Okayama Daigaku Hōbungakubu gakujutsu kiyō,* 5 (March 1956), 73-89.

———, "Namboku-chō nairanki ni okeru Yamana-shi no dōkō," in *Okayama Daigaku Hōbungakubu gakujutsu kiyō,* 13 (May 1960), 57-70.

———, "Shugo Akamatsu-shi no ryōkoku shihai to Kakitsu no hen," *Shirin,* 42.2 (February 1959), 254-281.

Murai Yasuhiko, "Myō seiritsu no rekishiteki zentei," *Rekishigaku kenkyū,* 215 (January 1958), 4-17.

Murao Jirō, "Ritsuryō seido no hyōka ni kansuru mittsu no mondaiten," *Rekishi kyōiku,* 11.5 (1963), 11-18.

Nagahara Keiji, "Namboku-chō no nairan," *Nihon rekishi kōza, 3, Chūsei-kinsei* (1957), 17-44.

Nagahara Keiji and Sugiyama Hiroshi, "Shugo ryōkokusei no tenkai," in *Shakaikeizaishigaku,* 17 (February 1951), 103-134.

Nakamura Kichiji, "Sengoku-daimyō ron," in *Iwanami kōza, Nihon rekishi, 8, Chūsei, 4* (1963), 189-237.

————, "Rekishi, kodai," in Sonrakushakai Kenkyūkai, *Sonraku kenkyū no seika to kadai,* 146-158.

Naoki Kōjirō, "Ritsuryōsei no dōyō," in *Nihon rekishi kōza, 2, Kodai-chūsei* (1959), 19-48.

Niino Naoyoshi, "Ritsuryō-sei ka in okeru 'kuni-no-miyatsuko,'" *Rekishi kyōiku,* 9.5 (1961), 42-47.

Nishikawa Hiroshi, "Kofun bunka ni arawareta chiiki shakai," in *Nihon kōkogaku kōza,* 5 (Tokyo, 1955).

Nishioka Toranosuke, "Shōensei no hattatsu," in *Shōenshi no kenkyū,* 1 (1957), 1-68.

————, "Shugo daimyō ryōka no jiryō shōen—Daitokuji-ryō Harima-no-kuni Oyake-no-shō Sanshiki-kata," in *Nomura Hakase kanreki kinen rombunshū, Hōken-sei to shihonsei* (Tokyo, 1959), 73-119.

Nitta Hideharu, "Kamakura-bakufu no gokenin-seido," in *Nihon rekishi kōza, 2, Kodai-chūsei* (1959), 229-255.

Nomura Tadao, "Ritsuryō kanjin no kōsei to shutsuji," in Ōsaka Rekishi Gakkai, *Ritsuryō kokka no kiso kōzō,* 235-292.

Ōishi Shinzaburō, "Sengoku jidai," in *Nihon rekishi kōza, 3, Chūsei-kinsei* (1957), 159-184.

Okuda Shinkei, "Bushi kaikyū no seiritsu hatten," *Shin Nihonshi kōza* (1948).

Okuno Takahiro, "Shōensei yori daimyōsei e," *Nippon rekishi,* 39 (August 1948), 50-53.

Ōyama Kyōhei, "Kokugaryō jitō no ichi-keitai," *Nihon rekishi,* 158 (August 1961), 58-66.

Sakamoto Keiichi, "Suiden shakai no seikaku," *Jimbun gakuhō,* 3 (March 1953), 143-164.

Satō Saburō, "Chūsei bushi-shakai ni okeru zokuteki danketsu—Kii, Suda-no-shō Suda ichizoku no kōsatsu," *Shakaikeizaishigaku,* 8. 3 (June 1938), 344-374.

Satō Shin'ichi, "Bakufu ron," *Shin Nihonshi kōza* (1951).

————, "Shoki hōkenshakai no keisei," *Shin Nihonshi taikei, 3, Chūsei shakai* (1954), 1-80.

————, "Shugo-ryōkokusei no tenkai," *Shin Nihonshi taikei, 3, Chūsei shakai* (1954), 81-127.

Seno Seiichirō, "Hizen-no-kuni ni okeru Kamakura gokenin," *Nihon rekishi,* 117 (March 1958), 30-39.

Shibata Hajime, "Sengoku dogō-sō to Taikō kenchi—Ukita ryō ni okeru jirei," *Rekishi kyōiku,* 8.8 (August 1960), 52-63.

Shimizu Mitsuo, "Kokugaryō to bushi," *Shirin,* 27.4 (1937). Reprinted in *Jōdai no tochi kankei* (Tokyo, 1943), 133-161.

Sugiyama Hiroshi, "Muromachi bakufu," *Nihon rekishi kōza, 3, Chūsei-kinsei* (1957), 45-67.

———, "Shōen ni okeru shōgyō," in *Nihon rekishi kōza, 3, Chūsei, 1* (1951), 200-218.

Suzuki Ryōichi, *Doikki ron,* in *Shin Nihonshi kōza* (1948).

———, "Shokuhō seikenron," *Nihon rekishi kōza, 4, Chūsei, 2* (1952), 86-102.

Suzuki Hisashi, "Hatamoto-ryō no kōzō," *Rekishigaku kenkyū,* 208 (June 1957), 12-29.

Takao Kazuhiko, "Shōen to kōryō," in *Nihon rekishi kōza, 2, Kodai-chūsei* (1959), 49-83.

Takayanagi Mitsutoshi, "Genna ikkoku-ichijō rei," *Shigaku zasshi,* 33.11 (1922), 863-888.

Takeuchi Rizō, "Bushi hassei-shi jō ni okeru zaichō to rusudokoro no kenkyū," *Shigaku zasshi,* 48.6 (June 1937), 671-719.

———, "Heike oyobi Insei seiken to shōensei," *Rekishigaku kenkyū* 225 (November 1958), 28-33.

———, "Manyō-jidai no shomin-seikatsu," in *Ritsuryō-sei to kizoku seiken, 1* (1959), 183-213.

———, "Ritsuryo kan-i sei ni okeru kaikyūsei," in *Ritsuryō-sei to kizoku seiken, 1* (1959), 156-182.

———, "Shōensei to hōkensei—Nihon no baai," *Shigaku zasshi,* 62.12 (December 1953), 1075-1087.

———, "Zaichō kanjin no bushika," in *Nihon hōkensei seiritsu no kenkyū,* 1-42. Originally published in *Shigaku zasshi,* 48.6 (1937).

Taniguchi Sumio, "Bizen-han no chigyō seido," *Shigaku kenkyū,* 62 (August 1956), 17-40.

———, "Bizen hansei no kakuritsu katei," *Okayama Daigaku Kyōiku-gakubu kenkyū shūroku,* 2 (1956), 1-15.

———, "Han kashindan no keisei to kōzō—Okayama-han no baai," *Shigaku zasshi,* 66.6 (June 1957), 594-615.

———, Hansei kakuritsu-ki no shomondai—Okayama-han no baai," *Shakaikeizaishigaku,* 24.2 (1958), 205-228.

———, "Jōkamachi Okayama no seiritsu," in Uozumi Sōgorō, *Daimyō ryōkoku to jōkamachi,* 131-163.

Toyoda Takeshi, "Sengoku-daimyo-ryō no keisei," in *Shin Nihonshi taikei, 3, Chūsei shakai* (1952), 197-223.

———, "Shokuhō seiken," in *Nihon rekishi kōza, 3, Chūsei-kinsei* (1957), 185-208.

Ueda Masaaki, "Asuka no kyūtei," *Nihon rekishi kōza, 1, Genshi-kodai* (1958), 133-159.

Wajima Seiichi, "Kofun bunka no henshitsu," *Iwanami kōza, Nihon rekishi, 2, Kodai, 2* (1962), 123-184.

Wakamori Tarō and Nagano Masashi, "Reimeiki Nihon no shakei to seikatsu," in *Shin Nihonshi taikei, 1, Kokka no seisei* (1952), 118-229.

Watanabe Nobuo, "Kōbu kenryoku to shōensei," *Iwanami kōza, Nihon rekishi, 5, Chūsei, 1* (1962), 188-226.

INDEX